ORACLE® *Oracle Press*™

Oracle PL/SQL 101

About the Author

Over the last 20 years Christopher Allen has provided computer consulting services for clients such as IBM, Microsoft, the California Institute of Technology, the Department of Justice, Universal Studios, and Dell. He has programmed hundreds of custom applications, and has taught over a thousand computer classes for professionals. He is an Oracle Certified Professional DBA and Application Developer. This is his eighth book on computer topics.

ORACLE®   *Oracle Press*™

Oracle PL/SQL 101

Christopher Allen

Osborne/**McGraw-Hill**

Berkeley New York St. Louis San Francisco
Auckland Bogotá Hamburg London Madrid
Mexico City Milan Montreal New Delhi Panama City
Paris São Paulo Singapore Sydney Tokyo Toronto

Osborne/**McGraw-Hill**
2600 Tenth Street
Berkeley, California 94710
U.S.A.

For information on translations or book distributors outside the U.S.A., or to arrange bulk purchase discounts for sales promotions, premiums, or fund-raisers, please contact Osborne/**McGraw-Hill** at the above address.

Oracle PL/SQL 101

1234567890 DOC DOC 01987654321

ISBN 0-07-212606-X

Publisher
  Brandon A. Nordin

Vice President & Associate Publisher
  Scott Rogers

Acquisitions Editor
  Jeremy Judson

Project Editors
  Betsy Manini
  Madhu Prasher
  Claire Splan

Acquisitions Coordinators
  Monika Faltiss
  Ross Doll

Technical Editors
  Beethoven Cheng
  Warren Li
  Ravindra Dani

Proofreader
  Pat Mannion

Indexer
  David Heiret

Series Design
  Jani Beckwith

Computer Designers
  Tara Davis
  Elizabeth Jang

Illustrator
  Michael Mueller

This book was composed with Corel VENTURA ™ Publisher.

For Grace

Contents at a Glance

vii

Table of Contents

PART II
Advanced SQL

PART III
Creating Programs Using PL/SQL

PART IV
Appendix

Acknowledgments

nce again I find myself privileged to be part of the distinguished Oracle Press collection. A tip of the hat to Publisher Brandon Nordin and Vice President and Associate Publisher Scott Rogers for guiding the Oracle Press line to become the quality series that it is. I'm honored to be in such company.

Thanks go to Monika Faltiss, Ross Doll, Claire Splan, and Lisa McClain for making the production process as painless as possible. A special thanks to Ravindra Dani for invaluable editorial input. And a hearty handshake to Jeremy Judson, who remains a voice of sanity and a very cool guy.

Finally, I want to thank my wife Grace, whose own PL/SQL studies helped make it clear why a book like this would be valuable. This time her support extended beyond keeping me happy during the grueling writing process, and included reading through each chapter and making valuable suggestions. She is the matriarch of Team Allen, and rightly so.

Introduction

ot too long ago my lovely wife decided she wanted to learn more about SQL and Oracle. I thought that was a great idea, so I gave her the three or four books I had on SQL and PL/SQL, and we bought two or three more as time went on. By this time we had just about every major SQL book on the market. In the months that followed we both came to the conclusion that while the books contained…("paper," my wife just said, as she looks over my shoulder now—I was thinking more along the lines of "lots of information")…none of them seemed to be written for a beginner. Many assumed prior knowledge of SQL, Oracle, or a programming language like C++. They offered plenty of examples showing features producing results that had no particular value, and many of the books jumped around from topic to topic without bringing everything together into a bigger picture that relates to normal work life.

Around that time I had a conversation with Scott Rogers, Associate Publisher and Editor in Chief for Oracle Press. Scott was telling me about his vision for a new line of books they were calling the 101 Series. When he said the series needed a book on PL/SQL, I interrupted him with "I want to do that book." (Scott, I never apologized for interrupting…sorry about that.) He listened to my ideas for such a book, and the book you are now holding is the result.

What I present here is my best effort at presenting SQL and PL/SQL in a way that makes sense. I have worked to create examples that demonstrate not only *how* to use each feature, but also *why*. I've provided exercises that mirror the kinds of tasks you'll be asked to accomplish if you make SQL and PL/SQL part of your work. And I've done my best to make the writing reasonably interesting to read, so your flame of interest in this fascinating topic stays burning. If you have ideas about how I could make this book better, e-mail me at **plsql101@yahoo.com**. I'll do my best to remember that you're doing me a favor giving positive *or* negative feedback. You can also write me there to get the scripts used in this book.

All the best in your SQL endeavors,
Christopher Allen

PART
I

Database Basics

CHAPTER

1

Introduction to Databases

elcome to the wonderful world of databases. "Huh?" you might say to yourself. "What's so wonderful about databases?" The answer lies not with databases themselves, but with what they contain: information. Information that can make your life easier, transform a mountain of chaos into a manageable chunk of order, and help you discover things you would never have the time to find out otherwise. When you learn how to use databases knowledgeably, you learn how to control the way you receive information. More and more, this fundamental skill is becoming the difference between getting the answers you need and not.

What Exactly Is a Database?

Stripped down to its most basic form, a *database* is a list of information. Or a set of lists that work together. A database program is a fancy list manager.

Databases are a regular part of just about everyone's life. For example, a telephone book is a paper representation of a database. It provides you with specific pieces of information about people, and it sorts that information into an order designed to help you find what you want quickly. If the telephone book contains business listings—often called the "yellow pages"—the information there will be sorted by business type, and within each business type, it will be sorted by name.

You probably have an address book—it's a database too. So is your checkbook register. If your local television provider has a channel that shows what's playing on each channel, that information is coming from a database.

You have probably used databases on the Internet too. If you have looked for a book or CD using a Web site, the information that came back to you was pulled from a database. (I recently designed just such a database for the world's largest music-publishing company.) Online auction sites are large databases containing information about buyers, sellers, items, bids, and feedback. Internet search engines such as AltaVista and Yahoo! are enormous databases containing key information about millions of Web pages.

Tables

Databases are always designed to store a particular type of information. For instance, in the case of a telephone book, the information is about people (in the white pages) and about businesses (in the yellow pages). A database would generally store such information by having one *table* containing all the information about people, and another table containing the information about businesses. Each of these tables would look a lot like a spreadsheet, with individual columns for each type of information being stored (name, address, number, and so on) and a row for each person or business. For instance, a simple employee table might look like this:

```
EMPLOYEE_ID   FIRST_NAME      LAST_NAME          SALARY    HIRE_DATE
-----------   -------------   --------------     ---------  ---------
       1024   Scott           Campbell            63000     17-FEB-98
       2048   Linda           Hammond             68000     15-JAN-99
       3072   Dave            Anthony             69000     11-APR-00
       4096   Tiff            Berlin              66000     24-DEC-01
```

The most important thing to remember about a table is this: *It stores information about **one** type of thing.* A table about people will not store information about lawnmowers! A table about school classes will not store information about the people who take those classes. If a database needs to store information about more than one type of thing—and it almost always will—it does so by using more than one table. For example, to properly track school classes, a database would have (at the very least) a table for faculty, another one for classes, a third one for classrooms, and a fourth one for students. Keeping the different types of information separate allows a database to store information very efficiently, and in a highly organized (and therefore easy-to-use) manner.

Rows/Records

The simple employee table shown earlier contains information about four people. Each person's information is on a line of its own. Each line is called a *row*, and the data it contains is called a *record*. Each row will contain the information for one—and only one—of the items defined by the table's name. For instance, in an employee table, each row contains information for only one employee. Similarly, each employee's information is stored on just one row. You design the table so that it only takes one row to hold all of the information specific to each of whatever the table's name says it holds. (You'll be doing this yourself very soon.)

Columns/Fields

Each row contains several pieces of information. In the employee example, those pieces included employee ID, first name, and so on. In a table, these pieces of information are stored in *columns*. The junction point of a row and a column—for instance, a particular person's first name—is called a *field*. A field contains a single piece of information about something—for instance, a telephone number for one person.

Let's think about a concrete example. Imagine that you want to put information for five of your friends onto 3" × 5" index cards. Each friend will get his or her own index card, so you'll use a total of five cards. By doing this, you're creating a small database. It's a physical database, as opposed to one on a computer, but it's a database nonetheless, and the concepts of tables, records, and fields still apply. Figure 1-1 shows the relationships between the index cards and these terms.

Now let's say you've put the information for the same five friends into a spreadsheet. Figure 1-2 shows how the terms you've just learned would apply to that situation.

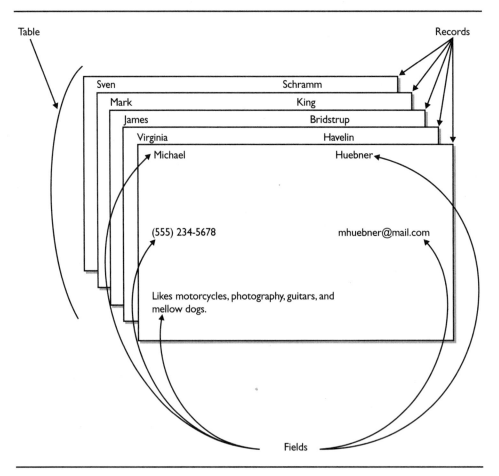

FIGURE 1-1. *Friend information laid out on index cards*

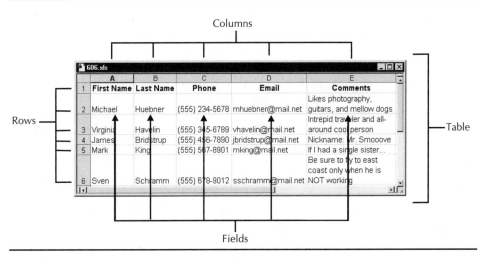

FIGURE 1-2. *Friend information laid out in a spreadsheet*

How Is a Database Different from a Spreadsheet?

Based on the "list of friends" example, it would be easy to think "Well, why not just keep the list in a spreadsheet?" For a list like the one shown, you could. A database becomes appropriate when the lists get more complicated, or when they need to be used in a more sophisticated environment. What follows are several distinctive features that databases offer.

Many Rows

Since spreadsheets are designed primarily for financial calculations—essentially, they function as ledger sheets with formulas where the answers go—they aren't designed to accommodate the number of rows that a business database will need. It's common for a spreadsheet to have a limit of 65,536 on the number of rows it can contain. While that is a lot of rows for a spreadsheet, it isn't really that many for a database. (For example, I just used a Web site to find out how many Internet newsgroup messages contain the world "Oracle." There were approximately 1,200,000 matching messages, and every one of those messages is stored in the Web site's database. That Web site's database contains over a million records about Oracle messages alone; imagine how many records it contains in total!) It's not uncommon for a business database to contain a million rows or more, and large businesses have databases containing billions of rows. No spreadsheet is going to handle that!

Many Users Simultaneously

Because databases are at the core of many businesses, it's essential that they allow lots of people to access to the same data simultaneously. To understand why, imagine a retail store chain that has a hundred computerized cash registers distributed among its stores. On a busy sale day, many of those registers are going to be doing transactions at the same time. If you had to wait for all of the other transactions to be completed before yours could go through, you would probably get frustrated and leave, and so would a lot of other people—and sales would suffer. On a bigger scale, airline reservation systems can deal with thousands of requests every second— if each of those had to wait for all the others, the reservation system would be very slow and annoying. The ability to accommodate large numbers of simultaneous users is one of the key characteristics of a database. A well-designed database can answer requests from thousands—or even millions—of users simultaneously and still provide satisfactory performance.

Security

Databases contain some of the most sensitive information in a business: salaries, customer information, and project schedules, for instance. If this information were to be deleted, changed, or revealed to coworkers or competitors, it could cause problems ranging from embarrassment to failure of the business itself. Because of this, databases have extremely robust security systems. You won't find any passwords stored in easily snooped text files in a database system; everything is encrypted, including the information sent between the database and a user's computer when he or she logs in.

Even valid users of a database don't necessarily get access to everything the database contains. Users can be given privileges to specific tables, and not to others. It's even possible to make some columns within a table visible to all users, and other columns visible to only a select group. In addition, a database can be instructed to filter a table's rows so that some users see only certain rows, while other users see all rows.

A database's security features go even further. In addition to controlling who can see what information, a database allows you to specify who can insert new information, update existing information, or delete information. This helps ensure that people who have no business reason to change or delete data, for instance, cannot do so accidentally (or not so accidentally).

In a large database system—say, one with 1,000 users or more—managing all of these different kinds of privileges would quickly become impossible if they had to be set on a user-by-user basis. Fortunately, databases like Oracle allow you to gather a specific set of privileges into something called a *role*. That way, whenever users are added to the database, they are assigned one or more roles, and those roles carry the privileges the users can exercise. This works well because businesses generally have specific job descriptions, and the privileges each user will need relate directly to his or her job description. An accounting clerk will need the ability to enter data from bills, but perhaps only the accounting managers will have the ability to change data once it's been entered. Similarly, perhaps only accounting executives can do anything at all with the company's salary data. Each of these three job descriptions would be a good candidate for a database role. For instance, an "accounting clerk" role would be assigned to all of the accounting clerks. Security roles help ensure that everyone has exactly the privileges they need. Roles also make it very easy to assign a new privilege to a group: You just add the privilege to that group's role, and the job is done.

Relational Abilities

Since a database employs separate tables to store different types of data—remember the example of a school's database having individual tables for faculty, classes, classrooms, and students—there must be a way to connect records in one table with relevant records in the other tables. Databases accommodate this by letting you define *relationships* between the tables.

For example, let's consider an order-entry system. The core of this type of system is the business' inventory, so there will always be a table containing information about products. The PRODUCT table will store each piece of information pertaining to an inventory item, including description, manufacturer, price, and quantity currently in stock. The PRODUCT table will also store a unique identifier for each product, as a way of unquestionably identifying one product as opposed to another. Let's say for the sake of discussion that in the PRODUCT table, the unique identifier is the Stock Keeping Unit (SKU).

Now that we have a table in which to store products, we need another table in which to store orders for those products. Each row in the ORDER table will store the date, time, location, and total order value. The ORDER table must also identify what product the order is for, and it can do this simply by storing the product's SKU as part of the order record. Here's where the relationship comes in: *The only product information an order contains is the product's SKU.* The product's description, price, and other information are not stored in the ORDER table. Why? It would waste space, among other reasons, because each product's description, price, and so on are already available in the PRODUCT table. The only requirement to making this work is that the database must be told that an order's SKU is the unique identifier in the PRODUCT table. Once it knows that, the database can join information from both tables, and present the combined information on a single line, as if it came from one table.

A database that employs this technique of relating records in separate tables is called a *relational database*. It's not uncommon for business databases to contain tables that have relationships to dozens of other tables. There are many reasons for doing this, and they will be discussed in depth in Chapter 6. The opposite of this approach is a single large table that repeats information every time it is needed. This type of table is called a *flat file*, indicating that it is two-dimensional—just rows and columns, no related tables.

Constraints to Ensure Data Quality

Sometimes the data stored in a database comes directly from other machines: automated sensors, timers, or counters. Most of the data in a database, though, is entered by people. And people make mistakes. (Not you, of course, but I'm sure you know others who do.) When designing a database, it's easy to define *constraints* identifying conditions that data in a particular field must meet before the database accepts the record. The constraint defines what must be true about the data in order for it to be accepted. These constraints can be very simple—like ensuring that a price is a positive number—or more involved, like ensuring that a SKU entered into an order actually exists in the PRODUCT table, or requiring that certain fields in a record be entered if other fields contain specific values. By automating these types of quality-control functions, the database helps guarantee that the data it contains is clean.

Review Questions

1. What is the most significant characteristic of a table?

2. Define the following terms: *row, record, column, field, table, database, constraint.*

3. What are the key features that make a database suitable for storing large amounts of data?

Hands-On Project

1. Gather four blank sheets of paper. The sheets can be any size—index cards will work as well as 8.5" × 11" sheets.

2. On each sheet, write the first name, last name, phone number, and e-mail address of a friend or associate (you will do this for a total of four people— one per sheet).

3. After you have written the information onto the sheets, lay the sheets on a table—separately, so that they do not touch each other.

4. Move the sheets right next to each other, so they form a grid that is two sheets wide and two sheets high. In this arrangement, each sheet will touch two other sheets.

5. Tape the sheets together in this arrangement.

6. Take a pen that is a different color and on the top-left sheet, circle each item that would be stored in a database field. Write the word "Fields" at the bottom of the sheet, and draw arrows to each of the circled fields.

7. Next, put a rectangle around each item in the four-sheet grid that would relate to a row in a database. Write the word "Rows" in the center of the four-sheet grid, and draw arrows from the word to each square.

8. Finally, write "e-mail column" wherever on the four-sheet grid you have some space. Then draw one long line that connects that phrase to every item in the grid that would be stored in a table's e-mail column.

How Will Knowing This Help You?

Everybody is busy these days, and if you are reading a book about PL/SQL, you are probably busier than most. It's reasonable that you will want to know how something is going to help you before investing the time to learn it. What follows is a list of the ways that learning PL/SQL can help you in different situations.

When Doing Database Administration

It's impossible to be an Oracle database administrator (DBA) without knowing SQL, and very difficult without knowing Oracle's SQL superset named PL/SQL. This is because many of the tasks that are generally done by a DBA are accomplished using SQL, and quite a few require the programming capabilities of PL/SQL, as well. While Oracle does provide a number of software programs enabling administrators to perform tasks using a nice graphic user interface (GUI), these tools have their fair share of bugs. In addition, some tasks can just be done faster when using SQL directly, and in some database installations, connections to databases are accomplished using text-based terminals that cannot run the pretty GUI tools. The importance of SQL is reflected in the fact that Oracle's own DBA certification program, which consists of five separate exams, devotes the entire first exam to SQL and PL/SQL.

When Developing Software

Whether you develop programs using Java, C++, or Oracle's own Forms Developer product, the chances are high that at some point you will need to write some SQL code to interact with a database directly. Many developers stumble through this, making mistakes that cost them time and performance. Investing the time to learn SQL properly will pay for itself many times over. The documentation supplied with Oracle includes sections dedicated to interacting with Oracle via Java, C, C++, and COBOL.

When Doing Business Analysis

Being able to slice and dice huge mounds of data into the information you need is an essential part of a business analyst's job. Lots of people do this by getting an extract of their company's database, putting it in a spreadsheet, and manually creating the analyses they need. This approach is flexible, but it can be time consuming. Some companies also provide their analysts with software tools designed to make data analysis quick and easy. But even these tools don't provide every imaginable way of looking at the information; they provide the subsets that their designers think are the most likely to be used. The chances are good that you will want to look at the data in some way that the tool doesn't support. Often a single SQL query can provide the information you need.

If You Just Want to Know How to Use Databases Better

Recently I visited Silicon Valley and, when I had some free time, decided to go to a movie. I purchased a local newspaper and turned to the movie listings. I was struck by what I saw: *two* sets of listings, one sorted by geographic area, and the other sorted by movie title. So if you wanted to find out what was showing near you, you would use one listing; if you wanted to find out where a specific movie was playing, you would use the other. This simple, powerful idea made the listings a real pleasure to use. I'm positive it was thought up by someone with database experience, someone who was familiar with the idea that the content of the data and how it is displayed are two different things.

These days, practically everything is built around a database. If you understand how databases work, you understand how a lot of businesses function. This can be extremely useful. For instance, if you call a company's customer service department but don't have your customer number with you, you might think to ask "What else can you search on to find my record?" When you use a Web search site to locate information, you will get the results you want much more quickly if you understand how databases interpret search terms. (My friends are regularly amazed at how quickly I can find relevant information using search sites. My only trick: educated decisions about what to enter as search criteria.) Understanding databases is becoming a lot like being able to do basic math quickly in your head: It isn't essential, but it sure comes in handy a lot.

History of SQL

A little bit of history is useful to give perspective, and the history of SQL parallels the history of relational databases. In 1969, Dr. Edgar F. Codd published an IBM

Research Report with the catchy title *Derivability, Redundancy, and Consistency of Relations Stored in Large Data Banks*. This paper described an approach to structuring databases with related tables, which was quite different than the flat-file approach used by databases at the time. The paper was stamped with IBM's Limited Distribution Notice, so it wasn't widely read. Codd revised the concepts and published them in a 1970 article named "A Relational Model of Data for Large Shared Data Banks" in the journal of the Association of Computer Machinery. The relational model described by Codd was used in a prototype relational database management system (RDBMS) called System R in 1974. Describing the system's query language in a November 1976 article in the *IBM Journal of R&D*, IBM used the name Structured English QUEry Language (SEQUEL). The language and its name evolved, becoming Structured Query Language (SQL, pronounced either "sequel" or "S-Q-L"). The first commercially available version of SQL was released in 1979 by Oracle Corporation (although the company's name was Relational Software, Inc. at the time).

In 1986, the American National Standards Institute (ANSI) stepped in and published a formal SQL standard, which it identified as ANSI X3.135-1986. The International Standards Organization (ISO) picked up this standard the following year and published it as ISO 9075-1987. The specification was expanded in 1992, and then again in 1999. The current specification is in five parts, named ANSI/ISO/IEC 9051-1-1999 through 9051-5-1999.

SQL has become the de facto standard language for querying databases. Each database company modifies it a bit to suit its needs, but the core SQL functions remain essentially unchanged. This is good news for database users and developers, because the time invested in learning SQL will reap benefits for years to come, across software revision after software revision, and even to other products.

The bottom line is: SQL is a versatile and essential tool for anyone who works with databases regularly.

SQL Command Categories

SQL commands fall into functional groups that help make them easy to remember. These groups include:

- Data Definition

- Data Manipulation

- Data Control

- Data Retrieval

- Transaction Control

Your work with these commands will start in Chapter 2, and will continue throughout the book. Here's an overview of the categories of commands you will learn to use.

Data Definition

Oracle, and all major database programs, are database platforms—meaning that they provide an environment that supports working with tables very well, but that they don't provide any tables already created for your use. You get to define what data will be stored and in what configuration. SQL provides a collection of commands for these purposes: CREATE, ALTER, DROP, RENAME, and TRUNCATE.

These commands fall into a group called Data Definition Language, which is routinely referred to as DDL.

Data Manipulation

Okay, you learn how to create some tables. What's the next step? Putting data into them. SQL provides an INSERT command enabling you to add data to tables. After the data has been inserted, you can change it using the UPDATE command, or remove it using the DELETE command.

This category of commands is called SQL's Data Manipulation Language, more often referred to as DML.

Data Control

Remember the security features discussed earlier in this chapter? (I'm sure you do, but if anyone reading over your shoulder doesn't remember it, it's in the section titled "How Is a Database Different from a Spreadsheet?".) The ability to let some users use particular tables while other users cannot is enforced by assigning users *privileges* for specific tables or activities. An *object privilege* allows a user to perform specified actions on a table (or on other database objects, which will be covered in other parts of this book). An example of an object privilege would be the ability to insert records into an EMPLOYEE table. In contrast, a *system privilege* enables a user to perform a particular type of action anywhere in the database. An example of a system privilege would be the ability to insert records into *any* table in the database.

Database privileges are assigned and removed using the SQL commands GRANT and REVOKE. These commands fall into the category of Data Control Language (DCL).

Data Retrieval

The whole point of putting information into a database is getting it out again in a controlled fashion. There is just one command in this category—SELECT—but it has a wealth of parameters that provide a *lot* of flexibility. The SELECT command is the command you're likely to use more than any other, especially if you plan to use SQL from another programming language like Java or C++.

Transaction Control

Oracle's SQL provides an undo capability enabling you to cancel any recent DML commands before they are applied to the database. (Quick quiz: What commands are DML commands? If you need a reminder, take another look at the section titled "SQL Command Categories," earlier in this chapter.) After performing one or more DML commands, you can either issue a COMMIT command to save your changes to the database, or issue a ROLLBACK command to undo them.

The undo capability provides multiple levels, too: You can reverse just the last DML transaction, or the last several, or whatever level you need. Taking advantage of this multiple-level redo takes a little more forethought than it does in your favorite word processor, however. If you want to be able to undo to intermediate points, you have to mark those points by issuing a SAVEPOINT command at whatever point you want to be able to roll back to.

Chapter Summary

Stripped down to its most basic form, a database is a list of information. Or a set of lists that work together. A database program is a fancy list manager. Familiar databases include telephone books, checkbook registers, and Web sites providing online auctions, ordering, and searching.

Databases are always designed to store a particular type of information. For instance, in the case of a telephone book, the information is about people (in the white pages), and about businesses (in the yellow pages). A database would generally store such information by having one table containing all the information about people, and another table containing the information about businesses. Each of these tables would look a lot like a spreadsheet, with individual columns for each type of information being stored (name, address, number, and so on) and a row for each person or business.

The most important thing to remember about a table is this: *It stores information about **one** type of thing.* If a database needs to store information about more than one type of thing—and it almost always will—it does so by using more than one table. Keeping the different types of information separate allows a database to store information very efficiently, and in a highly organized (and therefore easy-to-use) manner.

Each line in a table contains information about one instance of whatever the table is designed to store. Each line is called a *row*, and the data it contains is called a *record*. You design the table so that it only takes one row to hold all of the information that is specific to each item the table contains.

Each row contains several pieces of information. In a table, these pieces of information are stored in *columns*. The junction point of a row and a column—for instance, a particular person's first name—is called a *field*. A field contains a single piece of information about something—for example, the last name for one person.

While a table in a database stores data in rows and columns like a spreadsheet, there are many characteristics that make a database more appropriate when the data gets more complicated, or when it needs to be used in a more sophisticated environment. These include the ability to handle billions of rows, accommodate thousands of simultaneous users, provide object-specific security, relate many tables together, and constrain the content of incoming data to ensure quality information.

Understanding how to use SQL can benefit you in a number of different areas. It's an essential skill if you're planning to be an Oracle DBA, because many DBA tasks are executed using SQL commands. When developing software, it's likely you will need to write SQL commands to insert, select, update, and delete data within programs you write using Java, C, C++, and COBOL. When doing business analysis, knowing SQL enables you to interact directly with the database, slicing and dicing its information the way you want, without being limited by pre-designed queries created by someone else. And if you just want to know how to use databases better, understanding SQL will help you understand how to use a variety of products and services used in daily life.

SQL is based on concepts pioneered by Dr. Edgar F. Codd and first published in 1969. It has become the de facto standard language for interacting with all major database programs. Its commands fall into functional categories, which include data definition, data manipulation, data control, data retrieval, and transaction control. The Data Definition Language (DDL) commands are used to define how you want your data to be stored; these commands include CREATE, ALTER, DROP, RENAME, and TRUNCATE. The Data Manipulation Language (DML) commands enable you to work with your data; they include INSERT, UPDATE, and DELETE. The Data Control Language (DCL) commands control who can do what within the database, with object privileges controlling access to individual database objects and system privileges providing global privileges across the entire database. The DCL commands include GRANT and REVOKE. For data retrieval, SELECT is the sole command, but its many variations are likely to make it the most-used command in your arsenal. To control transactions, SQL provides the COMMIT command to save recent DML changes to the database; the ROLLBACK command to undo recent DML changes; and the SAVEPOINT command to let you undo some, but not all, of a string of DML commands.

Chapter Questions

1. Which of the following are examples of databases that you're likely to encounter in daily life?

A. Front page news

B. Telephone books

C. Checkbook registers

D. Web sites providing online auctions, ordering, and searching

E. Ads with sale prices

F. Movie listings

2. What is the most significant characteristic of a table?

A. It has rows and columns.

B. It can be related to other tables.

C. It stores information about one type of thing.

D. It contains records and fields.

3. Relate each term on the left with the appropriate description on the right.

Term	Description
Row	Stores all information about one type of thing (for instance, people or products)
Record	Defines what must be true about the data in order for it to be accepted by the database
Column	One line in a table
Field	Collection of one type of information stored in a table (for instance, all of the phone numbers or all of the last names)
Table	Data contained in a table row
Database	Contains a single piece of information about something
Constraint	Collection of related tables

4. Which of the following are reasons why a database is the best choice for handling large quantities of business data?

   A. Can handle billions of rows

   B. Runs only on PCs

   C. Can accommodate thousands of simultaneous users

   D. Provides object-specific security

   E. Can relate many tables together

   F. Allows you to define constraints defining conditions that data must satisfy before it is accepted into the database

5. Whose work pioneered relational database theory?

   A. E. F. Skinner

   B. Edgar Winter

   C. E. F. Codd

   D. Edgar Piece

6. Relate each SQL command category on the left with the appropriate commands on the right.

SQL Command Category	Commands
Data Definition Language (DDL)	GRANT and REVOKE
Data Manipulation Language (DML)	SELECT
Data Control Language (DCL)	CREATE, ALTER, DROP, RENAME, and TRUNCATE
Data Retrieval	COMMIT, ROLLBACK, and SAVEPOINT
Transaction Control	INSERT, UPDATE, and DELETE

Answers to Chapter Questions

1. B, C, D, F. Telephone books; checkbook registers; Web sites providing online auctions, ordering, and searching; and movie listings.

Explanation The essence of a database is a list that can be presented in a chosen order, and filtered to display only selected records. Front page news does not fit this description; it cannot be sorted or filtered. The same is true for ads. However, the other categories do fit this description.

2. C. It stores information about one type of thing.

Explanation Choices A and D are true, but they are also true of spreadsheets, so they cannot be a table's most significant characteristic. B is also true, but its importance does not compare with choice C. The single most important characteristic of a table is that it stores information about one type of thing.

3.	**Term**	**Description**
	Row	One line in a table
	Record	Data contained in a table row
	Column	Collection of one type of information stored in a table (for instance, all of the phone numbers or all of the last names)
	Field	Contains a single piece of information about something
	Table	Stores all information about one type of thing (for instance, people or products)
	Database	Collection of related tables
	Constraint	Defines what must be true about the data in order for it to be accepted by the database

4. A, C, D, E, F. Can handle billions of rows, can accommodate thousands of simultaneous users, provides object-specific security, can relate many tables together, allows you to define constraints defining conditions that data must satisfy before it is accepted into the database.

Explanation Each of the answers provided is a powerful reason for using a relational database to handle large quantities of information, with the exception of B. Large databases do not run only on PCs—for instance, Oracle is available for computers running Unix, Linux, Windows NT, and a variety of other operating systems. Even if it was available only on PCs, that would be a liability, not an asset, because the other operating systems are designed for industrial-strength use and tend to be more stable than PC-based systems.

5. C. E. F. Codd

Explanation Dr. Edgar F. Codd published ground-breaking papers about relational database theory in 1969. He is widely regarded as the father of relational database design.

6.

SQL Command Category	Commands
Data Definition Language (DDL)	CREATE, ALTER, DROP, RENAME, and TRUNCATE
Data Manipulation Language (DML)	INSERT, UPDATE, and DELETE
Data Control Language (DCL)	GRANT and REVOKE
Data Retrieval	SELECT
Transaction Control	COMMIT, ROLLBACK, and SAVEPOINT

CHAPTER 2

Storing and Retrieving Data: The Basics

his chapter is going to be a lot of fun, because you're going to step out of the realm of theory and start getting your hands dirty. The chapter starts with a quick exercise in which you will create a table, insert records into it, view those records, and then delete the table. This exercise is deliberately kept quick and simple; it's like testing the temperature of a lake before jumping in. Next, you will take an extended tour of these activities, learning many details about creating versatile tables, inserting various types of data into them, and viewing the information they contain in a myriad of ways.

Putting Your Toe in the Water

In this section, you will do a quick exercise to see, in a basic way, what a database does. This will be a very simple exercise; databases can do infinitely more than what you will see in the next few pages. The purpose of this step is to give you some of the "big picture" about how basic database techniques fit together. That framework will help you later in the chapter: As you learn more detailed techniques, you can put them into the context of the "big picture."

To perform the steps that follow, you need to be running SQL*Plus, the program supplied by Oracle that lets you communicate with a database. To do that, you will need to have been given a user ID, password, and database name by your database administrator, and shown how to start SQL*Plus on your own computer system. (Explaining how to set up an Oracle database and configure SQL*Plus is beyond the scope of this book. If you would like to learn more about it, check out *Oracle 8i for Windows NT Starter Kit* by Steve Bobrowski (Oracle Press, 2000) or your Oracle documentation.)

Assuming you have been given the necessary information and now have SQL*Plus showing a SQL> prompt, let's proceed.

Creating a Table

As you will recall from the first chapter, a table is constructed something like a spreadsheet: It is made up of columns, and you place rows of data into it. Before you can add the rows of data, you must define the columns that make up the table. You do this with the command CREATE TABLE. To see how this command works, enter the following code at the SQL> prompt:

```
CREATE TABLE plsql101_test_1 (
     first_name CHAR(15),
     last_name  CHAR(20)
     )
;
```

After you have typed this command, press the ENTER key. Your screen should look like the one shown in Figure 2-1.

This is SQL*Plus' way of telling you that the command was successful. (If you see any other response, check the spelling in your command and try again.) You now have a table in Oracle! The structure of the command you used to create the table will be discussed in detail later in this chapter. For now, let's proceed directly to using the table by entering some records into it.

Inserting Records

To place records in a table, use the INSERT command. In SQL*Plus, type the following line at the SQL> prompt:

```
INSERT INTO plsql101_test_1 VALUES ('Jane', 'Smith');
```

After you have typed this command, press the ENTER key. You should see a response similar to the one shown in Figure 2-2.

Your table now contains its first record. To add a second record, type the following line into SQL*Plus and press ENTER:

```
INSERT INTO plsql101_test_1 VALUES ('Christopher', 'Allen');
```

Now your table contains two separate records. As you may have noticed, INSERT places records into a table one at a time. How do you see those records? Read on.

```
Oracle SQL*Plus                                          _ □ ✕
File  Edit  Search  Options  Help
SQL> CREATE TABLE plsql101_test_1 (
  2        first_name CHAR(15),
  3        last_name  CHAR(20)
  4        )
  5  ;

Table created.

SQL>
```

FIGURE 2-1.   *Results of CREATE TABLE command*

```
Oracle SQL*Plus                                    _ □ ✕
File  Edit  Search  Options  Help
SQL> CREATE TABLE plsql101_test_1 (
  2        first_name CHAR(15),
  3        last_name  CHAR(20)
  4        )
  5  ;

Table created.

SQL>
SQL> INSERT INTO plsql101_test_1 VALUES ('Jane', 'Smith');

1 row created.

SQL>
```

FIGURE 2-2. *Results of INSERT command*

NOTE
*From this point on, the text will not tell you to press
the ENTER key after every command. It will simply
instruct you to enter one or more lines of SQL
commands. Press the ENTER key after every line
in order for SQL*Plus to accept the commands.*

Selecting Records

To see the records you have inserted into your table, enter the following command:

```
SELECT * FROM plsql101_test_1;
```

In response, you should see the two records you entered, as shown in Figure 2-3.

Deleting a Table

To complete this first foray into the world of databases, you will delete the table
you created.

```
Oracle SQL*Plus                                          _ □ ✕
File  Edit  Search  Options  Help
SQL> CREATE TABLE plsql101_test_1 (
  2         first_name CHAR(15),
  3         last_name  CHAR(20)
  4         )
  5  ;

Table created.

SQL>
SQL> INSERT INTO plsql101_test_1 VALUES ('Jane', 'Smith');

1 row created.

SQL> INSERT INTO plsql101_test_1 VALUES ('Christopher', 'Allen');

1 row created.

SQL>
SQL> SELECT * FROM plsql101_test_1;

FIRST_NAME       LAST_NAME
---------------  --------------------
Jane             Smith
Christopher      Allen

SQL> |
```

FIGURE 2-3.   *Results of SELECT command*

NOTE
*Deleting a table is a serious step! It is not reversible!
Only use this command when you are absolutely
certain you do not need the records the table
contains.*

To delete your table, enter the following command:

 DROP TABLE plsql101_test_1;

Your screen should show the response depicted in Figure 2-4.

```
Oracle SQL*Plus                                          _ □ ✕
File  Edit  Search  Options  Help
SQL> CREATE TABLE plsql101_test_1 (
  2          first_name CHAR(15),
  3          last_name  CHAR(20)
  4          )
  5   ;

Table created.

SQL>
SQL> INSERT INTO plsql101_test_1 VALUES ('Jane', 'Smith');

1 row created.

SQL> INSERT INTO plsql101_test_1 VALUES ('Christopher', 'Allen');

1 row created.

SQL>
SQL> SELECT * FROM plsql101_test_1;

FIRST_NAME      LAST_NAME
--------------- --------------------
Jane            Smith
Christopher     Allen

SQL> DROP TABLE plsql101_test_1;

Table dropped.

SQL>
```

FIGURE 2-4.   *Results of DROP TABLE command*

This response tells you that the command succeeded. You can double-check this by trying to select records from the table, using the command that follows:

```
SELECT * FROM plsql101_test_1;
```

You should see a display similar to the one shown in Figure 2-5. With this command, you are attempting to select records from a table that doesn't exist. In response, Oracle displays four lines of text. The first response line repeats the portion of your command where Oracle encountered a problem. (Since your command was only one line long, that is the line shown.) The second response line places an asterisk (*) beneath the spot in the command line where Oracle

```
Oracle SQL*Plus                                                    _□×
File  Edit  Search  Options  Help
SQL> CREATE TABLE plsql101_test_1 (
  2       first_name CHAR(15),
  3       last_name  CHAR(20)
  4       )
  5   ;

Table created.

SQL>
SQL> INSERT INTO plsql101_test_1 VALUES ('Jane', 'Smith');

1 row created.

SQL> INSERT INTO plsql101_test_1 VALUES ('Christopher', 'Allen');

1 row created.

SQL>
SQL> SELECT * FROM plsql101_test_1;

FIRST_NAME       LAST_NAME
---------------  --------------------
Jane             Smith
Christopher      Allen

SQL> DROP TABLE plsql101_test_1;

Table dropped.

SQL> SELECT * FROM plsql101_test_1;
SELECT * FROM plsql101_test_1
              *
ERROR at line 1:
ORA-00942: table or view does not exist


SQL> |
```

FIGURE 2-5. *Results when trying to select from a non-existent table*

started getting confused. The third response line announces that there was an error, and the fourth response line tells you what that error is—in this case, that the table you have named (PLSQL101_TEST_1) doesn't exist.

The steps you just took demonstrated the most basic functions of a table: to receive, store, and supply information. Good job! You're done with the book now.

Okay, not really. The steps you have taken show just a tiny part of what you can do with a database. To learn more, read on.

Creating Tables

Databases are all about storing data, and data is stored in tables. To make a database useful, you need to know how to create tables that are somewhat more sophisticated than the one you created in the prior exercise. You need to know how to create tables that:

- Store various types of data, such as text, numbers, and dates

- Enforce length limits on the data entered

- Prohibit records from being entered if specific columns are empty

- Ensure that the values being entered in specific columns fall within a reasonable range

- Relate in a sensible way to data stored in other tables

In this section you will learn how to create tables satisfying the first three of these points. The last two points will be covered in Chapter 7.

Guidelines for Naming Tables and Columns

There are certain guidelines you must follow regarding the names you give tables and columns. Some of them are hard-and-fast rules, while others are recommendations that will keep your tables from looking like they were created by a novice.

Rules

The following rules are true for any table or column. Do your best to memorize these *now* to save yourself some head-scratching later when you inadvertently try to specify a name that violates one or more of the rules. (It's a good idea to put a copy of these rules on a piece of paper that you can refer to while practicing your SQL commands.)

- The maximum length of a table or column name is 30 characters.

- Table or column names can include letters, numbers, and the underscore character (_). (There are a couple of other special characters that can be used if you employ an inconvenient workaround, but using them would be nothing but trouble, so you should stick with letters, numbers, and the underscore character.)

- Table or column names must start with an alphabetic character. A name can include numbers or underscores, but must start with a letter.

- Uppercase and lowercase characters are treated the same in table and column names.

- A table or column name cannot contain spaces.

- Tables in Oracle are assigned to users; by default, they are assigned to whatever user created them. Every one of a user's tables must have a name that is different than all the other tables the user owns. In other words, a user cannot have two tables with the same name. (It is okay for different users to create tables with the same names, however.) Within a table, all of the columns must have unique names.

- Certain words represent commands and parameters to Oracle itself, and therefore cannot be used to name a table or column. You probably won't memorize all these words, but it's good to get an idea of what they are. The restricted words are shown in Table 2-1.

TIP
Speaking just of table names, one way to ensure that a table name never matches an Oracle reserved word is to preface every table's name with an abbreviation denoting the system the table is part of. For instance, in an Accounts Payable system, each table's name could begin with "AP_".

Recommendations
The following items are good to keep in mind when designing your tables.

- Table names should be singular, not plural. I know the PRODUCT table is going to contain records for multiple products. So does everyone else, so you don't need to indicate that in the table's name. Keep the name singular so that when you are looking at a diagram showing the database's tables (discussed in Chapter 7), you can move from table to table saying things like "A PRODUCT is referenced by a PURCHASE ORDER..."

- Don't include the word TABLE or DATA in a table name. Experienced users understand that an object storing information in a database is a table, and that tables store data. You don't need to remind them by putting TABLE or DATA in the tables' names.

ACCESS	ACCOUNT	ACTIVATE	ADD	ADMIN	AFTER	ALL	ALL_ROWS
ALLOCATE	ALTER	ANALYZE	AND	ANY	ARCHIVE	ARCHIVELOG	ARRAY
AS	ASC	AT	AUDIT	AUTHENTICATED	AUTHORIZATION	AUTOEXTEND	AUTOMATIC
BACKUP	BECOME	BEFORE	BEGIN	BETWEEN	BFILE	BITMAP	BLOB
BLOCK	BODY	BY	CACHE	CACHE_INSTANCES	CANCEL	CASCADE	CAST
CFILE	CHAINED	CHANGE	CHAR	CHAR_CS	CHARACTER	CHECK	CHECKPOINT
CHOOSE	CHUNK	CLEAR	CLOB	CLONE	CLOSE	CLOSED_CACHED_OPEN_CURSORS	CLUSTER
COALESCE	COLUMN	COLUMNS	COMMENT	COMMIT	COMMITTED	COMPATIBILITY	COMPILE
COMPLETE	COMPOSITE_LIMIT	COMPRESS	COMPUTE	CONNECT	CONNECT_TIME	CONSTRAINT	CONSTRAINTS
CONTENTS	CONTINUE	CONTROLFILE	CONVERT	COST	COUNT	CPU_PER_CALL	CPU_PER_SESSION
CREATE	CURRENT	CURRENT_SCHEMA	CURRENT_USER	CURSOR	CYCLE	DANGLING	DATABASE
DATAFILE	DATAFILES	DATAOBJNO	DATE	DBA	DEALLOCATE	DEBUG	DEC
DECIMAL	DECLARE	DEFAULT	DEFERRABLE	DEFERRED	DEGREE	DELETE	DEREF
DESC	DIRECTORY	DISABLE	DISCONNECT	DISMOUNT	DISTINCT	DISTRIBUTED	DML
DOUBLE	DROP	DUMP	EACH	ELSE	ENABLE	END	ENFORCE
ENTRY	ESCAPE	ESTIMATE	EVENTS	EXCEPTIONS	EXCHANGE	EXCLUDING	EXCLUSIVE
EXECUTE	EXEMPT	EXISTS	EXPIRE	EXPLAIN	EXTENT	EXTENTS	EXTERNALLY

TABLE 2-1. Oracle Commands and Reserved Words That Cannot Be Part of Table or Column Names

FAILED_LOGIN_ATTEMPTS	FALSE	FAST	FILE	FIRST_ROWS	FLAGGER	FLOAT	FLUSH
FOR	FORCE	FOREIGN	FREELIST	FREELISTS	FROM	FULL	FUNCTION
GLOBAL	GLOBAL_NAME	GLOBALLY	GRANT	GROUP	GROUPS	HASH	HASHKEYS
HAVING	HEADER	HEAP	IDENTIFIED	IDLE_TIME	IF	IMMEDIATE	IN
INCLUDING	INCREMENT	IND_PARTITION	INDEX	INDEXED	INDEXES	INDICATOR	INITIAL
INITIALLY	INITRANS	INSERT	INSTANCE	INSTANCES	INSTEAD	INT	INTEGER
INTERMEDIATE	INTERSECT	INTO	IS	ISOLATION	ISOLATION_LEVEL	KEEP	KEY
KILL	LAYER	LESS	LEVEL	LIBRARY	LIKE	LIMIT	LINK
LIST	LOB	LOCAL	LOCK	LOG	LOGFILE	LOGGING	LOGICAL_READS_PER_
LOGICAL_READS_PER_CALL	LONG	MANAGE	MASTER	MAX	MAXARCHLOGS	MAXDATAFILES	MAXEXTENTS
MAXINSTANCES	MAXLOGFILES	MAXLOGHISTORY	MAXLOGMEMBERS	MAXSIZE	MAXTRANS	MAXVALUE	MEMBER
MIN	MINEXTENTS	MINIMUM	MINUS	MINVALUE	MODE	MODIFY	MOUNT
MOVE	MTS_DISPATCHERS	MULTISET	NATIONAL	NCHAR	NCHAR_CS	NCLOB	NEEDED

TABLE 2-1. *Oracle Commands and Reserved Words That Cannot Be Part of Table or Column Names (continued)*

NESTED	NETWORK	NEW	NEXT	NLS_CHARACTERSET	NLS_CALENDAR	NLS_ISO_CURRENCY	NLS_LANGUAGE
NLS_NUMERIC_CHARACTERS	NLS_SORT	NLS_TERRITORY	NOARCHIVELOG	NOAUDIT	NOCACHE	NOCOMPRESS	NOCYCLE
NOFORCE	NOLOGGING	NOMAXVALUE	NOMINVALUE	NONE	NOORDER	NOOVERIDE	NOPARALLEL
NORESETLOGS	NOREVERSE	NORMAL	NOS_SPECIAL_CHARS	NOSORT	NOT	NOTHING	NOWAIT
NULL	NUMBER	NUMERIC	NVARCHAR2	OBJECT	OBJNO	OBJNO_REUSE	OF
OFF	OFFLINE	OID	OIDINDEX	OLD	ON	ONLINE	ONLY
OPCODE	OPEN	OPTIMAL	OPTIMIZER_GOAL	OPTION	OR	ORDER	ORGANIZATION
OVERFLOW	OWN	PACKAGE	PARALLEL	PARTITION	PASSWORD	PASSWORD_LIFE_TIME	PASSWORD_LOCK_TIME
PASSWORD_REUSE_MAX	PASSWORD_REUSE_TIME	PASSWORD_VERIFY_FUNCTION	PASSWORD_GRACE_TIME	PCTFREE	PCTINCREASE	PCTTHRESHOLD	PCTUSED
PCTVERSION	PERCENT	PERMANENT	PLAN	PLSQL_DEBUG	POST_TRANSACTION	PRECISION	PRESERVE
PRIMARY	PRIOR	PRIVATE	PRIVATE_SGA	PRIVILEGE	PRIVILEGES	PROCEDURE	PROFILE
PUBLIC	PURGE	QUEUE	QUOTA	RANGE	RAW	RBA	READ
REAL	REBUILD	RECOVER	RECOVERABLE	RECOVERY	REF	REFERENCES	REFERENCING
REFRESH	RENAME	REPLACE	RESET	RESETLOGS	RESIZE	RESOURCE	RESTRICTED
RETURN	RETURNING	REUSE	REVERSE	REVOKE	ROLE	ROLES	ROLLBACK

TABLE 2-1. Oracle Commands and Reserved Words That Cannot Be Part of Table or Column Names (continued)

ROW	ROWID	ROWLABEL	ROWNUM	ROWS	RULE	SAMPLE	SAVEPOINT
SCAN_INSTANCES	SCHEMA	SCN	SCOPE	SD_ALL	SD_INHIBIT	SD_SHOW	SEG_BLOCK
SEG_FILE	SEGMENT	SELECT	SEQUENCE	SERIALIZABLE	SESSION	SESSION_CACHED_CURSORS	SESSIONS_PER_USER
SET	SHARE	SHARED	SHARED_POOL	SHRINK	SIZE	SKIM_UNUSABLE_INDEXES	SMALLINT
SNAPSHOT	SOME	SORT	SPECIFICATION	SPLIT	SQL_TRACE	SQLCODE	SQLERROR
STANDBY	START	STATEMENT_ID	STATISTICS	STOP	STORAGE	STORE	STRUCTURE
SUCCESSFUL	SUM	SWITCH	SYNONYM	SYSDATE	SYSDBA	SYSOPER	SYSTEM
TABLE	TABLES	TABLESPACE	TABLESPACE_NO	TABNO	TEMPORARY	THAN	THE
THEN	THREAD	TIME	TIMESTAMP	TO	TOPLEVEL	TRACE	TRACING
TRANSACTION	TRANSITIONAL	TRIGGER	TRIGGERS	TRUE	TRUNCATE	TX	TYPE
UBA	UID	UNARCHIVED	UNDER	UNDO	UNION	UNIQUE	UNLIMITED
UNLOCK	UNRECOVERABLE	UNTIL	UNUSABLE	UNUSED	UPDATABLE	UPDATE	USAGE
USE	USER	USING	VALIDATE	VALIDATION	VALUE	VALUES	VARCHAR
VARCHAR2	VARRAY	VARYING	VIEW	WHEN	WHENEVER	WHERE	VARCHAR
WITHOUT	WORK	WRITE	XID				WITH

TABLE 2-1. *Oracle Commands and Reserved Words That Cannot Be Part of Table or Column Names (continued)*

Creating a More Involved Table

When creating a table, you have to tell Oracle the *datatype* and length for each column. Oracle tables can store all kinds of data, including text, numbers, dates, pictures, sound files, and other items. Oracle has specific features related to each kind of data. By far, the most common types of data in a table are text, numbers, and dates. What follows are examples of how to specify each of these common datatypes, along with explanations of the features that differentiate one datatype from another.

How Oracle Stores Text

As a basis for this topic, it's important to be clear about what a database considers to be text. It might seem obvious, but it isn't always, because some text columns are meant to store nothing but numbers.

A text column can store letters, numbers, spaces, and special characters—anything you can type on the keyboard. When a number is entered into a text column, it is still text; it's just text that happens to display as a number character. Numbers in text columns cannot be added, averaged, or subjected to any other mathematical operation. (However, there are functions enabling you to convert numbers in text columns to numbers for math purposes...but we'll save that for later.)

So why would you ever put a number in a text column, if you can't do math with it? Because there are situations where numbers are used for things other than math. Telephone numbers, for instance. Consider this phone number:

(800) 555-1212

It consists of numbers and symbols which could be interpreted in a mathematical way—but doing so wouldn't make any sense. The same is true for zip codes (12345-6789) and Social Security numbers (123-45-6789). In each of these cases, the data is comprised of numbers and math symbols, but is never intended to be added, subtracted, and so on. This type of data is best stored in a text column.

TIP

When you want to store numbers in a table, how can you decide whether to use a number or text column? Ask yourself whether you will ever be adding the numbers, averaging them, or performing any other mathematical operations on them. If so, use a number column. If not, it's probably better to use a text column.

Oracle offers a number of different ways to store text, and each is appropriate for a different type of use. The most straightforward text datatype is the one you used when creating the table in the previous exercise; that datatype is called CHAR (short for "character"). When you define a CHAR column for a table, you also specify the maximum number of characters the column can hold. You accomplish this using a command constructed like the one that follows (don't enter this one yet—it is only an example):

```
CREATE TABLE table_name (column_name CHAR(n));
```

This simple example shows the language you would use to create a table with one CHAR column. Note that three locations in the example are italicized: the table name, the column name, and the number of characters the column can hold. When italics are used in an example command like this, they indicate locations where you would put in your own information, rather than typing exactly what is in the italicized text. In this case, the italics indicate where you would place your own table name, column name, and column length into the command. Examples like this that show how a command is constructed are demonstrating the command's *syntax*.

The column's length is indicated with the character "n." In the world of databases, "n" is used to represent a location in which a number will be placed. You fill in the number that is appropriate for your application.

TIP
It is possible to define a CHAR column without specifying its length. If you do, a default length of 1 will be assigned. However, it is considered sloppy technique to define a column without specifying its length explicitly. Be sure to specify the column's length in all situations, even if that length is 1.

The other column datatype for storing text is VARCHAR2 (short for "variable-length character"). Like CHAR, the VARCHAR2 datatype stores text, numbers, and special characters. So how is it different? When a CHAR column is designed to store, say, ten characters of text, it stores ten characters of text even if the data entered doesn't consume all of those characters. A CHAR column will pad the end of the data with spaces until it is the full length of the column. So the name "George" entered into a CHAR(10) column would actually be stored as "George" with four spaces following it. Since there is no point in storing additional spaces in a column whose contents will vary in length, CHAR columns are best suited for columns where the length of the text is known to be fixed, such as abbreviations for states, countries, or gender.

In contrast, a VARCHAR2 stores only as many characters as are typed. A VARCHAR2(10) column storing "George" would only store six characters of data. The VARCHAR2 datatype is best suited for columns where the length of the text cannot be precisely predicted for each record, which describes most text columns stored in a database, such as names, descriptions, and so on.

NOTE
Why is it called VARCHAR2 instead of VARCHAR? Good question. There is a datatype named VARCHAR as well, and in current versions of Oracle it behaves the same as VARCHAR2. However, Oracle Corporation says they may change the behavior of a VARCHAR column in the future—and we have no way of knowing how the "changed" VARCHAR will behave—so you should always specify the full VARCHAR2 datatype name.

To try out these two text datatypes, enter the following code into SQL*Plus:

```
CREATE TABLE plsql101_test_2 (
      name    VARCHAR2(20),
      gender CHAR(1)
      )
;

INSERT INTO plsql101_test_2 VALUES ('George', 'M');
INSERT INTO plsql101_test_2 VALUES ('Jane', 'F');

SELECT * FROM plsql101_test_2;

DROP TABLE plsql101_test_2;
```

When you are done, your SQL*Plus screen should look similar to the one shown in Figure 2-6.

TIP
You may have noticed that in an INSERT command, text is surrounded by single quotes. This holds true regardless of the type of SQL command you are using. Text data is always surrounded by single quotes. Numbers are not.

```
Oracle SQL*Plus                                                    _ □ ×
File  Edit  Search  Options  Help
SQL>  CREATE TABLE plsql101_test_2 (
  2        name    VARCHAR2(20),
  3        gender CHAR(1)
  4        )
  5  ;

Table created.

SQL>
SQL> INSERT INTO plsql101_test_2 VALUES ('George', 'M');

1 row created.

SQL> INSERT INTO plsql101_test_2 VALUES ('Jane', 'F');

1 row created.

SQL>
SQL> SELECT * FROM plsql101_test_2;

NAME                    G
--------------------    -
George                  M
Jane                    F

SQL>
SQL> DROP TABLE plsql101_test_2;

Table dropped.

SQL>
```

FIGURE 2-6. *Inserting records with CHAR and VARCHAR2 values*

There is also another column datatype designed to store text: LONG. The
LONG datatype can store up to 2,147,483,647 characters (two gigabytes) of text.
This immense capacity comes at a price, however: The LONG datatype has many
restrictions on how it can be used. Using this datatype is outside the scope of
a "101" book, but if you need that type of storage, you can find out everything
you need to know by checking Oracle's online documentation. (See Chapter 9
for tips on using Oracle's online documentation.)

TIP
In nerd language, a piece of text is called a string, which is a short way of saying "a string of characters." People who work with data a lot often used the terms "text" and "string" interchangeably. Another common term is ASCII, which stands for American Standard Code for Information Interchange. (It's pronounced "ask-ee".) ASCII is an agreed-upon standard for the computer values that represent text, numbers, the special characters on your keyboard, and a few special codes for controlling devices like printers. It's the "lowest common denominator" standard for transferring information between computers. In standard daily use, "ASCII" is used to indicate that a file essentially contains just text—no formatting, margins, boldface, or underlining. For instance, a Microsoft Word .doc file is not ASCII, but if you use Word's File | Save As command to save the file with a type of Text Only, the resulting file will be ASCII. ASCII files can be opened by any word processor or text editor.

How Oracle Stores Numbers

To define columns that will store numbers within a table, you use the NUMBER column datatype. When defining a NUMBER column, you also specify how many digits the column will need to store. This specification can be in two parts: the number of digits the column can store before a value's decimal point, and the number of digits it can store after the decimal point.

For instance, let's say you want to create a table that stores prices for products. All product prices are under a hundred dollars. Enter the following commands now to see how creating and using such a table would work:

```
CREATE TABLE plsql101_product (
     product_name   VARCHAR2(25),
     product_price NUMBER(4,2)
     )
;

INSERT INTO plsql101_product VALUES ('Product Name 1', 1);
INSERT INTO plsql101_product VALUES ('Product Name 2', 2.5);
INSERT INTO plsql101_product VALUES ('Product Name 3', 50.75);
INSERT INTO plsql101_product VALUES ('Product Name 4', 99.99);
```

```
SELECT * FROM plsql101_product;

DROP TABLE plsql101_product;
```

When you are through, your screen should look similar to Figure 2-7.

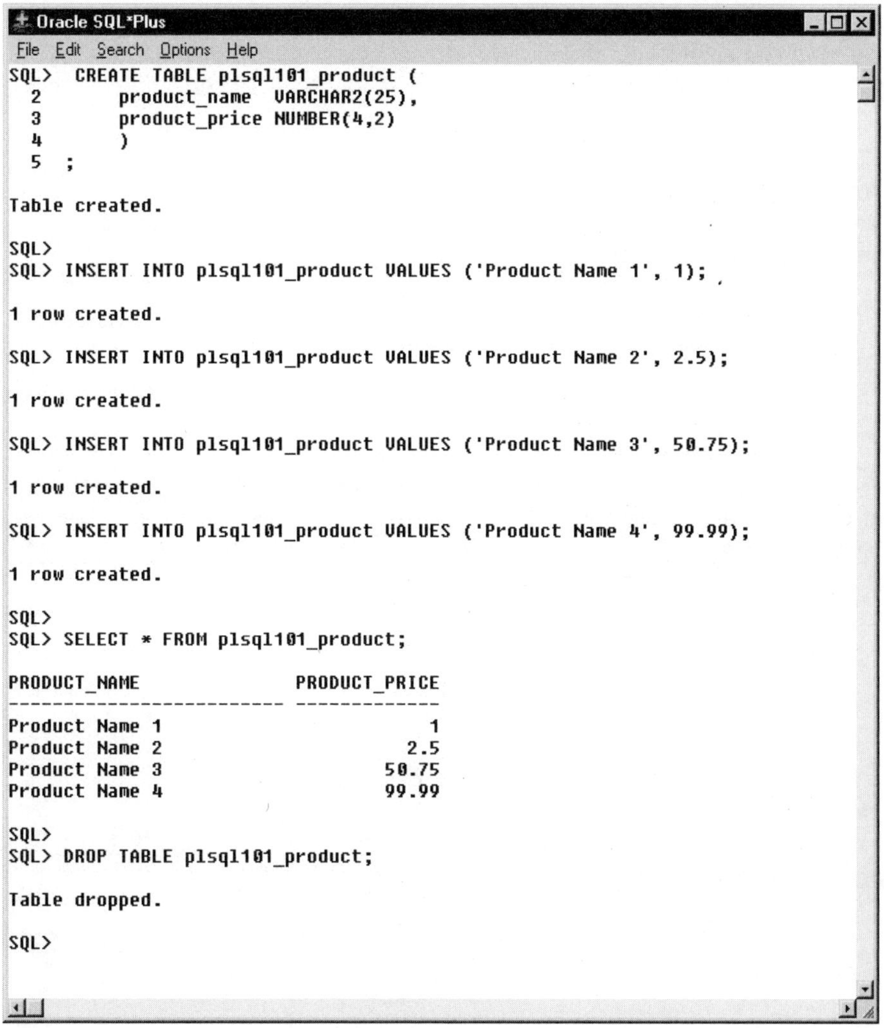

FIGURE 2-7. *Inserting records with NUMBER values*

As you probably noticed, the syntax of the NUMBER datatype is as follows:

NUMBER(*total_number_of_digits, digits_after_a_decimal_point*)

The NUMBER datatype can store truly huge numbers: the largest value it can store is 999,999,999,999,999,999,999,999,999,999,999,990,000,000,000, 000,000,000,000,000,000,000,000,000,000,000,000,000,000,000,000,000, 000,000,000,000,000,000,000,000. It can even store as many as 127 digits after a decimal place. This kind of industrial-strength capacity is one of the things that separates serious databases like Oracle from standard office productivity products such as spreadsheets.

How Oracle Stores Dates

Dates present an interesting problem for computers. For instance, consider a list of dates like the ones that follow:

January 15, 2002
February 15, 2002
March 15, 2002

You could store this list in a text column, but the dates will not sort properly, because text columns sort from left to right, and the "F" that begins February falls before the "J" for January and the "M" for March. To get around this problem, you might use numbers to represent the months, instead of month names. This would result in the following list:

01-15-2002
02-15-2002
03-15-2002

This would sort the months properly. If the dates within each month were different, this approach would handle that too, since the day-of-the-month characters follow the month characters. However, if the years are different, this approach has a problem. Consider this variation on the list:

01-15-2010
02-15-2005
03-15-2000

If these are stored in a text column and then sorted, they will sort into exactly the order shown, because text columns sort from left to right. As soon as Oracle sees that the second record's first two characters are "02," it's going to put it after the record whose first two characters are "01," no matter what characters follow.

A workaround to this problem would be to put the year first. This approach would make the list look as follows:

```
2010-01-15
2005-02-15
2000-03-15
```

From the standpoint of sorting, this would work quite well. With the characters being read from left to right, a sorted version of the list would look like this:

```
2000-03-15
2005-02-15
2010-01-15
```

That's a very nice solution, as long as all you need to do with dates is sort them into the proper chronological order. However, lots of business situations require you to do more with dates than just sort them. Accounting departments want to know what receivables are due during the next 15 days, and who is more than 30 days late in paying their bill. Executives want to know how this period's sales compare with the same period last year. Managers want to know how long a project will take if all of the lead times double. This type of work requires the ability to compare two dates and count how many days (or weeks, months, or years) separate them. This is called *date math*.

You can't do date math with dates stored as text, because the text representations have no intrinsic value as dates. They're just strings of text characters that we, as humans, have agreed to interpret as dates. What's needed for date math is a means of converting dates into numbers. Since most date math involves counting days, the most useful approach would be one in which each day has a unique number, and tomorrow's number will be one higher than today's. That way, if you subtract an earlier date from a later one, the difference will be the number of days between the two.

With humans being clever and all, an approach to keeping track of days in this manner already exists: *Julian dates*. When a system uses Julian dates, it specifies a starting date as day 1; the next day is called day 2, and so on. Since each subsequent day increments the count by one, this type of calendar is ideally suited for date math. Oracle supports Julian dates, and its starting date is January 1, 4712 BC. Oracle automatically handles the conversion of dates between the visual format we can understand (for example, '08-MAY-2004') and the Julian date equivalent. We just insert dates using a familiar text representation, and Oracle converts them to their Julian equivalent behind the scenes. When we select those dates back out from the table, they appear in the familiar form of days, months, and years. We never have to look at dates in their Julian form.

To get a taste of how dates work in Oracle, enter the commands that follow:

```
CREATE TABLE plsql101_purchase (
     product_name  VARCHAR2(25),
     product_price NUMBER(4,2),
     purchase_date DATE
     )
;

INSERT INTO plsql101_purchase VALUES
     ('Product Name 1', 1, '5-NOV-00');
INSERT INTO plsql101_purchase VALUES
     ('Product Name 2', 2.5, '29-JUN-01');
INSERT INTO plsql101_purchase VALUES
     ('Product Name 3', 50.75, '10-DEC-02');
INSERT INTO plsql101_purchase VALUES
     ('Product Name 4', 99.99, '31-AUG-03');

SELECT * FROM plsql101_purchase;
```

After completing this exercise, your screen should look like the one shown in Figure 2-8.

TIP
Dates must be surrounded by single quotes in SQL statements, just like text strings.

Julian dates have other benefits in addition to accommodating date math. For instance, if someone tries to insert the date February 29, 2002 into an Oracle date column, Oracle will prevent the insert from succeeding, because it recognizes that 2002 is not a leap year and therefore does not have a February 29. In addition, Julian dates can store time values. Time is stored as a decimal value following the integer that represents the date (or following 0 if the value is solely a time, with no date component). For instance, if a given day's Julian date value is 54321, then noon on that day would be stored as 54321.5 (the .5 shows that half of the day has gone by—the portion of the day necessary to reach noon). Oracle would store 6:00 A.M. on that same day as 54321.25, and 6:00 P.M. would be 54321.75. Other times would be stored as values that aren't nearly so tidy; for instance, 3:16 P.M. would add .636111111 to the day's Julian value. (You will have the opportunity to experiment with this feature in Chapter 6.)

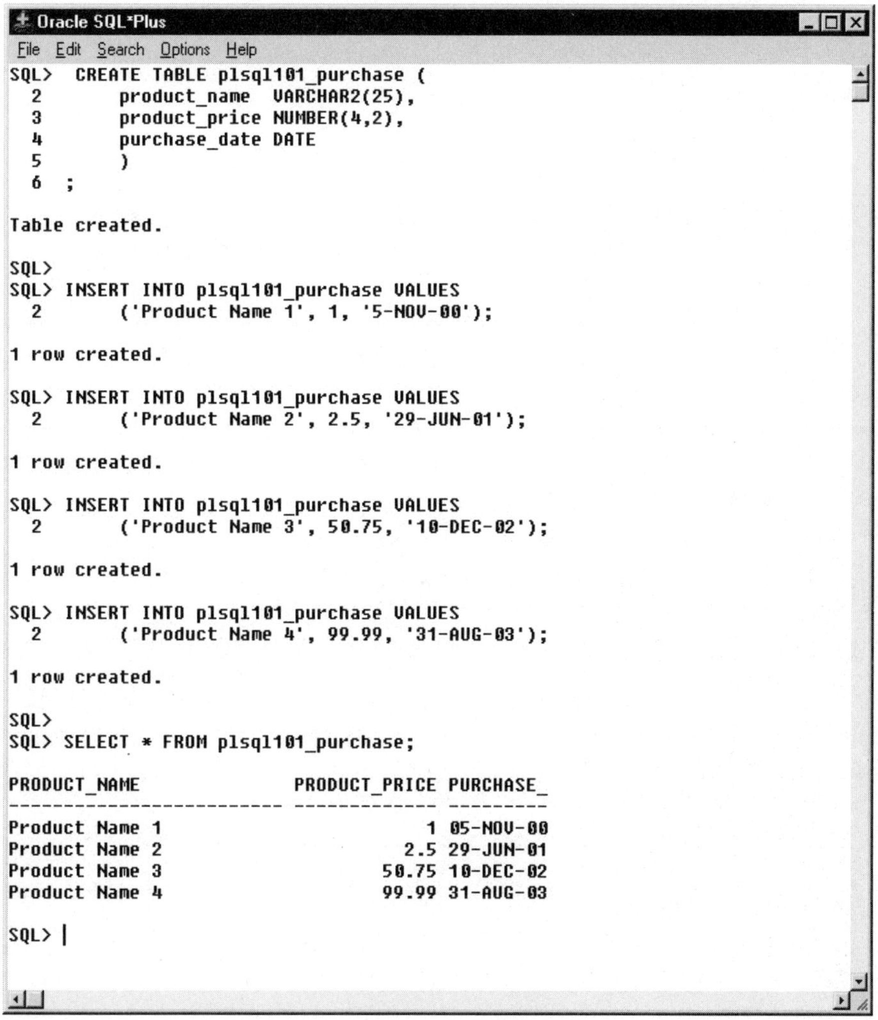

```
Oracle SQL*Plus                                                    _ □ ×
File  Edit  Search  Options  Help
SQL>  CREATE TABLE plsql101_purchase (
  2        product_name  VARCHAR2(25),
  3        product_price NUMBER(4,2),
  4        purchase_date DATE
  5        )
  6  ;

Table created.

SQL>
SQL> INSERT INTO plsql101_purchase VALUES
  2        ('Product Name 1', 1, '5-NOV-00');

1 row created.

SQL> INSERT INTO plsql101_purchase VALUES
  2        ('Product Name 2', 2.5, '29-JUN-01');

1 row created.

SQL> INSERT INTO plsql101_purchase VALUES
  2        ('Product Name 3', 50.75, '10-DEC-02');

1 row created.

SQL> INSERT INTO plsql101_purchase VALUES
  2        ('Product Name 4', 99.99, '31-AUG-03');

1 row created.

SQL>
SQL> SELECT * FROM plsql101_purchase;

PRODUCT_NAME              PRODUCT_PRICE PURCHASE_
------------------------- ------------- ---------
Product Name 1                        1 05-NOV-00
Product Name 2                      2.5 29-JUN-01
Product Name 3                    50.75 10-DEC-02
Product Name 4                    99.99 31-AUG-03

SQL> |
```

FIGURE 2-8.   *Inserting records with DATE values*

Determining a Table's Structure

When you create your own table, you know what its structure is...for a while.
Then other things take up that space in your memory and you forget. Moreover, if
the table was created by someone else, you won't know what its structure is at all.
What you need is a way to find out the structure of an existing table. You probably

won't be surprised to learn that Oracle provides a command that does just that. The command is DESCRIBE, which can be shortened to DESC. Its syntax is as follows:

DESC *table_name*

This is one of the few commands that does not need to be ended with a semicolon. However, including it doesn't hurt anything, so you may want to include the semicolon just to reinforce the habit.

To see how the DESC command works, enter the following command:

```
DESC plsql101_purchase
```

The display you see in response should look like the one shown in Figure 2-9. The DESC command's output consists of three columns: Name, Null?, and Type. The Name column lists each of the table's columns by name, in the order that the columns appear in the table. The Null? column's purpose will be explained in the next paragraph, and the Type column shows the datatype and length for each of the table's columns.

NULL and NOT NULL Columns

When you design tables to store information for a particular purpose (let's use the word *application* in place of "purpose"), you have the ability to exercise quite a bit of control over what can and cannot go into those tables. Because you have the ability, you also have the responsibility to use this capability in a way that will ensure that the data that makes it into your tables is of the highest quality possible.

```
Oracle SQL*Plus
File  Edit  Search  Options  Help
SQL> DESC plsql101_purchase
 Name                            Null?    Type
 ------------------------------- -------- ----
 PRODUCT_NAME                              VARCHAR2(25)
 PRODUCT_PRICE                             NUMBER(4,2)
 PURCHASE_DATE                             DATE

SQL>
```

FIGURE 2-9. *Results of the DESCRIBE command*

One of the first things to decide is which columns in a record must contain data, and which columns can be blank.

By default, every column in a table is optional. That means you can enter records that have data in some, but not all, of the columns. The columns without data are considered *null,* meaning "empty." A zero is not null, and a space is not null; both are real values that may or may not have significance in a particular context. When a column is null, it truly contains no value whatsoever.

It might seem like it would be a good idea to make every one of a table's columns required for entry. That is sometimes a good approach, but usually not: Most tables contain columns that won't necessarily be filled in, or that may be filled in later, after the initial entry of the record. For instance, consider a table that will store information about people. Let's say the people are employees within a company. The information you want to store about each person might look like this:

First Name
Last Name
Hire Date
Job Title
Department
Supervisor
Salary
Birth Date
Insurance Plan
Phone Extension

TIP

Individual pieces of information like First Name and Salary are called attributes in database language. Attributes are directly related to columns in a table. The column is the means of physical storage; the attribute is the content being stored in each column for each row.

Does every one of these attributes need to be filled in (or *populated*) in order for an employee's record to be acceptable? Not really. When a new person is hired, the company can't know what insurance plan the employee will choose. In addition, it's possible that his/her birth date and phone extension will not be immediately known. Requiring that these columns contain data in order for a record to be accepted would make the table unusable for its intended purpose.

On the other hand, it would be a very good idea to require data in some of the other columns. For instance, a record without a first name, last name, hire date, and salary is not likely to be usable, so those columns should be required.

You can specify which columns are required when you issue a CREATE TABLE command. (You can also change an existing table; that will be covered in Chapter 3.) Within the command, you identify a column as required by placing the words "NOT NULL" after the column's name and datatype. To see this in action, enter the following commands into SQL*Plus:

```
DROP TABLE plsql101_purchase;

CREATE TABLE plsql101_purchase (
     product_name  VARCHAR2(25) NOT NULL,
     product_price NUMBER(4,2)  NOT NULL,
     purchase_date DATE
     )
;
```

When you are done, your screen should look similar to Figure 2-10. To test the results of defining a column as NOT NULL, you need to know how to insert a record that does not contain data for every column in the table. That is the first topic in the next section.

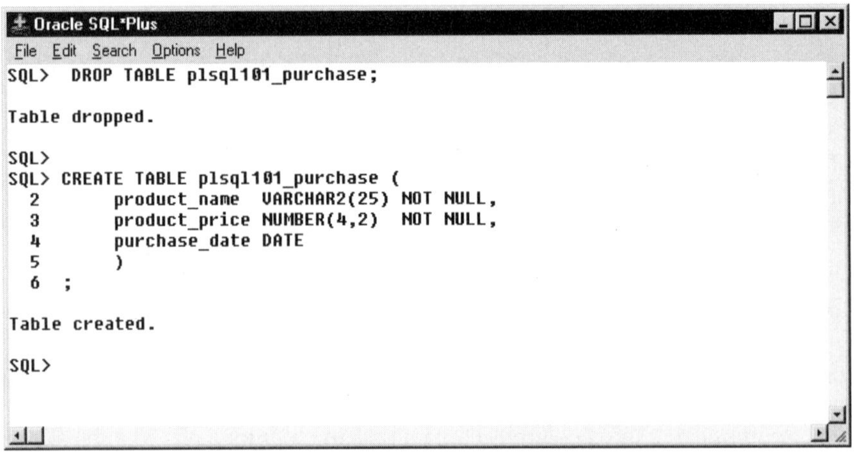

FIGURE 2-10. *Creating a table with NOT NULL columns*

Inserting Data—Additional Techniques

If you have done the exercises up to this point, you have already practiced the basics of inserting data into a table. Now it is time to learn some more advanced techniques. In this section, you will learn how to insert records containing data in some, but not all, columns, as well as how to insert data containing apostrophes.

How to Insert Records Containing Null Values

Earlier in the chapter you learned that a null value is an empty attribute—for instance, a blank birthday in a personnel record. You will probably run into a variety of situations that call for inserting records with null values in certain columns. There are two ways to accomplish this.

The first technique is to just use the word "NULL" in the INSERT statement wherever you would have specified a value. For instance, in the most recent table you created (PLSQL101_PURCHASE), the product name and product price are required, but the purchase date is not. Therefore, you could insert a record that populates just the first two attributes by entering the following commands:

```
INSERT INTO plsql101_purchase VALUES ('Product Name 1', 1, NULL);

SELECT * FROM plsql101_purchase;
```

Your screen should now look similar to the one shown in Figure 2-11. Notice that when SQL*Plus displays your record in response to the SELECT command, the record's third column is blank.

Now that you know how to insert records with null values, it is time to check whether the NOT NULL settings you defined for the table's first two columns are working. How can you check this? By trying to insert a record that omits values in either or both of the required columns. To be thorough, you should test all three variations: missing the product name, missing the product price, and missing both. Enter the following commands to perform these tests:

```
INSERT INTO plsql101_purchase VALUES
     (NULL, 2.5, '29-JUN-01');
INSERT INTO plsql101_purchase VALUES
     ('Product Name 3', null, '10-DEC-02');
INSERT INTO plsql101_purchase VALUES
     (NULL, NULL, '31-AUG-03');

SELECT * FROM plsql101_purchase;
```

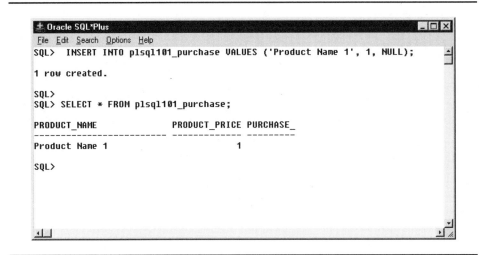

FIGURE 2-11. *Inserting records with null values—first technique*

The results of these commands should look similar to what you see in Figure 2-12. Each of the INSERT commands produced an Oracle error message reminding you in its friendly way that you can't insert null values into columns created as NOT NULL.

The second technique for inserting null values into a table produces exactly the same results as using NULL in your list of inserted values; it just achieves that result in a different way.

The technique uses a variation of the INSERT command syntax. In this variation, you explicitly name every column you are inserting data into. In all of your INSERT commands up to this point, you have not stated which columns you were inserting into; you just specified the values to be inserted. When you write INSERT commands in that way, Oracle makes two assumptions: You are inserting values into every column the table has, and the values you specify are in the same order as the columns in the table. By explicitly stating which columns you are populating, and in what order, you override both of those assumptions, and give yourself the ability to skip columns altogether.

To see this in action, enter the following commands:

```
INSERT INTO plsql101_purchase (product_name, product_price)
     VALUES ('Product Name 2', 2.5);
INSERT INTO plsql101_purchase (product_name, product_price)
```

```
     VALUES ('Product Name 3', 50.75);
INSERT INTO plsql101_purchase (product_price, product_name)
     VALUES (99.99, 'Product Name 4');

SELECT * FROM plsql101_purchase;
```

The results you see should be similar to those shown in Figure 2-13.

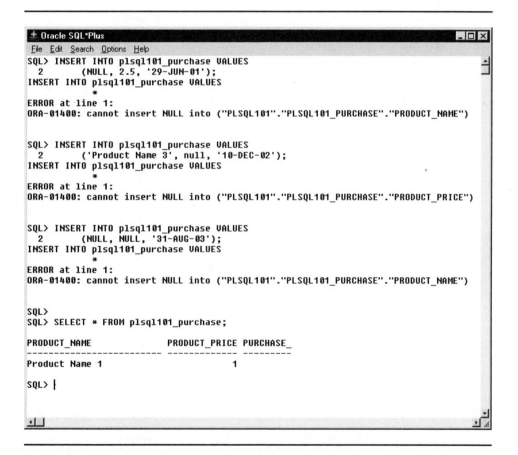

FIGURE 2-12.   *Results of attempting to insert null values into NOT NULL
columns*

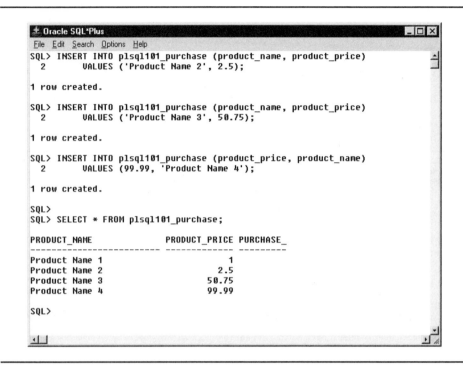

FIGURE 2-13.   *Inserting records with null values—second technique*

Notice that in the last of the INSERT commands you just performed, the columns are named in reverse order. It doesn't matter what order you specify the columns in, as long as the values are provided in the same order as the columns are named. Generally, you will want to specify the columns in the order they occur in the table—but it's good to know how to change the INSERT command's column order if you need to.

How to Insert Data that Contains Apostrophes

At some time or another, you will probably need to insert records with text that contains apostrophes. This presents a bit of a problem, since Oracle interprets apostrophes as the beginning or end of a text string. If you try to just place an apostrophe in the middle of a piece of text and then insert it, Oracle will think that the text string ends when it reaches the apostrophe and when it discovers that more text follows the apostrophe, it will get thoroughly confused. If you would like to see this in action, enter the following command:

```
INSERT INTO plsql101_purchase VALUES
    ('Fifth Product's Name', 25, '05-MAY-03');
```

In response, Oracle will display the error message shown in Figure 2-14. Clearly, this approach does not work. To make it work, you have to do two things: execute a SET SCAN OFF command before the INSERT, and place two apostrophes in a row at the location in the text string where you want the single apostrophe to be inserted. The resulting commands look like this:

```
SET SCAN OFF

INSERT INTO plsql101_purchase VALUES
    ('Fifth Product''s Name', 25, '05-MAY-03');

SET SCAN ON
```

Enter those commands, and then check how well they worked by entering this one:

```
SELECT * FROM plsql101_purchase;
```

You should see your newly inserted record, as reflected in Figure 2-15.

```
Oracle SQL*Plus                                              _□×
File  Edit  Search  Options  Help
SQL> INSERT INTO plsql101_purchase VALUES
  2       ('Fifth Product's Name', 25, '05-MAY-03');
ERROR:
ORA-01756: quoted string not properly terminated


SQL>
```

FIGURE 2-14.   *Result of trying to insert a text string containing an apostrophe*

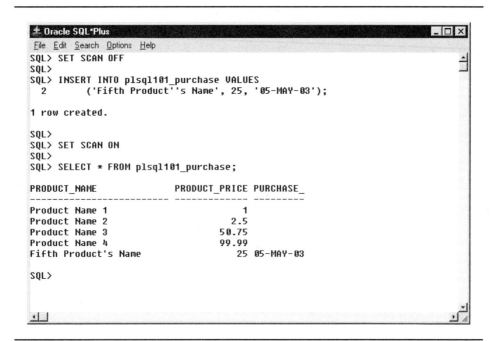

FIGURE 2-15. *Result of using correct technique to insert text containing an apostrophe*

Viewing Data—Additional Techniques

Now that you know how to do basic SELECT, it's time to learn some more sophisticated techniques for viewing data in a table. In this section, you will learn how to select specific columns out of a table, change the order in which selected columns are displayed, perform math using data in a table, connect text strings together, and change the names assigned to columns. Ready? Sure you are.

Selecting Specific Columns

As your tables get larger, it's likely that sometime you will want to view some, but not all, of the columns in a table. It's easy to do; you just name the columns you want in your SELECT statement, rather than specifying all of them using the "*" character, as you have done up to this point. To try out this technique, enter the following command to select just the first column from the table you created earlier:

```
SELECT product_name FROM plsql101_purchase;
```

In response, you should see a display like the one shown in Figure 2-16. To practice this technique further, take a moment now to execute SELECT commands for each of the other columns in the table.

To choose more than one column, name each column you want, and place a comma between each name. For instance, to choose the first and third columns from your PLSQL101_PURCHASE table, enter the following command:

```
SELECT product_name, purchase_date FROM plsql101_purchase;
```

Changing Column Order

Now that you know how to choose specific columns from a table, it's very easy to change the order in which those columns are shown. In your SELECT command, you just name the columns in the order you want them to appear.

For instance, to see the columns from the PLSQL101_PURCHASE table with the last column first and the first column last, enter this command:

```
SELECT purchase_date, product_price, product_name
FROM   plsql101_purchase;
```

In response, you should see output matching Figure 2-17. To help get familiar with this technique, take some time now to select records from your PLSQL101_PURCHASE table in varying column arrangements.

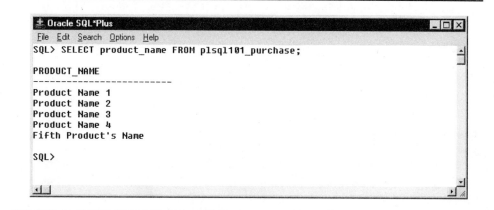

FIGURE 2-16. *Selecting specific columns*

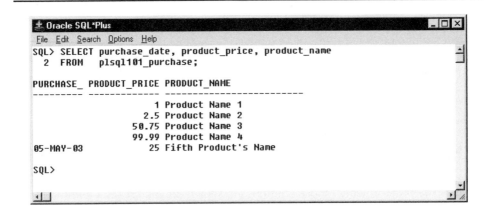

FIGURE 2-17. *Columns displayed in a custom arrangement*

Performing Math Using Data in a Table

There are many reasons why you might want to perform math operations using data stored in a table. For instance, you might want to see what the price of something would be if you increased it by 7 percent. Or you might want to calculate the amount an item costs including local tax, even if the tax isn't stored in the table. This is easy to do using SQL. You simply write SELECT statements that include the math operations.

For instance, let's say you wanted to see what the prices in the PLSQL101_ PURCHASE table would look like if they were increased by 15 percent. Type in the following command to accomplish this:

```
SELECT product_name, product_price * 1.15 FROM plsql101_purchase;
```

The results you see from this command should match what is shown in Figure 2-18.

Math Operators

The techie name for math symbols is *operators*. The plus sign is an operator, for instance; so is the minus sign. Oracle supports standard four-function math: addition, subtraction, multiplication, and division. As you saw in the last example, multiplication is identified with the asterisk character (*). Division results from the / character, while addition and subtraction are produced by the + and – characters, respectively. To try each of these out in a way that is reasonably relevant to real-life

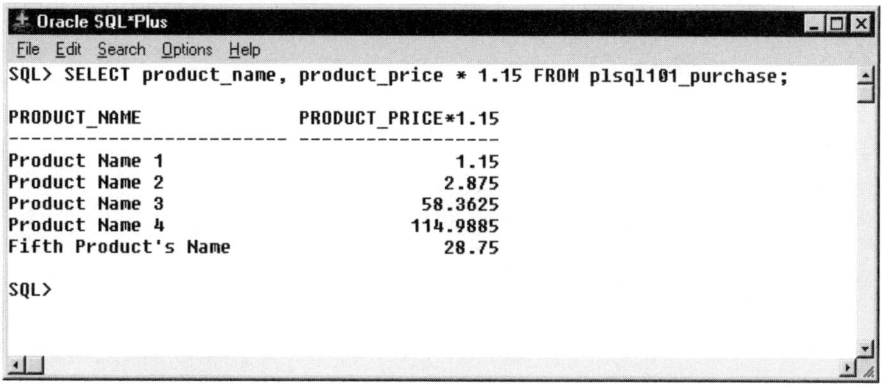

FIGURE 2-18. *Math operations: increasing a value by 15 percent*

work, we need to create a new table that has two number columns. The following set of commands will do this, as well as demonstrate the math operators.

```
DROP TABLE plsql101_purchase;

CREATE TABLE plsql101_purchase (
     product_name  VARCHAR2(25),
     product_price NUMBER(4,2),
     sales_tax     NUMBER(4,2),
     purchase_date DATE,
     salesperson   VARCHAR2(3)
     )
;

INSERT INTO plsql101_purchase VALUES
     ('Product Name 1', 1, .08, '5-NOV-00', 'AB');
INSERT INTO plsql101_purchase VALUES
     ('Product Name 2', 2.5, .21, '29-JUN-01', 'CD');
INSERT INTO plsql101_purchase VALUES
     ('Product Name 3', 50.75, 4.19, '10-DEC-02', 'EF');
INSERT INTO plsql101_purchase VALUES
     ('Product Name 4', 99.99, 8.25, '31-AUG-03', 'GH');

SELECT product_name, product_price + sales_tax FROM plsql101_purchase;
SELECT product_name, 100 - product_price FROM plsql101_purchase;
SELECT product_name, sales_tax / product_price FROM plsql101_purchase;
```

The results of the three SELECT commands should look similar to what is shown in Figure 2-19.

NOTE
This exercise demonstrates inserting dates with only two digits specifying the year. This is necessary in some versions of Oracle 7, which do not like seeing a four-digit year under normal circumstances. If you are using Oracle 8 or later, it is always a good idea to specify the full four digits of a year in any SQL command.

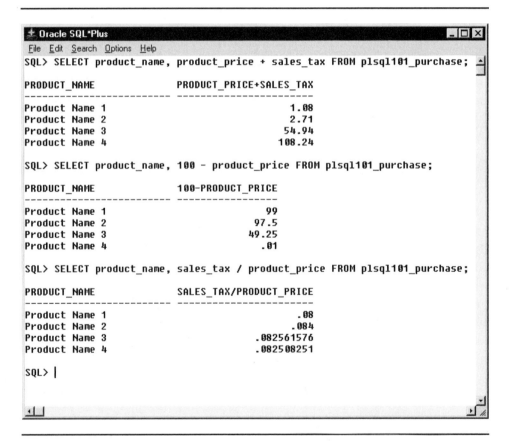

FIGURE 2-19. *SELECT commands using various math operators*

What Is an Expression?

Within the world of Oracle, the term *expression* is used to denote a variety of things. For our purposes, it refers to the portion of a command that consists of one or more column names, NULL, a value you have entered yourself (like the ".05" in the previous batch of commands, which would also be called a *constant* because its value is fixed), or a combination of any of those things connected by math operators. For instance, consider the following command:

```
SELECT product_name, product_price * 2 + 10 FROM plsql101_purchase;
```

In the preceding command, PRODUCT_NAME is an expression, and PRODUCT_PRICE * 2 + 10 is another expression.

Looking at that example, you might wonder: "How does Oracle handle a situation where an expression contains more than one math operator?" That brings us to the topic of *operator precedence*.

Operator Precedence

When an expression contains more than one math operator, Oracle does have a method to decide the order in which to perform the operations. Multiplication, division, and anything appearing in parentheses are done first and from left to right. Once they are calculated, addition and subtraction are done next, also left to right.

However, many people forget which math operators are calculated first, if they ever knew at all. Because of this, it's a good idea to identify calculation precedence explicitly in your statements by using parentheses. Surround the portion of the expression you want executed first in a pair of parentheses, and there will never be any question how the expression will be calculated.

For instance, a clearer way to write the preceding example would be as follows:

```
SELECT product_name, (product_price * 2) + 10 FROM plsql101_purchase;
```

Connecting Two or More Pieces of Text Together

There are many, many situations in the world of databases where it is desirable to display the contents of two or more text columns together in one connected string of text, while continuing to store the text pieces in separate columns. For instance, a mailing label has a person's last name following their first name, and the city, state, and zip code (or equivalents for your country) are all on the same line—but are stored in separate columns in the table. Connecting two pieces of text is called *concatenation*.

In Oracle SELECT statements, you can indicate that two columns should be concatenated by putting two vertical bars (||) between the column names. For instance, the following command would concatenate the contents of the product name and salesperson columns:

```
SELECT product_name || salesperson FROM plsql101_purchase;
```

However, this command's output would be hard to read, because the product name would be followed immediately by the salesperson's initials; there would be no space between them. A more readable variation would be to insert between the columns a fixed string of text written to support and clarify the data that will be on either side. To separate the fixed text from the data that will surround it, it often makes sense to place a space before the fixed text, and another space after it. As is the case with other text in SQL commands, the fixed text string will be surrounded with single quotes. Type in the following command to see how this works:

```
SELECT product_name || ' was sold by ' || salesperson
FROM    plsql101_purchase;
```

The results of this command should match what you see in Figure 2-20.

When you include fixed text in a command, the fixed text is called a *literal*. This means that it will be reproduced character for character, and not interpreted as the name of a table, column, or other object.

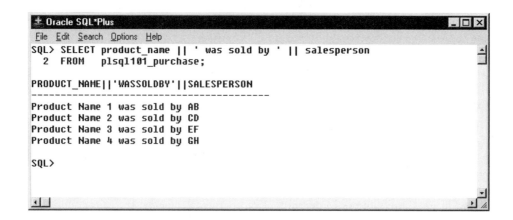

FIGURE 2-20. *Using string concatenation and literal text in a SELECT command*

Assigning Aliases to Columns

You may have noticed in the last command that the column's header has gotten out of hand. By default, column headers are the column names. However, when you execute a SELECT statement that includes concatenated columns, the entire expression that generates the concatenated output is displayed as the column's header. This is usually unattractive and rarely helpful. SQL lets you define what will be placed at the top of a column in a SELECT statement. It's easy: After the column name (or expression), you just type the text you want displayed at the top of the output column.

To see this in action, enter the following variation on the previous SELECT command:

```
SELECT product_name || ' was sold by ' || salesperson SOLDBY
FROM   plsql101_purchase;
```

The surrogate name you specify for the column is called a *column alias*. This particular column alias, SOLDBY, gives a more readable column name, but it's still a little clumsy. If you surround the alias in double quotes, you can include spaces in it, and use lowercase letters, too. (You have to use double quotes here so Oracle will not try to interpret the column alias as a column name to select.) You can see this work by entering the following command:

```
SELECT product_name || ' was sold by ' || salesperson "Sold By"
FROM   plsql101_purchase;
```

Your display should look similar to the one shown in Figure 2-21.

```
Oracle SQL*Plus                                              _ □ ×
File  Edit  Search  Options  Help
SQL> SELECT product_name || ' was sold by ' || salesperson "Sold By"
  2  FROM    plsql101_purchase;

Sold By
-------------------------------------------
Product Name 1 was sold by AB
Product Name 2 was sold by CD
Product Name 3 was sold by EF
Product Name 4 was sold by GH

SQL>
```

FIGURE 2-21. *Changing a column's header using a column alias*

Chapter Summary

This chapter has given you a good foundation in the basics of SQL. After doing a quick exercise demonstrating how a table is created, used, and dropped, you proceeded to learn and practice detailed techniques for each of these steps.

The name for a table or column can be up to 30 characters long. It must start with a letter, and can contain letters, numbers, and a small assortment of special characters, the most useful of which is the underscore "_", which you can use to visually separate words in the name. You cannot put a space in a table or column name. Oracle treats upper- and lowercase characters as identical values.

A number of words are reserved and cannot be used as table or column names; these include commands such as CREATE, as well as object names such as ROW. There are too many reserved words for most people to memorize; you will know if you accidentally use one of them because Oracle will display an error message stating "Invalid table name" or "Invalid column name" instead of completing the command. If you encounter this problem with a table name, add an abbreviation to the beginning of the name identifying what system the table is part of (for instance, AP_ADMIN instead of ADMIN). If you encounter the problem with a column name, add another word or two to the column name to more clearly describe what the column will contain.

Whenever you create a table, you are automatically assigned as the table's owner. The tables you own must all have unique names; you cannot own two tables that have the same name. (Two different Oracle users can have tables with the same name, however.) Within a table, each column must have a unique name. The same column name can be used in more than one table.

As a matter of general procedure, it is best to make table names singular, not plural: the employee table would be called EMPLOYEE, not EMPLOYEES. Also, there is no need to include the words TABLE and DATA in a table name, since both pieces of information are inferred by the fact that it is a table in the first place. When creating a table, you have to tell Oracle the datatype and length for each column. Oracle tables can store all kinds of data, including text, numbers, dates, pictures, sound files, and other items. Oracle has specific features related to each kind of data. By far, the most common types of data in a table are text, numbers, and dates.

Text columns can store letters, numbers, spaces, and special characters—anything you can type on the keyboard. When a number is entered into a text column, it is still text; it's just text that happens to display as a number character. Numbers in text columns cannot be added, averaged, or subjected to any other mathematical operation. It is common to put numbers in a text column when the numbers contain non-numeric characters, such as math symbols, alphabetic characters, or spaces. Data such as telephone numbers, Social Security numbers, and account numbers are familiar examples of text values that happen to contain a large percentage of numbers. If a numeric value is never going to be added, averaged, or in any other way involved in a mathematical operation, it is a good candidate for a text column.

There are two main types of text columns: fixed length and variable length. You can create a fixed-length column by specifying a datatype of CHAR in your CREATE TABLE command. A CHAR column places spaces after any data entered, so the total length of the data (plus spaces) is always equal to the length of the column. This can be wasteful of storage space, so fixed-length CHAR columns are only appropriate for columns whose entries will always be the same length, for instance, gender or state codes.

Most text columns will contain data of varying lengths, so you will want to use the VARCHAR2 datatype when creating those columns. If the data you need to store in a text column is longer than the 2,000-character limit of a VARCHAR2 column, you can employ a LONG datatype to store up to two billion characters per entry.

A text value is commonly referred to as a "string." When referring to strings in SQL commands, you must always surround the string in single quotes. Simple text containing just the characters you find on your keyboard—and no formatting characters such as the kind inserted by word processors and spreadsheets—is often called ASCII text (ASCII is the acronym for the American Standard Code for Information Interchange). ASCII is the "lowest common denominator" standard for transferring information between computers.

In contrast to text columns, Oracle offers one basic type of number column. Its datatype, appropriately enough, is NUMBER. When creating a number column, you simply specify the maximum number of digits it can hold, along with the number of decimal places its numbers will need. The largest number you can store is 999,999,999,999,999,999,999,999,999,999,999,990,000,000,000,000,000, 000,000,000,000,000,000,000,000,000,000,000,000,000,000,000,000,000, 000,000,000,000,000,000.

Oracle provides a DATE datatype that stores both dates and times. To store dates, Oracle converts date values (which are also surrounded by single quotes) into Julian dates. Oracle automatically handles the conversion of dates between the visual format we can understand (for example, '08-MAY-2004') and the Julian date equivalent. We just insert dates using a familiar text representation, and Oracle converts them to their Julian equivalent behind the scenes. When we select those dates back out from the table, they appear in the familiar form of days, months, and years. We never have to look at dates in their Julian form.

The DATE datatype can be used to perform date math. For instance, to produce a date one week away from a known date, you simply add 7 to the known date. Oracle also performs validity checking on dates; for instance, if someone tries to insert the date February 29, 2002 into an Oracle date column, Oracle will prevent the insert from succeeding, because it recognizes that 2002 is not a leap year and therefore does not have a February 29.

The DATE datatype stores time values as decimal amounts representing how much of a day has passed at the time being stored. For instance, if a given day's Julian date value is 33333, then 6:00 P.M. on that day would be stored as 33333.75 (the .75 shows that 75% of the day has gone by at 6:00 P.M.).

After learning about the common datatypes in Oracle, you learned how to use the DESC command to see the structure of an existing table. You also learned that your CREATE TABLE commands can include NOT NULL specifications for any or all columns, causing Oracle to require inserted or updated records to contain values in those columns before the records will be accepted.

When adding or changing data in tables whose columns *do* accept nulls, you can bypass entering a value in a column by specifying NULL in that column's location in the SQL statement. You can also skip columns in INSERT commands by naming every column you care about in the command, and simply not naming the column you do not intend to insert data into. To insert data containing apostrophes using the SQL*Plus program, precede your INSERT command with a SET SCAN OFF command. Once you have finished inserting data containing apostrophes, issue a SET SCAN ON command to return things to normal.

Next you learned some more sophisticated techniques for viewing data in a table. You can specify which of a table's columns you wish to view by naming the columns you want in your SELECT statement, rather than specifying all of them using the "*" character. If you would like to see columns in a different order, name them in the order you want them when writing your SELECT command.

To perform math using data stored in a table, write the math operators into your SELECT statement, with the column name you care about included as a math variable. The resulting expression looks like a math formula and produces answers utilizing data in your table. When writing math formulas, you must pay attention to operator precedence, that is, the order in which Oracle performs operations if the formula contains more than one math operator. Multiplication, division, and any operations appearing in parentheses are done first and from left to right. Once they are done, addition and subtraction are done next, also left to right. The best way to handle operator precedence is to specify it explicitly in your statements by using parentheses; surround the portion of the expression you want executed first in a pair of parentheses, and there will never be any question of how the expression will be calculated.

When you want to add text instead of numbers—that is, concatenate text from two columns together—you can do so by placing two verticals bars (||) between the column names in your SELECT statement. If you wish to place a space between the two pieces of text, you can do so by using ||' '|| between the column names. Doing so will probably result in a column heading that is long and difficult to read, so you might want to assign an alias to the column by placing the alias name after the concatenated expression.

That's quite a bit of progress for one chapter. Read on to learn more!

Chapter Questions

1. What is a datatype?

   A. Hard-coded information typed directly into a SQL command

   B. The method Oracle uses to store dates

   C. A declaration of whether a column will store text, numbers, dates, or other types of information

   D. A type of computer terminal, used before personal computers, that relied on the presence of a mainframe computer

2. What is the correct syntax for creating a table containing two columns?

   A.
   ```
   CREATE TABLE table_name
           column_name_1 datatype,
           column_name_2 datatype
       ;
   ```

   B.
   ```
   CREATE TABLE table_name
           FROM column_name_1 datatype,
                column_name_2 datatype
       ;
   ```

   C.
   ```
   CREATE TABLE table_name (
           column_name_1 datatype,
           column_name_2 datatype
           )
       ;
   ```

3. Which of the following is *not* a benefit of using Julian dates?

   A. Date math

   B. Validity checking

   C. Proper sorting

   D. Faster operation

   E. Ability to store times

4. On which line will the following command fail?

```
SELECT first_name ||
       " " ||
       last_name
       "Full Name"
FROM   plsql101_person;
```

A. 1

B. 2

C. 3

D. 4

E. 5

F. The command will succeed.

5. Which of the following are *not* operators you can use in a math formula within a SQL statement?

A. +

B. (

C.]

D. *

E. {

F. /

6. What is the proper syntax for assigning a column alias?

A. SELECT *column_name* ALIAS *alias_name*
FROM *table_name*;

B. SELECT *column_name* *alias_name*
FROM *table_name*;

C. SELECT *alias_name*
FROM *table_name*;

D. ASSIGN *alias_name* TO *column_name*;

Answers to Chapter Questions

1. C. A declaration of whether a column will store text, numbers, dates, or other types of information

Explanation A column's datatype defines the type—and often the length—of data that the column will store.

2. C. CREATE TABLE *table_name* (
      column_name_1 datatype,
      column_name_2 datatype
)
   ;

Explanation Please refer to the section titled "Creating a More Involved Table," and especially the code used in Figure 2-6, for a refresher on this subject.

3. D. Faster operation

Explanation Greater speed is not a reason to utilize Julian dates. They are used because they offer far greater functionality and versatility than any text-based alternative.

4. B. 2

Explanation The problem will be caused by the double quotes surrounding the space on line 2. The space is text, and text must be surrounded by single quotes, not double quotes. The sole exception to this is column aliases, which need to be surrounded by double quotes if they contain spaces or are mixed upper/lower case. In this usage, the double quotes help Oracle separate the column alias from the names that make up the column's contents.

5. C, E.], {

Explanation Math operators include math symbols such as +, - ,*, /, and ().

6. B. SELECT *column_name alias_name*
     FROM *table_name;*

Explanation To assign an alias to a selected column, simply place the alias after the column's name in the SELECT statement.

CHAPTER
3

Advanced Data Manipulation

n this chapter, you will explore more sophisticated ways to work with data. By "more sophisticated" I mean you will learn how to limit selected records to only those satisfying criteria you specify, how to sort records into whatever order you want, and how to make Oracle perform real-time calculations (like a calculator). In addition, you will learn how to change data already in a table, delete data from a table, select unique values from a table, and undo DML operations such as INSERT, UPDATE, and DELETE. Sounds exciting, eh? You bet it is.

Limiting Which Records You Select

One of the most common functions you will perform when selecting records is getting a specific subset of the records in a table. The subset you want will change constantly in order to answer questions like "What customers haven't heard from me for more than two weeks?" or "What products have sold more than 100 units in the last 30 days?" Filtering records in this fashion is accomplished by adding a clause to your SELECT statement. The clause is WHERE, and you follow it with a statement of whatever *conditions* must be true about records in order for them to be shown. The syntax is as follows:

SELECT *columns* FROM *table_name* WHERE *condition(s)*;

As an example, a condition could be that a person's last contact date is more than two weeks ago. Or it could be that a product's sale date is 30 or fewer days before today, and that the total quantity sold is greater than 100. Let's go through some exercises to show how this is done. To give you something to work with, let's re-create the PLSQL101_PRODUCT table with a few more columns, and place records in it using the following commands:

```
DROP TABLE plsql101_product;

CREATE TABLE plsql101_product (
     product_name      VARCHAR2(25),
     product_price     NUMBER(4,2),
     quantity_on_hand  NUMBER(5,0),
     last_stock_date   DATE
     )
;

INSERT INTO plsql101_product VALUES
     ('Small Widget', 99, 1, '15-JAN-03');
INSERT INTO plsql101_product VALUES
     ('Medium Wodget', 75, 1000, '15-JAN-02');
INSERT INTO plsql101_product VALUES
```

```
     ('Chrome Phoobar', 50, 100, '15-JAN-03');
INSERT INTO plsql101_product VALUES
     ('Round Chrome Snaphoo', 25, 10000, null);
```

Filtering Records Based on Numbers

There are several ways you can filter records based on values in number columns. You can tell Oracle to show you only records that have a specific value in a column, or to show records with values above or below an amount you specify, or to show records with values between a certain range.

Selecting Records Based on a Single Value

To select all the records from your test table that have a quantity of 1, enter the following command:

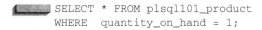

```
SELECT * FROM plsql101_product
WHERE   quantity_on_hand = 1;
```

The display you get in response should look like Figure 3-1. Take a moment now and practice this technique by selecting records whose price equals 25.

The next step is selecting records containing values above or below a specific amount. For instance, to find products that may need to be restocked, you could enter the following command:

```
SELECT * FROM plsql101_product
WHERE   quantity_on_hand < 500;
```

Enter this command now, and compare your results with those shown in Figure 3-2.

```
┌──────────────────────────────────────────────────────────────────────┐
│ ♨ Oracle SQL*Plus                                          _ □ ×      │
│ File  Edit  Search  Options  Help                                      │
│ SQL> SELECT * FROM plsql101_product                                    │
│   2  WHERE   quantity_on_hand = 1;                                     │
│                                                                        │
│ PRODUCT_NAME              PRODUCT_PRICE QUANTITY_ON_HAND LAST_STOC     │
│ ------------------------- ------------- ---------------- ---------     │
│ Small Widget                         99                1 15-JAN-03     │
│                                                                        │
│ SQL>                                                                   │
└──────────────────────────────────────────────────────────────────────┘
```

FIGURE 3-1. *Selecting records with values matching a specific number*

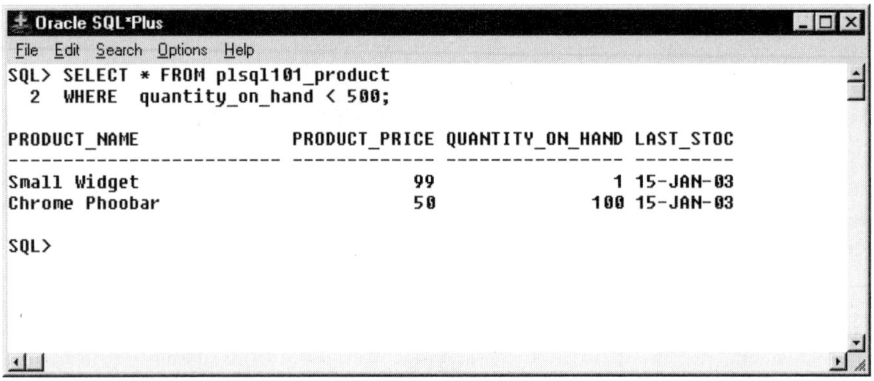

FIGURE 3-2. *Selecting records with values below a specific number*

The preceding command excludes records whose quantity on hand is exactly 500. If you want to select records that are less than or equal to a specific value, you can do so by adding an equals sign after the less-than sign. Try entering the following pair of commands to see the impact of this variation:

```
SELECT * FROM plsql101_product
WHERE  quantity_on_hand < 1000;

SELECT * FROM plsql101_product
WHERE  quantity_on_hand <= 1000;
```

The results from these two commands, shown in Figure 3-3, demonstrate the effect of adding the equals sign after the less-than sign. The first command, which states only that records with a quantity on hand less than 1000, does not include the record for the Medium Wodget, because that record's quantity on hand is exactly 1000, not less. The second command, by specifying that the values can be less than or equal to 1000, causes the record for the Medium Wodget to be included.

Extending this technique a bit further, you can select records containing values above a specific amount by using the greater-than sign instead of the less-than sign. Try out the following pair of commands to see this in action:

```
SELECT * FROM plsql101_product
WHERE  quantity_on_hand > 1000;

SELECT * FROM plsql101_product
WHERE  quantity_on_hand >= 1000;
```

```
Oracle SQL*Plus                                                    _ □ ✕
File  Edit  Search  Options  Help
SQL> SELECT * FROM plsql101_product
  2  WHERE   quantity_on_hand < 1000;

PRODUCT_NAME                 PRODUCT_PRICE QUANTITY_ON_HAND LAST_STOC
--------------------------   ------------- ---------------- ---------
Small Widget                            99                1 15-JAN-03
Chrome Phoobar                          50              100 15-JAN-03

SQL>
SQL> SELECT * FROM plsql101_product
  2  WHERE   quantity_on_hand <= 1000;

PRODUCT_NAME                 PRODUCT_PRICE QUANTITY_ON_HAND LAST_STOC
--------------------------   ------------- ---------------- ---------
Small Widget                            99                1 15-JAN-03
Medium Wodget                           75             1000 15-JAN-02
Chrome Phoobar                          50              100 15-JAN-03

SQL>
```

FIGURE 3-3. *Selecting records with values below or equal to a specific number*

Selecting Records Based on a Range of Values

The next step is selecting records containing values that fall within a range. To
define the range, you simply specify a bottom limit and a top limit. To do this, you
will learn a new technique: how to designate two separate conditions that must
both be satisfied in order for a record to make it through the filter. It's easy, really:
You just connect the two conditions with the word "AND." Try out the following
code to see how this works:

```
SELECT * FROM plsql101_product
WHERE  product_price >= 50
       AND
       product_price <= 100
;
```

Using AND between two criteria is the classic way to define a range of acceptable
values. It will work with practically every database in existence. Oracle offers an
alternative way to achieve the same result that is less traditional but easier to read: the
BETWEEN clause. Using BETWEEN, the preceding code could be rewritten as follows:

```
SELECT * FROM plsql101_product
WHERE  product_price BETWEEN 50 AND 100;
```

For practice purposes, create a series of SELECT statements now to determine whether the BETWEEN clause is exclusive or inclusive (that is, if the selected records include values that exactly match either of the numbers defined after the BETWEEN).

Excluding Records

What if you need to *exclude* a specific range from the selected records? No problem—just reverse the greater-than and less-than signs, and use OR instead of AND to connect the two conditions. This is shown in the following command:

```
SELECT * FROM plsql101_product
WHERE   product_price < 50
        OR
        product_price > 100
;
```

You can also use the BETWEEN clause to exclude a range of values; just precede it with the modifier "NOT." For example:

```
SELECT * FROM plsql101_product
WHERE   product_price NOT BETWEEN 50 AND 100;
```

The preceding example shows how to exclude a range of values from the records selected. If you just want to exclude one specific value, there is an easier way. By using the operators "<>" in your comparison, you state that records must be greater than or less than the value you specify, which is just another way of saying the records must be "not equal to" the value you define. To see how this approach works, enter the following command:

```
SELECT * FROM PLSQL101_PRODUCT
WHERE   PRODUCT_PRICE <> 99;
```

This traditional technique is understood by many different databases. Oracle also offers another way to produce the same result: using "!=" instead of "<>". Placing the exclamation point in front of the equals sign changes the meaning from "is equal to" to "is not equal to." To see how this works, enter the following commands:

```
SELECT * FROM PLSQL101_PRODUCT
WHERE   PRODUCT_PRICE = 99;

SELECT * FROM PLSQL101_PRODUCT
WHERE   PRODUCT_PRICE != 99;
```

As the last few commands demonstrate, using "<>" or "!=" instead of "=" for individual values causes Oracle to display exactly the records it would filter out if a "=" was used instead. You might be surprised how often this is useful.

Selecting Records Based on a Group of Acceptable Values

There may be times when you want to select records containing any of a group of values—for instance, every product whose color is either red *or* green *or* white. You could get that result from a command like this (don't try to enter this one—it is for example purposes only):

```
SELECT * FROM product
WHERE   COLOR = 'Red'
        OR
        COLOR = 'Green'
        OR
        COLOR = 'White'
;
```

However, this approach will quickly get tedious if you have large number values that can be matched. Instead, you can get the same result more easily by using the **IN** function, as demonstrated with this code (also an example only):

```
SELECT * FROM product
WHERE   COLOR IN ('Red', 'Green', 'White')
;
```

Note that the **IN** function is followed by an opening parenthesis, a list of acceptable values separated by commas, and then a closing parenthesis. Now let's look at how to apply the **IN** function to the PLSQL101_PRODUCT table you have built. Enter the following command to see how it works:

```
SELECT * FROM plsql101_product
WHERE   product_price IN (50, 99);
```

Filtering Records Based on Text

Now that you know how to create WHERE clause expressions evaluating numbers, it's easy to apply the same techniques to evaluating text columns. To find records containing values that match a specific text string, simply include a WHERE clause stating that the appropriate column equals the text string (which must be surrounded by single quotes, as all text is in SQL commands). Try the following command to see this in action:

```
SELECT * FROM plsql101_product
WHERE  product_name = 'Small Widget';
```

In response, you should get a display matching the one shown in Figure 3-4.

You can also specify a list of values to match by employing the **IN** function. The following command demonstrates this technique:

```
SELECT * FROM plsql101_product
WHERE  product_name IN ('Small Widget', 'Round Chrome Snaphoo');
```

Using Wildcards

When searching text, it is often useful to be able to find a small bit of text anywhere within a column—for instance, to find all records that contain the word "Chrome" anywhere within the product name, such as "Chrome Phoobar" or "Round Chrome Snaphoo." You can accomplish this by using *wildcards* to represent the portion of text that can vary. For instance, to find every record in your PLSQL101_PRODUCT table whose product name starts with "Chrome," use the following command:

```
SELECT * FROM plsql101_product
WHERE  product_name LIKE 'Chrome%';
```

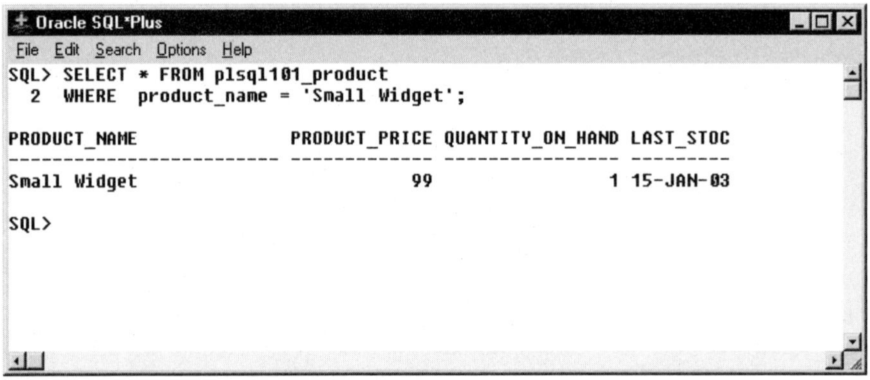

FIGURE 3-4. *Selecting records matching an explicit text string*

Note that the word "Chrome" is followed by a percent sign (%). The percent sign is the wildcard character, and when it follows a text string, it means "anything can follow this text string, and it will still be a match."

You may have noticed, however, that the previous example did not return every record that has the word "Chrome" in its product name. That's because in the other record containing "Chrome" there is text before the word "Chrome" as well as after. To include both records in your results, place percent sign wildcards before *and* after the word "Chrome," as demonstrated in the following command:

```
SELECT * FROM plsql101_product
WHERE  product_name LIKE '%Chrome%';
```

The results of the previous two commands should look like Figure 3-5. One important fact to point out here is that while the Oracle commands themselves are not case-sensitive—you will get the same result from SELECT, select, or SeLeCt— the text you put between single quotes for comparison purposes *is* case-sensitive. Searching for "Chrome" will not return records containing the word "chrome" or "CHROME." You will learn about a way around this in Chapter 5.

The % wildcard represents any amount of text—any number of characters can be replaced by a single % wildcard. There is also a wildcard that replaces just a single character: the underscore (_). You can see this wildcard in action by entering

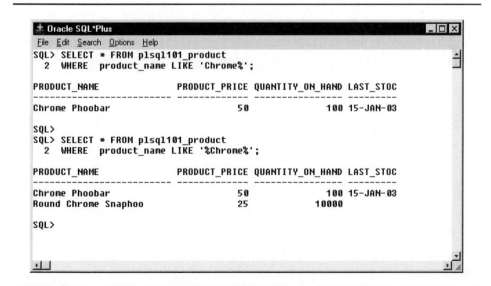

FIGURE 3-5. *Using wildcards to find text*

the following command, which retrieves every record containing a product name that contains the letter "W" followed by any character and a "d":

```
SELECT * FROM plsql101_product
WHERE  product_name LIKE '%W_d%';
```

Filtering Records Based on Dates

Selecting records based on the dates they contain works very similarly to selecting based on numbers. Since the values you're comparing are dates, however, you will need to remember to surround any date you specify with single quotes, just like you did when you inserted them.

For example, to find every record in your PLSQL101_PRODUCT table whose stock date is January 15, 2003, enter the following command:

```
SELECT * FROM plsql101_product
WHERE  last_stock_date = '15-JAN-03';
```

The results you see should match those shown in Figure 3-6. In newer versions of Oracle, you can also specify years using four digits, as demonstrated in this command:

```
SELECT * FROM plsql101_product
WHERE  last_stock_date = '15-JAN-2003';
```

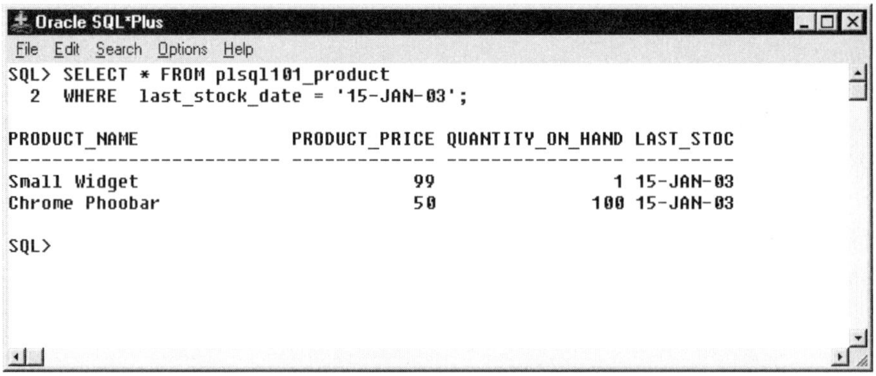

```
Oracle SQL*Plus
File  Edit  Search  Options  Help
SQL> SELECT * FROM plsql101_product
  2  WHERE  last_stock_date = '15-JAN-03';

PRODUCT_NAME               PRODUCT_PRICE QUANTITY_ON_HAND LAST_STOC
-------------------------- ------------- ---------------- ---------
Small Widget                          99                1 15-JAN-03
Chrome Phoobar                        50              100 15-JAN-03

SQL>
```

FIGURE 3-6. *Filtering records based on date*

If you want to find records containing dates before or after a specific date, you can do so using the familiar greater-than and less-than signs, as demonstrated in this code:

```
SELECT * FROM plsql101_product
WHERE  last_stock_date > '31-DEC-02';
```

You can also use the BETWEEN clause to find dates that fall within a range, as shown in the following command:

```
SELECT * FROM plsql101_product
WHERE  last_stock_date BETWEEN '01-JAN-03' and '31-DEC-03';
```

By adding the NOT clause, you can identify a range to be excluded rather than included:

```
SELECT * FROM plsql101_product
WHERE  last_stock_date NOT BETWEEN '01-JAN-03' and '31-DEC-03';
```

Selecting Records Based on Null Values

You may have noticed that even though the last two commands contain exactly the opposite criteria of each other, their combined outputs do not show every record in the database. How could there be a record that does not match either criterion, when one criterion is the opposite of the other? This situation arises when the database contains records with null values in a column named in the WHERE clause. A null value does not match any criterion, except one that checks for a null value. You can check for a null value by placing IS NULL in your WHERE clause, as shown in this command:

```
SELECT * FROM plsql101_product
WHERE  last_stock_date IS NULL;
```

To find records that contain data in a specific column, use IS NOT NULL, as shown in this code:

```
SELECT * FROM plsql101_product
WHERE  last_stock_date IS NOT NULL;
```

Try both of the previous commands, and compare the output you get with that shown in Figure 3-7.

The parameters IS NULL and IS NOT NULL work in expressions evaluating numbers and text, too; in fact, they work for any type of column.

```
Oracle SQL*Plus                                                  _□×
File  Edit  Search  Options  Help
SQL> SELECT * FROM plsql101_product
  2  WHERE  last_stock_date IS NULL;

PRODUCT_NAME              PRODUCT_PRICE QUANTITY_ON_HAND LAST_STOC
------------------------- ------------- ---------------- ---------
Round Chrome Snaphoo                25            10000

SQL>
SQL> SELECT * FROM plsql101_product
  2  WHERE  last_stock_date IS NOT NULL;

PRODUCT_NAME              PRODUCT_PRICE QUANTITY_ON_HAND LAST_STOC
------------------------- ------------- ---------------- ---------
Small Widget                        99                1 15-JAN-03
Medium Wodget                       75             1000 15-JAN-02
Chrome Phoobar                      50              100 15-JAN-03

SQL>
```

FIGURE 3-7. *Filtering for null values*

Changing the Order of Records

Most of the time, the order in which data is inserted into a table bears little
relevance to the order in which you want to view it. For instance, purchases are
inserted as they occur, but you may want to see them later in order by product or
store. Similarly, a company's employees are entered into its employee table in the
order the people are hired, but when you view a list of employees you will probably
want to see them sorted by name and/or department. To get results like these, you
need to know how to control the order in which selected records are displayed.

Interestingly, you won't actually change the order of records within whatever table
they're stored. At least not very often—doing so is a tedious, time-consuming task that
few applications benefit from. Instead, you just change the order in which they're
shown to you. Oracle fulfills this request by sorting a copy of the selected records
before displaying them, and then displaying the sorted copy. This allows you (and
thousands of other people connected to the database) to display records in any order
you want without constantly rewriting tables with newly re-sorted versions.

Sorting on Individual Columns

To change the order in which records are displayed, you just add an ORDER BY clause to your SELECT command. In the ORDER BY clause, you identify one or more columns which Oracle should sort the records by. The ORDER BY clause's syntax is as follows:

SELECT * FROM *table_name* ORDER BY *column_to_sort_by*;

To see this in action, enter the following command:

```
SELECT * FROM plsql101_product ORDER BY product_price;
```

In response, you should see a display similar to the one shown in Figure 3-8. Experiment with this technique further now by writing a SELECT command that sorts records by their quantity on hand.

Sorting on Multiple Columns

If you sort your PLSQL101_PRODUCT table by the LAST_STOCK_DATE column, you will see that a problem becomes evident: two of the table's records contain the same last stock date. How will Oracle know what order to place those records in? You can control it by specifying a second sort column in your SELECT command's ORDER BY clause.

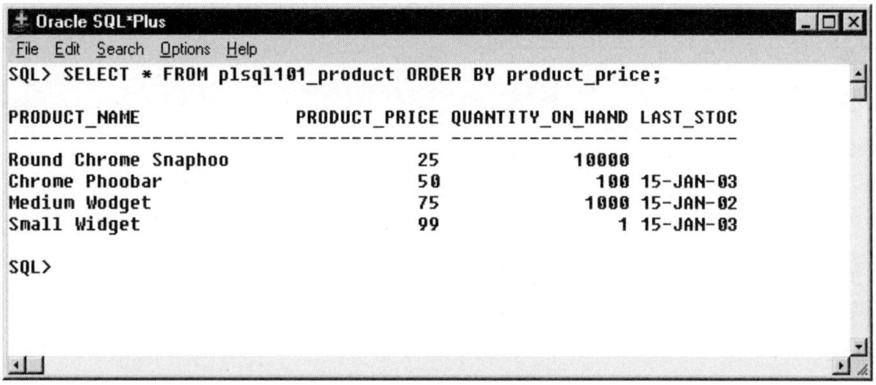

```
± Oracle SQL*Plus                                           _ □ ✕
 File  Edit  Search  Options  Help
SQL> SELECT * FROM plsql101_product ORDER BY product_price;

PRODUCT_NAME              PRODUCT_PRICE QUANTITY_ON_HAND LAST_STOC
------------------------- ------------- ---------------- ---------
Round Chrome Snaphoo                 25            10000
Chrome Phoobar                       50              100 15-JAN-03
Medium Wodget                        75             1000 15-JAN-02
Small Widget                         99                1 15-JAN-03

SQL>
```

FIGURE 3-8. *Sorting records by a single column*

TIP
When you specify two or more sort columns in an ORDER BY clause, the columns are not treated equally. The first column you name is the primary sort column, and it will determine all sorting until it reaches two or more records that have the same value in that column. Then the second sort column is applied to those records. If any of them have identical values in the second sort column, Oracle looks to see if you have defined a third sort column, and so on.

To see this in action, you will write a command that sorts product records by stock date, and within a given stock date, by product name. The command is as follows:

```
SELECT * FROM plsql101_product
ORDER BY last_stock_date, product_name;
```

The results you see from this command should match what is shown in Figure 3-9. Note that to define two sort columns, you simply separated the column names with a comma. This is the same method you used to separate column names when you wanted to select specific columns from a table.

```
± Oracle SQL*Plus                                                    _ □ X
 File  Edit  Search  Options  Help
SQL> SELECT * FROM plsql101_product
  2  ORDER BY last_stock_date, product_name;

PRODUCT_NAME                PRODUCT_PRICE QUANTITY_ON_HAND LAST_STOC
-------------------------   ------------- ---------------- ---------
Medium Wodget                          75             1000 15-JAN-02
Chrome Phoobar                         50              100 15-JAN-03
Small Widget                           99                1 15-JAN-03
Round Chrome Snaphoo                   25            10000

SQL>
```

FIGURE 3-9. *Sorting records by two columns*

In fact, let's combine the two techniques: selecting columns by name, and sorting records by column. In the previous exercise, the records were sorted based on the right-most column shown. That can easily confuse someone else looking at the data, because they will probably look at the first column, see that it isn't in order, and assume that the records are in no order whatsoever. Generally, you want order of columns to reflect the order the records are sorted in: the left-most column is the primary sort key, the next column is the secondary sort key (if a secondary sort key is needed), and so on. You can easily make this happen with the PLSQL101_PRODUCT table. Try out the following command as an example:

```
SELECT      last_stock_date,
            product_name,
            product_price,
            quantity_on_hand
FROM        plsql101_product
ORDER BY    last_stock_date,
            product_name
;
```

Your results should match those shown in Figure 3-10.

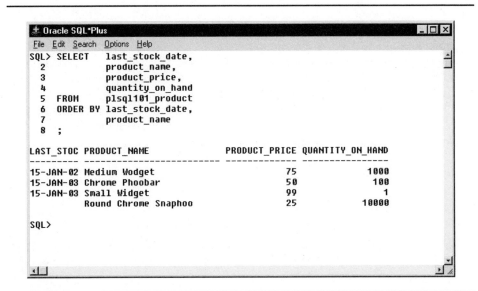

FIGURE 3-10. *Specifying column order to reflect sort order*

You can also sort columns in descending order, so that larger values are on top. While this is rarely useful for text columns, it is often handy for number or date columns. For instance, you could find the highest-priced products in your PLSQL101_PRODUCT table by entering the following command:

```
SELECT * FROM plsql101_product ORDER BY product_price DESC;
```

You can even sort by a column that isn't being selected. For instance, try out this command:

```
SELECT product_name FROM plsql101_product ORDER BY quantity_on_hand;
```

As a result, you see a list of product names. But without a column showing the quantity on hand, it's impossible to tell why the product names are sorted the way they are. This is why you will usually want to include the sort column in the columns displayed and, as mentioned earlier, put those columns in the same order as the sort order.

Showing Only Unique Values

There will probably be times when you want to know what values a column contains, but you only want to see one instance of each value. For instance, if you need to know which salesperson sold products during a particular period of time, there would be no point in having the salesperson's ID shown repeatedly, once for every sale made. You just want to know who is in that group and who isn't. Therefore, you only need to see one row for every salesperson who has at least one sales record within the timeframe you have specified. This type of approach is useful for answering questions like "Who is scheduled to work next week?" and "What products sold this weekend?".

To see this technique in action, you're going to re-create a transaction table and populate it with records. Then you will see how to get unique values out of the table. To create and populate the table, enter the following commands:

```
DROP TABLE plsql101_purchase;

CREATE TABLE plsql101_purchase (
    product_name   VARCHAR2(25),
    quantity       NUMBER(4,2),
    purchase_date  DATE,
    salesperson    VARCHAR2(3)
    )
```

```
;

INSERT INTO plsql101_purchase VALUES
     ('Small Widget', 1, '14-JUL-03', 'CA');
INSERT INTO plsql101_purchase VALUES
     ('Medium Wodget', 75, '14-JUL-03', 'BB');
INSERT INTO plsql101_purchase VALUES
     ('Chrome Phoobar', 2, '14-JUL-03', 'GA');
INSERT INTO plsql101_purchase VALUES
     ('Small Widget', 8, '15-JUL-03', 'GA');
INSERT INTO plsql101_purchase VALUES
     ('Medium Wodget', 20, '15-JUL-03', 'LB');
INSERT INTO plsql101_purchase VALUES
     ('Chrome Phoobar', 2, '16-JUL-03', 'CA');
INSERT INTO plsql101_purchase VALUES
     ('Round Snaphoo', 25, '16-JUL-03', 'LB');
INSERT INTO plsql101_purchase VALUES
     ('Chrome Phoobar', 2, '17-JUL-03', 'BB');
```

Selecting unique values from a table is similar to selecting a regular list of values; you just add the modifier DISTINCT to the SELECT command, as shown in the following pair of commands:

```
SELECT    product_name
FROM      plsql101_purchase
ORDER BY product_name;

SELECT DISTINCT product_name
FROM            plsql101_purchase
ORDER BY        product_name;
```

After you have entered both of these commands, compare the results you get with those shown in Figure 3-11.

You can also get the same results by using the modifier UNIQUE instead of DISTINCT, as shown in the following command:

```
SELECT  UNIQUE product_name
FROM            plsql101_purchase
ORDER BY        product_name;
```

The DISTINCT and UNIQUE modifiers produce identical results. Because DISTINCT tends to be more common, it will be used throughout this book.

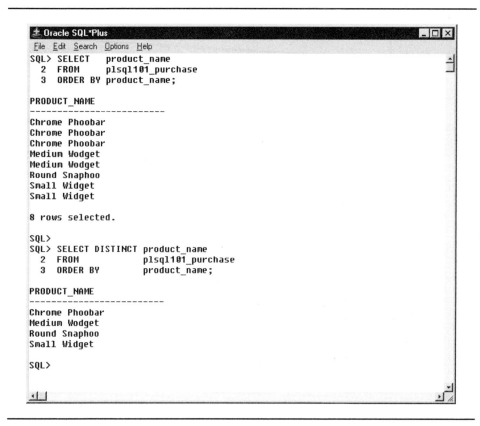

FIGURE 3-11. *Selecting unique values from a table*

Selecting unique values is especially useful when you limit the records to those matching a criterion that is important to you. For instance, to see who made sales during the first half of July, you could use the following command:

```
SELECT DISTINCT salesperson
FROM            plsql101_purchase
WHERE           purchase_date BETWEEN '01-JUL-03' AND '15-JUL-03'
ORDER BY        salesperson;
```

Selecting from DUAL

In Chapter 2 you saw that it was possible to perform math on values stored in a database, by defining the equation in your SELECT statement. The examples you tried in that chapter included the following (which will not work now, by the way, because the table they refer to no longer has a SALES_TAX column):

```
SELECT product_name, product_price + sales_tax FROM plsql101_purchase;
SELECT product_name, 100 - product_price FROM plsql101_purchase;
SELECT product_name, sales_tax / product_price FROM plsql101_purchase;
```

You can take this one step farther and have the SELECT statement specify all of the values that should be used in the calculation, meaning that no values are derived from the table at all. To see this in action, try this command, which calculates the result of increasing the value 18 by 5 percent:

```
SELECT 18*1.05 FROM plsql101_purchase;
```

As your display will undoubtedly show, the answer is getting calculated, all right—calculated once for every record in the table. Wouldn't it be convenient if there was a table set up that you knew would always have just one record? Well, the bright folks who designed Oracle thought about that, too, and in response they designed Oracle's installation process to create a table called DUAL that is available to all users. To see how DUAL is constructed, enter the following commands:

```
DESC DUAL;
SELECT * FROM DUAL;
```

As you can see, the DUAL table contains one column (named DUMMY) and one row (whose value is simply X). The DUAL table's data is never meant to be used directly. Instead, the DUAL table is provided to support on-the-fly queries like the one you just did. Try it out by entering the following command:

```
SELECT 18*1.05 FROM DUAL;
```

In response, you should see just one instance of the answer of 18.9 displayed, as shown in Figure 3-12.

You will have more opportunities to use the DUAL table in Chapter 5. Right now, it's time to move on, and learn how to change data already present in a table.

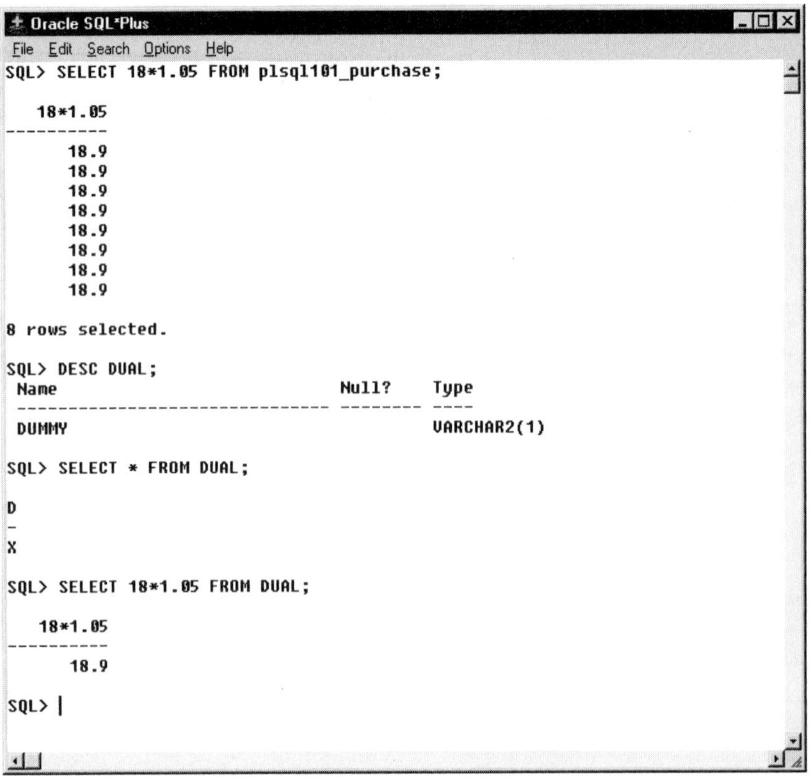

```
Oracle SQL*Plus                                              _ □ ✕
File  Edit  Search  Options  Help
SQL> SELECT 18*1.05 FROM plsql101_purchase;

   18*1.05
----------
      18.9
      18.9
      18.9
      18.9
      18.9
      18.9
      18.9
      18.9

8 rows selected.

SQL> DESC DUAL;
 Name                                    Null?    Type
 --------------------------------------- -------- ----
 DUMMY                                            VARCHAR2(1)

SQL> SELECT * FROM DUAL;

D
-
X

SQL> SELECT 18*1.05 FROM DUAL;

   18*1.05
----------
      18.9

SQL>
```

FIGURE 3-12. *Selecting values from DUAL*

Modifying Data In a Table

It's very easy to change data in an Oracle table. The command to perform this operation is UPDATE, and its syntax is as follows:

UPDATE *table_name* SET *column_name* = *new_value* WHERE *condition*;

For instance, to change all products named "Small Widget" to "Large Widget" in your PLSQL101_PURCHASE table, enter the following command:

```
SELECT * FROM plsql101_purchase;

UPDATE plsql101_purchase
```

```
SET     product_name = 'Large Widget'
WHERE   product_name = 'Small Widget';

SELECT * FROM plsql101_purchase;
```

Now select all the records in the PLSQL101_PURCHASE table. Your display should match Figure 3-13.

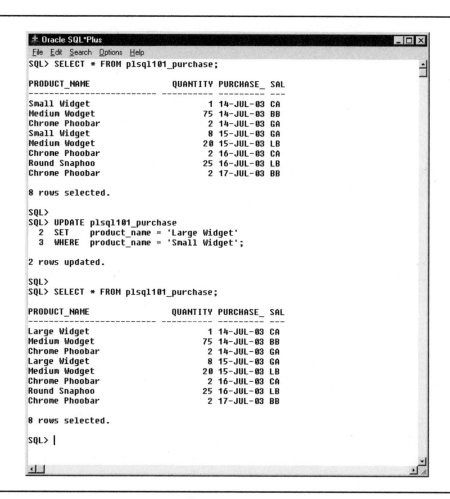

FIGURE 3-13. *Updating data in specific records*

NOTE
It is very important *that you include a WHERE condition in your UPDATE command. If you do not include a WHERE condition, every record in the table will be updated!*

Removing Records from a Table

The last of the fundamental skills you need while working with tables is the ability to delete records. The DELETE command uses the following syntax:

DELETE FROM *table_name* WHERE *condition*;

The DELETE command is easy to use—maybe too easy. Be sure you're thinking about the condition(s) you specify when using this command!

Deleting Rows Matching Specific Criteria

Let's start our experimentation with this command by deleting the newest records in your PLSQL101_PURCHASE table. Enter the following command to remove all records whose purchase date is later than July 15, 2003:

```
SELECT * FROM plsql101_purchase;

DELETE FROM plsql101_purchase
WHERE purchase_date > '15-JUL-03';

SELECT * FROM plsql101_purchase;
```

Your results should match those shown in Figure 3-14.
You can delete records using any column or columns in your condition clause. For instance, try the following command to delete the "Large Widget" records:

```
DELETE FROM plsql101_purchase
WHERE product_name = 'Large Widget';
```

Select all the records once again, and you will see that the only remaining records are those in which wodgets or phoobars were purchased July 15 or earlier.

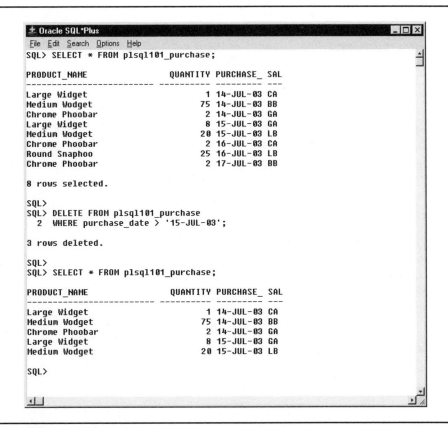

FIGURE 3-14. *Deleting records based on date*

Deleting All Rows

The final variation of deleting records is deleting all rows from a table. There are two ways to do this: using the DELETE command without specifying a WHERE condition, and using an entirely new command: TRUNCATE.

Deleting Records Without Specifying Criteria

The syntax for deleting all records in a table is as follows:

    DELETE FROM *table_name*;

While this command is easy to read and understand, it has a major drawback: Even though it says that every record should be deleted, it still forces Oracle to read every row before deleting it, as it would if you had included a WHERE condition. This can be extremely time consuming, wasting both your time and server resources. If you want to delete all records in a table, a more efficient method is to use the TRUNCATE command.

Truncating a Table

The advantage offered by the TRUNCATE command is speed. When Oracle executes this command, it does not evaluate the existing records within a table; it basically chops them off. In addition to speed, this command provides the added benefit of automatically freeing up the table space that the truncated records previously occupied.

The syntax of the command is:

TRUNCATE TABLE *table_name*;

To see this in action, truncate your PLSQL101_PURCHASE table and then view its contents, using the commands that follow:

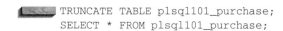
```
TRUNCATE TABLE plsql101_purchase;
SELECT * FROM plsql101_purchase;
```

NOTE
*The TRUNCATE command is not reversible! Use it
only when you really mean it!*

Transaction Control

So far in this chapter, you have created and dropped tables, inserted and deleted records, and generally done whatever you wanted, without having to think about how your actions may impact others. In real life you will be working with tables containing data that other people care about, and the changes you make will impact other users. To work responsibly, you need to understand how Oracle applies the changes you make. One of the immediate benefits of this is that you learn how to use Oracle's "undo" facility.

Undoing DML Transactions

When you insert, update, or delete data in a table, Oracle does not actually apply those changes to the table immediately. It appears to you that the changes are applied right away; if you do a SELECT command, the changes you made are reflected in the output. But those changes are being held in temporary storage, and will only be applied to the actual table in response to one of several different catalysts. You'll see what those catalysts are soon; for now, let's see how things work *before* one of those catalysts has occurred.

If you have just started reading in this chapter and don't yet have a PLSQL101_PURCHASE table to practice with, create one now using the following command:

```
CREATE TABLE plsql101_purchase (
      product_name  VARCHAR2(25),
      quantity      NUMBER(4,2),
      purchase_date DATE,
      salesperson   VARCHAR2(3)
      )
;
```

Oracle's undo capability comes via the command ROLLBACK. When you roll back one or more transactions, you tell Oracle to not apply them to the database. To see this in action, enter the following commands:

```
INSERT INTO plsql101_purchase VALUES
      ('Small Widget', 1, '14-JUL-03', 'CA');
INSERT INTO plsql101_purchase VALUES
      ('Medium Wodget', 75, '14-JUL-03', 'BB');

SELECT * FROM plsql101_purchase;

ROLLBACK;

SELECT * FROM plsql101_purchase;
```

Compare your results with those shown in Figure 3-15. The important part of this exercise is that your first SELECT returned records, while the second SELECT did not. The ROLLBACK command you issued removed the records from your local storage, and kept them from ever being written to the database table for permanent storage. The net result is that it is as if you never entered those two records.

The ability demonstrated by the ROLLBACK command is a useful undo mechanism, and it isn't limited to just one level of undo. By pairing ROLLBACK with another command, SAVEPOINT, you may specify any number of points to which a ROLLBACK command can return. The syntax of the SAVEPOINT command is as follows:

SAVEPOINT *savepoint_name;*

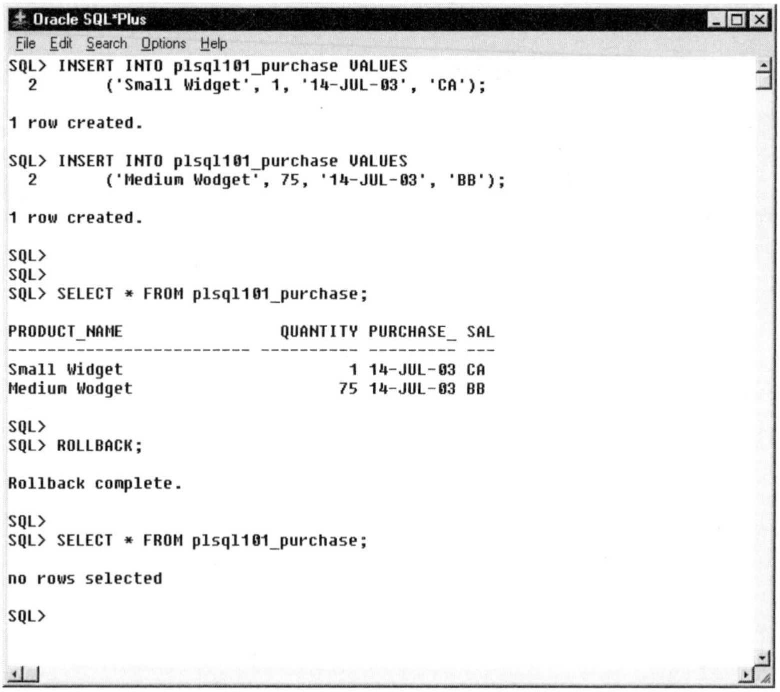

FIGURE 3-15. *Rolling back data changes*

Why would you need multiple return points? Flexibility. If you have a large batch of commands to execute, you can put a savepoint after the end of each logical group of commands, and if the next group of commands is unsatisfactory for any reason, you can still roll back to the most recent savepoint and apply your changes up to that point in the database.

To see this in action, you'll enter a series of records and place a separate savepoint after each one. Then you will roll back to each savepoint, and see how that affects the records returned to you by SELECT statements. The commands to do this are as follows:

```
INSERT INTO plsql101_purchase VALUES
     ('Small Widget', 1, '14-JUL-03', 'CA');
SAVEPOINT a;
INSERT INTO plsql101_purchase VALUES
     ('Medium Wodget', 75, '14-JUL-03', 'BB');
SAVEPOINT sp_2;
```

```
INSERT INTO plsql101_purchase VALUES
    ('Chrome Phoobar', 2, '14-JUL-03', 'GA');
SAVEPOINT third;
INSERT INTO plsql101_purchase VALUES
    ('Small Widget', 8, '15-JUL-03', 'GA');
SAVEPOINT final_sp;
INSERT INTO plsql101_purchase VALUES
    ('Medium Wodget', 20, '15-JUL-03', 'LB');
SELECT * FROM plsql101_purchase;
ROLLBACK TO final_sp;
SELECT * FROM plsql101_purchase;
ROLLBACK TO third;
SELECT * FROM plsql101_purchase;
ROLLBACK TO sp_2;
SELECT * FROM plsql101_purchase;
ROLLBACK TO a;
SELECT * FROM plsql101_purchase;
ROLLBACK;
SELECT * FROM plsql101_purchase;
```

Notice that the savepoint names in the preceding example don't really follow a methodical pattern. Actually, each name is an example of what could be a methodical pattern if it was applied to every savepoint name in the session. Savepoint names are just labels, so they can be anything you want. It is up to you to select savepoint names that make it obvious what data each savepoint covers. Savepoint names follow conventions similar to those for tables and columns: a maximum length of 30 characters, and the first character must be a letter.

Now that you know how to undo changes, you're ready to learn how to make changes permanent. The command to do this is COMMIT. Because the COMMIT command causes Oracle to write your changes to the database table—which renders rollbacks impossible—any savepoints present at the time of the commit are cleared. To see this in action, enter the following commands:

```
INSERT INTO plsql101_purchase VALUES
    ('Small Widget', 1, '14-JUL-03', 'CA');
SAVEPOINT A;
INSERT INTO plsql101_purchase VALUES
    ('Medium Wodget', 75, '14-JUL-03', 'BB');
SAVEPOINT B;
INSERT INTO plsql101_purchase VALUES
    ('Chrome Phoobar', 2, '14-JUL-03', 'GA');
SAVEPOINT C;
INSERT INTO plsql101_purchase VALUES
    ('Small Widget', 8, '15-JUL-03', 'GA');
SAVEPOINT D;
INSERT INTO plsql101_purchase VALUES
```

```
    ('Medium Wodget', 20, '15-JUL-03', 'LB');

COMMIT;

ROLLBACK TO D;

SELECT * FROM plsql101_purchase;
```

Your results should match those shown in Figure 3-16. Notice that Oracle complains about the ROLLBACK command, telling you it's never heard of a savepoint named "d," even though you created one. Oracle has forgotten about your savepoint because they were all cleared when the data changes were committed to the table.

Making Data Available to Others

Because the COMMIT command causes your changes to be written to the database shared by all other users, committing your work affects the data other users see. When you issue the COMMIT command, it makes your changes visible to other users. The flip side of that fact is that the changes you make will not be visible to other users until you commit those changes—you could insert a thousand new records, change a thousand more, and then delete another thousand, and none of those changes would be reflected in other users' SELECT statements until you commit your work.

If you want to test this for yourself, you can do so by opening a second SQL*Plus window (using the same username and password you used for the first one), changing some data in your first SQL*Plus window, and looking for the results of those changes in the second SQL*Plus window. Go ahead and open a second SQL*Plus window now, and enter the following commands in each window:

Commands for First SQL*Plus Window	**Commands for Second SQL*Plus Window**
SELECT * FROM plsql101_purchase;	
	SELECT * FROM plsql101_purchase;

INSERT INTO plsql101_purchase
    VALUES ('Round Snaphoo', 5,
    '16-JUL-03', 'CA');	

	SELECT * FROM plsql101_purchase;
COMMIT;	
	SELECT * FROM plsql101_purchase;

The results you see should be similar to those shown in Figure 3-17.

```
Oracle SQL*Plus                                                    _ □ ×
File  Edit  Search  Options  Help
SQL> INSERT INTO plsql101_purchase VALUES
  2        ('Small Widget', 1, '14-JUL-03', 'CA');

1 row created.

SQL> SAVEPOINT A;

Savepoint created.

SQL> INSERT INTO plsql101_purchase VALUES
  2        ('Medium Wodget', 75, '14-JUL-03', 'BB');

1 row created.

SQL> SAVEPOINT B;

Savepoint created.

SQL> INSERT INTO plsql101_purchase VALUES
  2        ('Chrome Phoobar', 2, '14-JUL-03', 'GA');

1 row created.

SQL> SAVEPOINT C;

Savepoint created.

SQL> INSERT INTO plsql101_purchase VALUES
  2        ('Small Widget', 8, '15-JUL-03', 'GA');

1 row created.

SQL> SAVEPOINT D;

Savepoint created.

SQL> INSERT INTO plsql101_purchase VALUES
  2        ('Medium Wodget', 20, '15-JUL-03', 'LB');

1 row created.

SQL>
SQL> COMMIT;

Commit complete.

SQL>
SQL> ROLLBACK TO D;
ROLLBACK TO D
             *
ERROR at line 1:
ORA-01086: savepoint 'D' never established


SQL>
SQL> SELECT * FROM plsql101_purchase;

PRODUCT_NAME              QUANTITY PURCHASE_ SAL
------------------------- -------- --------- ---
Small Widget                     1 14-JUL-03 CA
Medium Wodget                   75 14-JUL-03 BB
Chrome Phoobar                   2 14-JUL-03 GA
Small Widget                     8 15-JUL-03 GA
Medium Wodget                   20 15-JUL-03 LB

SQL> |
```

FIGURE 3-16. *Committing changes to a table*

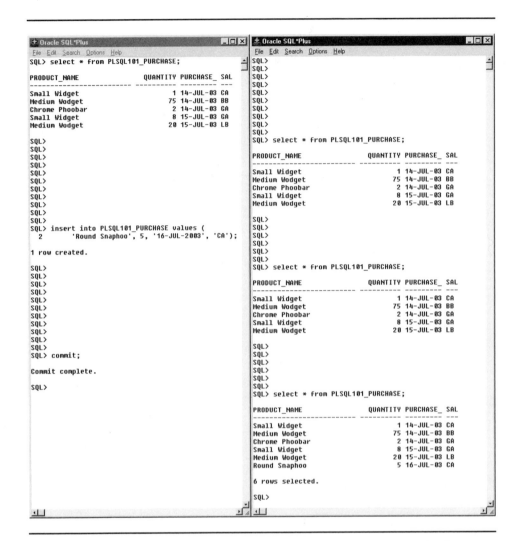

FIGURE 3-17. *Impact of the COMMIT command between different database sessions*

Implicit and Explicit **COMMITs**

By doing the exercises up to this point, you have performed several COMMIT commands. Entering the command explicitly, as you have, is one way to commit changes to the database—and there are other ways, too. Certain Oracle commands execute a COMMIT without waiting for you to tell them to—in other words, implicitly—before the new command is executed. To be specific, any DDL command (such as CREATE TABLE or DROP TABLE) will implicitly commit any unsaved data before executing the command's stated function. In addition, logging out of Oracle (or simply closing SQL*Plus) will automatically commit your changes.

Chapter Summary

You have covered a lot of ground in this chapter. You began by learning how to limit which records Oracle returns by including a WHERE clause in your SELECT statements. When filtering with a WHERE clause, you can use a variety of comparison operators in the filtering condition, including =, !=, >, <, <>, >=, <=, BETWEEN, and NOT. You can also create compound conditions by separating them with AND, or either/or conditions by separating them with OR. If you wish to select records whose values match any item within a group of satisfactory matching values, you can forego using multiple OR clauses by instead employing an **IN** function.

When searching text, you can specify wildcards in your search string by using "_" to represent single characters, and "%" to represent multiple characters, along with the LIKE operator. With any datatype, you can find or avoid records with empty columns by using the IS NULL or IS NOT NULL operator in your WHERE clause.

Once you have your SELECT statement producing just the records you want, you can change the order in which they are displayed by including an ORDER BY clause. In the clause you specify the column(s) by which the records should be sorted in the display. (Remember that ORDER BY only changes the order in which records are returned to you—it does not change their order in the actual table, because that would take much more time.) In general, you will want the left-most column displayed in your records to be the first sort column, and the next displayed column to be the next sort column, and so on; otherwise, it will be hard for people looking at the records to understand how they are sorted.

There may be times when you want to know what values a column contains, but you only want to see one instance of each value. You can accomplish this by adding the modifier DISTINCT right after the word SELECT in your query. You can also perform real-time calculations on data that isn't even in a table by selecting values from DUAL.

When the time comes to modify data in a table, you can employ the UPDATE command. When using this command, you identify the table to be updated, state what value should be assigned to what column, and then specify what condition a record must meet in order to receive the update. It is very important to include the WHERE condition, because if you don't, every record will be updated! The same is true when you are removing records with the DELETE command: If you do not include a WHERE clause, you will delete every record in the table. If that is your goal, a much faster approach is to use the TRUNCATE TABLE command, which doesn't bother reading every record in the table before deleting it.

Oracle offers an "undo" facility in the form of a group of commands that fall under the category of "transaction control." Most significant of these is the ROLLBACK command, which undoes any DML commands (INSERT, UPDATE, and DELETE) that have been performed since the last commit was performed. An explicit commit is performed whenever you issue the COMMIT command. An implicit commit occurs whenever you perform a DDL operation (including CREATE and DROP, among others), as well as when you exit from SQL*Plus.

Savepoints offer the ability to have a multilevel undo—that is, they let you decide just how far back in your DML commands you want to roll back. By issuing a SAVEPOINT command, you set a named marker that can later be rolled back to by using a ROLLBACK command along with the name of the desired savepoint. Savepoints remain active until the data is committed, after which they disappear. Once data changes are committed, the changed data is visible to other people and programs using the Oracle database. (Not understanding this can easily cause confusion if someone inserts/updates/changes some data and then doesn't understand why the changes aren't visible on a co-worker's computer—usually it means the first person forgot to commit his or her changes.)

In Chapter 4, you will learn a suitcase full of techniques for controlling the SQL*Plus program. These techniques will help you get your work done more quickly, produce output that is more attractive, and automate so you can easily re-create an action without having to type its code again.

Chapter Questions

1. What is the definition of a "savepoint"?

   A. A place within a set of DML commands where you want Oracle to save data to the server so it is visible to other users.

   B. A place where Oracle should stop processing until you tell it to continue.

   C. A place within a set of DML commands to which Oracle can return, nullifying changes made beyond that point.

   D. A parameter used to indicate when Oracle needs to back up and restore its database.

2. Which of the following is a valid condition?

   A. WHERE 'Smith'

   B. WHERE 'Job_Description' = 'Manager'

   C. WHERE SaLaRy = SYSDATE

    D. WHERE LAST_NAME BETWEEN 'K' AND 9

    E. WHERE HIREDATE BETWEEN '02-JAN-02' AND '01-JAN-01'

    F. WHERE PRICE LIKE 10%

3. Which of the following are *not* reasonable series of transaction-control commands?

    A. Insert some records, COMMIT, ROLLBACK

    B. ROLLBACK, insert some records, COMMIT

    C. SAVEPOINT, insert some records, ROLLBACK, ROLLBACK, COMMIT

    D. ROLLBACK, insert some records, COMMIT, COMMIT

4. Which of the following shows the wildcards for a single character and multiple characters, respectively?

    A. ?, *

    B. _, %

    C. ?, _

    D. ?, %

    E. %, _

    F. *, _

    G. *, ?

    H. *, %

5. On which line would a command using the following syntax fail?

```
UPDATE table_name
WHERE column_name = condition_to_be_met
SET column_name = new_value
ORDER BY column_name;
```

    A. 1

    B. 2

    C. 3

    D. 4

    E. The command would succeed.

Answers to Chapter Questions

1. **C.** A place within a set of DML commands to which Oracle can return, nullifying changes made beyond that point.

Explanation The SAVEPOINT command marks a place in a series of DML command that can be returned to later via a ROLLBACK command.

2. **E.** WHERE HIREDATE BETWEEN '02-JAN-02' AND '01-JAN-01'

Explanation Choice A does not compare anything with "Smith." Choice B has quotes around the column name. Choice C compares a column that obviously contains numbers (salary) with today's date, which makes no sense (the fact that "salary" has unusual case does not matter, because column names are not case-sensitive). Choice D tries to use a string and a number as the limiting ends of a BETWEEN operator, which does not make sense—the BETWEEN should be given with two values of the same datatype. Choice F uses the LIKE operator with a numeric column and numeric column value, but the LIKE operator only works with text.

3. **A, C, D.** Insert some records, COMMIT, ROLLBACK
SAVEPOINT, insert some records, ROLLBACK, ROLLBACK, COMMIT
ROLLBACK, insert some records, COMMIT, COMMIT

Explanation In Choice A, there is no reason to perform a ROLLBACK after a COMMIT, since there is no data to roll back to once the COMMIT has been done. In Choice C, there is no point in issuing a second ROLLBACK command. In Choice D, there is no point in performing a second COMMIT.

4. **B.** _, %

Explanation Please see the section titled "Using Wildcards" for a refresher on this topic.

5. **B.** 2

Explanation When issuing an UPDATE command, the SET clause must be included before the WHERE clause.

CHAPTER
4

Controlling SQL*Plus

his chapter presents a variety of useful techniques for getting the most out of the SQL*Plus program. You will learn how to save time and keystrokes by modifying and re-using old commands; get a "clean slate" in SQL*Plus by clearing the screen; customize the way SQL*Plus works and save those customizations so they are used automatically next time; improve the readability of data retrieved via SELECT commands; write selected data out to a disk file; and store commands in script files that can easily be re-run with very few keystrokes. Do less work and get more done! I think we can all agree that's worth learning about.

Editing Prior Commands

Up to this point, each time you have entered a SQL command into SQL*Plus you have had to type the command manually, even if it was similar to the prior command entered. SQL*Plus offers a variety of ways you can edit and re-use commands without having to completely retype them. We'll start with an approach that is likely to be very familiar, and then proceed to another approach that can be faster in certain situations.

Using a Text Editor

Even if you just started writing SQL commands when you began reading this book, I'll bet you have experienced a time when you wrote a SQL command that was a few lines long, entered it, and immediately discovered a minor mistake in the command. Wouldn't it be nice to be able to edit that command—like you edit text in a word processor—and have it automatically resubmitted for execution? You can. By typing the command EDIT (or its abbreviation, ED) at the next SQL> prompt, SQL*Plus will open your computer's default text-editing program and automatically place your last SQL command into it. You can edit the command, have it "saved" back into SQL*Plus, and then execute the edited version of the command.

I'm going to step you through an exercise that demonstrates how to do this. If you worked through the exercises in the last chapter, jump down to the heading "Using the EDIT Command." If you just started reading the book in this chapter—and therefore don't have the sample tables and data from the prior chapter created yet—enter the following SQL commands to create them before proceeding to the next section.

```
DROP TABLE plsql101_product;
CREATE TABLE plsql101_product (
     product_name      VARCHAR2(25),
     product_price     NUMBER(4,2),
     quantity_on_hand  NUMBER(5,0),
     last_stock_date   DATE
```

```
        )
;

INSERT INTO plsql101_product VALUES
    ('Small Widget', 99, 1, '15-JAN-03');
INSERT INTO plsql101_product VALUES
    ('Medium Wodget', 75, 1000, '15-JAN-02');
INSERT INTO plsql101_product VALUES
    ('Chrome Phoobar', 50, 100, '15-JAN-03');
INSERT INTO plsql101_product VALUES
    ('Round Chrome Snaphoo', 25, 10000, null);

DROP TABLE plsql101_purchase;
CREATE TABLE plsql101_purchase (
    product_name  VARCHAR2(25),
    salesperson   VARCHAR2(3),
    purchase_date DATE,
    quantity      NUMBER(4,2)
    )
;

INSERT INTO plsql101_purchase VALUES
    ('Small Widget', 'CA', '14-JUL-03', 1);
INSERT INTO plsql101_purchase VALUES
    ('Medium Wodget', 'BB', '14-JUL-03', 75);
INSERT INTO plsql101_purchase VALUES
    ('Chrome Phoobar', 'GA', '14-JUL-03', 2);
INSERT INTO plsql101_purchase VALUES
    ('Small Widget', 'GA', '15-JUL-03', 8);
INSERT INTO plsql101_purchase VALUES
    ('Medium Wodget', 'LB', '15-JUL-03', 20);
INSERT INTO plsql101_purchase VALUES
    ('Round Snaphoo', 'CA', '16-JUL-03', 5);
```

Using the EDIT Command

To see how the EDIT command works, take the following steps:

I. Enter the following command. Note that it contains some misspellings.

```
SELECT    product_nmae
FROM      plsql101_produtc
WHERE     quantity_on_hand >= 100
          AND
          last_stock_date IS NOT NULL
ORDER BY product_name;
```

2. In response, SQL*Plus should display the message "ORA-00942: table or view does not exist." This is Oracle's way of telling you that the name of the table you're selecting from is misspelled. You could retype the command, but six lines is a lot of retyping to correct two misspellings, so…

3. Type **edit** and press the ENTER key. You should see an editor window like the one shown in Figure 4-1. (The actual program that is opened to edit your text may vary from computer to computer. For instance, on Windows systems it will be Notepad by default, while on Unix systems it's likely to be ED or VI.) Your command will have been placed into a temporary file with a name like *afiedt.buf*. The name is irrelevant, because you aren't going to actually save your command to disk.

4. Correct the spelling of the column name on line 1, and the spelling of the table name on line 2.

5. Exit from the text-editing program (generally the File | Exit command will accomplish this). It will ask if you want to save your changes. Usually, a prompt like this means you are about to create (or update) a file on disk, but what's really going to happen is that the text-editing program will write your edited command back into SQL*Plus. Answer **Yes** to the prompt asking about saving your changes.

6. You will see that your edited command has automatically been written into SQL*Plus. To execute the newly edited command, type one forward slash (/) and press the ENTER key.

7. You will see that your newly edited command executes as though you had typed it manually.

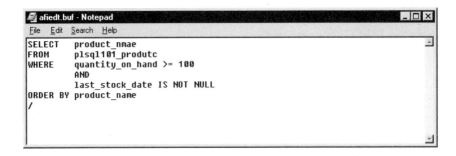

FIGURE 4-1. *Using the EDIT command to edit SQL commands*

Line-Level Editing

While it is very nice to be able to edit commands in a full-screen editor, sometimes the change you want to make is so small that you could retype the entire command in less time than it would take to open a text editor, make the change, and save it. In instances like these, you can employ a SQL*Plus feature allowing you to edit your previous command right in SQL*Plus. This approach doesn't offer the full features of a text editor, so it isn't well suited for multiline SQL commands, but it is the fastest way to make changes to short commands.

Using the CHANGE Command

The best way to understand this approach is to try it first, and afterward read an explanation of what you saw happen. Take the steps that follow to see how this approach to editing works:

1. Enter the following command. Notice that the column name is spelled incorrectly—be sure to type it that way.

   ```
   SELECT product_nmae FROM plsql101_product;
   ```

2. Notice that the error message displayed by SQL*Plus flags the column name PRODUCT_NMAE with an asterisk (*). This, of course, is because it is misspelled.

3. Type the following command:

   ```
   change/nmae/name
   ```

   Press the ENTER key to execute the CHANGE command. Notice that SQL*Plus re-displays the command, this time with "NAME" replacing the old "NMAE" in the column name.

4. To execute the newly modified command, type a slash (/) and press ENTER.

5. Compare the results you got with those shown in Figure 4-2.

As you can see from the preceding example, the CHANGE command allows you to replace any text string in a command with any other. CHANGE is not a SQL command; it works only within the SQL*Plus program.

In the previous exercise you started the command with "CHANGE." You can also abbreviate this to simply "C." The long and short versions of the command do the same thing; the "C" shortcut is simply a convenience.

The syntax of the CHANGE command is as follows:

C[HANGE] *separator_character old_text* [*separator_character new_text*]

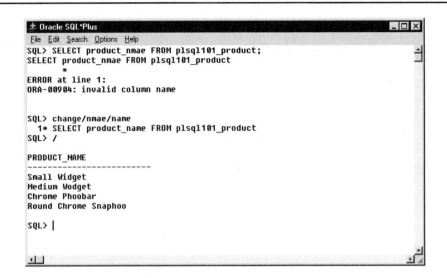

FIGURE 4-2. *Correcting a command line using the CHANGE command*

The square brackets represent portions of the command that are optional. The separator character that follows can be any character that is not a letter or a number. (In the previous exercise the separator character was the forward slash, and that is the most common character used as a separator.) After the separator character, you specify the old text that should be replaced. If you stop the command there and press ENTER, the old text will be removed and nothing will replace it. If you want to put something in place of the old text, just type the separator character again, followed by the new text to replace the old.

Take a moment now to experiment with this command. Enter a valid SQL statement, execute it, and then change it using the CHANGE command. Then enter an erroneous SQL statement and change it using the same technique.

Controlling Which Line Is Edited During Line-Level Editing

In the previous two examples, you used EDIT to modify multiple lines and CHANGE to modify single lines. The CHANGE command can also do multiline editing, but it works differently than EDIT. Instead of giving you a nice text-editing environment where you can move your cursor from line to line by just pressing arrow keys or clicking with your mouse, the CHANGE command continues to let you edit just one line at a time. To correct multiline statements with the CHANGE command, you must specify which line you want to work on before making any actual changes. You do this simply by entering the number of the line you want to change before using the CHANGE command. Entering the line number causes SQL*Plus to make that line current.

This may all seem a little abstract, because very few programs in the consumer world work this way. The best way to learn it, as usual, is to try it for yourself. Enter the following commands to do this:

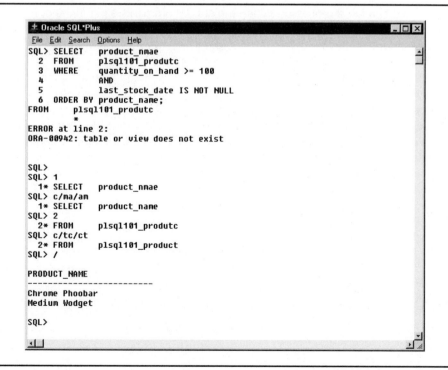

```
SELECT      product_nmae
FROM        plsql101_productc
WHERE       quantity_on_hand >= 100
            AND
            last_stock_date IS NOT NULL
ORDER BY product_name;

1
c/ma/am
2
c/tc/ct
/
```

Compare your results now with those shown in Figure 4-3. As you can see, each time you enter a number, SQL*Plus makes that line number from the prior SQL command current and allows you to modify the line using the CHANGE command.

FIGURE 4-3. *Using the CHANGE command for multiline editing*

Copying and Pasting

It's common to need to repeat a SQL command that you executed two, three, or even more commands ago. In these instances, the CHANGE and EDIT commands won't help you, because the command you want is no longer in SQL*Plus's command buffer. You can, however, leverage your prior typing in a different way. You can copy commands from the SQL*Plus display screen and re-use them by pasting them back in at the SQL> prompt. To see this in action, start by entering the following commands:

```
SELECT * FROM plsql101_product;

UPDATE plsql101_product
SET     product_name = 'Large Widget'
WHERE   product_name = 'Small Widget';
```

To check the results of your UPDATE command, you don't need to re-type the SELECT statement. You can just copy it. Move your computer's mouse so that it is just before the "S" of "SELECT." Hold down the left mouse button and drag the mouse along the entire length of the command, like you would if you wanted to copy it within a word processor. When the entire command is highlighted, let go of the mouse button and open SQL*Plus's Edit menu. Select the Copy command to place a duplicate of the command into the Windows copy buffer. Then execute the menu command Edit | Paste to paste the command back into SQL*Plus. Press ENTER to cause the command to execute. Your screen should now look similar to Figure 4-4.

You can also use your operating system's standard keyboard shortcuts for the Copy and Paste commands used in this approach. For instance, if you are running SQL*Plus in a Windows environment, you can hold down the CTRL key and tap the letter "C" to copy the selected command, then use CTRL-V to paste it.

There's an even quicker way, too. Let's try it out by making a copy of your last UPDATE command to change the product name back to its original value. Take the following steps:

1. Move your mouse pointer so it is just to the left of the "U" for "UPDATE" in the first line of the UPDATE command.

2. Hold down your left mouse button.

3. Drag the mouse over the entire first line of the original UPDATE command.

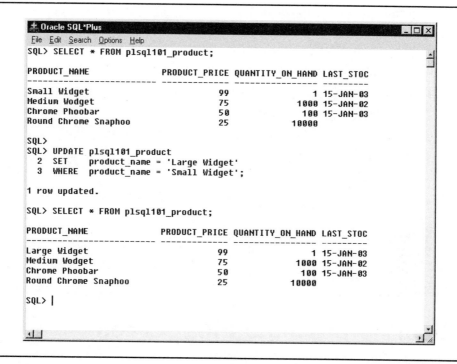

FIGURE 4-4. *Results of copying and pasting a SQL command*

4. While still holding down the left mouse button, click the right mouse button once. You will see the text you selected automatically copied to the SQL> prompt.

5. Press the ENTER key to start a new line at the SQL> prompt (its prompt will be "2").

6. Move your mouse pointer so it is just to the left of the "S" for "SET" in the second line of the original UPDATE command.

7. Hold down your left mouse button.

8. Drag the mouse over the second line up until it reaches the "L" of "Large." You want to include the single quote just before "Large," but not the "L."

9. While still holding down the left mouse button, click the right mouse button once. You will see the partial command you selected automatically copied to the SQL> prompt.

10. Type the word **Small** followed by a space.

11. Select the rest of the original UPDATE command's second line and copy it using the same double-mouse-button technique you have used twice already.

12. Press the ENTER key to start a new line at the SQL> prompt.

13. Perform a similar treatment on the original UPDATE command's third line, changing "Small" to "Large."

14. Press ENTER to run the command.

This technique works for commands that have scrolled off the top of your SQL*Plus window, too. You can scroll up to find a command, use this technique, and the command will be pasted next to your current SQL> prompt.

Clearing the SQL*Plus Screen

By now you have executed dozens or perhaps hundreds of SQL commands while practicing the things you've learned in this book. At any point have you wished you could clear up the SQL*Plus screen—return it to a blank slate, to reduce the clutter? You can, and it's easy to do. Just hold down the SHIFT key, and while holding it down, tap the DELETE key. You will see the dialog box shown in Figure 4-5. Click the OK button, and your SQL*Plus screen will clear to show just a SQL> prompt.

FIGURE 4-5.   *SQL*Plus dialog box for clearing the screen*

Customizing the SQL*Plus Environment

Many facets of SQL*Plus' behavior can be modified. You won't get much benefit from changing most of the facets, but a handful are very handy. We'll see how to change them using the SQL*Plus menu, and then see how to change a few using commands at the SQL*Plus prompt.

Customizing Using the SQL*Plus Menu

Within SQL*Plus, execute the Options | Environment menu command. This will cause a dialog box to appear that looks like the one shown in Figure 4-6. The left half of the Environment dialog box contains a scrolling list of options, while the right half contains two settings controlling how much data SQL*Plus keeps in its scroll-back buffer. By default, SQL*Plus remembers up to 100 characters of each line you type, and up to 1,000 such lines. Using the Environment dialog box, however, you can tell SQL*Plus to store up to 1,000 characters per line (occasionally useful) and up to 2,000 lines (often useful, since the lines of data that display in response to your commands are counted too). By changing these values, you can maximize the number of prior commands and results SQL*Plus stores, making it easier to go back and find commands to copy or results to compare.

To change the buffer width and length, type **1000** into the Buffer Width field, and **2000** into the Buffer Length field.

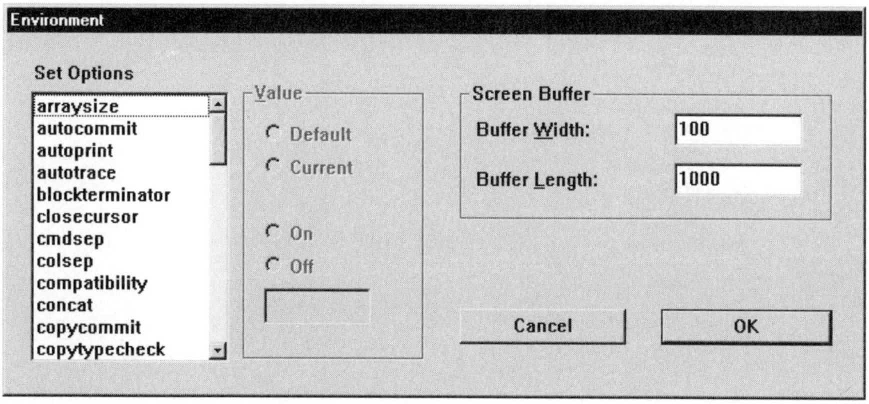

FIGURE 4-6. *SQL*Plus Environment dialog box*

On the left side of the Environment dialog box, two of the options in the Set Options list are useful at this time: linesize and pagesize. Linesize sets the maximum width SQL*Plus will provide for each line before wrapping. When the linesize is too small, the data you select may be wider than SQL*Plus can display on one line, in which case SQL*Plus will wrap columns to make them fit. It does make them fit, but it also makes them very difficult to read. Figure 4-7 shows an example of this problem. By setting a linesize large enough to accommodate the width of the data being displayed, you can make your listings more readable…to a point. The trade-off is that SQL*Plus doesn't scroll to the right, so any data not shown on your screen won't be viewable at all.

The linesize value is independent of the Buffer Width parameter modified earlier. Linesize controls how wide the lines can be, while Buffer Width determines how many characters of each line will be stored in memory for later retrieval. It makes sense for the two values to be the same, so that all of the data you see is being stored in the memory buffer.

To set the linesize value so it matches the Buffer Width, scroll down the Set Options list until you see the linesize option. Select it, and in the dialog box's Value box, click the Current radio button. This will enable the value field at the bottom of the dialog box's Value box. Enter **1000** into that field. Then click the OK button to close the Environment dialog box. Making this change will help ensure that the results you get look less like Figure 4-7 and more like Figure 4-8.

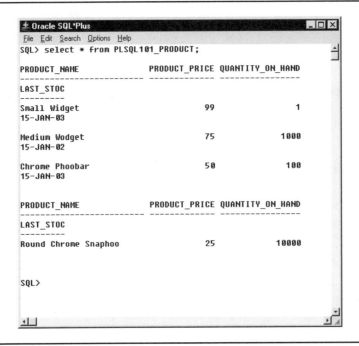

FIGURE 4-7. *Results of having data wider than the linesize*

```
± Oracle SQL*Plus                                          _ □ ×
 File  Edit  Search  Options  Help
SQL> select * from PLSQL101_PRODUCT;

PRODUCT_NAME              PRODUCT_PRICE QUANTITY_ON_HAND LAST_STOC
------------------------- ------------- ---------------- ---------
Small Widget                         99                1 15-JAN-03
Medium Wodget                        75             1000 15-JAN-02
Chrome Phoobar                       50              100 15-JAN-03
Round Chrome Snaphoo                 25            10000

SQL>
```

FIGURE 4-8.   *Results of setting a more accommodating linesize*

Another useful option is pagesize, which controls how many lines of data SQL*Plus will display in response to a SELECT command before it repeats the column headings. The default value is quite low, causing SQL*Plus to show numerous sets of headings per screen when running on a modern high-resolution display. I like changing the pagesize to 9999, so that only the longest lists of data contain more than one set of headers. You can try out this setting by entering **9999** into the pagesize option's value field.

Once you are done changing values in the Environment dialog box, click the OK button to close it.

Customizing Using Commands

All of the options shown in the Environment dialog box's Set Options list can be changed from SQL*Plus. To see this in action, enter the following commands at the SQL> prompt:

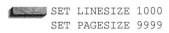

```
SET LINESIZE 1000
SET PAGESIZE 9999
```

Saving Environment Customizations

You can tell SQL*Plus to store all of its environment settings in a file that it will then read each time you start the program. This feature makes it easy to make changes that improve SQL*Plus' functionality, and have those changes automatically re-applied each time you start SQL*Plus. To accomplish this, take the following steps:

   1. Determine the file path of your *Oracle home*. The Oracle home is the folder WS(or *directory* in more traditional computer language) on your computer's

hard disk where Oracle program files are stored. If you are using Windows NT, open the Windows Explorer program (Start | Programs | Windows NT Explorer) and look for a directory with a name like "OraNT." If you use Windows 95, 98, 2000, or later versions to run SQL*Plus, you should look for a directory whose name is similar to "ORAWIN95." If you cannot determine which directory is the Oracle home on your computer, ask your database administrator.

2. Back in SQL*Plus, enter the following command.

```
STORE SET drive:oracle_home\DBS\LOGIN.SQL APPEND
```

Replace the *drive:oracle_home* portion of the command with the disk-drive letter and directory name of the Oracle home directory on your own computer. Note that this command does not need to end with a semicolon; that is because this command controls only the SQL*Plus program, and does not even get sent to the Oracle database.

The STORE command instructs SQL*Plus to save all of your current environment settings into a disk file. The login.sql file, located in the DBS directory underneath your Oracle home, is automatically read each time SQL*Plus starts. By storing your settings into that file, you ensure that they will be reinstated each time you start SQL*Plus.

Producing More Readable Output

You may have noticed by now that SQL*Plus does very little to beautify the records it displays. It doesn't align decimal places in numbers, cuts off column headings as it sees fit, and insists on showing the entire contents of a large text column in a single row, regardless of how wide the column must become in order to do so. With a few simple commands you can improve the appearance of SQL*Plus' output dramatically.

The trick to doing all of this is the COLUMN command. Like STORE, the COLUMN command does not get sent to the Oracle database. Its only job is to affect the way your own copy of SQL*Plus displays information. As such, COLUMN commands do not need to end with a semicolon like standard SQL commands do. In addition, they stay active only as long as your SQL*Plus session lasts—if you exit SQL*Plus and then restart it, the effect is gone until you issue the COLUMN commands again.

Before you start experimenting with the COLUMN command, it would be good to add a record that needs a lot of formatting to your PL/SQL 101 sample tables. Enter the following code to add such a record:

```
INSERT INTO plsql101_product VALUES (
    'Extra Huge Mega Phoobar +',
    9.95,
    1234,
    '15-JAN-04')
;
```

Formatting Numbers in SQL*Plus

There are three things that commonly need to be done to numbers:

- Align their decimals
- Place a separator between hundreds, thousands, and so on.
- Place a currency symbol with them

We'll look at each need individually, then combine them.

Aligning Decimals

The syntax of the COLUMN command to align decimals is as follows:

COLUMN *column_name* FORMAT *format_code*

You replace the *column_name* argument with the name of the column you wish to format. Note that there is no mention of which table the column is in! The COLUMN command affects all columns with the name you specify, regardless of the tables in which the columns reside. Fortunately, if two columns have the same name they probably contain similar data, so the formatting you apply to one generally makes sense for the other as well.

You replace the *format_code* argument with a representation of how the numbers should look. The representation consists of one "9" for every digit your numbers will require, along with a "." for the decimal place. (If your country's standard format uses a different character than "." to denote decimals, use "D" in the COLUMN command's *format_code* argument instead of ",", and the decimal indicator from your database's national configuration will be used.)

To see the COLUMN command in action, enter the following commands:

```
SELECT * FROM plsql101_product;

COLUMN product_price FORMAT 9999.99

SELECT * FROM plsql101_product;
```

Your screen should now look similar to the one shown in Figure 4-9. Notice how the values in the PRODUCT_PRICE column started out unaligned, and then became aligned after you issued the COLUMN command.

Adding a Group Separator

A *group separator* is a character that separates hundreds, thousands, and so on, within a number. Your PLSQL101_PRODUCT table has values in its QUANTITY_ON_HAND column that could benefit from having a comma separate the hundreds from the thousands. You can achieve this result with the same COLUMN syntax you used to get decimal alignment; you just need to change the format code. Try entering the following commands to see how it works.

```
COLUMN quantity_on_hand FORMAT 99,999

SELECT * FROM plsql101_product;
```

In response, you can see that the QUANTITY_ON_HAND column now includes commas when appropriate.

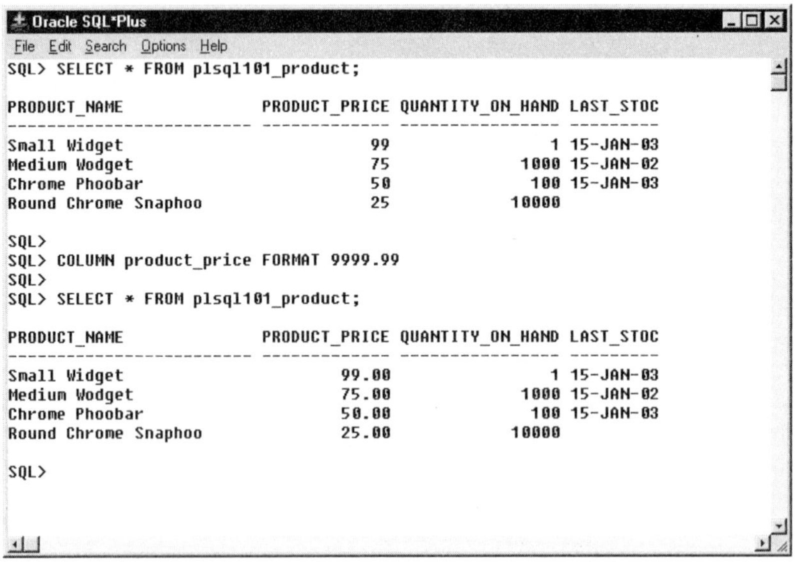

FIGURE 4-9. *Using the COLUMN command to align decimals*

Including a Currency Symbol

As you might suspect, this too is simply a variation on the format code. Try the following code to place a dollar sign ($) before each PRODUCT_PRICE value:

```
COLUMN product_price FORMAT $99.99

SELECT * FROM plsql101_product;
```

Other Useful Number Format Codes

Table 4-1 contains a list of the most important format codes you can use with numbers. Take a moment now and try out each one of these codes, so you can see firsthand what they do. Be sure to try the RN code for a little bit of fun.

Element	Example	Description
$	$9999	Places a dollar sign before the value
, (comma)	9,999	Places a comma in the position indicated
. (period)	99.99	Places a decimal point in the position indicated
MI	9999MI	Causes a minus sign (–) to be displayed after any negative value
S	S9999	Places a plus sign (+) for positive values and a minus sign (–) for negative values in position indicated
PR	9999PR	Causes negative values to be surrounded by angle brackets (<>)
D	99D99	Displays your country's decimal character in the position indicated
G	9G999	Displays your country's group separator in the position indicated
C	C999	Displays the ISO currency symbol in the position indicated
L	L999	Displays the local currency symbol in the position indicated

TABLE 4-1. *Number Format Codes*

Element	Example	Description
RN or rn	RN	Causes numbers to display as upper- or lowercase Roman numerals (limited to integers between 1 and 3,999)
0	0999	Displays one or more leading zeros
0	9990	Causes empty values to display as zeros

TABLE 4-1. *Number Format Codes* (continued)

Formatting Text in SQL*Plus

One of the most common things I hear people complaining about with SQL*Plus is that it doesn't wrap the contents of large text columns. This is a valid complaint, because it diminishes the program's usefulness. However, there is a simple way to make SQL*Plus wrap large text columns. It uses a variation on the COLUMN command. The syntax is as follows:

COLUMN *column_name* FORMAT A*nn* WORD_WRAP

You've probably figured out that you replace *column_name* with the name of the column you want to wrap. The other argument is *nn*, which is where you place a number representing how many characters wide the wrapped column should be. (The "A" preceding the number stands for "alphanumeric.")

Try out the following commands to see how this works:

```
SELECT * FROM plsql101_product;

COLUMN product_name FORMAT A10 WORD_WRAP

SELECT * FROM plsql101_product;
```

As you can see, the product names now fit easily into a narrow space. You might be thinking, "They fit before, too." That's true. This technique works best with columns that are wider: 30, 40, 50, 100, or even several hundred characters wide. So why didn't I create an exercise showing how it works with text that long?

Do *you* want to type in a bunch of hundred-character-long product names?

I didn't think so. Remember this technique, and when a situation arises where a wide column doesn't fit within the SQL*Plus screen, you'll know what to do.

Formatting Column Headings in SQL*Plus

While the techniques you've learned so far give you the ability to polish up the appearance of the records being displayed, the column headings above those records are still a mess. Besides being comprised entirely of capital letters, the column names are too long to fit within the width of some of the columns—so some of the names are cut off. A variation of the COLUMN command will take care of that. The new syntax is:

COLUMN *column_name* HEADING '*heading_text*' JUSTIFY LEFT

…or…

COLUMN *column_name* HEADING '*heading_text*' JUSTIFY CENTER

…or…

COLUMN *column_name* HEADING '*heading_text*' JUSTIFY RIGHT

In addition to letting you control what headings are displayed above columns, this technique offers a couple of other nice benefits: you can use a mixture of upper- and lowercase characters, and you can break the headings into multiple lines. Within the *heading_text* argument, a vertical bar (|) represents a line break. You can even specify whether the headings should be justified to the column's left margin, to its center, or to its right margin.

To see this in action, try the following commands:

```
SELECT * FROM plsql101_product;

COLUMN product_name HEADING 'Product|Name' JUSTIFY CENTER

SELECT * FROM plsql101_product;
```

You can put all of these COLUMN command options together and use them at the same time. Try out the following commands and compare your results with those shown in Figure 4-10:

```
SELECT * FROM plsql101_product;

COLUMN product_name FORMAT A10 WORD_WRAP HEADING 'Name' JUSTIFY CENTER
COLUMN product_price FORMAT $99.99 HEADING 'Price' JUSTIFY RIGHT
COLUMN quantity_on_hand FORMAT 99,999 HEADING 'On|Hand' JUSTIFY RIGHT
COLUMN last_stock_date HEADING 'Last|Stock|Date' JUSTIFY RIGHT

SELECT * FROM plsql101_product;
```

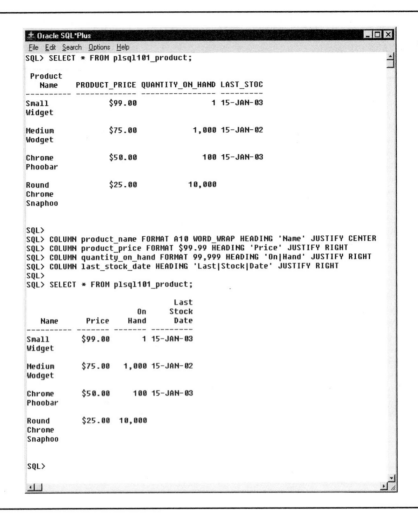

FIGURE 4-10. *Formatting text with a variety of COLUMN commands*

To turn off the formatting from the COLUMN command, you can use this syntax:

COLUMN *column_name* OFF

For instance, to make the columns in your PLSQL101_PRODUCT table display like they did before you applied any formatting, enter the following commands:

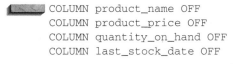

```
COLUMN product_name OFF
COLUMN product_price OFF
COLUMN quantity_on_hand OFF
COLUMN last_stock_date OFF

SELECT * FROM plsql101_product;
```

Spooling Output to Disk

Spooling is the process of writing information out to a file on a disk. There are
times when it's handy to do this from within SQL*Plus, either to make a record of
a series of commands and their results, or to store voluminous output from a single
command. (If the output fits within a single SQL*Plus screen, you can simply use
the mouse to select the information you want, copy it, and paste it into whatever
program you want. Once the information is pasted into the destination program,
you may need to apply a fixed-space font such as Courier New to it in order for its
lines to align properly.)

The syntax of the SPOOL command is as follows:

SPOOL *spool_file_name*

The spool file name can include a file extension if you wish (such as .sql or .prn).
If you do not specify one, the extension .lst will be appended to the end of the name
you specify. Also, you can include a *path* as part of the spool file name; the path is
the name of the disk drive and directory in which the spool file should be stored.
If you do not include a path, the spool file will be stored in the BIN directory
beneath your Oracle home directory.

To try the SPOOL command, enter the following commands. Note that because
SPOOL controls behavior within SQL*Plus—and does not affect the Oracle server—
you do not need to place a semicolon at the end of each SPOOL command.

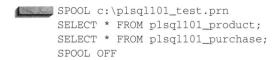

```
SPOOL c:\plsql101_test.prn
SELECT * FROM plsql101_product;
SELECT * FROM plsql101_purchase;
SPOOL OFF
```

TIP
*For those of you running SQL*Plus on Unix, the
path for the spool file will have a structure more
like this:*

/u01/user/plsql101_test.prn

*(Remember that path and file names in Unix are
case-sensitive.)*

After executing these commands, use Windows Explorer or the File Manager to navigate to the location where you stored your plsql101_test.prn file. Open the file and you will see a complete record of everything that crossed your SQL*Plus screen.

SQL Script Files

By this time, you have learned quite a few different SQL commands, and you have typed in many lines as you experimented with those commands. In a business environment, it's common to have certain operations that get performed in exactly the same way—or almost exactly the same way—many times. Retyping the same commands over and over can get tedious quickly. Instead, you can store the commands needed to accomplish a specific task in a disk file. This has three major benefits: it saves you time by eliminating the need to retype repetitive commands; it makes the procedure finish more quickly because commands are read from the disk file much more quickly than you could type them; and it ensures that the commands are executed in exactly the same way, with perfect syntax, each time.

Creating a Script File

A script file is just a plain text file. You can create one using any text editor or word processor. (If you use a word processor, be sure to use the Save As command to save the file in a "text only" format, so it will not contain any of the word processor's formatting codes.) You can even use SQL*Plus's EDIT command to start your system's default text editor to create a new script file. To see how this works, take the following steps:

1. In SQL*Plus, enter this command:

   ```
   EDIT c:\plsql101_test.sql
   ```

NOTE
Unix users should modify the file path to a location of your choosing. The same guideline will apply to subsequent exercises that involve file paths.

2. Within the text editor, enter the following commands into your plsql101_test.sql file:

   ```
   CREATE TABLE plsql101_temp (
        first_name VARCHAR2(15),
        last_name  VARCHAR2(25)
   ```

```
      )
   ;

   INSERT INTO plsql101_temp VALUES ('Joe', 'Smith');
   INSERT INTO plsql101_temp VALUES ('Jane', 'Miller');

   SELECT * FROM plsql101_temp;

   DROP TABLE plsql101_temp;
```

3. Exit from the text editor. When asked if you want to save the file you just created, answer Yes.

That's it! You now have a script file containing SQL commands. This particular script file contains commands that create a table, populate it with data, select data out of it, and then drop it. You would never create a script with these commands in real life, because the script is self-nullifying. However, it serves as an excellent example of the kinds of commands you can include in a script file to automate common actions.

Running a Script File

Running a script file in SQL*Plus is very easy. You simply precede the name of the file with the "at" sign (@). Enter the following command at the SQL> prompt to see this in action:

```
@c:\plsql101_test
```

In response, you should see a screen similar to the one shown in Figure 4-11. Notice that you did not need to include the .sql file extension in the command. If you do not specify a file extension in the @ command, the extension of .sql is assumed.

Using Variables In Script Files

Sometimes it is handy to be able to write a script file that can work in a variety of situations, changing what it does in each situation. You can accomplish this by using *variables* in your script files. A variable takes the place of a portion of your command, allowing you to "fill in" that portion when the script is run—thereby changing what the script does. (The opposite of this is information typed explicitly into the script file. This type of information is called *hard coded* because it cannot be changed when the script is run.) You can build variables into your SQL scripts in two different ways: using substitution variables, and using the ACCEPT command.

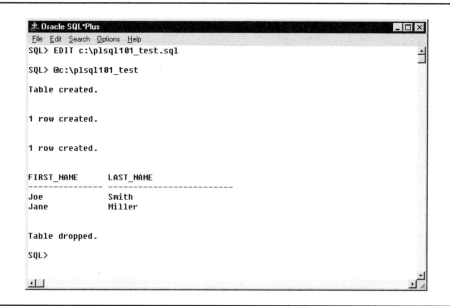

FIGURE 4-11. *Running a SQL script file*

Substitution Variables

Using a *substitution variable* is the simplest way to build a variable into your script. To see how this works, create a script file named plsql101_test2.sql, and place within it the following commands:

```
SET VERIFY OFF

SELECT product_name, quantity, purchase_date
FROM   plsql101_purchase
WHERE  quantity >= &minimum_quantity_sold
;

SET VERIFY ON
```

Save and run the script. You will see a brand-new prompt asking you to "Enter value for minimum_quantity_sold." The number that you type in will be placed into the script's WHERE clause as if it had been hard-coded into the script. Enter a value of **20** and see how the script performs. Then run it again (you can do that just by typing a slash (**/**) and pressing ENTER) and respond to the prompt with a value of **5**, to see how the script's behavior changes.

The SET VERIFY OFF and SET VERIFY ON commands in the script help improve its appearance when the script runs. Without them, SQL*Plus would insist on showing old and new values for the substitution variable before executing your SELECT command, which will confuse anyone running the script other than its creator—and will eventually annoy even its creator.

Substitution variables work just as well for text and dates, too. You must remember, though, that SQL requires text and dates to be surrounded by single quotes. Since it is unlikely that other people using your script will remember this, the best practice is to place the single quotes into the script itself. Consider the following code for an example:

```
SET VERIFY OFF

SELECT product_name, quantity, purchase_date
FROM    plsql101_purchase
WHERE   purchase_date = '&date_you_want_to_select'
;

SET VERIFY ON
```

Notice that the substitution variable in this example is surrounded by single quotes. Those quotes will surround whatever date the user types in, thereby making a properly formatted date.

Place this code in a script file named plsql101_test3.sql, and then run it to see how it works. (The table currently contains records whose dates are 14-JUL-03, 15-JUL-03, and 16-JUL-03.)

To sharpen your skills at this technique, create a script file that allows the user to specify two dates between which records will be selected. This will involve using the BETWEEN clause and two separate substitution variables.

The ACCEPT Command

You may have noticed that the prompt SQL*Plus displays to users when it encounters a substitution variable isn't exactly attractive. An alternative is the ACCEPT command, which allows you to define any prompt you want. The command's syntax is as follows:

accept *variable_name* prompt '*prompt text*'

To see how it works, create a script named plsql101_test4.sql and place the following commands within it:

```
SET VERIFY OFF
SET ECHO OFF

ACCEPT v_earliest_date
  PROMPT 'Earliest date you would like to see? (dd-mmm-yy): '
ACCEPT v_latest_date
  PROMPT 'Thank you. Latest date you would like to see? (dd-mmm-yy): '
SELECT product_name, quantity, purchase_date
FROM   plsql101_purchase
WHERE  purchase_date BETWEEN '&v_earliest_date' AND '&v_latest_date'
ORDER BY product_name, quantity
;

SET VERIFY ON
SET ECHO ON
```

This script employs one more pair of new commands: SET ECHO OFF and SET ECHO ON. The SET ECHO commands control whether commands in the script file are shown to the user. In this case, they ensure that the user only sees the prompts from the ACCEPT commands and does not see the commands themselves.

Chapter Summary

This chapter presented a variety of useful techniques for getting the most out of the SQL*Plus program. You began by learning how to edit and reuse commands. There are two ways to do this: using the ED command to invoke your system's default text editor, or using the CHANGE command to perform line-level editing. If the command you want to reuse doesn't need to be changed, you can simply copy it from the SQL*Plus screen and paste it back in at the cursor position to use it again.

After learning how to reuse prior commands, you saw that you can clear the SQL*Plus screen by using the SHIFT-DELETE key sequence. Then you learned how to customize numerous facets of the SQL*Plus environment using both the Options | Environment menu command and a variety of commands you enter directly at the SQL prompt. To ensure that your changes will be active in future sessions, you can use the STORE command to save them.

To make selected data easier to read, you can employ the COLUMN command to format the display of numbers, dates, and text, as well as the wording and justification of column headings. You can also use the SPOOL command to create a disk file containing everything you see go across your SQL*Plus screen.

Speaking of disk files, one of your most powerful tools for making your SQL work more efficient is storing often-used groups of commands in text files using the .sql extension. You can make SQL*Plus run these script files simply by typing an @ character at the SQL prompt, followed by the path and name of the file that contains the commands you want to run. To make the script files more versatile, you can include substitution variables and the ACCEPT command so you can enter criteria (or any other information) when the script is run.

Way to go! Now let's move on to the really hard stuff.

OK, I'm just kidding. The next chapter isn't hard at all. In fact, it contains some very cool functions that are easy to use and that dramatically increase what you can do with SQL. It just gets more and more interesting…

Chapter Questions

1. What editor is started when you execute the ED command from SQL*Plus?

   A. Oracle's internal editor

   B. Your system's default editor

   C. The EDIT program

   D. The VI program

2. Which of the following commands will *not* alter the way data is displayed on your screen?

   A. COLUMN

   B. SET LINESIZE

   C. SPOOL

   D. SET PAGESIZE

3. On which line will the following command fail?

```
SELECT product_name, quantity, purchase_date
FROM   plsql101_purchase
WHERE  quantity <= &maximum_quantity_sold;
```

   A. 1

   B. 2

   C. 3

   D. The command will succeed.

4. On which line will the following command fail?

```
SET VERIFY OFF
SET ECHO OFF
ACCEPT v_earliest_date PROMPT 'Earliest date? (dd-mmm-yy): '
ACCEPT v_latest_date PROMPT 'Latest date? (dd-mmm-yy): '
SELECT product_name, quantity, purchase_date
FROM   plsql101_purchase
WHERE  purchase_date BETWEEN '&earliest_date' AND '&latest_date'
ORDER BY product_name, quantity;
SET VERIFY ON
SET ECHO ON
```

A. 1

B. 3

C. 5

D. 7

E. 9

Answers to Chapter Questions

I. B.   Your system's default editor

Explanation   Oracle does not have an editor of its own. The ED command will start whatever editing program your system is configured to use by default.

2. C.   SPOOL

Explanation   The SPOOL command simply controls whether the data displayed on your SQL*Plus screen is also written out to a disk file. It does not alter the displayed data in any way.

3. D.   The command will succeed

Explanation   The only thing unusual about this SELECT command is its use of the & character on the third line. This character marks the name that follows (maximum_quantity_sold) as a substitution variable, which will cause a prompt to be displayed to the user when the command is run. This syntax is perfectly acceptable.

4. D.   7

Explanation   The names used in the substitution variables do not match those created by the ACCEPT commands.

PART II

Advanced SQL

CHAPTER
5

SQL Functions

his unit contains a wealth of advanced techniques you can use to make your Oracle applications easier to use, more powerful, and more efficient. Following this chapter, you will learn about Oracle indexes, constraints, and relationships in Chapter 6, and learn a variety of powerful real-life techniques in Chapter 7 to help you perform day-to-day database tasks in the most efficient way.

Before all that good stuff, though, is this chapter, which focuses on the fascinating world of SQL functions. A *function* is like a mini-command you can place within a larger SQL statement. Data goes into a function looking one way, and comes out looking another way, based on the purpose the function is designed to fulfill. For instance, functions can change the way data appears (like turning a date value into the related day of the week), subtotal the data in a way you specify, or alter the content of the data (like taking one set of codes and translating them into a different set of codes). By learning to use functions, you take a major step ahead of those who have merely been exposed to SQL, and toward the group of people who really understand how to make SQL dance for them.

The functions will be presented in two groups: single-row functions and group functions. Single-row functions perform operations that could affect the display of every row in a table. In contrast, group functions are designed to give you information about subsets of your data, with the groupings defined in any way you please.

If you just started reading in this chapter and have not done any of the exercises in the preceding chapters, you will need to create the sample tables built in prior chapters before you can do the exercises in this chapter. You can accomplish this by entering the following SQL commands:

```
DROP TABLE plsql101_product;
CREATE TABLE plsql101_product (
       product_name      VARCHAR2(25),
       product_price     NUMBER(4,2),
       quantity_on_hand  NUMBER(5,0),
       last_stock_date   DATE
       )
;

INSERT INTO plsql101_product VALUES
     ('Small Widget', 99, 1, '15-JAN-03');
INSERT INTO plsql101_product VALUES
     ('Medium Wodget', 75, 1000, '15-JAN-02');
INSERT INTO plsql101_product VALUES
     ('Chrome Phoobar', 50, 100, '15-JAN-03');
INSERT INTO plsql101_product VALUES
     ('Round Chrome Snaphoo', 25, 10000, null);
INSERT INTO plsql101_product VALUES
     ('Extra Huge Mega Phoobar +',9.95,1234,'15-JAN-04');
```

```
DROP TABLE plsql101_purchase;
CREATE TABLE plsql101_purchase (
     product_name  VARCHAR2(25),
     salesperson   VARCHAR2(3),
     purchase_date DATE,
     quantity      NUMBER(4,2)
     )
;

INSERT INTO plsql101_purchase VALUES
     ('Small Widget', 'CA', '14-JUL-03', 1);
INSERT INTO plsql101_purchase VALUES
     ('Medium Wodget', 'BB', '14-JUL-03', 75);
INSERT INTO plsql101_purchase VALUES
     ('Chrome Phoobar', 'GA', '14-JUL-03', 2);
INSERT INTO plsql101_purchase VALUES
     ('Small Widget', 'GA', '15-JUL-03', 8);
INSERT INTO plsql101_purchase VALUES
     ('Medium Wodget', 'LB', '15-JUL-03', 20);
INSERT INTO plsql101_purchase VALUES
     ('Round Snaphoo', 'CA', '16-JUL-03', 5);
```

Commonly Used Single-Row Functions

This section introduces you to single-row functions. These functions give you row-by-row control over how the data in your database is entered and presented. The functions fall into the following categories:

- System variables
- Number
- Character (text)
- Date
- Data conversion
- Miscellaneous

System Variables

System variables are maintained by Oracle to provide you with information about the environment in which the database is running. The three system variables presented here allow you to determine the system date and time, the ID of the user executing a SQL statement, and the name of the computer from which a user is executing commands. These functions can be very useful in a variety of ways, as you will see.

SYSDATE

The SYSDATE function returns the current date and time. To be more specific, it returns the current date and time from the Oracle server's point of view, so if the server happens to be in another time zone, that time zone's information will be returned. To see the function in action, enter the following command:

```
SELECT SYSDATE FROM DUAL;
```

In response, you will see the current date appear on your screen. A more interesting way to use this command is in DML statements. For instance, you can cause the current date to be inserted into any date field by specifying SYSDATE in the INSERT statement. Try the command shown below to see how this works:

```
INSERT INTO plsql101_purchase VALUES
     ('Small Widget', 10, sysdate, 'SH');
```

After you have entered this command, use a SELECT statement to see all the records in your PLSQL101_PURCHASE table, and you will see that your new record has been added with today's date in the PURCHASE_DATE column. (Actually, the value entered in that column contains both the date and the time—you will see how to display the time component of the value later in this chapter.)

Let's extend this idea a bit further by using some date math in the INSERT statement. Enter the following commands:

```
INSERT INTO plsql101_purchase VALUES
     ('Medium Wodget', 15, sysdate-14, 'SH');
INSERT INTO plsql101_purchase VALUES
     ('Round Snaphoo', 25, sysdate-7, 'SH');
INSERT INTO plsql101_purchase VALUES
     ('Chrome Phoobar', 10, sysdate+7, 'SH');
```

With these commands, you can see that today's date can be manipulated simply by adding and subtracting days. For instance, by subtracting 7 from today's SYSDATE value, you get the date value for exactly a week ago.

SYSDATE is also useful when you want to view records containing dates that have a certain relationship to today. For instance, to see all the sales that occurred in the last 30 days, you could use a command like the one that follows.

```
SELECT * FROM plsql101_purchase
WHERE  purchase_date BETWEEN (SYSDATE-30) AND SYSDATE;
```

The results you get from this command should be similar to those you see in Figure 5-1.

Take a few moments now to experiment with SYSDATE. For instance, try selecting all the records that have been entered in the last two weeks, the last six months, and the last year. When you are done, delete the records used for this SYSDATE section by issuing the following command:

```
DELETE FROM plsql101_purchase
WHERE   SALESPERSON = 'SH';
```

USER

Before explaining what the USER function does, I want to tell you that I won't be able to demonstrate a good use for this function until later in the book. The same is true for the USERENV function that follows. These functions are both useful when you want to audit activity on a table—that is, keep track of who is inserting, updating, and deleting records. Doing that is a relatively sophisticated operation, and you will learn how to do it in Chapter 9. To keep all the functions in one chapter, though, I'm presenting these two functions now. I recommend that you treat them as interesting novelties for the time being. When you encounter them again later in the book, they'll be familiar.

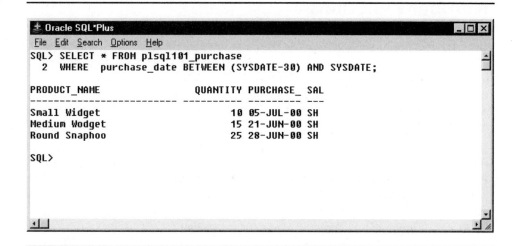

FIGURE 5-1.   *Selecting records using SYSDATE in the WHERE clause*

That having been said, let's learn about the USER function. It returns the Oracle user ID of the person who issues the command containing a USER function. Try the following command to see what I mean:

```
SELECT USER FROM DUAL;
```

In response, you will see the name you logged in as when you started SQL*Plus. As I said earlier, this is nothing more than an interesting novelty at the moment, but later on it will be useful when you want Oracle to store the user ID of a person making changes to the database.

USERENV

The USERENV function can return a variety of different facts about the computer environment of the person who issued the command containing the USERENV function. The most useful of these facts is the name of the computer the person is working on. Enter the following command to see what I mean:

```
SELECT USERENV('TERMINAL') FROM DUAL;
```

In response, you will see your computer's name. This function, combined with the USER function you just learned, enables you to determine who took an action and from what computer. Add a SYSDATE function to the mix, and you have the beginning of a detailed audit record. You'll learn how to put these to use in this capacity in Chapter 9.

Number Functions

Number functions manipulate numeric values, changing them to suit your needs. The functions presented here provide common mathematical features. If the data you work with is mostly text-oriented, you might not see a need to know these functions. I recommend that you learn them anyway. A big part of growing more valuable as a technical person is being familiar with what a system *can* do, so that when a new need arises, you know what tools are available to you for taking care of that need.

ROUND

The ROUND function rounds numbers to whatever degree of precision you specify. Its syntax is as follows:

ROUND(*input_value, decimal_places_of_precision*)

To use the ROUND function—and every other function that modifies a value—you "wrap" it around the value you want to modify. Since this is usually done in a SELECT statement, you accomplish this by wrapping the function around the column name containing the values to be modified.

Let's look at an example. The PLSQL101_PRODUCT table contains prices for the products. Some of those prices are integers with no decimal values—but not all. Try this pair of commands to see the ROUND function in action:

```
SELECT product_name, product_price
FROM   plsql101_product;

SELECT product_name, ROUND(product_price, 0)
FROM   plsql101_product;
```

The results you get should look similar to those shown in Figure 5-2.

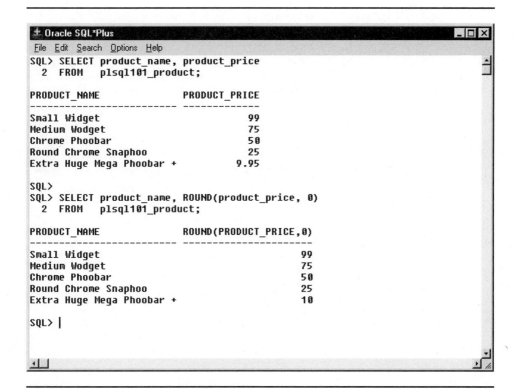

FIGURE 5-2. *The ROUND function*

This example shows one of the most common uses for the ROUND function. Another would be rounding detailed values that contain a lot of decimal places down to dollars and cents; that would require specifying a decimal precision value of 2. You can specify any number of decimals of precision you want, but certain values make more sense than others. If you specify a negative number, the ROUND function starts rounding *before* the decimal point, resulting in numbers that are rounded to the nearest 10, 100, 1000, and so on.

The best way to see the relationship between the ROUND function's decimal places of precision and the change the function makes in the value it processes is to use it on numbers containing many decimal places. Since your test tables don't contain any records whose values have many decimal places—and it wouldn't make sense to create product records with prices like that—we'll use DUAL to demonstrate what ROUND does with such numbers. Enter the following commands to see the relationship between the ROUND function's decimal places of precision and the way the function rounds the number it is given. The results are summarized in Table 5-1.

```
SELECT ROUND(1234.5678, 4) FROM DUAL;
SELECT ROUND(1234.5678, 3) FROM DUAL;
SELECT ROUND(1234.5678, 2) FROM DUAL;
SELECT ROUND(1234.5678, 1) FROM DUAL;
SELECT ROUND(1234.5678, 0) FROM DUAL;
SELECT ROUND(1234.5678, -1) FROM DUAL;
SELECT ROUND(1234.5678, -2) FROM DUAL;
SELECT ROUND(1234.5678, -3) FROM DUAL;
```

TRUNC

The TRUNC function truncates precision from a number. The difference between this and rounding becomes apparent when a number contains decimal values of .5 or higher. Rounding the number would cause it to move up to the next higher number, while truncating it does not. Enter the following series of commands to see how this works. The results are summarized in Table 5-2.

```
SELECT TRUNC(1234.5678, 4) FROM DUAL;
SELECT TRUNC(1234.5678, 3) FROM DUAL;
SELECT TRUNC(1234.5678, 2) FROM DUAL;
SELECT TRUNC(1234.5678, 1) FROM DUAL;
SELECT TRUNC(1234.5678, 0) FROM DUAL;
SELECT TRUNC(1234.5678, -1) FROM DUAL;
SELECT TRUNC(1234.5678, -2) FROM DUAL;
SELECT TRUNC(1234.5678, -3) FROM DUAL;
```

ROUND Function	Resulting Number
ROUND(1234.5678, 4)	1234.5678
ROUND(1234.5678, 3)	1234.568
ROUND(1234.5678, 2)	1234.57
ROUND(1234.5678, 1)	1234.6
ROUND(1234.5678, 0)	1235
ROUND(1234.5678, -1)	1230
ROUND(1234.5678, -2)	1200
ROUND(1234.5678, -3)	1000

TABLE 5-1. *ROUND Function Precision Results*

TRUNC Function	Resulting Number
TRUNC(1234.5678, 4)	1234.5678
TRUNC(1234.5678, 3)	1234.567
TRUNC(1234.5678, 2)	1234.56
TRUNC(1234.5678, 1)	1234.5
TRUNC(1234.5678, 0)	1234
TRUNC(1234.5678, -1)	1230
TRUNC(1234.5678, -2)	1200
TRUNC(1234.5678, -3)	1000

TABLE 5-2. *TRUNC Function Precision Results*

Text Functions

Text functions, referred to in Oracle as *character functions*, manipulate text strings. The most common things to do with text strings are changing their case (between uppercase, lowercase, and mixed case); separating a long string into a number of shorter substrings; and cleaning up text coming in from an external source that is padded with extra spaces. By learning the character functions that follow, you will learn how to do each of those things.

UPPER, LOWER, and INITCAP

These three functions change the case of the text you give them. Since their functions are reasonably self-explanatory, I'll let them do the talking:

```
SELECT UPPER(product_name) FROM plsql101_product;
SELECT LOWER(product_name) FROM plsql101_product;
SELECT INITCAP(product_name) FROM plsql101_product;
```

The results you get from these commands should match what you see in Figure 5-3. As you may have noticed, the INITCAP function doesn't really do anything in this example, because the product names already have the first character of each word capitalized. The function's ability to clean up messy text is better demonstrated by the following command:

```
SELECT INITCAP('this TEXT hAd UNpredictABLE caSE') FROM DUAL;
```

Of the three case-changing character functions, you will probably use UPPER the most. One very handy use for it is in SELECT statements, when you are not sure what case your desired text will be in. For those instances, you just wrap an UPPER function around the name of the column you're searching, and then specify the text you want to match in uppercase letters. To demonstrate this technique, you need to change your test records a little, so there are records containing the same word but with different case. The following code makes this change, demonstrates how to use the UPPER function to overcome the difference in case, and then changes the data back so the case is once again the same. Enter the commands and compare the results of your SELECT command with those shown in Figure 5-4.

```
UPDATE plsql101_product
SET    product_name = 'chrome phoobar'
WHERE  product_name = 'Chrome Phoobar';

SELECT * FROM plsql101_product
WHERE  UPPER(product_name) LIKE '%PHOOBAR%';
```

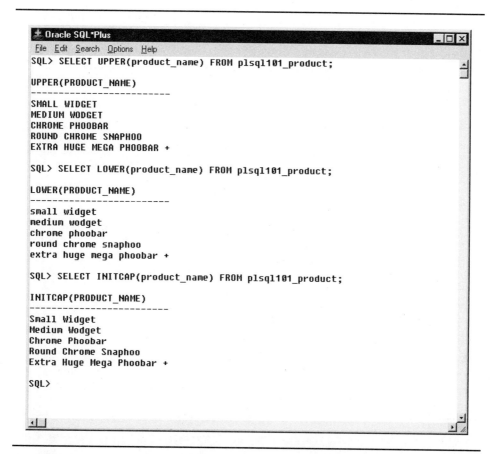

FIGURE 5-3. *Results of the UPPER, LOWER, and INITCAP functions*

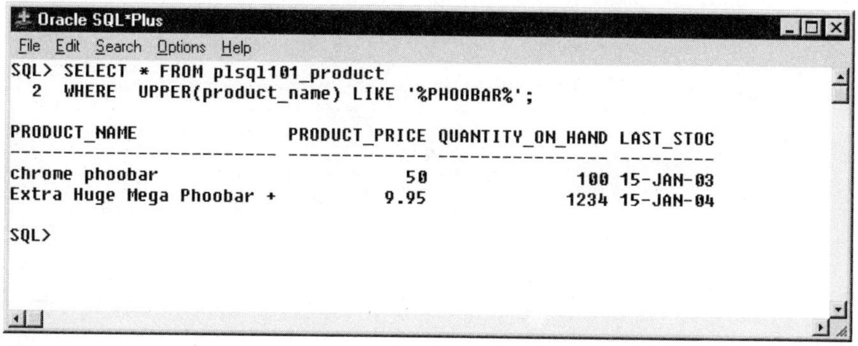

FIGURE 5-4. *Using the UPPER function to simplify text searches*

Using the UPPER function in this way can make it a lot easier to find the text you want when you don't know the case in which it was originally entered. However, as you can see in Figure 5-4, the data displayed as a result is still inconsistent in its use of upper- and lowercase characters. The solution is to wrap an INITCAP function around the PRODUCT_NAME column to clean it up. Enter the following code to see how this works:

```
SELECT  INITCAP(product_name),
        product_price,
        quantity_on_hand,
        last_stock_date
FROM    plsql101_product
WHERE   UPPER(product_name) LIKE '%PHOOBAR%';
```

After you have compared the results you got with those shown in Figure 5-5, enter the following code to return your product names to the state they were in before this exercise:

```
UPDATE plsql101_product
SET    product_name = 'Chrome Phoobar'
WHERE  product_name = 'chrome phoobar';
```

LENGTH

There are times when it is useful to determine the lengths of data stored in a database column. The LENGTH function provides this capability. Imagine, for

```
Oracle SQL*Plus                                              _ □ ×
File  Edit  Search  Options  Help
SQL> SELECT INITCAP(product_name),
  2         product_price,
  3         quantity_on_hand,
  4         last_stock_date
  5  FROM   plsql101_product
  6  WHERE  UPPER(product_name) LIKE '%PHOOBAR%';

INITCAP(PRODUCT_NAME)       PRODUCT_PRICE QUANTITY_ON_HAND LAST_STOC
--------------------------- ------------- ---------------- ---------
Chrome Phoobar                         50              100 15-JAN-03
Extra Huge Mega Phoobar +            9.95             1234 15-JAN-04

SQL>
```

FIGURE 5-5. *Using the INITCAP function to clean up mixed-case data*

example, that you are using a table similar to the PLSQL101_PRODUCT table in your business, and the table feeds product names into the catalog department. They are considering using a smaller page size for the catalog, and the new page size requires them to reduce the length of product names from 25 characters to 15 characters. To help in their decision, they would like to know how many product names they would need to change. You can produce a list of the names that would need to be changed by employing a command such as this:

```
SELECT    product_name, LENGTH(product_name) NAME_LENGTH
FROM      plsql101_product
WHERE     LENGTH(product_name) >15
ORDER BY product_name;
```

NOTE
This example applies the alias NAME_LENGTH to the column containing product-name lengths, in order to make the column headings more readable.

The LENGTH function is also useful for determining the size of the largest entry in a column, as well as the size of the average entry in a column. You will see how to do both of these things a bit later in this section.

SUBSTR
There will be times in your Oracle career when you encounter data with a column containing multiple bits of data that you need to separate in discrete segments. In plain language, you will need to turn a column like this:

ITEM_ID

LA-101

LA-102

LA-103

LA-104

NY-101

NY-102

NY-103

NY-104

into multiple columns like this:

MANUFACTURER LOCATION	MANUFACTURER ITEM NUMBER
LA	101
LA	102
LA	103
LA	104
NY	101
NY	102
NY	103
NY	104

Since text is referred to as a *string* in the computer world, a smaller portion of text derived from a larger piece of text is called a *substring*. In the example just shown, the strings in the ITEM_ID column were broken out into two substrings each. This process is called *parsing* strings.

Oracle provides a function named SUBSTR to do this. Whenever you want to cut strings up into substrings, you need to specify the point at which the substring should start, as well as the length that the substring should be. For instance, in the preceding example, the first substring was the manufacturer's location. Its values start at the first character position in the ITEM_ID column, and extend for two characters. The next substring was the manufacturer's item number, whose values start at the fourth character position within the ITEM_ID and extend for three characters.

None of your current sample tables from this book contain data that calls for parsing. I'm sure you know what that means: That's right, you get to practice your CREATE TABLE command. Enter the following commands to create an appropriate table and records:

```
CREATE TABLE plsql101_old_item (
    item_id   CHAR(20),
    item_desc CHAR(25)
    )
;

INSERT INTO plsql101_old_item VALUES
    ('LA-101', 'Can, Small');
INSERT INTO plsql101_old_item VALUES
    ('LA-102', 'Can, Large');
```

```
INSERT INTO plsql101_old_item VALUES
     ('LA-103', 'Bottle, Small');
INSERT INTO plsql101_old_item VALUES
     ('LA-104', 'Bottle, Large');
INSERT INTO plsql101_old_item VALUES
     ('NY-101', 'Box, Small');
INSERT INTO plsql101_old_item VALUES
     ('NY-102', 'Box, Large');
INSERT INTO plsql101_old_item VALUES
     ('NY-103', 'Shipping Carton, Small');
INSERT INTO plsql101_old_item VALUES
     ('NY-104', 'Shipping Carton, Large');
```

Now that you have data that can use parsing, it's time to learn the syntax of the SUBSTR command. It is:

SUBSTR(*source_text, starting_character_position, number_of_characters*)

The *source_text* value will usually be the name of the column that needs to be parsed. The *starting_character_position* is the first character in the column to include, and the *number_of_characters* is the number of characters to get. To parse the item ID into a manufacturer location and item number, enter the following command:

```
SELECT SUBSTR(item_id, 1, 2) MFGR_LOCATION,
       SUBSTR(item_id, 4, 3) ITEM_NUMBER,
       item_desc
FROM   plsql101_old_item
;
```

After you have entered this command, compare the results you get with those shown in Figure 5-6.

Parsing strings is a very common part of transferring data from one application to another, because the two applications never store data in exactly the same way. Later in this chapter you will become familiar with this process by learning how to copy records from one table to another, and part of the process will include parsing the data along the way.

INSTR

Using SUBSTR as shown in the previous exercise works great when you know exactly how long each substring will be. Often, however, you will be called upon to parse strings like those in the ITEM_DESC column of your PLSQL101_OLD_ITEM table—strings whose substrings vary in length. This means that not only is the length

```
┌─────────────────────────────────────────────────────────────────────┐
│ ± Oracle SQL*Plus                                          _ □ ×      │
├─────────────────────────────────────────────────────────────────────┤
│ File  Edit  Search  Options  Help                                     │
│ SQL> SELECT  SUBSTR(item_id, 1, 2) MFGR_LOCATION,            ▲         │
│   2           SUBSTR(item_id, 4, 3) ITEM_NUMBER,            ▓         │
│   3           item_desc                                               │
│   4  FROM    plsql101_old_item                                        │
│   5  ;                                                                 │
│                                                                       │
│ MF ITE ITEM_DESC                                                      │
│ -- --- ------------------------                                       │
│ LA 101 Can, Small                                                     │
│ LA 102 Can, Large                                                     │
│ LA 103 Bottle, Small                                                  │
│ LA 104 Bottle, Large                                                  │
│ NY 101 Box, Small                                                     │
│ NY 102 Box, Large                                                     │
│ NY 103 Shipping Carton, Small                                         │
│ NY 104 Shipping Carton, Large                                         │
│                                                                       │
│ 8 rows selected.                                                      │
│                                                                       │
│ SQL> |                                                       ▼         │
│                                                                       │
│ ◄└┘                                                         ►         │
└─────────────────────────────────────────────────────────────────────┘
```

FIGURE 5-6.   *Parsing data using the SUBSTR function*

of the first substring unknown, but the starting position of the second substring can also vary. The only way to parse a string like this is to find out the location of the character (or characters) separating the items you want to parse. Oracle provides a function named INSTR that does just that.

INSTR searches for the text you specify and returns a number identifying the starting position of that text within a string. By using the number returned by INSTR to control the length of your first SUBSTR function, as well as the starting position of the next substring, you can reliably slice and dice long strings no matter how they are divided.

The INSTR function's syntax is as follows:

INSTR(*source_text, text_to_locate, starting_character_position*)

The *source_text* is generally the name of the column containing the long string you want to parse. The *text_to_locate* is the text you want to find, and the *starting_character_position* specifies the character number in the source text at which you want to start searching (to start at the beginning of the text, use a *starting_character_position* value of 1).

The INSTR function can help us separate the PLSQL101_OLD_ITEM table's ITEM_DESC column into two pieces. All we have to do is tell it to locate the comma that separates the item category from the item size. By using the number it returns, we can specify the proper size for the item category, as well as the starting point for the item size.

If we're going to have the INSTR function help us separate the PLSQL101_OLD_ITEM table's ITEM_DESC column into two pieces, we need to understand what information the function provides for each record. Enter the following command to see the INSTR function in action:

```
SELECT item_desc,
       INSTR(item_desc,
             ',',
             1
             )
FROM   plsql101_old_item;
```

As Figure 5-7 shows, the INSTR function returns a number identifying the location of the comma in each record's item description. We could use that number

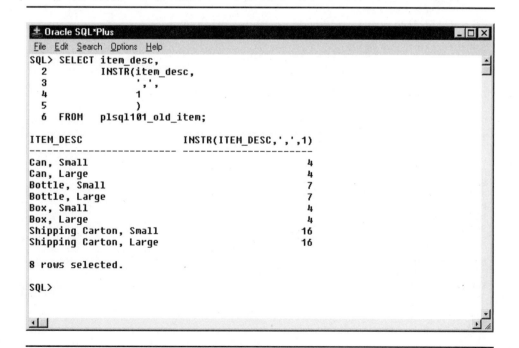

FIGURE 5-7. *Results of the INSTR function*

as the length of our SUBSTR function to get the item category, but if we did, the category would include the comma. Therefore we will want to subtract 1 from the INSTR function's value. The following code demonstrates how to do this:

```
SELECT item_desc,
       SUBSTR(item_desc,
              1,
              INSTR(item_desc,
                    ',',
                    1
                    ) -1
              )
FROM   plsql101_old_item;
```

Enter the code and compare your results with those shown in Figure 5-8. As you can see, you now have a means to get a clean item category from each item record.

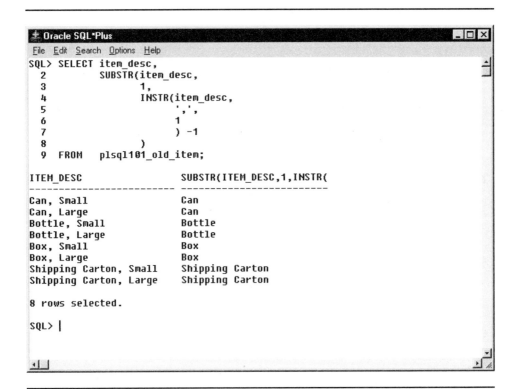

FIGURE 5-8. *Parsing a variable-length substring*

You have just had your first experience using one function within another one. This is called *nesting* functions. In a nested function, the inner function returns a value that is then used by the outer function. This is a powerful capability.

Getting back to the subject at hand, you still need to extract the item size from the ITEM_DESC column. The tricky part of this is the starting position for the size's SUBSTR function. Once again the INSTR function provides the solution by identifying the location of the comma preceding the size. However, that comma is located two characters before the actual start of the size, so you will want to add 2 to the value returned by the INSTR function. Enter the code that follows to get a nice clean list of each item's size:

```
SELECT  item_desc,
        SUBSTR(item_desc,
               INSTR(item_desc,
                      ',',
                      1
                     ) +2,
               99
              )
FROM    plsql101_old_item;
```

In this case, the length of the substring is not a concern, because you are extracting the last portion of text in the overall string. To signify this, I specified a length of 99, which can help serve as a reminder that the SUBSTR function is pulling out the last text in the overall string.

Now that you have seen how to parse each item's category and size, it's time to do both in one command. The code that follows will include two SUBSTR functions: one for category, and the other for size. To help keep things clear, I'm placing a column alias after each SUBSTR function identifying which attribute it is producing.

```
SELECT  item_desc,
        SUBSTR(item_desc,
               1,
               INSTR(item_desc,
                      ',',
                      1
                     ) -1
              ) CATEGORY,
        SUBSTR(item_desc,
               INSTR(item_desc,
                      ',',
                      1
                     ) +2,
               99
              ) ITEM_SIZE
FROM    plsql101_old_item;
```

The results you get from this command should match those shown in Figure 5-9. The formatting used in the code just shown uses indenting to help clarify how the portions of each function and nested function are grouped together. It's useful to do this when you are learning about functions, because it helps you keep clear about what part of which function you are dealing with at any given location in the command. Oracle doesn't care how the command is formatted, and will produce identical results from the following code, which contains exactly the same command in a more compact form:

```
SELECT item_desc,
       SUBSTR(item_desc, 1, INSTR(item_desc, ',', 1) -1)  CATEGORY,
       SUBSTR(item_desc, INSTR(item_desc, ',', 1) +2, 99) ITEM_SIZE
FROM   plsql101_old_item;
```

```
+ Oracle SQL*Plus                                                      _ □ X
 File  Edit  Search  Options  Help
SQL> SELECT item_desc,
  2          SUBSTR(item_desc,
  3                  1,
  4                  INSTR(item_desc,
  5                          ',',
  6                          1
  7                  ) -1
  8          ) CATEGORY,
  9          SUBSTR(item_desc,
 10                  INSTR(item_desc,
 11                          ',',
 12                          1
 13                  ) +2,
 14                  99
 15          ) ITEM_SIZE
 16  FROM    plsql101_old_item;

ITEM_DESC                    CATEGORY                   ITEM_SIZE
--------------------------   ------------------------   -----------------------
Can, Small                   Can                        Small
Can, Large                   Can                        Large
Bottle, Small                Bottle                     Small
Bottle, Large                Bottle                     Large
Box, Small                   Box                        Small
Box, Large                   Box                        Large
Shipping Carton, Small       Shipping Carton            Small
Shipping Carton, Large       Shipping Carton            Large

8 rows selected.

SQL> |
```

FIGURE 5-9.   *Parsing multiple variable-length substrings*

You will get a chance to work with substrings more a little later in the chapter, when you learn how to copy records from one table to another.

LTRIM and RTRIM

The best way to explain what these functions do is show you the problem they solve. Enter the following code and compare your results with those in Figure 5-10.

```
SELECT 'Item   ' ||
       item_id ||
       ' is described as a ' ||
       item_desc ||
       '.'   "Item Description Sentence"
FROM    plsql101_old_item;
```

Why is there so much space after the ITEM_ID and ITEM_DESC values? Because both columns are defined as CHAR datatypes. Remember the difference between the VARCHAR2 datatype and the CHAR datatype? VARCHAR2 is variable length, while CHAR is fixed length. This means that data stored in a CHAR column is padded with spaces to fill the data out to the column's defined length. Those spaces become a problem when you want to concatenate the column's contents

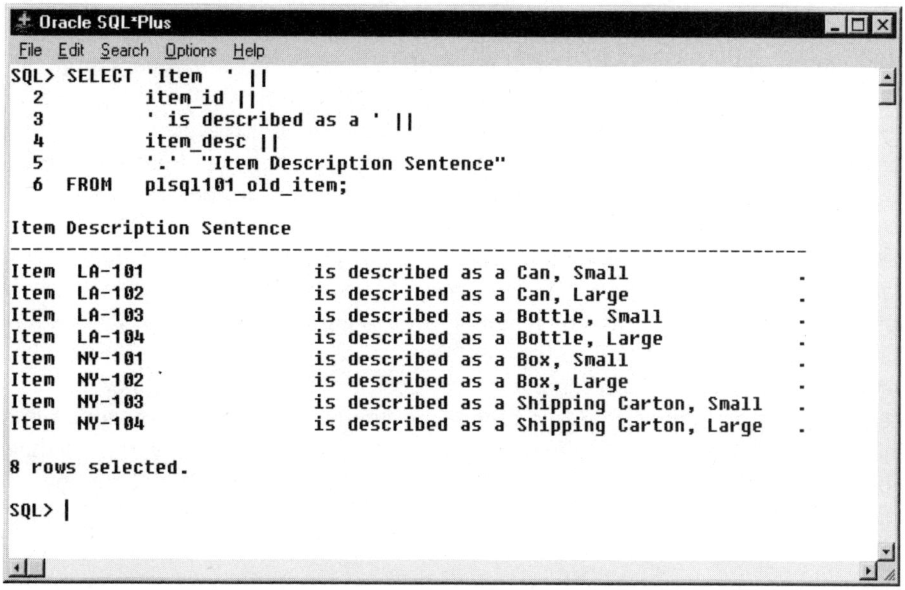

FIGURE 5-10. *Concatenating text from CHAR columns*

with anything else. They can also be unnecessary space-wasters when importing fixed-length data from another database system into your own tables.

Functions to the rescue. The process of removing extra spaces from the beginning or end of a text string is called *trimming,* and Oracle provides two functions that do it: LTRIM and RTRIM. The LTRIM function removes spaces from the beginning of a string, while the RTRIM function removes spaces from the end. The syntax for both functions is essentially identical:

LTRIM(*column_name*)

RTRIM(*column_name*)

In the ITEM_ID and ITEM_DESC columns, the problem is extra spaces at the end of each entry. The RTRIM function is the answer to this problem. You just wrap an RTRIM function around each column's name, as shown in the following code:

```
SELECT 'Item  ' ||
       RTRIM(item_id) ||
       ' is described as a ' ||
       RTRIM(item_desc) ||
       '.'  "Item Description Sentence"
FROM   plsql101_old_item;
```

Try this code, and compare the results with those you see in Figure 5-11.

Ready to test your skills? Combine the SUBSTR and INSTR skills you learned earlier in this section with the RTRIM function to create a SELECT statement that produces these results from the PLSQL101_OLD_ITEM table shown in Figure 5-12.

There's nothing new about the techniques necessary to produce the listing shown in Figure 5-12. You just need to combine what you have already learned in a new way. I would provide an appropriate listing as an answer, but the fact is *it doesn't matter how you produce the answer, as long as the result matches the defined goal.* This is an important thing to know as you move into this line of work. Very few people will ever look at your code. They will only look at your results. I'm confident that you can create the results shown in Figure 5-12 using what you have learned so far. It will probably take a few test runs to work out the bugs, but you can do it. To make it simpler, create the code to produce just the first portion of the sentence—up to the size description—and work with that until you get it right. Then add the code to include the category…nothing further. When you have that working, add the item ID. This "piece-by-piece" process is a good idea for any code that is too complicated to just type from memory.

```
Oracle SQL*Plus                                                    _ □ ×
File  Edit  Search  Options  Help
SQL> SELECT 'Item   ' ||
  2         RTRIM(item_id) ||
  3         ' is described as a ' ||
  4         RTRIM(item_desc) ||
  5         '.' "Item Description Sentence"
  6  FROM   plsql101_old_item;

Item Description Sentence
----------------------------------------------------------------
Item  LA-101 is described as a Can, Small.
Item  LA-102 is described as a Can, Large.
Item  LA-103 is described as a Bottle, Small.
Item  LA-104 is described as a Bottle, Large.
Item  NY-101 is described as a Box, Small.
Item  NY-102 is described as a Box, Large.
Item  NY-103 is described as a Shipping Carton, Small.
Item  NY-104 is described as a Shipping Carton, Large.

8 rows selected.

SQL>
```

FIGURE 5-11.   *Trimming fixed-length text values*

```
Oracle SQL*Plus                                                    _ □ ×
File  Edit  Search  Options  Help

Item ID sentence
--------------------------------------------------------------------------------
The Item ID for a Small Can is: LA-101.
The Item ID for a Large Can is: LA-102.
The Item ID for a Small Bottle is: LA-103.
The Item ID for a Large Bottle is: LA-104.
The Item ID for a Small Box is: NY-101.
The Item ID for a Large Box is: NY-102.
The Item ID for a Small Shipping Carton is: NY-103.
The Item ID for a Large Shipping Carton is: NY-104.

8 rows selected.

SQL>
```

FIGURE 5-12.   *Hone your skills by producing these results!*

Date

Oracle offers a number of functions designed to make it easier to work with dates. This section will start by showing you how to combine two functions you already know to create a new result that is useful in a lot of situations. Next, you will see how to use simple functions to do date tricks that would otherwise require a *lot* of thought and coding.

SYSDATE and TRUNC

To see the problem you're about to learn how to solve, enter the following code:

```
INSERT INTO plsql101_product VALUES
     ('Square Zinculator', 45, 1, SYSDATE);

SELECT * FROM plsql101_product;
```

Looks fine so far, right? You see the new record for the zinculator, and all the data for it appears correct. Now enter the following command, replacing the *dd-mmm-yy* with the current date (the one shown in your zinculator record):

```
SELECT * FROM plsql101_product
WHERE  last_stock_date = 'dd-mmm-yy';
```

If you enter these commands correctly, the result should be...no records displayed! Why isn't your zinculator record showing when you can see very clearly that it contains today's date?

The answer, of course, is that the date placed into the zinculator record was generated by using SYSDATE, and SYSDATE returns more than just the current date; it also returns the current time. Even though you can't see the time component of the date value (you will learn how to see time very soon), it is still there and it keeps the record's value from matching the date value for the current day. It's like trying to match 1 and 1.4 in a column that is formatted to not show decimal places: the difference is there, even if it doesn't show.

The solution: Use the TRUNC function to make your WHERE clause ignore the time value within the last stock date. To make this happen, you must wrap the TRUNC function around the reference to the LAST_STOCK_DATE column, as shown in the modified SELECT statement below:

```
SELECT * FROM plsql101_product
WHERE  TRUNC(last_stock_date) = 'dd-mmm-yy';
```

This will produce the results you expected the first time. This technique is very handy when you need to work with a table containing a column with date and time combined together.

An alternative use of the TRUNC function is to ensure that the date value stored in the database doesn't have a time component in the first place. Enter the following commands to see how this would work, and notice how the INSERT statement has a TRUNC function wrapped around its SYSDATE function:

```
DELETE FROM plsql101_product
WHERE   product_name = 'Square Zinculator';

INSERT INTO plsql101_product VALUES
    ('Square Zinculator', 45, 1, trunc(sysdate));

SELECT * FROM plsql101_product
WHERE   last_stock_date = 'dd-mmm-yy';
```

How can you decide whether to use the TRUNC function at the input stage or the output stage? It depends on the application. The time something occurs could be an important piece of information when you are recording transactions, tracking events, or storing auditing information. On the other hand, it may not be important at all if you are recording when something arrived, or identifying a follow-up date that is *nn* days from today. If you have an application that calls for automatic entry of today's date but is not concerned with time of day, you will save yourself (and others) a lot of confusion and extra work if you truncate the SYSDATE value before inserting it.

ADD_MONTHS

The ADD_MONTHS function returns a date that has the same day of the month as the original date it was provided, but is a specified number of months in the future (or the past). The function's syntax is as follows:

ADD_MONTHS('*starting_date*', *number_of_months*)

The *starting_date* can be today's date (using TRUNC(SYSDATE)), or it can be the name of a column in a table. The *number_of_months* is an integer representing the number of months you want added to or subtracted from the starting date. (If you want months subtracted, specify a negative value for the number of months.)

If want to see the function in action, try entering the following commands:

```
SELECT ADD_MONTHS(SYSDATE,1) FROM DUAL;
SELECT ADD_MONTHS(SYSDATE,12) FROM DUAL;
```

One interesting thing about the ADD_MONTHS function is that it is smart enough to understand when the day it's been given is the last day of the month and adjust accordingly. To see what that means, enter the following commands and compare your results with those in Figure 5-13:

```
SELECT ADD_MONTHS('28-NOV-00', 1) FROM DUAL;
SELECT ADD_MONTHS('29-NOV-00', 1) FROM DUAL;
SELECT ADD_MONTHS('30-NOV-00', 1) FROM DUAL;
SELECT ADD_MONTHS('31-DEC-00', -1) FROM DUAL;
```

Notice that in the last sample command, a month is subtracted from December 31. If you were to guess quickly, you might say the answer should be November 31—until you remembered that November only has 30 days. The ADD_MONTHS function is smart enough to know that and adjust accordingly. This adjustment only occurs when its starting date is the last day of a month. You can see in the preceding three sample commands that ADD_MONTHS adds precisely one month until it is given a starting date that is the last day of a month.

One example of when this would be useful might be a tickler file, where you want to record a date a month away when you will check up on something or get

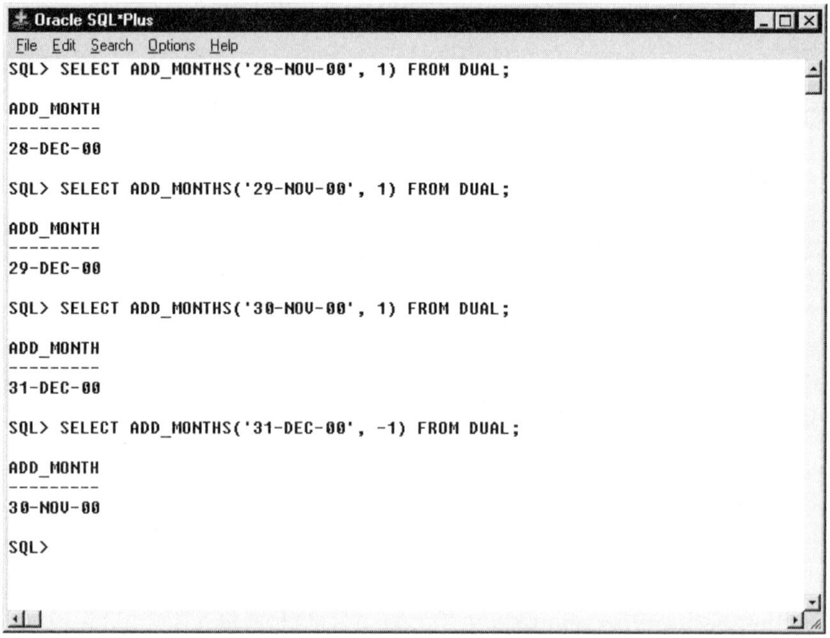

FIGURE 5-13. *Using the ADD_MONTHS function*

back in touch with someone. You can cause your INSERT or UPDATE statement to place the proper date in your table by including this in the statement:

```
ADD_MONTHS(TRUNC(SYSDATE), 1)
```

LAST_DAY

The LAST_DAY function performs a simple task that would be a lot more work to have to program yourself: It returns the last day of whatever month is included in the date it is given. Its syntax is:

LAST_DAY('*date*')

Like any other date function, it can be tested using SYSDATE as the *date* value. Try this series of commands to see the results it produces:

```
SELECT LAST_DAY(SYSDATE) FROM DUAL;
SELECT LAST_DAY('01-JAN-02') FROM DUAL;
SELECT LAST_DAY('15-JAN-02') FROM DUAL;
SELECT LAST_DAY('31-JAN-02') FROM DUAL;
```

There are a number of business situations where this type of function can be handy. For instance, in many companies a new employee's health insurance coverage begins on the first day of whatever month follows their hire date—meaning that if they started working on April 1 their insurance starts on May 1, and if they started working on April 30 their insurance still starts on May 1. Take a moment now and think: how can a date function that returns the last day of a month be modified to instead return the first day of the following month?

The answer is to simply add 1 to the value returned by the LAST_DAY function. To see this in action, you will need to create a new table that contains people and hire dates. You can do this with the following commands:

```
CREATE TABLE plsql101_person (
    person_code VARCHAR2(3),
    first_name  VARCHAR2(15),
    last_name   VARCHAR2(20),
    hire_date   DATE
    )
;

INSERT INTO plsql101_person VALUES
    ('CA', 'Charlene', 'Atlas', '01-FEB-02');
INSERT INTO plsql101_person VALUES
    ('GA', 'Gary', 'Anderson', '15-FEB-02');
INSERT INTO plsql101_person VALUES
```

```
        ('BB', 'Bobby', 'Barkenhagen', '28-FEB-02');
INSERT INTO plsql101_person VALUES
        ('LB', 'Laren', 'Baxter', '01-MAR-02');
```

Now that you have a suitable table, you can see how the LAST_DAY function can be useful for this purpose. Enter the SELECT command that follows, noting how the LAST_DAY function is used to determine the first day of the month following each person's hire date:

```
SELECT first_name,
       last_name,
       hire_date,
       LAST_DAY(hire_date)+1 INSURANCE_START_DATE
FROM   plsql101_person;
```

When you are done, the results of your SELECT statement should look like Figure 5-14.

You can produce some very interesting results by nesting date functions together. Consider this example: each record in your PLSQL101_PRODUCT table contains a date indicating when the item was last restocked. Let's say that in the fictional company you're working at, three months must go by before an item is restocked. To get the restock date, you could just use the ADD_MONTHS function

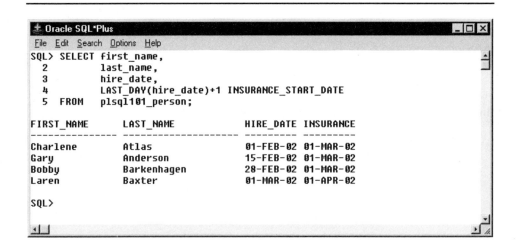

FIGURE 5-14. *Using the LAST_DAY function to determine the first day of the following month*

to produce dates that are three months after the last restock date. But there's a twist...ordering only happens on the first of each month. So what you really want are dates that are three months after the last restock date, moved forward to the first day in whatever month follows. How can you accomplish this?

By combining the two techniques you just learned: adding a specified number of months to a date, and using the LAST_DAY function to get the last day of a month and add 1 to it. The resulting nested function syntax looks like this:

```
LAST_DAY(
     ADD_MONTHS(
          column_containing_restock_date,
          number_of_months_forward
     )
  )
    +1
```

Look at the code that follows, paying particular attention to the fourth item being selected. Note how the syntax just shown is used with the LAST_STOCK_DATE column and the three-month interval. To make it more realistic, the example code limits the products to those whose stock is low, and it sorts the records so the product names are listed alphabetically. Enter the code now and compare your results with those shown in Figure 5-15.

```
SELECT product_name,
       quantity_on_hand,
       last_stock_date,
       LAST_DAY(ADD_MONTHS(last_stock_date, 3))+1 RESTOCK_DATE
FROM   plsql101_product
WHERE  quantity_on_hand <= 100
ORDER BY product_name;
```

MONTHS_BETWEEN

MONTHS_BETWEEN is a simple little function that returns the number of months between any two dates. Its syntax is as follows:

MONTHS_BETWEEN(*later_date, earlier_date*)

This command is most useful for comparing two date columns, or for comparing one date column with today's date. For instance, if you wanted to see how long

```
± Oracle SQL*Plus                                                    _ □ X
File  Edit  Search  Options  Help
SQL> SELECT product_name,
  2          quantity_on_hand,
  3          last_stock_date,
  4          LAST_DAY(ADD_MONTHS(last_stock_date, 3))+1 RESTOCK_DATE
  5   FROM   plsql101_product
  6   WHERE  quantity_on_hand <= 100
  7   ORDER BY product_name;

PRODUCT_NAME               QUANTITY_ON_HAND LAST_STOC RESTOCK_D
-------------------------- ---------------- --------- ---------
Chrome Phoobar                          100 15-JAN-03 01-MAY-03
Small Widget                              1 15-JAN-03 01-MAY-03
Square Zinculator                         1 09-JUL-00 01-NOV-00

SQL> |
```

FIGURE 5-15. *Nesting date functions*

items in your PLSQL101_PRODUCT table have been in stock, you could do so
with this command:

```
SELECT product_name,
       last_stock_date,
       MONTHS_BETWEEN(SYSDATE, last_stock_date) STOCK_MONTHS
FROM   plsql101_product;
```

If you wanted to make the months a little bit easier to read, you could do so by
wrapping a ROUND function around the MONTHS_BETWEEN function, like this:

```
SELECT product_name,
       last_stock_date,
       ROUND(MONTHS_BETWEEN(SYSDATE, last_stock_date),0) STOCK_MONTHS
FROM   plsql101_product;
```

If you wanted to see how many months you have been on this planet, you could
do so with a command like this (fill in your birthdate where it says *birthdate,* and be
sure to use a four-digit year):

```
SELECT MONTHS_BETWEEN(SYSDATE, birthdate) FROM DUAL;
```

Congratulations on surviving all those months! Makes the rest of this chapter
seem like a walk in the park, doesn't it?

Data Conversion

Data conversion is the label used to describe converting information from one datatype to another—usually between text and dates, times, or numbers. Within your own Oracle database there will be relatively little need for converting datatypes, but the data conversion functions will still be useful for two reasons:

■ They enable you to change the way dates, times, and numbers are displayed.

■ They simplify importing data from other sources.

In this section you will learn about functions designed to convert numbers, dates, times, and text.

TO_CHAR

The TO_CHAR function converts dates, times, or numbers to text. Its main value is giving you quite a bit of control over how dates, times, and numbers are displayed; the fact that they are text is irrelevant when they are scrolling across a SQL*Plus screen.

You may have noticed that when you select data containing numbers from a table, the numbers don't have any particular formatting applied to them; they display with however many decimals they contain, so the list is not decimal-aligned. Dates, too, have their problems: They're displayed in a way that few of us would use on a daily basis, and they do not display any time component. TO_CHAR gives you the means to correct both of these situations.

Formatting Date and Time Values   The syntax for a TO_CHAR function designed to change the way dates and times are displayed is as follows:

TO_CHAR(*input_value*, *format_code*)

The *input_value* can be written directly into the TO_CHAR function, but is more commonly derived by referring to a column in a table. The *format_code* consists of one or more elements identifying how you want the function to represent portions of a date or time.

Enter the SELECT statement that follows to see a simple example of the TO_CHAR function in action:

```
SELECT TO_CHAR(SYSDATE, 'MM-DD-YYYY HH24:MI:SS') NOW
FROM DUAL;
```

As you can see from the results in SQL*Plus, the *format_code* portion of this example causes the current date to be displayed using a format that is familiar to many people, and it gives a way to (finally) see the time portion of SYSDATE. You can make up any format code you want, combining elements as your needs dictate. The elements you can use are shown in Table 5-3. Take a moment to look at the table now and, if you are like me, marvel at the incredible number of ways Oracle can display dates and times.

Element	Meaning
- / , . ; : 'any text'	Punctuation and quoted text is reproduced in the result.
AD A.D.	AD indicator with or without periods.
AM A.M.	Meridian indicator with or without periods.
BC B.C.	BC indicator with or without periods.
CC SCC	One greater than the first two digits of a four-digit year; "S" prefixes BC dates with "-". For example, '20' from '1900'.
D	Day of week (1-7).
DAY	Name of day, padded with blanks to length of nine characters.
DD	Day of month (1-31).
DDD	Day of year (1-366).
DY	Abbreviated name of day.
E	Abbreviated era name (Japanese Imperial, ROC Official, and Thai Buddha calendars).
EE	Full era name (Japanese Imperial, ROC Official, and Thai Buddha calendars).

TABLE 5-3. *TO_CHAR Date and Time Format Code Elements*

Element	Meaning
HH	Hour of day (1-12).
HH12	Hour of day (1-12).
HH24	Hour of day (0-23).
IW	Week of year (1-52 or 1-53) based on the ISO standard.
IYYY	Four-digit year based on the ISO standard.
IYY IY I	Last three, two, or one digit(s) of ISO year.
J	Julian day; the number of days since January 1, 4712 BC. Number specified with 'J' must be an integer.
MI	Minute (0-59).
M	Month (01-12; JAN = 01).
MON	Abbreviated name of month.
MONTH	Name of month, padded with blanks to length of nine characters.
PM P.M.	Meridian indicator with or without periods.
Q	Quarter of year (1, 2, 3, 4; JAN-MAR = 1).
RM	Roman numeral month (I-XII; JAN = I).
RR	Given a year with two digits, returns a year in the next century if the year is <50 and the last two digits of the current year are >=50; returns a year in the preceding century if the year is >=50 and the last two digits of the current year are <50.
RRRR	Round year. Accepts either four-digit or two-digit input. If two-digit, provides the same return as RR. If you don't want this functionality, simply enter the four-digit year.
SS	Second (0-59).
SSSSS	Seconds past midnight (0-86399).
WW	Week of year (1-53) where week 1 starts on the first day of the year and continues to the seventh day of the year.

TABLE 5-3. *TO_CHAR Date and Time Format Code Elements* (continued)

Element	Meaning
W	Week of month (1-5) where week 1 starts on the first day of the month and ends on the seventh.
Y,YYY	Year with comma in this position.
YEAR SYEAR	Year, spelled out; "S" prefixes BC dates with "-".
YYYY SYYYY	Four-digit year; "S" prefixes BC dates with "-".
YYY YY Y	Last three, two, or one digit(s) of year.

TABLE 5-3.   *TO_CHAR Date and Time Format Code Elements* (continued)

The DD format element that displays the day of the month has a couple of optional suffixes that add some nice cosmetic polish. You can follow the DD element with TH to have Oracle display "1ST" instead of "1" for the day (and "2ND" instead of "2", and so on). Try the following command to see how this works:

```
SELECT TO_CHAR(SYSDATE, 'MONTH DDTH')
FROM DUAL;
```

You can also follow the DD format element with SP to have Oracle spell out the day of the month. Enter the following code for an example:

```
SELECT TO_CHAR(SYSDATE, 'MONTH DDSP')
FROM DUAL;
```

By combining these two suffixes, you can make Oracle spell out the day of the month *and* include "st", "nd", "rd", or "th" after it. The following command demonstrates this:

```
SELECT TO_CHAR(SYSDATE, 'MONTH DDSPTH')
FROM DUAL;
```

You may notice in these last three examples that the resulting date formats could use a little more cosmetic help. For instance, the MONTH format element always pads the month name to nine characters in length, so there is a lot of space between the month and the date if you are dealing with a date whose month name is short. Also, the entire result is capitalized, giving it a somewhat glaring look. You can solve these problems by using some of the other functions you have already learned. A complete list of the cosmetic problems follows:

- Month is followed by unnecessary spaces.

- Month name is all caps.

- Suffix following date is all caps (for example, "TH" instead of "th")

- When SP format code element suffix is used, spelled-out date is all caps.

Let's look at how to use the functions you've learned to solve each problem step by step. For this example, we'll correct the display of this date format:

```
SELECT TO_CHAR(SYSDATE, 'MONTH DDTH')
FROM DUAL;
```

To remove the extra spaces after the month name, you can use the RTRIM function. To do this, however, you will need to separate the month from the date that follows it. You can easily do that by selecting them as two separate items that are concatenated together. The following command shows how to separate the month name from the date. Enter it now, and you will see that the output it produces looks identical to that produced by the prior command.

```
SELECT TO_CHAR(SYSDATE, 'MONTH') ||
       ' ' ||
       TO_CHAR(SYSDATE, 'DDTH')
FROM DUAL;
```

Now it's time to get rid of the extra spaces following the month name. Wrap an RTRIM function around the TO_CHAR function that produces the month name, as shown in the code that follows:

```
SELECT RTRIM(TO_CHAR(SYSDATE, 'MONTH')) ||
       ' ' ||
       TO_CHAR(SYSDATE, 'DDTH')
FROM DUAL;
```

This produces the desired spacing. Next you want to change the capitalization of the month name, so that only its first letter is capitalized. The INITCAP function does just that. Surround the entire month-name portion of your SELECT statement with an INITCAP function, as shown in the following code:

```
SELECT INITCAP(RTRIM(TO_CHAR(SYSDATE, 'MONTH'))) ||
       ' ' ||
       TO_CHAR(SYSDATE, 'DDTH')
FROM DUAL;
```

The last change is making the date's TH element produce a lowercase suffix after the day of the month. I'd bet that you already have an idea how to do this. That's right: You place a LOWER function around the date portion of the SELECT statement, as shown in this code:

```
SELECT INITCAP(RTRIM(TO_CHAR(SYSDATE, 'MONTH'))) ||
       ' ' ||
       LOWER(TO_CHAR(SYSDATE, 'DDTH'))
FROM DUAL;
```

Using the techniques you just practiced, take a moment now to "get it into your fingers" by improving the appearance of the date displayed by this code:

```
SELECT TO_CHAR(SYSDATE, 'MONTH DDSPTH')
FROM DUAL;
```

Formatting Number Values   The TO_CHAR function can also standardize the way numbers are displayed. For instance, look at the output produced by this command:

```
SELECT * FROM plsql101_product;
```

The product prices are not decimal-aligned, which makes them harder to read than they need to be. By placing a simple TO_CHAR function around the reference to product price in your SELECT command, you can fix this problem. Try the following code to see how this works:

```
SELECT product_name,
       TO_CHAR(product_price, '$9,999.00') "Price",
       quantity_on_hand,
       last_stock_date
FROM   plsql101_product;
```

The results you get should look similar to those shown in Figure 5-16.

As was the case with date formats, number formats are made up of one or more elements that each represent a facet of the formatting being applied. Those elements are shown in Table 5-4. Take a moment to look over the number format code

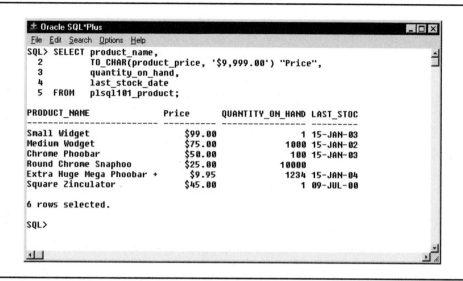

FIGURE 5-16. *Using the TO_CHAR function to improve appearance of numbers*

Element	Example	Description
$	$9999	Places a dollar sign before the value
, (comma)	9,999	Places a comma in the position indicated
. (period)	99.99	Places a decimal point in the position indicated
MI	9999MI	Causes a "–" to be displayed after any negative value
S	S9999	Places a "+" for positive values and a "–" for negative values, in position indicated
PR	9999PR	Causes negative values to be surrounded by <angle brackets>
D	99D99	Displays your country's decimal character in the position indicated

TABLE 5-4. *Number Format Code Elements*

Element	Example	Description
G	9G999	Displays your country's group separator in the position indicated
C	C999	Displays the ISO currency symbol in the position indicated
L	L999	Displays the local currency symbol in the position indicated
RN or rn	RN	Causes numbers to display as upper- or lowercase Roman numerals (limited to integers between 1 and 3999)
0	0999	Displays one or more leading zeros
0	9990	Causes empty values to display as zeros

TABLE 5-4.   *Number Format Code Elements* (continued)

elements offered, and then practice your skills by producing a SELECT statement that formats your PLSQL101_PRODUCT table's QUANTITY_ON_HAND column so that it is more readable. While you're at it, the LAST_STOCK_DATE column could stand a makeover too. Try to make your command produce output whose format matches that shown in Figure 5-17. Note that the LAST_STOCK_DATE column has been pushed to the right a couple of spaces to make it easier to

```
Oracle SQL*Plus                                          _ □ X
File  Edit  Search  Options  Help

PRODUCT_NAME               Price    On Hand  Last Stocked
-------------------------  -------  -------  ---------------
Small Widget                $99.00        1  JAN 15, 2003
Medium Wodget               $75.00    1,000  JAN 15, 2002
Chrome Phoobar              $50.00      100  JAN 15, 2003
Round Chrome Snaphoo        $25.00   10,000
Extra Huge Mega Phoobar +    $9.95    1,234  JAN 15, 2004
Square Zinculator           $45.00        1  JUL 09, 2000

6 rows selected.

SQL>
```

FIGURE 5-17.   *Output formatted with various TO_CHAR functions*

visually separate from the QUANTITY_ON_HAND column; I'll give you a hint and tell you that concatenation made that possible.

TO_DATE

The TO_DATE function converts text that looks like a date (and/or time) into an actual Oracle date/time value. While its primary use is for importing text files containing dates and times from other databases, it is also handy when you want to enter a date manually using a format other than Oracle's default of DD-MON-YY, or a time. The syntax of the function is as follows:

TO_DATE(*input_value, format_code*)

The TO_DATE function uses a subset of the format code elements used by the TO_CHAR function. The TO_DATE function's elements are shown in Table 5-5.

Element	Meaning
– / , . ; : `'any text'`	Punctuation and quoted text is reproduced in the result.
AD A.D.	AD indicator with or without periods.
AM A.M.	Meridian indicator with or without periods.
BC B.C.	BC indicator with or without periods.
D	Day of week (1-7).
DAY	Name of day, padded with blanks to length of nine characters.
DD	Day of month (1-31).
DDD	Day of year (1-366).
DY	Abbreviated name of day.

TABLE 5-5.   *Date and Time Format Code Elements*

Element	Meaning
HH	Hour of day (1-12).
HH24	Hour of day (0-23).
J	Julian day; the number of days since January 1, 4712 BC. Number specified with 'J' must be an integer.
MI	Minute (0-59).
MM	Month (01-12; JAN = 01)
MON	Abbreviated name of month.
MONTH	Name of month, padded with blanks to length of nine characters.
PM P.M.	Meridian indicator with or without periods.
RM	Roman numeral month (I-XII; JAN = I).
RR	Given a year with two digits, returns a year in the next century if the year is <50 and the last two digits of the current year are >=50; returns a year in the preceding century if the year is >=50 and the last two digits of the current year are <50.
RRRR	Round year. Accepts either four-digit or two-digit input. If two-digit, provides the same return as RR. If you don't want this functionality, simply enter the four-digit year.
SS	Seconds (0-59).
SSSSS	Seconds past midnight (0-86399).
Y,YYY	Year with comma in this position.
YYYY SYYYY	Four-digit year; "S" prefixes BC dates with "-".
YYY YY Y	Last three, two, or one digit(s) of year.

TABLE 5-5. *Date and Time Format Code Elements* (continued)

To see how the TO_DATE function enables you to insert dates and times more
flexibly, enter the following code and compare your results with Figure 5-18:

```
SELECT product_name,
       product_price,
       quantity_on_hand,
       TO_CHAR(last_stock_date, 'MM-DD-YYYY HH24:MI') "Last Stocked"
FROM   plsql101_product;

UPDATE plsql101_product
SET    last_stock_date = TO_DATE('December 31, 2002, 11:30 P.M.',
                                 'Month dd, YYYY, HH:MI P.M.')
WHERE  product_name LIKE '%Zinc%';

SELECT product_name,
       product_price,
       quantity_on_hand,
       TO_CHAR(last_stock_date, 'MM-DD-YYYY HH24:MI') "Last Stocked"
FROM   plsql101_product;
```

Other Functions

This section presents a group of SQL functions whose only common trait is that
they don't fit easily into any other group. That doesn't make them any less useful,
though, and every one of these functions provides a valuable service that you are
likely to use over and over.

DECODE

One of the differences between the SQL you have been learning and the PL/SQL
programming language you will soon start to learn is that SQL has no "flow control"
abilities: no loop, no "goto," no if-then-else. A SQL script starts at the top and goes
straight to the bottom, one line at a time, with no variation. It has no decision-
making abilities. However, it does offer one function that approximates the function
of an if-then-else statement: DECODE. The DECODE function translates from one
set of values to another set, using "before" and "after" values that you define. You
could characterize what it does by saying that if the incoming value equals "A"
then the DECODE function returns "B", and if the incoming value equals "C" the
function returns "D". You define what the values are for "A", "B", "C", and "D".
This can be immensely helpful when translating data from one database system to
another, because different systems usually use different sets of codes to represent
similar information.

```
Oracle SQL*Plus                                                    _ □ ×
File  Edit  Search  Options  Help
SQL> SELECT product_name,
  2          product_price,
  3          quantity_on_hand,
  4          TO_CHAR(last_stock_date, 'MM-DD-YYYY HH24:MI') "Last Stocked"
  5  FROM    plsql101_product;

PRODUCT_NAME              PRODUCT_PRICE QUANTITY_ON_HAND Last Stocked
------------------------- ------------- ---------------- ----------------
Small Widget                         99                1 01-15-2003 00:00
Medium Wodget                        75             1000 01-15-2002 00:00
Chrome Phoobar                       50              100 01-15-2003 00:00
Round Chrome Snaphoo                 25            10000
Extra Huge Mega Phoobar +          9.95             1234 01-15-2004 00:00
Square Zinculator                    45                1 07-09-2000 00:00

6 rows selected.

SQL>
SQL> UPDATE plsql101_product
  2  SET     last_stock_date = TO_DATE('December 31, 2002, 11:30 P.M.',
  3                            'Month dd, YYYY, HH:MI P.M.')
  4  WHERE   product_name LIKE '%Zinc%';

1 row updated.

SQL>
SQL> SELECT product_name,
  2          product_price,
  3          quantity_on_hand,
  4          TO_CHAR(last_stock_date, 'MM-DD-YYYY HH24:MI') "Last Stocked"
  5  FROM    plsql101_product;

PRODUCT_NAME              PRODUCT_PRICE QUANTITY_ON_HAND Last Stocked
------------------------- ------------- ---------------- ----------------
Small Widget                         99                1 01-15-2003 00:00
Medium Wodget                        75             1000 01-15-2002 00:00
Chrome Phoobar                       50              100 01-15-2003 00:00
Round Chrome Snaphoo                 25            10000
Extra Huge Mega Phoobar +          9.95             1234 01-15-2004 00:00
Square Zinculator                    45                1 12-31-2002 23:30

6 rows selected.

SQL>
```

FIGURE 5-18. *Using TO_DATE to insert dates and times flexibly*

The syntax of the DECODE function is as follows:

```
DECODE(incoming_source,
       incoming_value_1, outgoing_result_1,
```

> *incoming_value_2, outgoing_result_2,*
> *...*
> *last_incoming_value, last_outgoing_result,*
> [*default_outgoing_result_if_no_match*]
>)

A few words about interpreting the syntax example just given:

■ After specifying the *incoming_source*—usually a column name within some table—you define a series of incoming/outgoing pairs. The incoming side contains one of the values you know will be coming from the source data, and the outgoing side defines what you want that value translated into. You define as many of these as you want (that's what the "..." in the middle of the syntax example means).

■ After defining the incoming/outgoing pairs, you can specify a single, final outgoing result with no incoming value. That outgoing result will be returned if the DECODE function encounters an incoming value that is not found in the list of incoming/outgoing pairs you have defined. (This is similar to the "else" portion of an if-then-else statement.) This part of the function is optional (which is why it's surrounded by square brackets "[" and "]"). It's usually a good idea to include one of these, so you will know if the incoming data contained anything you didn't expect.

To see how the DECODE function works, let's say that you have been given the PLSQL101_OLD_ITEM table and told you need to produce from it some listings of records. However, the structure of your company has changed since the old items were in use, and now, instead of identifying items by the city they came from ("NY-101", and so on), you need to show regions. Items with "NY" in their item ID belong to the "Eastern" region, while "LA" items come from the "Western" region. The three-digit item numbers that follow each city abbreviation in the original data still need to be displayed, so you'll also employ your knowledge of the SUBSTR function to parse them out as substrings. Look over the following code to see how the DECODE function is used to translate from cities to regions, and then enter it to try it out. Your results should match those shown in Figure 5-19.

```
SELECT DECODE(SUBSTR(item_id, 1, 2),
             'LA', 'Western',
             'NY', 'Eastern',
             '* Unknown *'
             ) "Region",
       SUBSTR(item_id, 4,3) "Item ID",
```

```
        item_desc
FROM    plsql101_old_item;
```

To see how the DECODE and other functions you have been learning get used in real life, read through the code listing in the box that follows. It is extracted from a data-transfer script I wrote for a client. It contains several items worth noting:

- Almost every column was given a new name. This was to match the old system's column names with those used by the new system.

- The old system stored dates in standard Oracle format, but the new system needed to have them inserted as text strings with the format YYYYMMDD.

- Social security numbers in the old system did not contain any dashes, while the new system wanted to see them with dashes. The solution was to parse the old number into pieces using SUBSTR functions and concatenate them with dashes. The resulting string was then given the name PATIENT_ID.

```
Oracle SQL*Plus                                                    _ □ ✕
File  Edit  Search  Options  Help
SQL> SELECT DECODE(SUBSTR(item_id, 1, 2),
  2                'LA', 'Western',
  3                'NY', 'Eastern',
  4                '* Unknown *'
  5                ) "Region",
  6          SUBSTR(item_id, 4,3) "Item ID",
  7          item_desc
  8   FROM   plsql101_old_item;

Region      Ite ITEM_DESC
----------- --- ------------------------
Western     101 Can, Small
Western     102 Can, Large
Western     103 Bottle, Small
Western     104 Bottle, Large
Eastern     101 Box, Small
Eastern     102 Box, Large
Eastern     103 Shipping Carton, Small
Eastern     104 Shipping Carton, Large

8 rows selected.

SQL> |
```

FIGURE 5-19. *Using the DECODE function to translate data*

■ The old system defined gender using the codes M, F, O (other—the client was in Los Angeles), and U (unknown). The new system wanted to see those values represented as 1, 2, 3, or 4. A classic DECODE scenario.

■ The old system identified five different locations where patients were admitted. The new system just wanted to know which of the two local counties the facility was in—it didn't care which facility was used. In this case, the DECODE function still had one incoming/outgoing pair for every possible incoming code—for a total of five pairs—but there were only two different outgoing values generated by all those pairs (one for each county). Used in this way, the DECODE function serves as a grouping mechanism.

■ Many of the original system's items were entered sloppily, with unnecessary spaces before and/or after the actual data. This was cleaned up by wrapping the problematic columns in LTRIM and RTRIM functions.

■ The old system stored the patient's age at their time of entry to a facility. Unfortunately, some facilities stored the age in years, some in months, and some in days. Fortunately, they had enough foresight to include a code indicating which age increment was being used in each record. Essentially, they wanted to convert old data laid out like this:

SOCIAL_SECURITY_NUMBER	AGE_TYPE	AGE_AT_ENTRY
111223333	Y	28
222334444	Y	65
333445555	M	18
444556666	D	3
555667777	D	10

into new data laid out like this:

PATIENT_ID	AGE_YRS	AGE_MOS	AGE_DAYS
111-22-3333	28		
222-33-4444	65		
333-44-5555		18	
444-55-6666			3
555-66-7777			10

This was accomplished using three separate DECODE functions. The first one looks in the old system's AGE_TYPE column and, if it finds a "Y" there, places the old system's AGE_AT_ENTRY value into the new system under a column named AGE_YRS. If the DECODE function does not find "Y" in the AGE_TYPE column, it leaves the AGE_YRS column blank. The next two DECODE functions do the same thing, looking for AGE_TYPE values of "M" and "D", and placing the AGE_AT_ENTRY values into the AGE_MOS or AGE_DAYS column, depending on what they find. These DECODE functions demonstrate a couple of interesting facts: more than one DECODE function can refer to a given column, and a DECODE function can return a value based on a column other than the one it looked at for decision-making purposes.

Example: Real-Life Use of the Functions You Have Learned

```
select to_char(EXIT_DATE, 'YYYYMMDD')              DISCHARGE_DATE,
       substr(SOCIAL_SECURITY_NUMBER,1,3) ||'-'||
       substr(SOCIAL_SECURITY_NUMBER,4,2) ||'-'||
       substr(SOCIAL_SECURITY_NUMBER,6,4)          PATIENT_ID,
       decode(GENDER,
              'M', '1',
              'F', '2',
              'O', '3',
              'U', '4')                            GENDER,
       substr(ZIP_CODE,1,5)                        ZIPCODE,
       decode(ltrim(rtrim(SITE)),
              '300', 'LA',
              '350', 'OC',
              '410', 'LA',
              '420', 'OC',
              '440', 'LA',
              '*N/A*')                             COUNTY,
       ltrim(rtrim(PHYSICIAN))                     PHYSICIAN
       to_char(DATE_OF_BIRTH, 'YYYYMMDD')          DOB,
       decode(AGE_TYPE,
              'Y', AGE_AT_ENTRY,
              '')                                  AGE_YRS,
       decode(AGE_TYPE,
              'M', AGE_AT_ENTRY,
              '')                                  AGE_MOS,
       decode(AGE_TYPE,
              'D', AGE_AT_ENTRY,
              '')                                  AGE_DAYS,
from   ENCOUNTER
;
```

NVL

The NVL function performs a simple but useful function: Whenever it is presented with a value that is null, it returns a value of your choosing instead. This ability to fill in blank values automatically can help give your output a more finished look. The NVL function's syntax is as follows:

NVL(*input_value, result_if_input_value_is_null*)

As is often the case with functions, the *input_value* is usually the name of a column. The *result_if_input_value_is_null* can be anything you specify: a literal (that is, hard-coded) value, a reference to another column, or any other expression you want.

Enter the following example to see the NVL function in action. Your results should match what you see in Figure 5-20.

```
SELECT  product_name,
        last_stock_date
FROM    plsql101_product;

SELECT  product_name,
        NVL(last_stock_date, '01-JAN-2001') "Last Stocked"
FROM    plsql101_product;
```

As you can see from the example, the NVL function replaced the Round Chrome Snaphoo's empty LAST_STOCK_DATE value with the date specified in the NVL function. You could have had it replace the null value with today's date instead, by using this code:

```
SELECT  product_name,
        NVL(last_stock_date, TRUNC(SYSDATE)) "Last Stocked"
FROM    plsql101_product;
```

NOTE
The NVL function does not actually update any values in a table. The source data is left untouched.

One quirk with the NVL function is that it expects the datatypes for the *input_value* and *result_if_input_value_is_null* to be the same; if the *input_value* is a date, the *result_if_input_value_is_null* should also be a date, and so on. This becomes an issue if you want the function to display the popular "N/A" whenever it finds a null value, because "N/A" is text. If the column it gets as an *input_value* is a text column, then everything is fine. However, if the function is checking for nulls in a date or

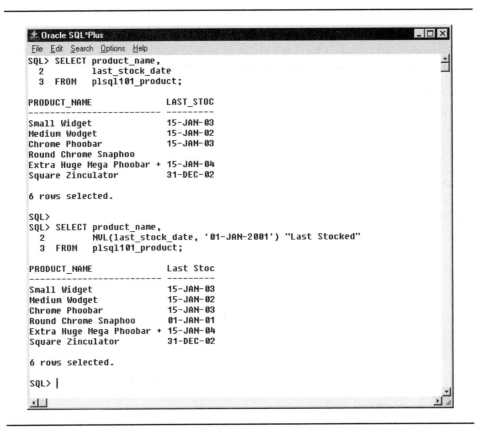

FIGURE 5-20. *NVL function filling null date with a default date*

number column, you will need to wrap a TO_CHAR function around the *input_value* column name, so that the input value is also text. The following code demonstrates this: The first version of the command will fail, while the second one will succeed. Enter the code and compare your results with those shown in Figure 5-21.

```
SELECT product_name,
       NVL(last_stock_date, 'N/A') "Last Stocked"
FROM   plsql101_product;

SELECT product_name,
       NVL(TO_CHAR(last_stock_date), 'N/A') "Last Stocked"
FROM   plsql101_product;
```

```
 Oracle SQL*Plus                                                    _ □ ✕
File  Edit  Search  Options  Help
SQL> SELECT product_name,
  2          NVL(last_stock_date, 'N/A') "Last Stocked"
  3  FROM    plsql101_product;
       NVL(last_stock_date, 'N/A') "Last Stocked"
                          *
ERROR at line 2:
ORA-01858: a non-numeric character was found where a numeric was expected


SQL>
SQL> SELECT product_name,
  2          NVL(TO_CHAR(last_stock_date), 'N/A') "Last Stocked"
  3  FROM    plsql101_product;

PRODUCT_NAME                 Last Stoc
-------------------------    ---------
Small Widget                 15-JAN-03
Medium Wodget                15-JAN-02
Chrome Phoobar               15-JAN-03
Round Chrome Snaphoo         N/A
Extra Huge Mega Phoobar +    15-JAN-04
Square Zinculator            31-DEC-02

6 rows selected.

SQL>
```

FIGURE 5-21.   *Using the NVL function with different datatypes*

Inserting Comments in SQL Scripts

In Chapter 4 you learned how to create and run SQL script files. These files are
essentially programs—simple programs at this stage, but programs nonetheless.
And programs need to be documented. SQL scripts are rarely long enough to justify
an external document explaining what they do, so the most common method of
documenting a script file is to place comments directly within the file. When done
correctly, these comments are ignored by Oracle, so you can leave them in the
script file and still run the file as you normally would.

There are two types of comments. The first type is a single line long, and is good
for little reminders, or to temporarily disable a portion of code you don't want to run
but also don't want to delete. The second type can be as many lines long as you want,
but is not quite as obvious, and therefore doesn't "jump out at you" when reading the
script file. Both types have their place, and many script files incorporate both.

To create a single-line comment, you simply make the first two characters on the line a pair of dashes. Whatever follows the dashes is ignored by Oracle. Enter the following SQL lines to see this in action:

```
SELECT * FROM plsql101_product;
-- This line will be ignored.  Oracle will not try to run it.
SELECT * FROM plsql101_purchase;
```

The results you see should match those shown in Figure 5-22. You can use this approach for any number of lines, whether they are separate or grouped together.

TIP
A single-line comment can also be created by starting the line with "REM " instead of "--". This technique is used in other programming languages, and is thus familiar to programmers who are learning SQL after learning some other language. However, from a visual standpoint the "REM " does not catch your eye as easily as "--". Perhaps this is the reason that "--" is more common.

```
± Oracle SQL*Plus                                                    _ □ ×
 File  Edit  Search  Options  Help
SQL> SELECT * FROM plsql101_product;

PRODUCT_NAME              PRODUCT_PRICE QUANTITY_ON_HAND LAST_STOC
------------------------- ------------- ---------------- ---------
Small Widget                         99                1 15-JAN-03
Medium Wodget                        75             1000 15-JAN-02
Chrome Phoobar                       50              100 15-JAN-03
Round Chrome Snaphoo                 25            10000
Extra Huge Mega Phoobar +          9.95             1234 15-JAN-04
Square Zinculator                    45                1 31-DEC-02

6 rows selected.

SQL> -- This line will be ignored.  Oracle will not try to run it.
SQL> SELECT * FROM plsql101_purchase;

PRODUCT_NAME                QUANTITY PURCHASE_ SAL
------------------------- ---------- --------- ---
Small Widget                       1 14-JUL-03 CA
Medium Wodget                     75 14-JUL-03 BB
Chrome Phoobar                     2 14-JUL-03 GA
Small Widget                       8 15-JUL-03 GA
Medium Wodget                     20 15-JUL-03 LB
Round Snaphoo                      5 16-JUL-03 CA

6 rows selected.

SQL>
```

FIGURE 5-22. *Commenting out single lines in a SQL script*

If you are going to have several lines of comments in a group, however, you may want to employ the other type of comment. In this approach, you place the characters "/*" at the start of the comment section, and "*/" at the end. The lines in between are ignored. Try the following code to see this:

```
/*
This script is designed to show how multiple-line commenting works.
It is used in the PL/SQL 101 book by Oracle Press.
*/

SELECT * FROM plsql101_product;

SELECT * FROM plsql101_purchase;
```

The results you see should match those shown in Figure 5-23.

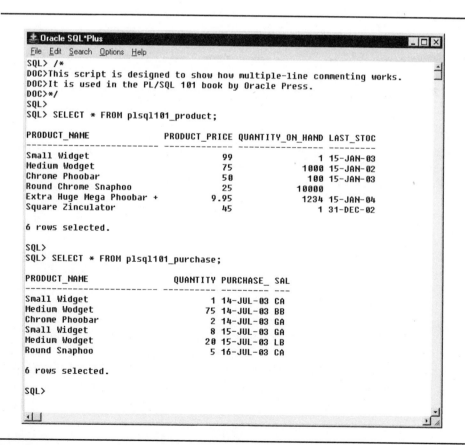

FIGURE 5-23   *Commenting out groups of lines in a SQL script*

Commonly Used Group Functions

So far, every function you have learned was designed to work on a row-by-row basis with records. Oracle also has *group functions* that return values useful when you are analyzing groups of records. A group of records is any collection of records that share something in common; for instance, they are for the same product, or the same department, or the same time range. You define what constitutes a group, and the group functions will provide you with totals, record counts, and average, smallest, and largest values within each group. These functions are very useful for statistical analysis.

This section will start by presenting the most-used group functions, and then it will show you how to define record groups so the functions return statistical information for each group. Since you will not know how to group records when you're first introduced to the functions, they will return values representing the entire set of records within your table.

SUM

The SUM function adds values and returns the total. Enter the following SQL statements to see it in action:

```
SELECT * FROM plsql101_purchase;
SELECT SUM(quantity) FROM plsql101_purchase;
```

COUNT

The COUNT function...you guessed it, counts records. You might be surprised how often this is useful. For instance, the easiest way to find out if a table contains any records is to use a command like this one:

```
SELECT COUNT(*) FROM plsql101_purchase;
```

Now that I've shown you this command, let me tell you why you shouldn't use it. (I know, I know...I led you into this, and I'll lead you right out of it.) By specifying "*" as the function's column set, you inadvertently force Oracle to read the entire table before returning an answer. That's not a problem with the small practice tables used in this book, but it is a problem in a system with a hundred thousand records, and a bigger problem in a system with, say, a billion records. Forcing a full-table scan will cause the count to be returned to you much more slowly than it could be, and it makes Oracle divert computing resources from the work the database was actually designed to do, which slows down operations for the rest of the business. It's much better to specify a single column for the COUNT function to count, like this:

```
SELECT COUNT(product_name) FROM plsql101_purchase;
```

Usually, the preferred column name is the first column in the table, for reasons which will be explained in the next chapter. An even simpler way is to define a literal value instead of a column name as the COUNT function's argument, like this:

```
SELECT COUNT(1) FROM plsql101_purchase;
```

Strictly speaking, this causes Oracle to return the value "1" for every record in the table. You could just as easily put "Hi There" in the COUNT function instead of the "1"; it doesn't matter what literal value is in the function, because the function ignores the literal value itself. It just counts the records and tells you how many it found.

One interesting facet of the COUNT function is that if you specify a column in the table whose records you are counting, the COUNT function only counts records that actually have a value in that column. You can use this to determine what percentage of records in a table are null in a specific column. As you enter the code that follows, notice that the first command tells the total number of records in the table; the second command produces the same number, because no records have a blank product name; the third command tells how many of the records have the LAST_STOCK_DATE column populated; and the final command gives you the percentage of records with that column populated. This kind of information can be handy if you are determining how useful a particular column is. After entering your commands, compare your results with those shown in Figure 5-24.

```
SELECT COUNT(1) FROM plsql101_product;

SELECT COUNT(product_name) FROM plsql101_product;

SELECT COUNT(last_stock_date) FROM plsql101_product;

SELECT COUNT(last_stock_date) / COUNT(product_name) "Populated Records"
FROM plsql101_product;
```

AVG

The AVG function returns the average of the values in the column you specify. Since the function has to actually read the column values in order to do its job, there is no point in specifying "1" or any other literal value as the function's argument; you must specify a column name. For instance, to get the average price of the items in your PLSQL101_PRODUCT table's inventory, enter the following statement:

```
SELECT AVG(product_price) FROM plsql101_product;
```

```
Oracle SQL*Plus                                                      _|□|×|
File  Edit  Search  Options  Help
SQL> SELECT COUNT(1) FROM plsql101_product;

  COUNT(1)
----------
         6

SQL>
SQL> SELECT COUNT(product_name) FROM plsql101_product;

COUNT(PRODUCT_NAME)
-------------------
                  6

SQL>
SQL> SELECT COUNT(last_stock_date) FROM plsql101_product;

COUNT(LAST_STOCK_DATE)
----------------------
                     5

SQL>
SQL> SELECT COUNT(last_stock_date) / COUNT(product_name) "Populated Records"
  2  FROM plsql101_product;

Populated Records
-----------------
        .833333333

SQL>
```

FIGURE 5-24.   *Using the COUNT function*

MIN

The MIN function returns the smallest value found in the column specified in its argument. For instance, to get the price of the cheapest item in the table of products, you could issue this command:

 `SELECT MIN(product_price) FROM plsql101_product;`

MAX

As you have probably guessed, the MAX function returns the largest value found in the column specified in its argument. For instance, to see the highest price in the table of products, you could use this command:

```
SELECT MAX(product_price) FROM plsql101_product;
```

The MAX function has a variety of useful capabilities. For example, there may be a time in the future when you are considering reducing the length of a text column in an existing table. You would want to know how much of the column's width is actually being used, and therefore need to know the length of the longest item within that column. You can do this easily by specifying the length of the column as a MAX function's argument, as shown in the second command in this set:

```
DESC plsql101_purchase;
SELECT MAX(LENGTH(product_name)) FROM plsql101_purchase;
```

Grouping Data via the GROUP BY Clause

Now that you know about group functions, it's time to learn how to create groups. You accomplish this by adding the clause GROUP BY to the SELECT statement, as shown in the following example:

```
SELECT * FROM plsql101_purchase;

SELECT product_name, SUM(quantity)
FROM    plsql101_purchase
GROUP BY product_name;
```

After entering this code, compare the results you get with those shown in Figure 5-25. Note that after the GROUP BY clause you simply state what column contains the values you want the groups to be based on. Generally, this is the first column in the SELECT list.

You can include several different group functions within a single SELECT statement. For instance, you could have the statement tell you the total quantity, count, average, and lowest and highest values within each group, all with a single SELECT command. The following code provides an example of how to do this. The code uses the SUBSTR function to narrow the PRODUCT_NAME column, in order to help the results fit on the screen.

```
SELECT SUBSTR(product_name, 1, 15) "Product",
       SUM(quantity) "Total Sold",
       AVG(quantity) "Average",
       COUNT(quantity) "Transactions",
       MIN(quantity) "Fewest",
       MAX(quantity) "Most"
FROM    plsql101_purchase
GROUP BY product_name;
```

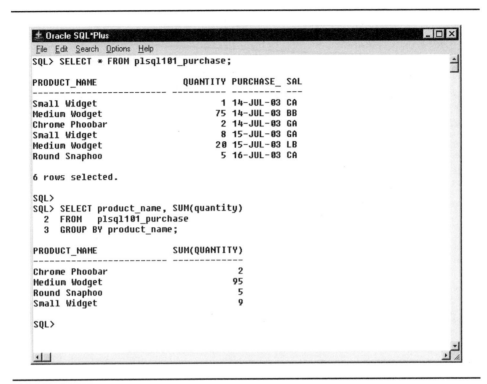

FIGURE 5-25. *Using the GROUP BY clause*

After entering this command, compare the results you get with those in Figure 5-26.

Including and Excluding Grouped Rows via the HAVING Clause

You probably remember that a WHERE clause can filter which records are returned by a SELECT statement. (If you don't remember that, review Chapter 3 and then come back. I'll wait.) A WHERE clause works the same way when you are grouping records: It filters individual records, keeping them from ever being factored into the calculations done by the group functions.

Once the groups are created, however, there is a new need: to be able to filter the groups themselves, based on group information. For instance, let's say that your

```
Oracle SQL*Plus                                                    _ □ ×
File  Edit  Search  Options  Help
SQL> SELECT  SUBSTR(product_name, 1, 15) "Product",
  2          SUM(quantity) "Total Sold",
  3          AVG(quantity) "Average",
  4          COUNT(quantity) "Transactions",
  5          MIN(quantity) "Fewest",
  6          MAX(quantity) "Most"
  7  FROM    plsql101_purchase
  8  GROUP BY product_name;

Product          Total Sold    Average Transactions      Fewest       Most
---------------  ----------  ---------- ------------  ----------  ----------
Chrome Phoobar            2           2            1           2           2
Medium Wodget            95        47.5            2          20          75
Round Snaphoo             5           5            1           5           5
Small Widget              9         4.5            2           1           8

SQL>
```

FIGURE 5-26.   *Using multiple group functions in one SELECT statement*

company is running out of warehouse space, and wants to reduce the number of products it carries in stock. To support this effort, you need to produce a list of the products that are selling poorly…products that have sold fewer than five items, for example. This is where the HAVING clause comes in. It filters *groups* based on *group values*. While the WHERE clause filters records before they are grouped, the HAVING clause filters entire groups. To see this in action, enter the following code (this command is identical to the prior one, with addition of a single line at the end, so you can save time by using the EDIT command and just adding the line containing the HAVING clause):

```
SELECT  SUBSTR(product_name, 1, 15) "Product",
        SUM(quantity) "Total Sold",
        AVG(quantity) "Average",
        COUNT(quantity) "Transactions",
        MIN(quantity) "Fewest",
        MAX(quantity) "Most"
FROM    plsql101_purchase
GROUP BY product_name
HAVING SUM(quantity) < 5;
```

As you can see, this causes the SELECT statement to include only those products that have been selling poorly. What if you wanted the opposite: a list of strong-selling products, with the performers excluded? Just change the criterion in the HAVING clause, as shown in the following code:

```
SELECT SUBSTR(product_name, 1, 15) "Product",
       SUM(quantity) "Total Sold",
       AVG(quantity) "Average",
       COUNT(quantity) "Transactions",
       MIN(quantity) "Fewest",
       MAX(quantity) "Most"
FROM   plsql101_purchase
GROUP BY product_name
HAVING SUM(quantity) >= 5;
```

Chapter Summary

This chapter has covered a lot of ground! You started by learning about single-row SQL functions. These include system variables (SYSDATE, USER, and USERENV), number functions (ROUND and TRUNC), text functions (UPPER, LOWER, INITCAP, LENGTH, SUBSTR, INSTR, LTRIM, and RTRIM), date functions (ADD_MONTHS, LAST_DAY, and MONTHS_BETWEEN), conversion functions (TO_CHAR and TO_DATE), and useful but hard-to-categorize functions such as DECODE and NVL. You also learned about group functions such as SUM, COUNT, AVG, MIN, and MAX, and you saw how you can get subtotal values from your data by including a GROUP BY clause in your SELECT statement. Finally, you saw how to exclude entire groups of subtotals from your output by placing a HAVING clause in your SELECT statement.

The next chapter has plenty of fascinating new things to learn. You will see how to speed up access to large tables, enforce your own requirements on the quality of data coming into a table, create relationships between tables, and use multiple-table groups to produce some pretty sophisticated results.

Chapter Questions

1. On which line will the following command fail?

```
INSERT INTO plsql101_product (
    product_name,
    product_price,
```

```
        quantity_on_hand,
        last_stock_date )
VALUES (
        'New Product',
        1.95,
        10,
        TO_CHAR(USER) )
    ;
```

   A. 1

   B. 2

   C. 7

   D. 10

   E. The command will succeed.

2. Which statement below is true?

   A. ROUND(4.5, 0) < TRUNC(4.5, 0)

   B. ROUND(4.1, 0) < TRUNC(4.2, 0)

   C. ROUND(8.9, 0) > TRUNC(8.9, 0)

   D. ROUND(8.9, 1) > TRUNC(8.95, 2)

3. What would be the result of the following DECODE function?

```
        DECODE('B',
            'A', 'One',
            'E', 'Five',
            'I', 'Nine',
            'O', 'Fifteen',
            'U', 'Twenty-one',
            'N/A'
        )
```

   A. One

   B. Two

   C. Five

   D. N/A

4. What will be the result of the following SUBSTR function when presented with an input value of 'Psychic trance, Medium' in the ITEM_DESC column?

```
SUBSTR(item_desc,
        INSTR(item_desc,
            ' ',
            1
        ) +2,
    99
    )
```

   A. Medium

   B. Psychic trance

   C. Psychic trance, Medium

5. Which of the following functions would return the last day of the year 2002?

   A. SELECT ADD_MONTHS(LAST_DAY('14-OCT-02'), 1) FROM DUAL;

   B. SELECT ADD_MONTHS(LAST_DAY('15-OCT-02'), -1) FROM DUAL;

   C. SELECT ADD_MONTHS(LAST_DAY('16-OCT-02'), 2) FROM DUAL;

   D. SELECT ADD_MONTHS(LAST_DAY('17-OCT-02'), -2) FROM DUAL;

Answers to Chapter Questions

I. D. 10

Explanation Even if the TO_CHAR function shown contained the formatting codes it needs, it would not work as an input value for a date column.

2. C. ROUND(8.9, 0) > TRUNC(8.9, 0)

Explanation Choice A resolves to 5 < 4, which is false. Choice B resolves to 4 < 4, which is also false. Choice D resolves to 8.9 > 8.95, which...you guessed it. Choice C resolves to 9 > 8, which is true.

3. D. N/A

Explanation Because the input value ('B') is text, it must find an exact match in the DECODE options, or else it will return the "else" value at the end of the function. In this case, there are no exact matches, so the 'N/A' value is the one returned.

4. A. Medium

Explanation For a refresher on this topic, review the section titled "Text Functions."

5. C

Explanation Since the LAST_DAY function is involved, you can ignore the day portion of the date supplied—all four LAST_DAY functions will resolve to October 31, 2002. Adding two months to that date, as the ADD_MONTHS function in choice C does, brings you to December 31, 2002.

CHAPTER
6

Using Indexes
and Constraints

uilding on the fundamental knowledge of tables, columns, and SQL that you have acquired, this chapter introduces you to concepts and techniques that are squarely in the realm of database geeks. (Wear the label proudly, and don't forget to mention it at your next salary review.) The chapter starts by explaining what indexes are, and then shows you how to use them to help your database operate more quickly. Next you will see how to create database constraints that check incoming data and stop any command that attempts to insert data that doesn't meet the requirements you specify. After that, you will learn about relationships between tables, which ushers you into the fascinating world of relational database design. Finally, you will see how to write queries that incorporate other queries, which can produce some pretty sophisticated results with very little code.

If you just started reading in this chapter and have not yet created the test tables used in prior chapters, you can use the following code to create the test tables before proceeding.

```
DROP TABLE plsql101_person;
CREATE TABLE plsql101_person (
    person_code VARCHAR2(3),
    first_name  VARCHAR2(15),
    last_name   VARCHAR2(20),
    hire_date   DATE
    )
;

INSERT INTO plsql101_person VALUES
    ('CA', 'Charlene', 'Atlas', '01-FEB-02');
INSERT INTO plsql101_person VALUES
    ('GA', 'Gary', 'Anderson', '15-FEB-02');
INSERT INTO plsql101_person VALUES
    ('BB', 'Bobby', 'Barkenhagen', '28-FEB-02');
INSERT INTO plsql101_person VALUES
    ('LB', 'Laren', 'Baxter', '01-MAR-02');

DROP TABLE plsql101_product;
CREATE TABLE plsql101_product (
    product_name     VARCHAR2(25),
    product_price    NUMBER(4,2),
    quantity_on_hand NUMBER(5,0),
    last_stock_date  DATE
    )
;

INSERT INTO plsql101_product VALUES
    ('Small Widget', 99, 1, '15-JAN-03');
```

```
INSERT INTO plsql101_product VALUES
    ('Medium Wodget', 75, 1000, '15-JAN-02');
INSERT INTO plsql101_product VALUES
    ('Chrome Phoobar', 50, 100, '15-JAN-03');
INSERT INTO plsql101_product VALUES
    ('Round Chrome Snaphoo', 25, 10000, null);
INSERT INTO plsql101_product VALUES
    ('Extra Huge Mega Phoobar +',9.95,1234,'15-JAN-04');
INSERT INTO plsql101_product VALUES ('Square Zinculator',
    45, 1, TO_DATE('December 31, 2002, 11:30 P.M.',
                    'Month dd, YYYY, HH:MI P.M.')
    )
;

DROP TABLE plsql101_purchase;
CREATE TABLE plsql101_purchase (
    product_name  VARCHAR2(25),
    salesperson   VARCHAR2(3),
    purchase_date DATE,
    quantity      NUMBER(4,2)
    )
;

INSERT INTO plsql101_purchase VALUES
    ('Small Widget', 'CA', '14-JUL-03', 1);
INSERT INTO plsql101_purchase VALUES
    ('Medium Wodget', 'BB', '14-JUL-03', 75);
INSERT INTO plsql101_purchase VALUES
    ('Chrome Phoobar', 'GA', '14-JUL-03', 2);
INSERT INTO plsql101_purchase VALUES
    ('Small Widget', 'GA', '15-JUL-03', 8);
INSERT INTO plsql101_purchase VALUES
    ('Medium Wodget', 'LB', '15-JUL-03', 20);
INSERT INTO plsql101_purchase VALUES
    ('Round Snaphoo', 'CA', '16-JUL-03', 5);

DROP TABLE plsql101_old_item;
CREATE TABLE plsql101_old_item (
    item_id   CHAR(20),
    item_desc CHAR(25)
    )
;

INSERT INTO plsql101_old_item VALUES
    ('LA-101', 'Can, Small');
INSERT INTO plsql101_old_item VALUES
    ('LA-102', 'Can, Large');
INSERT INTO plsql101_old_item VALUES
```

```
      ('LA-103', 'Bottle, Small');
INSERT INTO plsql101_old_item VALUES
      ('LA-104', 'Bottle, Large');
INSERT INTO plsql101_old_item VALUES
      ('NY-101', 'Box, Small');
INSERT INTO plsql101_old_item VALUES
      ('NY-102', 'Box, Large');
INSERT INTO plsql101_old_item VALUES
      ('NY-103', 'Shipping Carton, Small');
INSERT INTO plsql101_old_item VALUES
      ('NY-104', 'Shipping Carton, Large');
```

Indexes

You are undoubtedly familiar with the concept of an index at the back of a book. In fact, the book you are reading has an index; take a moment now and look at it.

What did you see? A word or two defining each subject or idea, followed by one or more page numbers. You can look a subject up in the index, find the page numbers related to that subject, and go directly to those pages. Indexes are useful because they let you find something specific within a book without having to look through every one of the book's pages.

Indexes in Databases

You can apply the same indexing concept to a table in a database. When a table contains a lot of records, it can take a long time for Oracle (or any other database program) to look through the table to locate specific records—just like it would take a long time to look at every page in a book to find pages discussing a specific topic. Oracle has an easy-to-use feature that creates a second, hidden table containing one or more important columns from the main table, along with pointers to rows in the main table. In this case, instead of page numbers, the pointers in the hidden second table—which I'm going to start calling the main table's index—will be row numbers. By looking in the index, Oracle can know exactly what rows to jump to in order to find a specific piece of data (as long as the data being asked for is in the columns that make up the index). Since the index is much smaller than the table it refers to—just like a book's index is much smaller than the book's complete text—finding data in a table with an index can be dramatically faster than in a table without an index. For example, while I was writing this I ran a little SQL routine that inserted one million rows into a test table. (You will learn how to create a routine like this in Chapter 8.) Selecting records matching a specific value from this million-record table takes 18.9 seconds. After creating an index on the table, the same query takes only 0.6 seconds to finish. Adding an index to the table made it possible for the table to answer queries 31 times faster!

Figure 6-1 shows how a standard index on the PLSQL101_PERSON table would look. In this figure, the PLSQL101_PERSON table has been indexed, with the PERSON_CODE column being the basis of the index. Note that the index is sorted by PERSON_CODE, even though the table stores records in the order they were entered. An index always sorts its entries by the columns it contains. The index's ROWNUM column keeps track of each row's original location in the table.

Figure 6-2 shows a similar relationship between the PLSQL101_PURCHASE table and two indexes. That's right, a table can have more than one index. Why would you want to do that? The answer is well demonstrated by the PLSQL101_PURCHASE table. It contains at least two columns that are likely candidates for indexes: product and salesperson. It's very likely that queries against the table will often be based on a particular product, and it's just as likely that other queries will often be based on salesperson. By creating a separate index for each of these columns, you generate the same improvement in access speed described earlier for a table with one index...but that improvement is available when searching by product name *or* by salesperson.

Once you have created an index on a table, Oracle automatically keeps the index synchronized with that table. Any INSERT, UPDATE, or DELETE on the table automatically changes the index as well, and any SELECT on the table will automatically be routed through an index, if one exists containing the columns needed by the SELECT statement. You can add or drop indexes without affecting the table's operations—any program that used the table before will still operate. It may operate more slowly, however. If you drop a table, any indexes associated with that table will automatically be dropped too, since an index has no purpose without its associated table.

The syntax for dropping an index is as follows:

DROP INDEX *index_name*;

PLSQL101_PERSON TABLE

PERSON_CODE	FIRST_NAME	LAST_NAME	HIRE_DATE
CA	Charlene	Atlas	01-Feb-02
GA	Gary	Anderson	15-Feb-02
BB	Bobby	Barkenhagen	28-Feb-02
LB	Laren	Baxter	01-Mar-02

PERSON_CODE INDEX

PERSON_CODE	ROWNUM
BB	3
CA	1
GA	2
LB	4

FIGURE 6-1. *Table with one index*

PLSQL101_PURCHASE TABLE

PRODUCT_NAME	QUANTITY	PURCHASE_DATE	SALESPERSON
Small Widget	1	14-Jul-03	CA
Medium Wodget	75	14-Jul-03	BB
Chrome Phoobar	2	14-Jul-03	GA
Small Widget	8	15-Jul-03	GA
Medium Wodget	20	15-Jul-03	LB
Round Snaphoo	5	16-Jul-03	CA

PRODUCT_NAME INDEX

PRODUCT_NAME	ROWNUM
Chrome Phoobar	3
Medium Wodget	2
Medium Wodget	5
Round Snaphoo	6
Small Widget	1
Small Widget	4

SALESPERSON INDEX

SALESPERSON	ROWNUM
BB	3
CA	2
CA	5
GA	6
GA	1
LB	4

FIGURE 6-2. *Table with indexes on two different columns*

When Do Indexes Help?

Indexes improve the response time of commands that have to read a table's contents in order to perform their operations. That means SELECT, UPDATE, and DELETE commands can all work more quickly if the table they're working on has an index relevant to the commands.

Adding indexes to a table will *not* speed up data entry via INSERT commands; in fact, the opposite is true. Why would the presence of an index make an insert take longer? Remember that an index is really a table itself. So when you add a record to a table that has an index, Oracle has to add a record to both the table and the index—in essence, Oracle has to perform *two* inserts for every record. Because of this, adding an index to a table will cause inserts to take a little more than twice as long (the time doubles for the two inserts, plus a little extra time is needed for handling the coordination between them). Adding two indexes makes inserts take three times as long, three indexes makes indexes take four times as long, and so on.

So the use of indexes is a trade-off. They make data entry take longer, but make reading data faster. Therefore an application in which data entry must happen as quickly as possible is not a good candidate for adding indexes to tables. For example, store point-of-sale systems need their cash registers to turn around sales transactions (which, in case you haven't thought about it, are inserts into a database) as rapidly as possible. In this case, placing an index on the table storing transactions would be a mistake, because it would make the inserts slower. On the other hand, at the same time the same business could have executives who want to run queries analyzing transactions, and these queries would benefit greatly from having well-indexed tables. How do you handle these conflicting needs? In many systems, the transactions are copied out of the transaction table automatically every night, and the duplicates are placed into a well-indexed table that is used the next day for analysis. The inserts into the well-indexed table take much longer than they did for the index-free transaction table, but nobody cares because the stores are closed, no customers are waiting, and computers are doing the work.

The larger a table, the more benefit you will see from creating indexes on that table. For instance, the tables you have created so far in this book are so small that everything you do to them is essentially instantaneous. As a result, indexes on those tables will not produce a noticeable benefit. As tables get larger, the benefit increases. Using the million-record table once again as an example, Table 6-1 shows how long various DML operations took with and without an index on the table. The first row of statistics repeats the SELECT information you read earlier, while the subsequent rows show the impact of an index on UPDATE and DELETE commands. All times are measured in seconds. Look at how much faster the operations are, and imagine what kind of a hero you would be if you started a new job and in the first day reduced the time required for a database process from hours to minutes.

How to Create Indexes

Creating an index is very easy. The syntax for the command is as follows:

CREATE INDEX *index_name* ON *table_name* (*column_name*);

Operation	Without Index	With Index	Speed Increase
SELECT 50 records	18.9	0.6	31.5 times faster
UPDATE 50 records	19.7	0.5	39.4 times faster
DELETE 50 records	19.6	0.06	326.7 times faster

TABLE 6-1. *Execution Times for DML Operations With and Without an Index*

If you want the index to contain more than one column from the table, the syntax would look like this:

> CREATE INDEX *index_name* ON *table_name* (
>   *first_column_name,*
>   *second_column_name*
>   )
>   ;

Applying this to your own test tables, you can create the index shown in Figure 6-1 by issuing the following command:

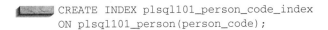

```
CREATE INDEX plsql101_person_code_index
ON plsql101_person(person_code);
```

This index would be most useful in searches referring to the PERSON_CODE in the WHERE clause. If, on the other hand, most of your searches were going to be based on a person's first and last name, an index based on those columns would be more useful. The following command would create such an index:

```
CREATE INDEX plsql101_person_name_index
ON plsql101_person(last_name, first_name);
```

This is an example of a *composite index* (sometimes called a *concatenated index*). A composite index is simply an index based on more than one column in a table. It is appropriate whenever the table contains columns that are likely to be used together in a query's WHERE clause—for instance, first and last name, or city, state, and zip code. As long as the WHERE clause includes either *all* of the columns in the composite index or the *first* column in the composite index, Oracle will use the index and your query will return more quickly. You can place columns in the index in any order you want—they don't have to be in the same order as in the table—so if you need to rearrange them to make the first column the one you're most likely to name in a WHERE clause, you can. Columns in a composite index do not have to be next to each other in the table they came from.

NOTE
The largest number of columns you can include in a standard Oracle index is 32.

Take a moment now to practice creating indexes by writing commands to produce the two indexes shown back in Figure 6-2.

Different Index Types

As you have probably deduced by now, an index is basically a way to summarize the locations of records based on what those records contain. The contents of a database can vary dramatically from system to system, and different kinds of content benefit from different kinds of organization. Oracle offers several different types of indexes, each using a different organizational approach. This section describes the two most common types of indexes; the others are used only in highly complicated databases and are better suited for a book on database administration.

B*-Tree Indexes

The default index type in Oracle organizes records into what is called a B*-Tree. Figure 6-3 shows how a B*-Tree index organizes records.

When creating a B*-Tree index, Oracle analyzes the values in the column(s) being indexed and determines how to split the table into *leaf blocks* with equal numbers of records. It then creates layers of *branch blocks* enabling records in the lower leaf blocks to be located in as few steps as possible.

TIP
In the example shown in Figure 6-3, the branch blocks split the alphabet evenly. In real life, the branch points are determined by the values in the records. For instance, if a table contained many more records whose names started with "A" than any other letter, an entire branch block might be devoted to "A," with the next branch block starting at "B."

The beauty of a B*-Tree index is that it quickly allows Oracle to identify records it does not need to read. By minimizing the amount of data that must be read—and therefore the amount of work it has to do—Oracle can return answers to you much more quickly. (Remember that the improvements listed in Table 6-1 were realized using Oracle's default index type of B*-Tree.) For example, consider a table that contains a billion records, and you want to see the record that has a specific ID number. The table isn't necessarily sorted by ID number, so Oracle may have to read as many as a billion records to find the one you want. If a B*-Tree index is defined for the table, however, Oracle can find the record in a maximum of 31 steps. Each step eliminates half of the records in the table, so Oracle can reduce the job to manageable proportions very quickly. Table 6-2 shows how quickly a B*-Tree index reduces the number of records involved in an operation.

Database Table

ROWNUM	LAST_NAME
1	Norton
2	Gutwirth
3	Trumble
4	Fletcher
5	Zoraster
6	Moss
7	Allen
8	Smith

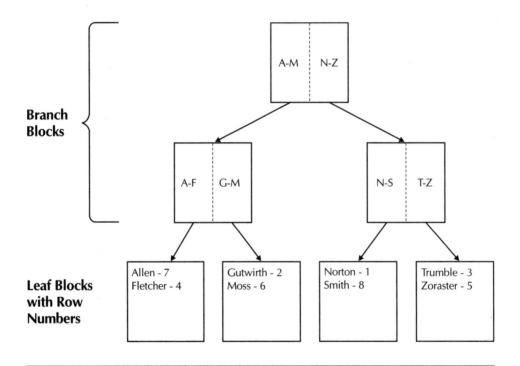

Branch Blocks

Leaf Blocks with Row Numbers

FIGURE 6-3. *How a B*-Tree index organizes records*

Since a B*-Tree index works by dividing data into sets and subsets based on content, this type of index works best when the column being indexed contains a wide variety of values, such as names or dates. For columns that contain a narrow

Step	Number of Records That Must Be Searched to Find Desired Value
1	1,000,000,000
2	500,000,000
3	250,000,000
4	125,000,000
5	62,500,000
6	31,250,000
7	15,625,000
8	7,812,500
9	3,906,250
10	1,953,125
11	976,563
12	488,281
13	244,141
14	122,070
15	61,035
16	30,518
17	15,259
18	7,629
19	3,815
20	1,907
21	954
22	477
23	238
24	119
25	60
26	30
27	15
28	7
29	4
30	2
31	1

TABLE 6-2. *Number of Steps Needed for a B*-Tree Index to Find a Specific Value*

range of values—such as gender, for instance—a bitmap index is a better choice. Read on to learn more about bitmap indexes.

Bitmap Indexes

If a B*-Tree index structure is optimal for indexing a column containing many unique values, then it stands to reason that a different index structure may be better suited for a column that contains only a few unique values. For example, a gender column would probably contain just three possible values: "M," "F," or "U" (for "Unknown"). Placing this small number of unique values into a B*-Tree index structure would not make sense, because the "divide into subgroups step by step" approach that makes the B*-Tree structure so useful for diverse values offers little benefit when there are only a few unique values. In this situation, using a bitmap index makes more sense. Figure 6-4 contains a somewhat simplified depiction of how a bitmap index is designed.

TIP
The term cardinality *refers to the number of unique values a column contains. A column that can contain very few unique values—like gender or any true/false column—has low cardinality. A column with many unique values—like price or name—has high cardinality.*

In SELECT queries in which the WHERE clause is a low-cardinality column (such as gender or any other column with only a few possible values), creating a bitmap index on that column beforehand can greatly decrease the time it takes to

	Database Table			Bitmap Index on Gender		

ROWNUM	LAST_NAME	GENDER
1	Norton	F
2	Gutwirth	M
3	Trumble	M
4	Fletcher	M
5	Zoraster	F
6	Moss	M
7	Allen	F
8	Smith	U

ROWNUM	FEMALE	MALE	UNKNOWN
1		1	
2			1
3			1
4			1
5	1		
6			1
7	1		
8			1

FIGURE 6-4. *How a bitmap index organizes records*

get your answers. The speed increase is the result of two factors: bitmap indexes can be quite small (because bits require only a fraction of the storage space needed by other datatypes that would be in a standard index), and the "1" or "0" value stored in a bitmap index can be evaluated very quickly by a computer.

The syntax for creating a bitmap index is almost identical to that for a standard index; you just add the word "BITMAP," as shown in the following example:

```
CREATE BITMAP INDEX index_name ON table_name(column_name);
```

Ensuring Data Integrity: Constraints

One of your most important jobs when designing tables is ensuring that the data people put into those tables is of the highest quality possible. "Dirty data" contains invalid codes, numbers that are too big or too small, dates that don't make any sense, or values that are simply left blank rather than filled in. You can exercise a lot of control over what goes into a table.

What's a Constraint?

A *constraint* is a way for you to define one or more conditions that a user's entry must satisfy before Oracle accepts the data into your table. Constraints are stored as part of a table's definition, and once created, they operate automatically. When someone attempts to perform an INSERT or UPDATE command that contains data violating a constraint, Oracle interrupts the command, rolls back the INSERT or UPDATE, and presents an error message.

How to Create Constraints

In this section you will learn how to create three different kinds of constraints. When used together, these constraints can go a long way toward ensuring that the data in your tables is "clean."

Not Null

You learned how to specify one type of constraints in Chapter 2, by specifying that one or more columns are NOT NULL in a CREATE TABLE command. To save you from having to flip pages back to that chapter for a refresher, the command employed was this:

```
CREATE TABLE plsql101_purchase (
     product_name  VARCHAR2(25) NOT NULL,
     product_price NUMBER(4,2)  NOT NULL,
     purchase_date DATE
     )
;
```

Now it's time to learn how to alter existing tables so that columns no longer accept null values when records are inserted or updated. The syntax for changing an existing column to NOT NULL status is as follows:

ALTER TABLE *table_name* MODIFY (*column_name* NOT NULL);

Let's try this out on one of your own tables. The PLSQL101_PERSON table contains FIRST_NAME and LAST_NAME columns, and it's reasonable to say that a record without these names would be unsatisfactory. To make those columns mandatory, enter the following commands, and compare your results with those shown in Figure 6-5:

```
ALTER TABLE plsql101_person MODIFY (first_name NOT NULL);
ALTER TABLE plsql101_person MODIFY (last_name NOT NULL);
```

Now test the constraint by entering the following code. Compare the results you get with those shown in Figure 6-6.

```
INSERT INTO plsql101_person VALUES (
       'XL', 'Xaviera', NULL, '15-NOV-03'
       )
   ;
```

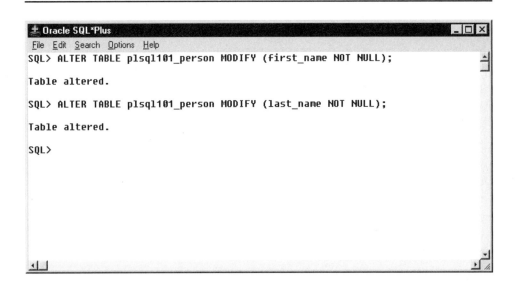

FIGURE 6-5. *Altering an existing table to make columns mandatory*

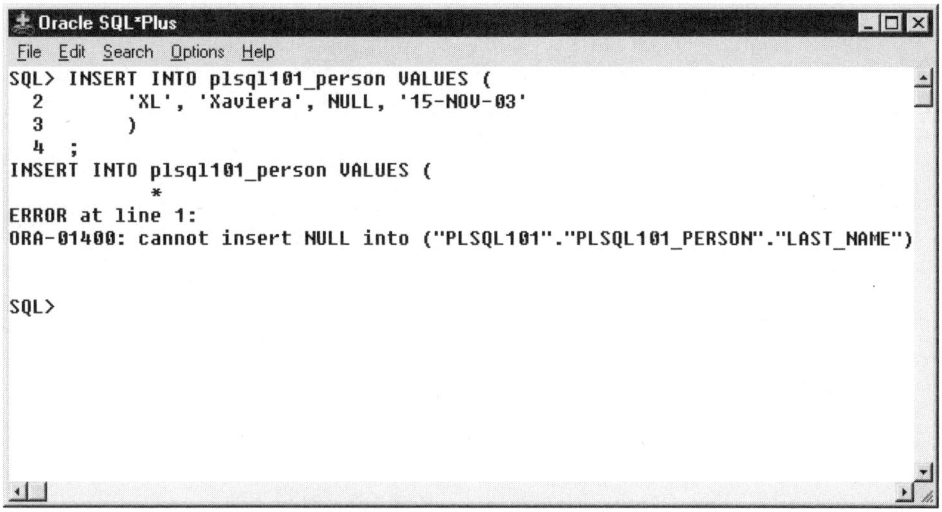

```
Oracle SQL*Plus                                                    _ □ ×
File  Edit  Search  Options  Help
SQL> INSERT INTO plsql101_person VALUES (
  2          'XL', 'Xaviera', NULL, '15-NOV-03'
  3          )
  4  ;
INSERT INTO plsql101_person VALUES (
            *
ERROR at line 1:
ORA-01400: cannot insert NULL into ("PLSQL101"."PLSQL101_PERSON"."LAST_NAME")


SQL>
```

FIGURE 6-6.   *Testing a NOT NULL constraint*

As you can see from the results on your screen (or in the figure), Oracle interrupts the operation and tells you, in its own clunky way, what the problem is. (In Chapter 8 you will learn how to intercept Oracle's error messages and instead show the user messages that are a little easier to understand.)

Unique

With the last exercise you ensured that records going into the PLSQL101_PERSON table will contain a first and last name. However, nothing is keeping a user from entering a person more than once. Do you think they'd know better? In an ideal world, they would. But people get interrupted, forget what they've already done, and sometimes just aren't paying attention; part of the human condition is that we make mistakes. Remember this motto:

<blockquote>
If they *can* do it,
they *WILL* do it.
</blockquote>

I don't mean that a given person will make every possible mistake. What I'm saying is that over the course of a database's life, many people are going to use it, and within that group, every possible mistake is likely to be made by *somebody*. Part of your job is thinking ahead and making sure that their unintentional attempts to enter bad data do not succeed.

Which brings us back to the subject of creating constraints that guarantee a record doesn't get entered twice. In the case of the PLSQL101_PERSON table, the first impulse might be to create a unique constraint stating that a given combination of first and last name can only be entered once. That's a good start, but limiting just by name might prove to be unreasonably restrictive—there are a lot of Bob Smiths out there, and it's very possible your company could hire more than one of them. The solution is to include the hire date in the equation, because it's extremely unlikely that two people with the same name would be hired on the same day.

With that in mind, take a look at the syntax used to add a constraint that guarantees unique values:

```
ALTER TABLE table_name
ADD CONSTRAINT constraint_name UNIQUE
(column_names);
```

Applying that syntax to the subject at hand, we get the following code. Enter this code now and compare your results with those shown in Figure 6-7.

```
ALTER TABLE plsql101_person
ADD CONSTRAINT plsql101_person_unique UNIQUE (
    first_name,
    last_name,
    hire_date
    )
;
```

Now test your new constraint by entering the following commands. Note that even though the second command has a different person code, it still fails because its first name, last name, and hire date are identical to those in the first command, as shown in Figure 6-8.

```
INSERT INTO plsql101_person VALUES (
    'LN', 'Linda', 'Norton', '01-JUN-03');

INSERT INTO plsql101_person VALUES (
    'NL', 'Linda', 'Norton', '01-JUN-03');
```

As you can see, the second record is rejected. Even though it had a different person code than the first record, the person's name and hire date were the same, so the record was not accepted.

Note also that the error message includes the name of the constraint that is stopping the record from being inserted (PLSQL101_PERSON_UNIQUE). Because of this, it's a good idea to make the constraint name as clear as possible (within the 30 characters you are allowed for the name). I recommend starting the

```
Oracle SQL*Plus                                          _ □ ×
File  Edit  Search  Options  Help
SQL> ALTER TABLE plsql101_person
  2   ADD CONSTRAINT plsql101_person_unique UNIQUE (
  3         first_name,
  4         last_name,
  5         hire_date
  6         )
  7  ;

Table altered.

SQL>
```

FIGURE 6-7.   *Creating a unique constraint*

```
Oracle SQL*Plus                                          _ □ ×
File  Edit  Search  Options  Help
SQL> INSERT INTO plsql101_person VALUES (
  2       'LN', 'Linda', 'Norton', '01-JUN-03');

1 row created.

SQL>
SQL> INSERT INTO plsql101_person VALUES (
  2       'NL', 'Linda', 'Norton', '01-JUN-03');
INSERT INTO plsql101_person VALUES (
            *
ERROR at line 1:
ORA-00001: unique constraint (PLSQL101.PLSQL101_PERSON_UNIQUE) violated


SQL>
```

FIGURE 6-8.   *Testing a unique constraint*

constraint name with the name of the table, followed by an indication of the purpose of the constraint.

When you create a unique constraint, Oracle creates a *unique index* behind the scenes. The index contains the columns you specified in your ALTER TABLE...ADD CONSTRAINT command, and it has the same name you gave the constraint. Oracle uses the unique index to help it identify duplicate records. When Oracle creates the unique index, it reads all existing records in the table and represents them in the index. Because of this, creating a unique constraint will only succeed if the records already in the table do not violate the constraint. If the table contains any records with duplicate values in the columns you specify, the ALTER TABLE...ADD CONSTRAINT command will fail with an error message explaining the problem.

Check

A *check constraint* allows you to define what must be true about incoming data in order for it to be accepted into your Oracle database. You can define a check constraint for each column in a table. This allows you to state that an entry for a price column must be a positive number, for instance, while also requiring that values for a date column be within a certain range. Check constraints are one of your most powerful tools for ensuring that your database will contain clean data.

The syntax for creating a check constraint on a column in an existing table is as follows:

```
ALTER TABLE table_name ADD
        CONSTRAINT [constraint_name]
        CHECK(column_name condition_to_satisfy)
    ;
```

The *table_name* parameter identifies the table whose column should be checked, of course. The optional *constraint_name* parameter lets you assign your own name to the constraint. If you omit this parameter, Oracle will assign a name to the constraint itself, and the name it assigns will have no inherent meaning—so it will essentially be indecipherable. It's better to assign a constraint name yourself, so that when a user violates the constraint, the resulting Oracle error will refer to *your* constraint name, which will presumably be more informative than the one Oracle would have assigned.

The *column_name* parameter is where you identify the column to which the constraint applies. Finally, the *condition_to_satisfy* parameter is where you define what must be true about the data attempting to make its way into that column in order for the attempt to succeed. Together, the *column_name* and *condition_to_satisfy* parameters look just like a condition you would place after the word WHERE in a SELECT statement's WHERE clause.

Now it's time to create a check constraint of your own. This first exercise will help keep data in your PLSQL101_PURCHASE table clean by ensuring that only reasonable purchase dates are accepted. (For the purposes of this exercise, we're defining "reasonable" as June 30, 2000. In the real world, the definition of a "reasonable" date varies from application to application.) A few things are noteworthy in the following exercise:

- The check constraint evaluates two different conditions before letting data pass through. The two conditions are connected by an AND clause, of course.

- The first condition ensures that the column contains a value (if you do not include this condition, the check constraint will only evaluate records that have values in the constraint's column, thereby allowing records with null values in that column to pass through).

- The second condition wraps a TO_CHAR function around the column being evaluated. This is due to an undocumented flaw—er, feature—in the current version of Oracle that causes an error to appear if you try to establish a check constraint referring directly to a date column. To work around this "feature," the check constraint must convert the date column to text and evaluate it in that format. Since it is in text format, however, it is no longer looked at as a date, but rather evaluated as a text string, meaning that "FEB" would be considered earlier than "JAN," because "F" comes before "J" in the alphabet. The solution to this is to format both the column and the date written into the check constraint as numbers, with the year coming first, followed by the month (in numeric form), followed by the day.

Enter the following commands, and compare the results you see with those shown in Figure 6-9.

```
ALTER TABLE plsql101_purchase ADD (
    CONSTRAINT reasonable_date CHECK(
        purchase_date IS NOT NULL
        AND
        TO_CHAR(purchase_date, 'YYYY-MM-DD') >= '2000-06-30'
        )
    )
;

INSERT INTO plsql101_purchase VALUES (
    'Small Widget', 'GA', '28-FEB-00', 10);
```

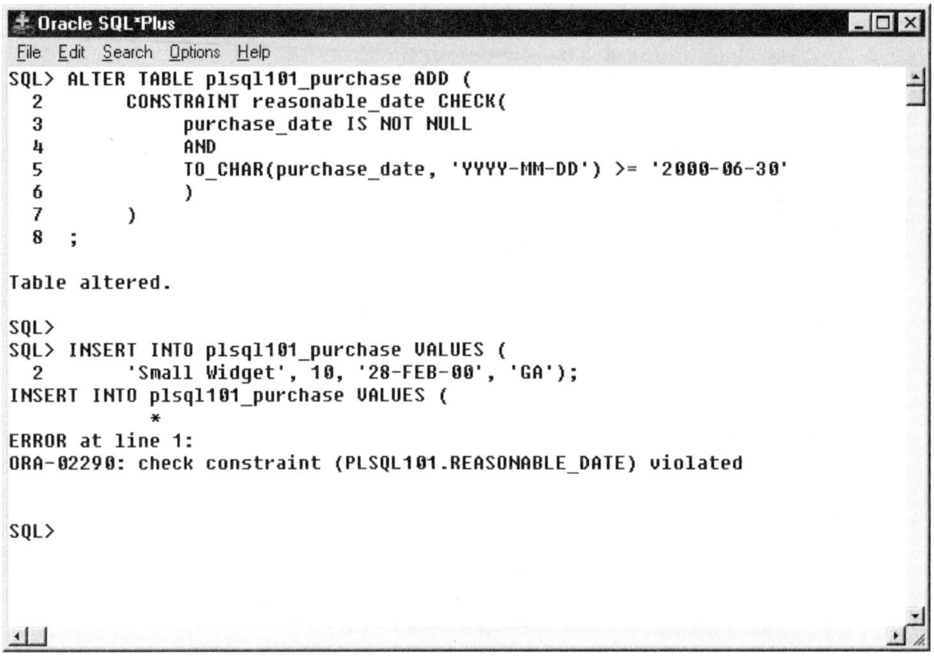

```
Oracle SQL*Plus                                                    _ □ ×
File  Edit  Search  Options  Help
SQL> ALTER TABLE plsql101_purchase ADD (
  2        CONSTRAINT reasonable_date CHECK(
  3            purchase_date IS NOT NULL
  4            AND
  5            TO_CHAR(purchase_date, 'YYYY-MM-DD') >= '2000-06-30'
  6            )
  7        )
  8  ;

Table altered.

SQL>
SQL> INSERT INTO plsql101_purchase VALUES (
  2        'Small Widget', 10, '28-FEB-00', 'GA');
INSERT INTO plsql101_purchase VALUES (
            *
ERROR at line 1:
ORA-02290: check constraint (PLSQL101.REASONABLE_DATE) violated


SQL>
```

FIGURE 6-9. *Using a check constraint to require entry of a valid date*

There may also be times when you would like to assign a check constraint to a column, but still allow null values; in other words, the column can be empty, but if it does contain a value, the value must satisfy one or more conditions. That is how Oracle interprets check constraints by default. As long as you do not include an IS NOT NULL clause in the check constraint, null values will still be accepted. Enter the following code to see this in action, and compare the results you get with those shown in Figure 6-10.

```
ALTER TABLE plsql101_product ADD (
    CONSTRAINT reasonable_stock_date CHECK(
        TO_CHAR(last_stock_date, 'YYYY-MM-DD') >= '2001-12-31'
        )
    )
;


INSERT INTO plsql101_product VALUES (
    'Anodized Framifier', 49, 5, NULL)
;
```

```
INSERT INTO plsql101_product VALUES (
     'Spring-Loaded Pit Puller', 49, 5, '30-DEC-01')
;
```

In the examples you have done so far, check constraints have always been
added after a table has been created. You don't have to wait until a table is
created to define check constraints; you can do that when you create the table.
You simply added the check constraint information to the definition of the relevant
column, following the column's datatype and null option. The following code
segment demonstrates how to do this. (Because the code creates tables you already
have, don't try to run it. Just look it over and note how the check constraint
information is included.)

```
CREATE TABLE plsql101_person (
     person_code  VARCHAR2(3) NULL,
     first_name   VARCHAR2(15) NOT NULL,
     last_name    VARCHAR2(20) NOT NULL,
     hire_date    DATE NULL
                  CONSTRAINT reasonable_hire_date CHECK (
                       TO_CHAR(hire_date, 'YYYY-MM-DD') >= '1930-01-01'
                  )
     )
;


CREATE TABLE plsql101_product (
     product_name     VARCHAR2(25) NULL,
     product_price    NUMBER(4,2) NULL
                      CONSTRAINT valid_price CHECK (
                           product_price BETWEEN 0 AND 10000
                      ),
     quantity_on_hand NUMBER(5) NULL
                      CONSTRAINT positive_quantity CHECK (
                           quantity_on_hand >=0
                      ),
     last_stock_date  DATE NULL
                      CONSTRAINT reasonable_stock_date CHECK (
                           TO_CHAR(last_stock_date, 'YYYY-MM-DD')
                                >= '2001-12-31'
                      )
     )
;
```

As a final option, you can also write a check constraint that compares values in
more than one column. This is useful for performing "reality checks" on values that
have some logical relationship to each other. None of the tables you have created
from this book so far contain columns that lend themselves to this type of check.

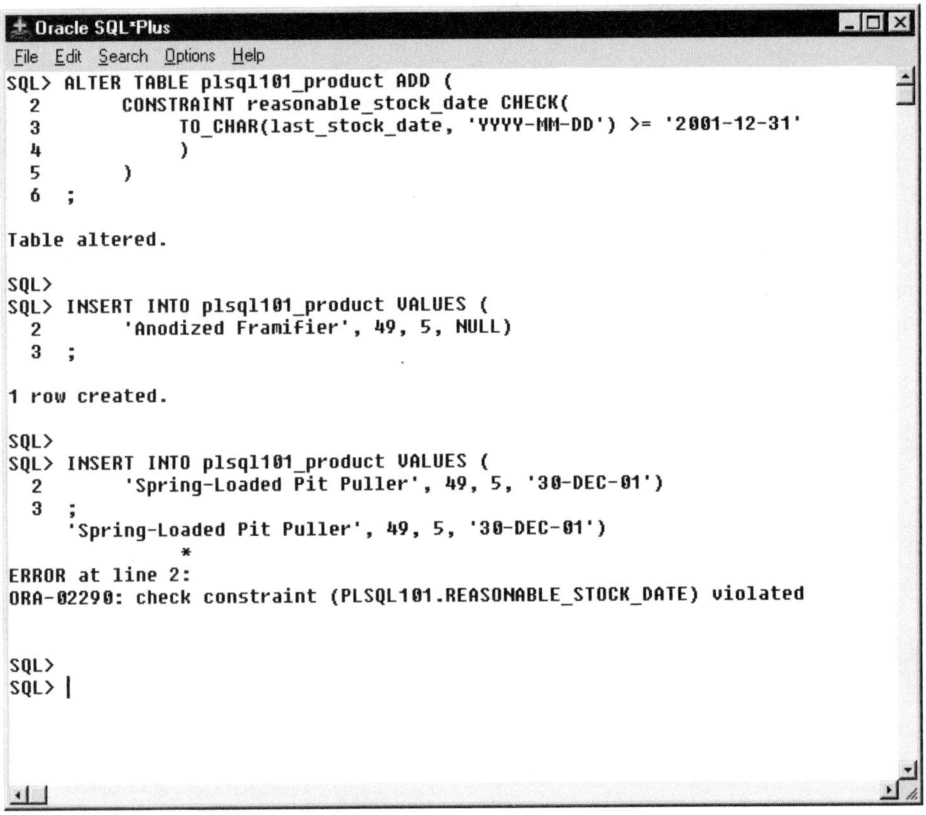

```
Oracle SQL*Plus                                                    _ □ ×
File  Edit  Search  Options  Help
SQL> ALTER TABLE plsql101_product ADD (
  2        CONSTRAINT reasonable_stock_date CHECK(
  3            TO_CHAR(last_stock_date, 'YYYY-MM-DD') >= '2001-12-31'
  4            )
  5        )
  6   ;

Table altered.

SQL>
SQL> INSERT INTO plsql101_product VALUES (
  2        'Anodized Framifier', 49, 5, NULL)
  3   ;

1 row created.

SQL>
SQL> INSERT INTO plsql101_product VALUES (
  2        'Spring-Loaded Pit Puller', 49, 5, '30-DEC-01')
  3   ;
      'Spring-Loaded Pit Puller', 49, 5, '30-DEC-01')
              *
ERROR at line 2:
ORA-02290: check constraint (PLSQL101.REASONABLE_STOCK_DATE) violated


SQL>
SQL> |
```

FIGURE 6-10. *Adding a check constraint that allows null values*

The following example shows how you could create a constraint in the fictional
table EMPLOYEE that ensures an employee's current salary is at least as much as
he or she was making the year before, but not more than 25% more than the prior
year's amount:

```
ALTER TABLE employee ADD (CONSTRAINT realistic_current_salary CHECK (
    salary BETWEEN prior_year_salary AND (prior_year_salary*1.25))
    )
;
```

Enabling and Disabling Existing Constraints

There are times when it is useful to temporarily disable constraints, and then re-enable them later. For instance, when loading data from an external source, you could know beforehand that some of the data does not satisfy a particular constraint, but prefer to fix the offending data within Oracle. In times like this, you can use an ALTER TABLE command to turn a constraint off temporarily without dropping it permanently. You can then load the data you know contains undesirable values, fix the values, and re-enable the constraint.

The syntax of the command is as follows:

ALTER TABLE *table_name* DISABLE CONSTRAINT *constraint_name*;

Similarly, the syntax of the command to re-enable constraints is as follows:

ALTER TABLE *table_name* ENABLE CONSTRAINT *constraint_name*;

To see the impact of disabling and enabling constraints, enter the following commands. The first command attempts to insert a record whose LAST_STOCK_DATE value is too early to satisfy the constraint on that column. The next command disables the constraint, and the following one attempts to insert the record again—this time successfully. The subsequent command tries to re-enable the constraint but fails because a record in the table fails to satisfy the constraint's condition. Once that record's value is changed, the constraint is successfully re-enabled. As you go through these commands, compare the results of each one with those shown in Figure 6-11.

```
INSERT INTO plsql101_product VALUES (
     'Red Snaphoo', 1.95, 10, '30-DEC-01')
;

ALTER TABLE plsql101_product DISABLE CONSTRAINT reasonable_stock_date;

INSERT INTO plsql101_product VALUES (
     'Red Snaphoo', 1.95, 10, '30-DEC-01')
;

ALTER TABLE plsql101_product ENABLE CONSTRAINT reasonable_stock_date;

UPDATE plsql101_product
SET    last_stock_date = '31-DEC-01'
WHERE  last_stock_date = '30-DEC-01';

ALTER TABLE plsql101_product ENABLE CONSTRAINT reasonable_stock_date;
```

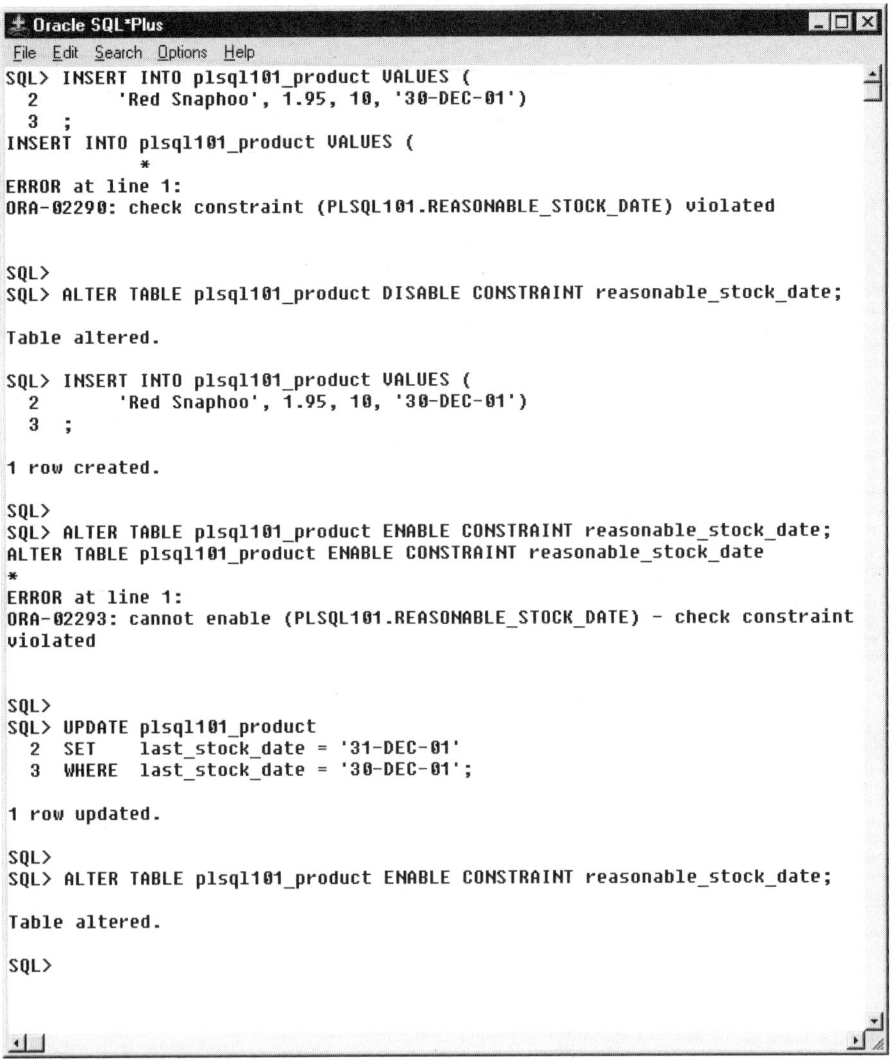

```
± Oracle SQL*Plus                                          _ □ ×
 File  Edit  Search  Options  Help
SQL> INSERT INTO plsql101_product VALUES (
  2       'Red Snaphoo', 1.95, 10, '30-DEC-01')
  3  ;
INSERT INTO plsql101_product VALUES (
            *
ERROR at line 1:
ORA-02290: check constraint (PLSQL101.REASONABLE_STOCK_DATE) violated


SQL>
SQL> ALTER TABLE plsql101_product DISABLE CONSTRAINT reasonable_stock_date;

Table altered.

SQL> INSERT INTO plsql101_product VALUES (
  2       'Red Snaphoo', 1.95, 10, '30-DEC-01')
  3  ;

1 row created.

SQL>
SQL> ALTER TABLE plsql101_product ENABLE CONSTRAINT reasonable_stock_date;
ALTER TABLE plsql101_product ENABLE CONSTRAINT reasonable_stock_date
*
ERROR at line 1:
ORA-02293: cannot enable (PLSQL101.REASONABLE_STOCK_DATE) - check constraint
violated


SQL>
SQL> UPDATE plsql101_product
  2  SET    last_stock_date = '31-DEC-01'
  3  WHERE  last_stock_date = '30-DEC-01';

1 row updated.

SQL>
SQL> ALTER TABLE plsql101_product ENABLE CONSTRAINT reasonable_stock_date;

Table altered.

SQL>
```

FIGURE 6-11. *Impact of disabling and enabling constraints*

Altering and Dropping Existing Constraints

Life is unpredictable, requirements change, and at some point you will need to
modify or remove existing constraints on a table. For instance, it's very common to

need to change whether a column accepts null values. The syntax to tell a column it should start accepting null values is as follows:

ALTER TABLE *table_name* MODIFY (*column_name* NULL);

The syntax to tell a column it should *stop* accepting null values is as follows:

ALTER TABLE *table_name* MODIFY (*column_name* NOT NULL);

To see this concept in action, enter the following commands and compare the results you get with those shown in Figure 6-12:

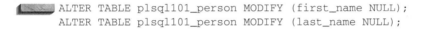

```
ALTER TABLE plsql101_person MODIFY (first_name NULL);
ALTER TABLE plsql101_person MODIFY (last_name NULL);
```

If you want to drop a constraint entirely, you can do so using the following syntax.

ALTER TABLE *table_name* DROP CONSTRAINT *constraint_name*;

TIP
Keep in mind that dropping a constraint is a permanent action. If you think you may need the constraint again later, consider disabling it instead of dropping it.

```
Oracle SQL*Plus                                                    _ □ ×
File  Edit  Search  Options  Help
SQL> ALTER TABLE plsql101_person MODIFY (first_name NULL);

Table altered.

SQL> ALTER TABLE plsql101_person MODIFY (last_name NULL);

Table altered.

SQL>
```

FIGURE 6-12. *Changing a column's NULL status*

To see this technique in action, enter the following series of commands, and compare the results you get with those shown in Figure 6-13:

```
INSERT INTO plsql101_product VALUES (
    'Blue Snaphoo', 1.95, 10, '30-DEC-01')
;

ALTER TABLE plsql101_product DROP CONSTRAINT reasonable_stock_date;

INSERT INTO plsql101_product VALUES (
    'Blue Snaphoo', 1.95, 10, '30-DEC-01')
;
```

Should a Constraint be in the Database, in the Software That Uses the Database, or Both?

This section has introduced you to techniques for enforcing constraints from within the database. It is also possible to enforce constraints on the *front end*—that is,

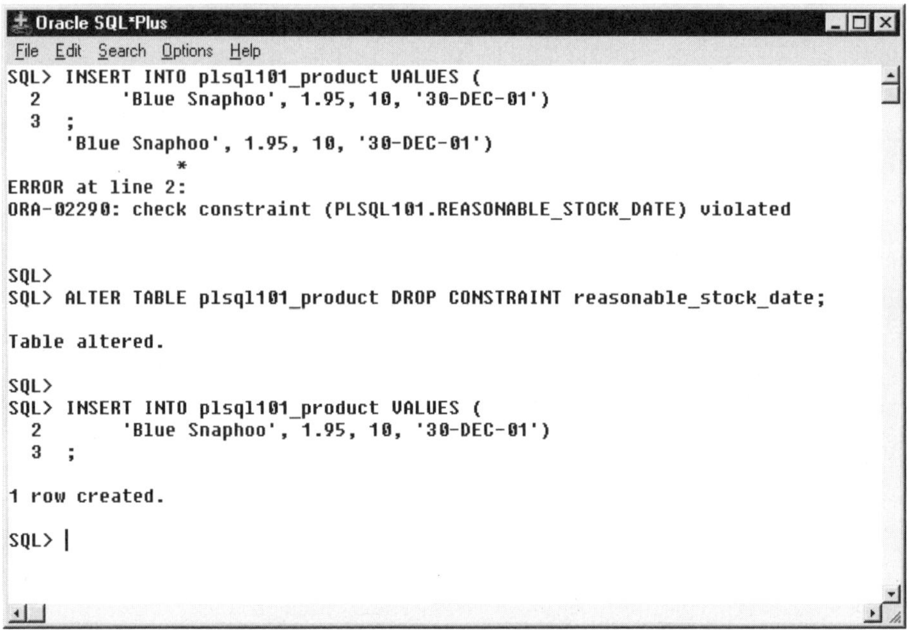

FIGURE 6-13. *Impact of dropping a constraint*

within the entry form people use to enter data. (The database is called the *back end* of a system.) There are benefits to both approaches.

When constraints are placed on the front end, they can be evaluated without having to make a trip to the database server. This eliminates unnecessary network traffic (because faulty data isn't being transmitted), reduces the load on the database, and allows constraints to be checked instantaneously. The result is a system that operates quickly and uses its network and server resources efficiently. This is ideal for systems that cannot wait for server processing (like a point-of-sale system in cash registers), use slow network connections (like Internet applications), or have a lot of users.

However, what happens if someone connects to the database using some means other than the approved entry forms? You have seen how easy it is to connect to a database using SQL*Plus, and it is almost as easy using office-productivity products such as Microsoft Access or Excel. If the database's constraints are only enforced by the approved data-entry forms, then a person connecting to the database using another method can make changes that do not necessarily satisfy the constraints. This can cause major problems such as sales orders referring to products that no longer exist, or personnel whose employment-start dates are in the 1800s. Remember: If people *can* do it, someone *will* do it. Including constraints in the database is the only way to ensure they will be enforced regardless of the method used to connect to the database.

From my perspective, the question really isn't whether to enforce constraints on the front end or the back end. Enforcing them on the back end is essential, period. The question is whether to *also* enforce them on the front end. If your application will have many users or a slow network connection and needs extremely fast response, consider having the programmers build the constraints into their front-end application as well.

NOTE
If you do include constraints on both the front end and the back end, you will need to establish standards for changing them. Otherwise, they will surely get out of sync as the application is revised and a back-end designer forgets to tell a front-end designer about a change, or vice versa.

Relationships Between Tables

In this section, you will learn how to make Oracle enforce relationships between tables, so that (for instance) a purchase record must refer to a product that actually exists in the product table. You will also learn how to select information from more than one table at a time, so you can retrieve related information from multiple tables simultaneously and present it in a single spreadsheet-like list.

Introduction to Data Modeling

The tables you have been working on throughout this book already have implied relationships with each other. The product names in PLSQL101_PRODUCT are used in each record in PLSQL101_PURCHASE, and the person codes in PLSQL101_PERSON are referred to in PLSQL101_PURCHASE within the SALESPERSON column. These types of relationships form the basis of a relational database system. They allow you to enter data in one table and then refer to that data in other tables, thereby eliminating the need to enter it again.

Figure 6-14 shows a logical representation of how the tables are related. The lines connecting one table to another represent relationships allowing, for instance, a product name in a purchase record to be used to find out more information about that product in the product table. In the example shown in Figure 6-14, the PLSQL101_PRODUCT table is the *parent table*, and PLSQL101_PURCHASE is the *child table*. Similarly, PLSQL101_PERSON and PLSQL101_PURCHASE have a *parent/child relationship*. In a parent/child relationship, a single record in the parent table can be referred to by any number of records in the child table. In this example, a person can make any number of sales, so a person code in one PLSQL101_PERSON record could be referred to in the salesperson column of any number of PLSQL101_PURCHASE records. Looking from the other direction, a PLSQL101_PURCHASE record can refer to only one salesperson, simply because it does not have the ability to store more than one salesperson code per purchase record. This is the most common type of relationship between tables, and it is called a *one-to-many relationship* (indicating that one record in the person table can be referred to by many records in the purchase table).

You may have noticed that the relationship lines between tables in the figure have a solid circle on one end of each line. This circle identifies the "many" end of a one-to-many relationship. There are a variety of standards for depicting relationships such as these. The one used in Figure 6-14 uses a standard called IDEF1X—the "IDEF" part of the name stands for "Integration DEFinition for Information Modeling," and the "1X" identifies which of the IDEF standards this is (there are other IDEF standards describing how other types of diagrams should look). Another common standard is called IE, which stands for "Information Engineering." This standard, which is shown in Figure 6-15, is often referred to as the "Crow's Foot" methodology because of the three-line "V" shape it uses to identify the "many" end of a one-to-many relationship.

Diagrams like those shown in Figures 6-14 and 6-15 are known as *Entity Relationship Diagrams* or *ERDs*. They are also commonly referred to as *data models*. They are the most effective way to depict the design of a database.

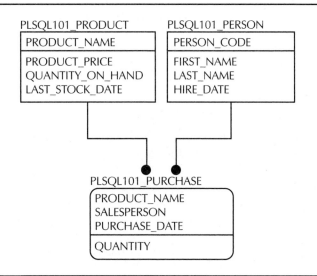

FIGURE 6-14.   *Relationships of PL/SQL 101 tables (IDEF1X display)*

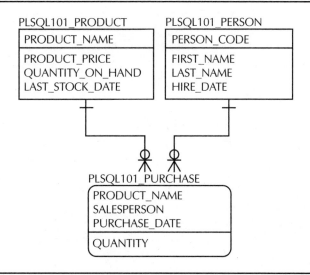

FIGURE 6-15.   *Relationships of PL/SQL 101 tables (IE display)*

Using Constraints to Enforce Relationships Between Tables

In order for a relationship to exist between two tables, two things must be true:

- The parent table must have a column (or set of columns) that uniquely identifies every record it contains.

- The child table must have an identical column (or set of columns) to contain the values that uniquely identify the parent record.

For example, in the PLSQL101_PRODUCT table each product has a product name. That value is what uniquely identifies each product record. It is called the table's *primary key*. The primary key is the main way you refer to records in a table. The primary key in the PLSQL101_PERSON table is the person code.

There are many examples of primary keys in daily life. Walk into a store— or call your local pizza-delivery service—and if you already have an account with them, they will probably ask for your phone number to look up the account. In their database's list of people, the phone number is the primary key—the main way of uniquely identifying each person in the list. Schools assign their students ID numbers, employers assign their employees employee numbers, and mail-order catalogs ask for product numbers. All of these are primary keys for their respective tables.

In order for a parent table's primary key to be used in a relationship, it must be referred to in the child table. This is done by including a column (or set of columns) in the child table that has exactly the same datatype(s) as the parent table's primary key. When you want to create a child-table record referring to a parent-table record, you include the parent record's primary-key value(s) in the child record. For instance, to identify what product was purchased in a transaction, you must include the product's name or number—whichever is used as the primary key in the product table—in the transaction record.

The child-table columns that contain primary-key values from a parent table are called *foreign keys*. A foreign key allows a child record to refer to a parent record. For instance, in the PLSQL101_PURCHASE table, the product name column is a foreign key back to the PLSQL101_PRODUCT table. Similarly, the salesperson column in PLSQL101_PURCHASE is a foreign key back to the PLSQL101_PERSON table. The following illustration shows a data model of your test tables with the foreign keys marked with "(FK)."

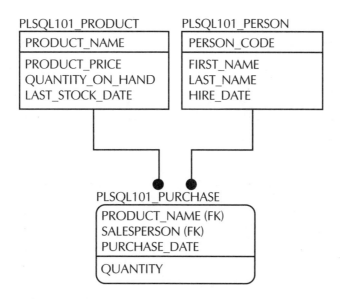

NOTE
There are several excellent books explaining how to design relational databases properly. Further discussion of the topic is beyond the scope of this book, so I'll include references in the bibliography at the end of the book.

Creating a Primary Key

The syntax for specifying what column(s) to use as the primary key in an existing table is as follows:

```
ALTER TABLE table_name
ADD PRIMARY KEY (column_name_1, column_name_2, …);
```

NOTE
When you create a primary key, Oracle automatically creates an index on the column(s) in the primary key. This will cause data entry to slow down slightly, and will speed up any queries that use the primary-key column(s) as the first column(s) in a WHERE clause.

To create a primary key on the PLSQL101_PRODUCT column, enter the following command, and compare your results with those shown in Figure 6-16:

```
ALTER TABLE plsql101_product
ADD PRIMARY KEY (product_name);
```

Using this technique, you can create primary keys in the other two tables by entering the following commands:

```
ALTER TABLE plsql101_person
ADD PRIMARY KEY (person_code);

ALTER TABLE plsql101_purchase
ADD PRIMARY KEY (product_name,
                 salesperson,
                 purchase_date
                 )
;
```

It is also possible to define a primary key when you first create a table. For example, the following code shows how to create a table with the same structure as the PLSQL101_PRODUCT table and define its primary key all in one command:

```
CREATE TABLE plsql101_product2 (
      product_name     VARCHAR2(25) PRIMARY KEY,
      product_price    NUMBER(4,2),
      quantity_on_hand NUMBER(5,0),
      last_stock_date  DATE
      )
;
```

```
± Oracle SQL*Plus                                                    _ □ ×
File  Edit  Search  Options  Help
SQL> ALTER TABLE plsql101_product
  2  ADD PRIMARY KEY (product_name);

Table altered.

SQL>
```

FIGURE 6-16. *Adding a primary key to an existing table*

Creating a Foreign Key Constraint

Primary keys and foreign keys are the physical components that make a relationship between tables possible. However, by themselves they do not enforce relational integrity—meaning that even if the columns in the primary key and foreign key have exactly the same names and datatypes, Oracle does not assume they are related until you say they are. This last step is crucial: You must define a constraint on the child table so it checks the parent table's primary key before accepting values into its foreign key. Without such a constraint, a user can enter values into the child table's foreign key that do not actually exist in the parent table.

As a matter of fact, your test tables contain a record with this problem already. Enter the following code, compare your results with Figure 6-17, and see if you can find the child record with the rogue product name:

```
SELECT product_name
FROM   plsql101_product
ORDER BY product_name;

SELECT DISTINCT product_name
FROM   plsql101_purchase
ORDER BY product_name;
```

As you can see, the PLSQL101_PURCHASE table contains a transaction for a "Round Snaphoo," while no such product exists in the PLSQL101_PRODUCT table. You will need to change the product name in the purchase table before you can create a foreign-key constraint to the product table. Before you do, though, go ahead and try to create the constraint, in order to see how Oracle responds to the situation. The syntax for creating a foreign-key constraint is:

```
ALTER TABLE child_table_name
ADD CONSTRAINT constraint_name
      FOREIGN KEY (column_name(s)_in_child_table)
      REFERENCES parent_table_name
;
```

Applying this syntax to your product and purchase tables produces the following command:

```
ALTER TABLE plsql101_purchase
ADD CONSTRAINT plsql101_purchase_fk_product
            FOREIGN KEY (product_name)
            REFERENCES plsql101_product
;
```

Enter this command now, and you will see the results shown in Figure 6-18. The error message's "Parent key not found" phrase is your clue that the child table

FIGURE 6-17. *Manually locating a child record with no matching parent record*

contains one or more product names that are not in the parent table. To make the constraint work, you will need to update the rogue product name in the child table. Enter the following commands to do this and re-try the constraint creation:

```
UPDATE plsql101_purchase
SET    product_name = 'Round Chrome Snaphoo'
WHERE  product_name = 'Round Snaphoo';

ALTER TABLE plsql101_purchase
ADD CONSTRAINT plsql101_purchase_fk_product
             FOREIGN KEY (product_name)
             REFERENCES plsql101_product;
```

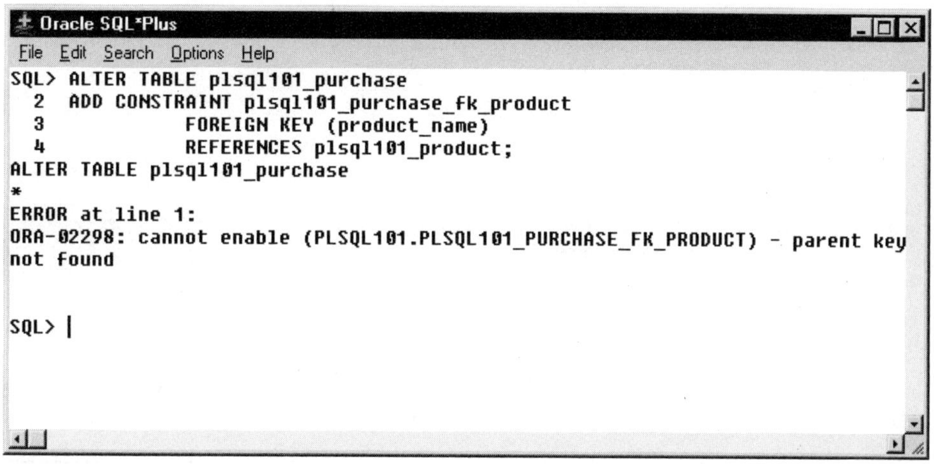

FIGURE 6-18. *Attempting to create a foreign-key constraint with non-matching child values*

To test your new foreign-key constraint, try entering a record using the following command:

```
INSERT INTO plsql101_purchase VALUES (
     'Small Widgee', 'CA', '17-JUL-03', 1)
;
```

Compare your results with those shown in Figure 6-19. As you can see, the purchase table will no longer accept records containing product names that do not exist in the product table. Try this corrected command to see what happens when the product name does exist in the product table:

```
INSERT INTO plsql101_purchase VALUES (
     'Small Widget', 'CA', '17-JUL-03', 1)
;
```

Using the technique you just learned, create a foreign-key constraint on the PLSQL101_PURCHASE table so that it checks the PLSQL101_PERSON table before accepting values into its SALESPERSON column.

```
┌─────────────────────────────────────────────────────────────────┐
│ ≛ Oracle SQL*Plus                                        _ □ ×    │
├─────────────────────────────────────────────────────────────────┤
│ File  Edit  Search  Options  Help                                │
│ SQL> INSERT INTO plsql101_purchase VALUES (             ▲        │
│   2        'Small Widgee', 'CA', '17-JUL-03', 1)        ▒        │
│   3   ;                                                           │
│                                                                   │
│ *                                                                 │
│ ERROR at line 3:                                                  │
│ ORA-02291: integrity constraint (PLSQL101.PLSQL101_PURCHASE_FK_PRODUCT) │
│ violated - parent key not found                                  │
│                                                                   │
│                                                                   │
│ SQL>                                                              │
│                                                         ▼        │
│ ◄                                                       ►        │
└─────────────────────────────────────────────────────────────────┘
```

FIGURE 6-19.   *Attempting to enter a child record without a matching parent record*

NOTE
When creating a foreign-key constraint, you usually only need to name the child table, parent table, and child table's foreign-key column(s) in the ALTER TABLE command. You do not need to name the parent table's primary-key columns, because Oracle can determine the table's primary key based on the table name. If the columns are not in the same order, however, you will need to name them for both the child table and the parent table.

Writing SELECT Statements to Display Data from More Than One Table

Now that you have seen how to create relationships between tables, it's time to learn how to join information from these related tables together. For instance, what if you want to get a list of purchases that identifies the salespeople by name, rather than by their person code? This type of need is very common, and it's easy to fulfill. The syntax of a SELECT statement that draws from two tables is as follows:

    SELECT table_1_name.column_name,
        table_2_name.column_name

```
FROM   table_1_name,
     table_2_name
WHERE parent_table_name.primary_key = child_table_name.foreign_key
;
```

Being the perceptive reader that you are, you probably noticed that even though the SELECT statement is supposed to join data from only two tables, the example syntax I've written refers to *four* different generic table names: TABLE_1_NAME, TABLE_2_NAME, PARENT_TABLE_NAME, and CHILD_TABLE_NAME. The four generic names do apply to only two tables. The reason I've used more than one generic name per table is that when you are specifying columns, you can do them in any order: the parent table's column(s) can be first, or the child table's column(s) can be first, or you can mix them—it doesn't matter, as long as you identify which table each column comes from (by preceding the column name with the name of its table and a period). However, when you write the WHERE clause of the command, it is essential that you identify the primary key column(s) in the *parent* table, and the foreign key column(s) in the *child* table. By describing the parent/child relationship in your SELECT statement, you allow Oracle to understand how information in the parent table should be linked to information in the child table.

Let's put this theory into practice by getting a list of purchases with the full names of their salespeople. You can achieve this result by entering the following command:

```
SELECT  plsql101_purchase.product_name,
        plsql101_person.last_name,
        plsql101_person.first_name,
        plsql101_purchase.quantity
FROM    plsql101_purchase,
        plsql101_person
WHERE   plsql101_person.person_code = plsql101_purchase.salesperson
;
```

Compare your results with those shown in Figure 6-20.

Writing a command that combines data from more than one table into a single list is called creating a *join*. The most important thing to remember about a join is this: *You must include a WHERE clause describing how the parent table's primary key relates to the child table's foreign key.* If you do not, Oracle will join *every* record in the parent table with *every* record in the child table, creating what could be a very, very long list. (This type of mistake can slow a database to a crawl while it is processing the incorrectly written request, so it is to be avoided.) To see the results of a join without a WHERE clause, enter the following code and compare your results with those shown in Figure 6-21.

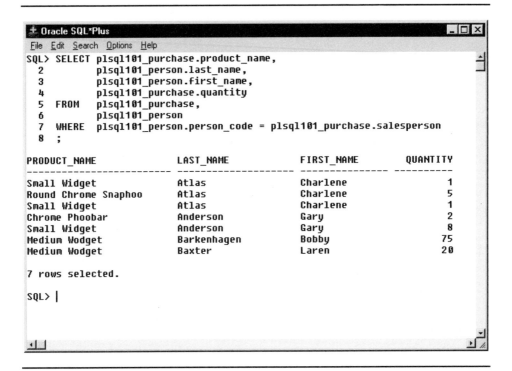

FIGURE 6-20. *Writing a SELECT statement that joins records from two tables*

```
SELECT plsql101_purchase.product_name,
       plsql101_person.last_name,
       plsql101_person.first_name,
       plsql101_purchase.quantity
FROM   plsql101_purchase,
       plsql101_person
;
```

With five records in the PLSQL101_PERSON table and seven records in the PLSQL101_PURCHASE table, the join produces 35 rows of completely useless results. This type of result, created by issuing a join without a WHERE clause, is called a *Cartesian product*.

You can join records from many different tables into a single SELECT statement. To do so, you simply have to ensure that (a) the tables are logically related via primary-key/foreign-key relationships, and (b) you define each of those relationships in the WHERE clause of the SELECT statement.

```
Oracle SQL*Plus                                                  _ □ ×
File  Edit  Search  Options  Help
SQL> SELECT plsql101_purchase.product_name,
  2         plsql101_person.last_name,
  3         plsql101_person.first_name,
  4         plsql101_purchase.quantity
  5  FROM   plsql101_purchase,
  6         plsql101_person
  7  ;

PRODUCT_NAME              LAST_NAME             FIRST_NAME        QUANTITY
------------------------- --------------------- ---------------- ----------
Small Widget              Atlas                 Charlene                 1
Medium Wodget             Atlas                 Charlene                75
Chrome Phoobar            Atlas                 Charlene                 2
Small Widget              Atlas                 Charlene                 8
Medium Wodget             Atlas                 Charlene                20
Round Chrome Snaphoo      Atlas                 Charlene                 5
Small Widget              Atlas                 Charlene                 1
Small Widget              Anderson              Gary                     1
Medium Wodget             Anderson              Gary                    75
Chrome Phoobar            Anderson              Gary                     2
Small Widget              Anderson              Gary                     8
Medium Wodget             Anderson              Gary                    20
Round Chrome Snaphoo      Anderson              Gary                     5
Small Widget              Anderson              Gary                     1
Small Widget              Barkenhagen           Bobby                    1
Medium Wodget             Barkenhagen           Bobby                   75
Chrome Phoobar            Barkenhagen           Bobby                    2
Small Widget              Barkenhagen           Bobby                    8
Medium Wodget             Barkenhagen           Bobby                   20
Round Chrome Snaphoo      Barkenhagen           Bobby                    5
Small Widget              Barkenhagen           Bobby                    1
Small Widget              Baxter                Laren                    1
Medium Wodget             Baxter                Laren                   75
Chrome Phoobar            Baxter                Laren                    2
Small Widget              Baxter                Laren                    8
Medium Wodget             Baxter                Laren                   20
Round Chrome Snaphoo      Baxter                Laren                    5
Small Widget              Baxter                Laren                    1
Small Widget              Norton                Linda                    1
Medium Wodget             Norton                Linda                   75
Chrome Phoobar            Norton                Linda                    2
Small Widget              Norton                Linda                    8
Medium Wodget             Norton                Linda                   20
Round Chrome Snaphoo      Norton                Linda                    5
Small Widget              Norton                Linda                    1

35 rows selected.

SQL>
```

FIGURE 6-21.   *Creating a join without a WHERE clause*

For example, let's say you want to get a list of each purchase, the price of the product purchased, and the last name of the salesperson who made the sale. This information resides in three different tables. The code to perform this join is as follows:

```
SELECT plsql101_purchase.product_name,
       plsql101_product.product_price,
       plsql101_purchase.quantity,
       plsql101_person.last_name
FROM   plsql101_product,
       plsql101_person,
       plsql101_purchase
WHERE  plsql101_product.product_name = plsql101_purchase.product_name
       and
       plsql101_person.person_code = plsql101_purchase.salesperson
;
```

Enter this code now and review your results. Now try to create a SELECT statement that displays each purchase's date and quantity, the last stock date for the item purchased, and the last name of the salesperson.

You may have noticed while entering these commands that it can become tedious to enter the table names over and over. You can assign a short *table alias* to each table, and refer to the tables by their aliases throughout the command. The table alias goes right after the table name in the FROM section of the statement. Using this approach, the most recent command could be rewritten as follows:

```
SELECT c.product_name,
       a.product_price,
       c.quantity,
       b.last_name
FROM   plsql101_product   a,
       plsql101_person     b,
       plsql101_purchase c
WHERE  a.product_name = c.product_name
       and
       b.person_code = c.salesperson
;
```

This is definitely less typing, but the command is hard to read, because you have to keep checking which table is represented by alias a, b, or c. It's much better to make each alias something that immediately reminds you what table the alias refers to, so an abbreviation of the table's name is commonly used. Since the tables in this example all have names that are very similar, it isn't possible to create one-letter aliases that intuitively remind you which table they refer to. Instead, we'll have to use a few letters for each alias. The result of this modification follows.

```
SELECT  purc.product_name,
        prod.product_price,
        purc.quantity,
        pers.last_name
FROM    plsql101_product  prod,
        plsql101_person   pers,
        plsql101_purchase purc
WHERE   prod.product_name = purc.product_name
        and
        pers.person_code = purc.salesperson
;
```

To save further keystrokes, you can also skip identifying the tables of any columns whose names are unique among the tables being selected from. In other words, if Oracle can look at a column name and see that it exists in only one of the tables, then you don't need to specify which table it is in. However, I don't recommend using this shortcut in joins, for two reasons: It slows down the processing somewhat (because Oracle has to look in all tables before determining that a column can only come from one of them), and it makes the command harder to read.

Outer Joins

To understand the problem this topic solves, enter the following code:

```
SELECT product_name FROM plsql101_product ORDER BY product_name;
```

```
SELECT  prod.product_name,
        prod.product_price,
        purc.purchase_date,
        purc.quantity
FROM    plsql101_product  prod,
        plsql101_purchase purc
WHERE   prod.product_name = purc.product_name
ORDER BY prod.product_name;
```

Look closely at the product names in the two lists, and you will see that there are several product names that do not show up in the second list. This is because the WHERE clause in the SELECT statement requires an exact match on the product names in both tables, and any product name that is in one table but not the other will not be shown.

There are times when that is desirable—for instance, when you want a list of what has actually sold. However, there will be many situations where you will want (for instance) a complete list of products, along with information about transactions—and the list needs to show every product, even if there are no transactions for some of them. In order to achieve this result, you must tell Oracle that the child table may not have records to match every record in the parent table. You can do this by placing the characters **(+)** after the child table's name in the WHERE clause. The resulting command looks like this:

```
SELECT product_name FROM plsql101_product ORDER BY product_name;

SELECT prod.product_name,
       prod.product_price,
       purc.purchase_date,
       purc.quantity
FROM   plsql101_product  prod,
       plsql101_purchase purc
WHERE  prod.product_name = purc.product_name (+)
ORDER BY prod.product_name;
```

Enter this code, and you will see that the listing it produces contains every product name, even if there have been no sales transactions for a product. This is called creating an *outer join*. When creating an outer join, you place the **(+)** characters after the name of one table in each of the *parent_table_name.primary_ key = child_table_name.foreign_key* statements in the WHERE clause. The **(+)** characters identify which table may not have matching records for every record in the other table. In other words, you place the **(+)** characters after the table that may produce some blanks for the column being matched. Generally, you will place the **(+)** characters after the name of the child table, and not the parent table. This is because if your referential integrity is working properly (meaning you have foreign-key constraints in place), the parent table can contain records that are not matched in the child table, but the child table should never contain records that are not matched by records in the parent table.

Join Operators

Now that you know how to make a traditional join between tables, it is time to show you some alternative types of joins. These are useful for different situations: times when you want to combine the contents of multiple tables that have similar layouts, or when you want to compare records in different tables and see which ones either are in both or are in one but not the other.

You can accomplish this by using *join operators* to connect two SELECT statements. There are four different join operators, and they are shown in Table 6-3. The following illustration gives a graphical representation of the results produced by each join operator.

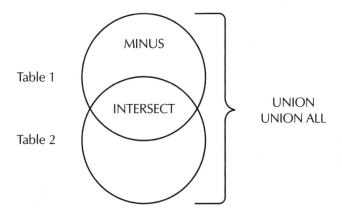

In order to see the join operators work in a way that is useful, you will need to create a new table and populate it with a few records. The following commands will give you the data you need to try the next examples.

```
CREATE TABLE plsql101_purchase_archive (
    product_name   VARCHAR2(25),
    salesperson    VARCHAR2(3),
    purchase_date  DATE,
    quantity       NUMBER(4,2)
    )
;

INSERT INTO plsql101_purchase_archive VALUES
    ('Round Snaphoo', 'BB', '21-JUN-01', 10);
INSERT INTO plsql101_purchase_archive VALUES
    ('Large Harflinger', 'GA', '22-JUN-01', 50);
INSERT INTO plsql101_purchase_archive VALUES
    ('Medium Wodget', 'LB', '23-JUN-01', 20);
INSERT INTO plsql101_purchase_archive VALUES
    ('Small Widget', 'ZZ', '24-JUN-02', 80);
INSERT INTO plsql101_purchase_archive VALUES
    ('Chrome Phoobar', 'CA', '25-JUN-02', 2);
INSERT INTO plsql101_purchase_archive VALUES
    ('Small Widget', 'JT', '26-JUN-02', 50);
```

UNION

The UNION join operator performs the useful task of combining data from multiple tables into a single list. This differs from the relational techniques you used earlier in this chapter in that the UNION join operator is usually used when the *structure* of the two tables is similar or identical, but the *content* of the tables differs. The

Join Operator	Results Produced
UNION	All rows from both SELECT statements, with duplicate values removed
UNION ALL	All rows from both SELECT statements, with duplicate values shown
INTERSECT	Rows that were returned by both SELECT statements
MINUS	Rows that were returned by the first SELECT statement, minus those returned by the second one

TABLE 6-3. *Join Operators*

UNION join operator provides a way to easily combine the contents of such tables into one listing.

To see this in action, enter the following commands and compare your results with those shown in Figure 6-22:

```
SELECT product_name FROM plsql101_purchase
ORDER BY product_name;
SELECT product_name FROM plsql101_purchase_archive
ORDER BY product_name;

SELECT product_name FROM plsql101_purchase
UNION
SELECT product_name FROM plsql101_purchase_archive
ORDER BY product_name;
```

Note that each of the tables being queried contains products the other table does not. The PLSQL101_PURCHASE table contains a Round Chrome Snaphoo not found in the PLSQL101_PURCHASE_ARCHIVE table, while the latter contains a Large Harflinger that is absent from the former. The list of product names produced by the UNION join operator contains both, as well as all the other products shared by both tables.

UNION ALL
The UNION ALL join operator functions similarly to the UNION join operator, except that UNION ALL causes every row to be returned, instead of just one

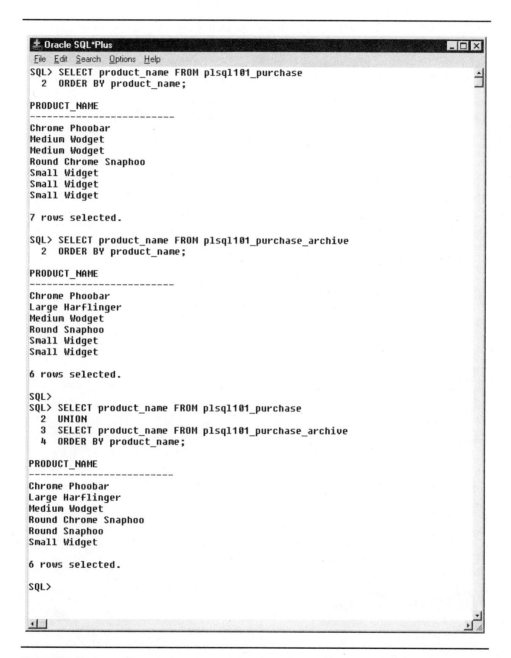

```
Oracle SQL*Plus                                                    _ □ ×
File  Edit  Search  Options  Help
SQL> SELECT product_name FROM plsql101_purchase
  2  ORDER BY product_name;

PRODUCT_NAME
------------------------
Chrome Phoobar
Medium Wodget
Medium Wodget
Round Chrome Snaphoo
Small Widget
Small Widget
Small Widget

7 rows selected.

SQL> SELECT product_name FROM plsql101_purchase_archive
  2  ORDER BY product_name;

PRODUCT_NAME
------------------------
Chrome Phoobar
Large Harflinger
Medium Wodget
Round Snaphoo
Small Widget
Small Widget

6 rows selected.

SQL>
SQL> SELECT product_name FROM plsql101_purchase
  2  UNION
  3  SELECT product_name FROM plsql101_purchase_archive
  4  ORDER BY product_name;

PRODUCT_NAME
------------------------
Chrome Phoobar
Large Harflinger
Medium Wodget
Round Chrome Snaphoo
Round Snaphoo
Small Widget

6 rows selected.

SQL>
```

FIGURE 6-22.   *The UNION join operator*

distinct row for each unique value. To see the difference this makes, enter the following command:

```
SELECT product_name FROM plsql101_purchase
UNION ALL
SELECT product_name FROM plsql101_purchase_archive
ORDER BY product_name;
```

This can be useful when you would like to count the number of instances of each value in more than one table.

INTERSECT

The INTERSECT join operator returns only the values that are present in *both* tables. If a value is found in one table but not the other, it is ignored by the INTERSECT join operator. This is very useful when you need to find out what values are shared in common by a pair of tables. An example of this join operator follows:

```
SELECT product_name FROM plsql101_purchase
INTERSECT
SELECT product_name FROM plsql101_purchase_archive
ORDER BY product_name;
```

MINUS

The MINUS join operator does essentially the opposite task from the INTERSECT join operator you just tried. The MINUS join operator shows you records in one table that are *not* in another table. Being able to easily uncover records in one table that are not being used in a second table is useful when you want to know what zero-activity items can be archived, or when you need to find out what values in one table are not being represented in another. The MINUS join operator works as shown in this code example:

```
SELECT product_name FROM plsql101_purchase
MINUS
SELECT product_name FROM plsql101_purchase_archive
ORDER BY product_name;
```

Writing Subqueries

Continuing with our theme of multiple-table operations, this section covers *subqueries*. Within this section you will learn what a subquery is, when to use them, and how to write them.

What Is a Subquery?

A subquery is a standard SELECT query that is nested within a SELECT, UPDATE, or DELETE command. It is used to provide data for the FROM or WHERE portions of the parent statement.

A subquery can even contain subqueries within itself. The Oracle documentation claims that you can nest subqueries to an infinite number of levels of depth. Usually a specification of "unlimited" translates to "it depends on the amount of computer resources available, but in any case it's likely to be more than you will ever use."

Types of Problems Subqueries Can Solve

A subquery enters the picture when one question must be answered before a larger question can be addressed. For instance, to find out which products are selling better than average, you must first determine what "average" is. To find out how much money has been made by your top salesperson, you first need to know who the top salesperson is. To identify products that are selling less than they did a year ago, you need to know what they sold a year ago. These are all situations where a subquery can provide the needed information.

Single-Row Subqueries

Let's consider an example. You've discovered that the most recent shipment of Small Widgets was intercepted while on its way to you, and replaced with cheap knockoffs. You want to know what else arrived that day, so you can check those products, as well. You don't know what date the Small Widgets arrived, so you can't specify the date explicitly in the WHERE clause. You can, however, have Oracle derive that date for you and use it as if you had typed it in by hand. You'll accomplish this by telling the SELECT statement's WHERE clause that it must retrieve the last stock date for the Small Widgets itself, and then use that date to filter other product records for you. Enter the following command, and compare your results with those shown in Figure 6-23:

```
SELECT *
FROM    plsql101_product
WHERE   last_stock_date = (
        SELECT last_stock_date
        FROM    plsql101_product
        WHERE   product_name = 'Small Widget'
        )
;
```

```
Oracle SQL*Plus
File  Edit  Search  Options  Help
SQL> SELECT *
  2  FROM   plsql101_product
  3  WHERE  last_stock_date = (
  4         SELECT last_stock_date
  5         FROM   plsql101_product
  6         WHERE  product_name = 'Small Widget'
  7         )
  8  ;

PRODUCT_NAME               PRODUCT_PRICE QUANTITY_ON_HAND LAST_STOC
-------------------------- ------------- ---------------- ---------
Small Widget                          99                1 15-JAN-03
Chrome Phoobar                        50              100 15-JAN-03

SQL>
```

FIGURE 6-23.   *Subquery based on last stock date*

To practice this technique further, create a new SELECT statement that returns all product records that have the same price as the Red Snaphoo. Your results should match those shown in Figure 6-24. Be sure not to simply type the price of 1.95 into the WHERE clause; make the statement find out for itself what the Red Snaphoo's price is.

A key characteristic of the subqueries you just wrote is that they are capable of returning only one value. For example, when you write a subquery that finds the last stock date for a Small Widget, only a single value can be returned; the Small Widget cannot have more than one last stock date, because there's only one column set aside to store that value in the product table. Since you can be sure that the subquery will return only one value, you can write the WHERE clause with an equals sign between the parent statement's WHERE clause and the subquery. You could not use the equals sign if the subquery had the potential for returning multiple values, because the parent statement's last stock date could never equal more than one value. This type of subquery is called a *single-row subquery*, because the subquery can only return one row of answers. (The parent statement can return any number of rows based on the subquery's one answer, of course.)

The subquery and the parent statement can refer to completely different tables, if you wish. For example, let's say you wanted to see all the sales made by Gary Anderson. You know the salesperson's name, but not the code that would be used to represent him or her in the purchase table. (That part may not make much sense

```
Oracle SQL*Plus                                                    _ □ X
File  Edit  Search  Options  Help

PRODUCT_NAME              PRODUCT_PRICE QUANTITY_ON_HAND LAST_STOC
------------------------- ------------- ---------------- ---------
Red Snaphoo                        1.95               10 31-DEC-01
Blue Snaphoo                       1.95               10 30-DEC-01

SQL>
SQL>
SQL>
```

FIGURE 6-24.   *Subquery based on product price*

with these test tables, where the person code is simply the person's initials, but in a
real database the person would most likely be represented by a number that had no
obvious relation to who the person is, and would therefore be difficult to guess.)
You can make the SELECT statement go and find Gary Anderson's code for you,
and still show you his sales records. Enter the following code to see how to
make this happen:

```
SELECT * FROM plsql101_purchase
WHERE   salesperson = (
        SELECT person_code
        FROM   plsql101_person
        WHERE  first_name = 'Gary' AND last_name = 'Anderson'
        )
;
```

As a last example of a single-row subquery, consider a situation where you
want to know which of your products are the most expensive. You can accomplish
this by writing a subquery that determines the average price of a product, as
shown in this code:

```
SELECT *
FROM   plsql101_product
WHERE  product_price > (
        SELECT AVG(product_price)
        FROM   plsql101_product
        )
;
```

Multirow Subqueries

As you may have guessed, a *multirow subquery* is one in which the subquery has the potential of returning more than one row of answers. The reason you need to think about this ahead of time is that it affects what comparison operator you use: You cannot compare something using an equals sign if the subquery is going to return more than one row of answers. Instead of the equals sign, you can use the **IN** function for multirow subqueries.

For example, let's say you want to know which products are not selling. To do that, you can tell your subquery to get a list of all the product names in the purchase table, and then provide that list back to the parent statement so those product names can be excluded from the product records returned to you. To see this in action, enter the following code and compare your results with those shown in Figure 6-25:

```
SELECT *
FROM   plsql101_purchase
ORDER BY product_name;

SELECT *
FROM   plsql101_product
WHERE  product_name NOT IN (
       SELECT DISTINCT product_name
       FROM   plsql101_purchase
       )
ORDER BY product_name
;
```

As mentioned earlier, you can also use subqueries in UPDATE and DELETE statements. For example, let's say you have been instructed to make a 10 percent reduction in the price of any item that has not sold. You can do that with a single UPDATE command by placing a subquery in its WHERE clause to determine which products have not sold. Enter the following code to see how this works:

```
SELECT * FROM  plsql101_product;

UPDATE plsql101_product
SET    product_price = product_price * .9
WHERE  product_name NOT IN (
       SELECT DISTINCT product_name
       FROM   plsql101_purchase
       )
;

SELECT * FROM  plsql101_product;
```

Notice that after the UPDATE command has been run, the prices have been changed only on those products that were not selling. Handy, eh?

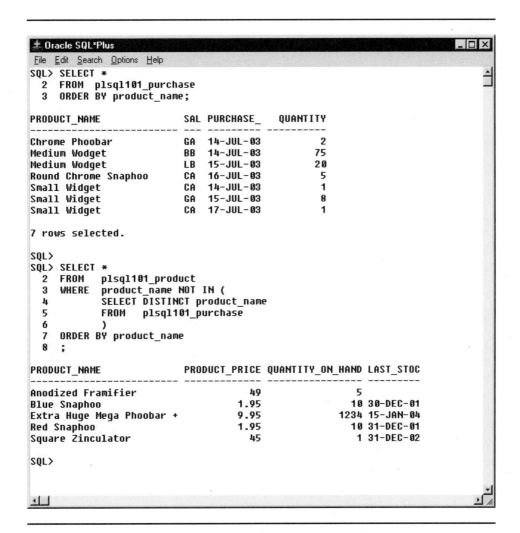

```
Oracle SQL*Plus                                                    _ □ ×
File  Edit  Search  Options  Help
SQL> SELECT *
  2  FROM  plsql101_purchase
  3  ORDER BY product_name;

PRODUCT_NAME              SAL PURCHASE_   QUANTITY
------------------------- --- ---------- ----------
Chrome Phoobar            GA  14-JUL-03         2
Medium Wodget             BB  14-JUL-03        75
Medium Wodget             LB  15-JUL-03        20
Round Chrome Snaphoo      CA  16-JUL-03         5
Small Widget              CA  14-JUL-03         1
Small Widget              GA  15-JUL-03         8
Small Widget              CA  17-JUL-03         1

7 rows selected.

SQL>
SQL> SELECT *
  2  FROM    plsql101_product
  3  WHERE   product_name NOT IN (
  4          SELECT DISTINCT product_name
  5          FROM    plsql101_purchase
  6          )
  7  ORDER BY product_name
  8  ;

PRODUCT_NAME              PRODUCT_PRICE QUANTITY_ON_HAND LAST_STOC
------------------------- ------------- ---------------- ---------
Anodized Framifier                   49                5
Blue Snaphoo                       1.95               10 30-DEC-01
Extra Huge Mega Phoobar +          9.95             1234 15-JAN-04
Red Snaphoo                        1.95               10 31-DEC-01
Square Zinculator                    45                1 31-DEC-02

SQL>
```

FIGURE 6-25. *Using a multirow subquery to find unmatched records*

Multicolumn Subqueries

Each of the subqueries you have seen so far retrieves just a single column of data.
It's possible to use subqueries that return multiple columns of data, too. To
demonstrate this, the following code evaluates the product names and purchase
dates in the PLSQL101_PURCHASE table to return only the most recent purchase
of each product. (When I interview people for PL/SQL jobs, I give a little quiz
that includes a question that requires this technique to answer; *very* few people
get it right.)

```
SELECT *
FROM   plsql101_purchase
ORDER BY product_name, purchase_date;

SELECT *
FROM   plsql101_purchase
WHERE  (product_name, purchase_date)
IN     (SELECT product_name, MAX(purchase_date)
        FROM   plsql101_purchase
        GROUP BY product_name
        )
;
```

Chapter Summary

This chapter has given you a thorough grounding in how to use indexes and constraints in Oracle. Database indexes work similarly to the index in a book: A database index contains key information from each row in a table, along with pointers to the related rows in that table. This provides a much quicker way to find rows matching a specific characteristic—as long as that characteristic is in the index. Once you have created an index on a table, Oracle automatically handles keeping the index synchronized with that table. Any INSERT, UPDATE, or DELETE on the table automatically changes the index as well, and any SELECT on the table will automatically be routed through an index, if one exists containing the columns needed by the SELECT statement. You can add or drop indexes without affecting the table's operations—any program that used the table before will still operate. It may operate more slowly, however. If you drop a table, any indexes associated with that table will automatically be dropped too, since an index has no purpose without its associated table.

Indexes improve the response time of commands that have to read a table's contents in order to perform their operations. Adding indexes to a table will *not* speed up data entry via INSERT commands; in fact, indexes slow down entry into the indexed table, because data must also be inserted into the table's index(es). So the use of indexes is a trade-off. They make data entry take longer, but make reading data faster.

The most common types of indexes are B*-Tree indexes and bitmap indexes. B*-Tree indexes are Oracle's default type, and they are appropriate for columns that contain a large number of unique values—for instance, names, person IDs, or phone numbers. Bitmap indexes make more sense on columns that contain a small number of unique values, such as gender or any kind of yes/no column. For columns with low cardinality, bitmap indexes are faster than B*-Tree indexes.

When the time comes to think about the quality of your database's data, you can use constraints to ensure that data meets certain minimum standards. When creating a constraint you define one or more conditions that a user's entry must satisfy before Oracle accepts the data into your table. Constraints are stored as part of a table's definition, and once created, they operate automatically. When someone attempts to perform an INSERT or UPDATE command that contains data violating a constraint, Oracle interrupts the command, rolls back their INSERT or UPDATE, and presents them with an error message.

A constraint can be as simple as requiring that a column contain data—any data. Or it can check to ensure that values in a column are all unique, with no duplicate entries. It can even check the values being entered and accept only those that satisfy any condition you specify, which can be useful to eliminate things like product prices that are below zero, transaction dates from a hundred years ago, or states that don't exist. This last example reflects Oracle's ability to have a constraint compare values being inserted in one table against values that are already present in another table, which is a good way to avoid problems like sales transactions for products that don't actually exist.

Once you have related data in separate tables, you need a way to reconnect that data and present it in a single list. You can do this in your SELECT statements by including a WHERE clause that identifies the primary key (unique identifying column(s)) in the parent table and the related foreign key in the child table.

Chapter Questions

1. Which of the following is NOT a benefit of indexes?

   A. Faster operation during INSERT commands

   B. Faster operation during UPDATE commands

   C. Faster operation during SELECT commands

   D. Faster operation during DELETE commands

2. On which line will the following command fail?

```
CREATE INDEX plsql101_purchase_pk ON plsql101_purchase (
    product_name,
    salesperson,
    purchase_date
    );
```

   A. 1

   B. 2

   C. 3

   D. 4

   E. The command will succeed.

3. Which of the following index types is best suited for a column with high cardinality?

  A. Composite

  B. B*-Tree

  C. Bitmap

  D. Other

4. Which of the following commands would ensure that products entered into a purchase record exist in the product table?

  A. CREATE INDEX *index_name* ON *table_name(column_name)*;

  B. ALTER TABLE *table_name* MODIFY (*column_name* NOT NULL);

  C. ALTER TABLE *table_name* ADD CONSTRAINT *constraint_name* UNIQUE (*column_name*);

  D. ALTER TABLE *table_name* ADD CONSTRAINT *constraint_name* CHECK (*column_name condition_to_satisfy*);

  E. ALTER TABLE *table_name* ADD CONSTRAINT *constraint_name* FOREIGN KEY (*column_name*) REFERENCES *parent_table_name*;

5. What will be the result of the following command if table 1 contains five records and table 2 contains ten records?

```
SELECT  table_1_name.column_name_1,
        table_2_name.column_name_2
FROM    table_1_name,
        table_2_name
;
```

  A. The five records from table 1 will display.

  B. The ten records from table 2 will display.

  C. Fifteen records will display, with data from both tables.

  D. Fifty records will display, with data from both tables.

  E. The number of records displayed will depend on how many records in table 1 share values with records in table 2.

Answers to Chapter Questions

1. A. Faster operation during INSERT commands

Explanation Because indexes are essentially additional tables, they slow down INSERT commands because the insert effort is being duplicated. The purpose of indexes is not to speed up inserts; it is to speed up any command that reads the data afterward.

2. E. The command will succeed.

Explanation For a refresher on the syntax for the CREATE INDEX command, refer to the section titled "How to Create Indexes."

3. B. B*-Tree

Explanation A composite index simply means that many columns are indexed at once, which isn't an issue related to the columns' cardinality. Bitmap indexes are designed for columns with low cardinality—that is, columns with a small number of different values. The "other" category (choice D) is meaningless, so the remaining choice is B*-Tree, which is designed for columns with a large number of different values.

4. E. ALTER TABLE *table_name* ADD CONSTRAINT *constraint_name* FOREIGN KEY (*column_name*) REFERENCES *parent_table_name*;

Explanation The tipoff here is the word "REFERENCES" in the command. This is the essential ingredient for creating a mechanism to enforce referential integrity between two tables.

5. D. Fifty records will display, with data from both tables.

Explanation Because the SELECT statement draws from two tables but does not include a WHERE clause to explain how they should be joined, it will produce a Cartesian product. Every *table_1_name.column_name_1* value will be joined with every *table_2_name.column_name_2* value, resulting in 5*10, or 50, records.

CHAPTER
7

Other Useful
Oracle Techniques

his chapter is a "catch-all" that presents a variety of tips and tools that will round out your knowledge of Oracle from a SQL standpoint. In it you will learn how to transfer data between tables; rename tables and change their structure; use the Oracle data dictionary; and create and use views, sequences, and synonyms. Once you know the information in this chapter, you will be well equipped for the upcoming chapters on PL/SQL programming.

If you have not done the examples from the previous chapter, enter the following code to create the tables and data used in this chapter. (If you already have these tables and data, jump over the following code listing and go directly to the section titled "Transferring Data Between Tables".)

```
DROP TABLE plsql101_purchase;
DROP TABLE plsql101_product;
DROP TABLE plsql101_person;
DROP TABLE plsql101_old_item;
DROP TABLE plsql101_purchase_archive;

CREATE TABLE plsql101_person (
     person_code VARCHAR2(3) PRIMARY KEY,
     first_name  VARCHAR2(15),
     last_name   VARCHAR2(20),
     hire_date   DATE
     )
;

CREATE INDEX plsql101_person_name_index
ON plsql101_person(last_name, first_name);

ALTER TABLE plsql101_person
ADD CONSTRAINT plsql101_person_unique UNIQUE (
     first_name,
     last_name,
     hire_date
     )
;

INSERT INTO plsql101_person VALUES
     ('CA', 'Charlene', 'Atlas', '01-FEB-02');
INSERT INTO plsql101_person VALUES
     ('GA', 'Gary', 'Anderson', '15-FEB-02');
INSERT INTO plsql101_person VALUES
     ('BB', 'Bobby', 'Barkenhagen', '28-FEB-02');
INSERT INTO plsql101_person VALUES
     ('LB', 'Laren', 'Baxter', '01-MAR-02');
```

```
INSERT INTO plsql101_person VALUES (
    'LN', 'Linda', 'Norton', '01-JUN-03');

CREATE TABLE plsql101_product (
    product_name    VARCHAR2(25) PRIMARY KEY,
    product_price   NUMBER(4,2),
    quantity_on_hand NUMBER(5,0),
    last_stock_date  DATE
    )
;

ALTER TABLE plsql101_product ADD CONSTRAINT positive_quantity CHECK(
    quantity_on_hand IS NOT NULL
    AND
    quantity_on_hand >=0
    )
;

INSERT INTO plsql101_product VALUES
    ('Small Widget', 99, 1, '15-JAN-03');
INSERT INTO plsql101_product VALUES
    ('Medium Wodget', 75, 1000, '15-JAN-02');
INSERT INTO plsql101_product VALUES
    ('Chrome Phoobar', 50, 100, '15-JAN-03');
INSERT INTO plsql101_product VALUES
    ('Round Chrome Snaphoo', 25, 10000, null);
INSERT INTO plsql101_product VALUES
    ('Extra Huge Mega Phoobar +',9.95,1234,'15-JAN-04');
INSERT INTO plsql101_product VALUES ('Square Zinculator',
    45, 1, TO_DATE('December 31, 2002, 11:30 P.M.',
                   'Month dd, YYYY, HH:MI P.M.')
    )
;
INSERT INTO plsql101_product VALUES (
    'Anodized Framifier', 49, 5, NULL);
INSERT INTO plsql101_product VALUES (
    'Red Snaphoo', 1.95, 10, '31-DEC-01');
INSERT INTO plsql101_product VALUES (
    'Blue Snaphoo', 1.95, 10, '30-DEC-01')
;


CREATE TABLE plsql101_purchase (
    product_name  VARCHAR2(25),
    salesperson   VARCHAR2(3),
    purchase_date DATE,
    quantity      NUMBER(4,2)
    )
```

```
;

ALTER TABLE plsql101_purchase
ADD PRIMARY KEY (product_name,
                 salesperson,
                 purchase_date
                 )
;

ALTER TABLE plsql101_purchase ADD CONSTRAINT reasonable_date CHECK(
     purchase_date IS NOT NULL
     AND
     TO_CHAR(purchase_date, 'YYYY-MM-DD') >= '2000-06-30'
     )
;

ALTER TABLE plsql101_purchase
     ADD CONSTRAINT plsql101_purchase_fk_product FOREIGN KEY
     (product_name) REFERENCES plsql101_product;

ALTER TABLE plsql101_purchase
     ADD CONSTRAINT plsql101_purchase_fk_person FOREIGN KEY
     (salesperson) REFERENCES plsql101_person;

CREATE INDEX plsql101_purchase_product
ON plsql101_purchase(product_name);

CREATE INDEX plsql101_purchase_salesperson
ON plsql101_purchase(salesperson);

INSERT INTO plsql101_purchase VALUES
     ('Small Widget', 'CA', '14-JUL-03', 1);
INSERT INTO plsql101_purchase VALUES
     ('Medium Wodget', 'BB', '14-JUL-03', 75);
INSERT INTO plsql101_purchase VALUES
     ('Chrome Phoobar', 'GA', '14-JUL-03', 2);
INSERT INTO plsql101_purchase VALUES
     ('Small Widget', 'GA', '15-JUL-03', 8);
INSERT INTO plsql101_purchase VALUES
     ('Medium Wodget', 'LB', '15-JUL-03', 20);
INSERT INTO plsql101_purchase VALUES
     ('Round Chrome Snaphoo', 'CA', '16-JUL-03', 5);
INSERT INTO plsql101_purchase VALUES (
     'Small Widget', 'CA', '17-JUL-03', 1)
;

UPDATE plsql101_product
SET    product_price = product_price * .9
WHERE  product_name NOT IN (
```

```
        SELECT DISTINCT product_name
        FROM    plsql101_purchase
        )
;

CREATE TABLE plsql101_old_item (
     item_id   CHAR(20),
     item_desc CHAR(25)
     )
;

INSERT INTO plsql101_old_item VALUES
     ('LA-101', 'Can, Small');
INSERT INTO plsql101_old_item VALUES
     ('LA-102', 'Can, Large');
INSERT INTO plsql101_old_item VALUES
     ('LA-103', 'Bottle, Small');
INSERT INTO plsql101_old_item VALUES
     ('LA-104', 'Bottle, Large');
INSERT INTO plsql101_old_item VALUES
     ('NY-101', 'Box, Small');
INSERT INTO plsql101_old_item VALUES
     ('NY-102', 'Box, Large');
INSERT INTO plsql101_old_item VALUES
     ('NY-103', 'Shipping Carton, Small');
INSERT INTO plsql101_old_item VALUES
     ('NY-104', 'Shipping Carton, Large');


CREATE TABLE plsql101_purchase_archive (
     product_name   VARCHAR2(25),
     salesperson    VARCHAR2(3),
     purchase_date DATE,
     quantity       NUMBER(4,2)
     )
;

INSERT INTO plsql101_purchase_archive VALUES
     ('Round Snaphoo', 'BB', '21-JUN-01', 10);
INSERT INTO plsql101_purchase_archive VALUES
     ('Large Harflinger', 'GA', '22-JUN-01', 50);
INSERT INTO plsql101_purchase_archive VALUES
     ('Medium Wodget', 'LB', '23-JUN-01', 20);
INSERT INTO plsql101_purchase_archive VALUES
     ('Small Widget', 'ZZ', '24-JUN-02', 80);
INSERT INTO plsql101_purchase_archive VALUES
     ('Chrome Phoobar', 'CA', '25-JUN-02', 2);
INSERT INTO plsql101_purchase_archive VALUES
     ('Small Widget', 'JT', '26-JUN-02', 50);
```

Transferring Data Between Tables

Now that you have done all of the basic DML commands, you are ready to put them to use performing a fundamental, and very necessary, function: copying records from one table to another. Being able to do this is important for a number of reasons:

■ **Importing Data from a Legacy System**   A regular part of SQL activities is transferring data from an existing system into a new system. Sometimes the existing system is being replaced by the new system. Other times the data has been purchased from an external source, and needs to be mapped and transferred into your own system. Often, the original data must be modified on its way to the new tables, which can involve using functions such as **UPPER, LOWER, LTRIM, RTRIM, SUBSTR, INSTR, TO_CHAR**, and **DECODE**.

■ **Loading Summaries into a Data Warehouse**   The basic function of a data warehouse is to store pre-calculated answers to often-asked questions—the kind of questions that can be answered with **SUM, COUNT, AVG, MIN**, and **MAX** functions along with **GROUP BY** clauses. These answers are usually stored in a separate set of tables, and that set of tables is usually populated using SQL queries.

■ **Copying Relational Data into Flat Files for Faster Access**   Relational databases are the most efficient way to store data, but retrieving data out of relational tables can take longer because the tables need to be joined, and table joins can be time consuming. In some applications, it makes sense to place a copy of related data from multiple tables into a single *flat-file* table where the joins have already been done. The flat-file table consumes more storage space than the relational tables from which it is derived, but it can be accessed more quickly because joins are unnecessary.

Transferring Data Using INSERT

This popular technique utilizes an INSERT command with a subquery that causes the inserted data to come from another table. To give yourself a destination for this technique, enter the following command:

```
CREATE TABLE plsql101_purchase_log (
    purchase_date     DATE,
    product_name      VARCHAR2(25),
    product_price     NUMBER(4,2),
    quantity          NUMBER(4,2),
    sales_first_name  VARCHAR2(15),
    sales_last_name   VARCHAR2(20)
    )
;
```

The PLSQL101_PURCHASE_LOG table is a flat-file representation of the important information from each purchase: date, product name and price, quantity purchased, and full name of salesperson. A table like this serves well as the basis for queries to answer business questions such as "Who sold the largest and smallest quantities of the Red Snaphoo?" Placing a complete compilation of the information necessary to answer these queries into a single table allows the answers to be produced more quickly, and it helps ensure that access to the tables that store transactions is not slowed down by questions from people who need to analyze those transactions as a group.

Now that you have a flat-file table suitable for storing records to be analyzed, it's time to populate that table with data. You will do that using an INSERT command that joins records from the PERSON, PRODUCT, and PURCHASE tables. The syntax for the command is as follows:

```
INSERT INTO table_name (
    SELECT statement
    )
;
```

The *SELECT statement* portion of the syntax example will be whatever SELECT command will produce the data you want in a structure that matches that of the destination table. To see how this works with your PLSQL101 tables, enter the following command, and check your results with those shown in Figure 7-1:

```
INSERT INTO plsql101_purchase_log (
    SELECT purc.purchase_date,
           prod.product_name,
           prod.product_price,
           purc.quantity,
           pers.first_name,
           pers.last_name
    FROM   plsql101_product  prod,
           plsql101_person   pers,
           plsql101_purchase purc
    WHERE  prod.product_name = purc.product_name
           AND
           pers.person_code = purc.salesperson
    )
;

SELECT * FROM plsql101_purchase_log;
```

As you can see, the PLSQL101_PURCHASE_LOG table contains an easy-to-use collection of information about each transaction in the PLSQL101_PURCHASE table.

```
┌─────────────────────────────────────────────────────────────────────┐
│ ± Oracle SQL*Plus                                        _ □ ×        │
├─────────────────────────────────────────────────────────────────────┤
│ File  Edit  Search  Options  Help                                     │
│     2        SELECT  purc.purchase_date,                              │
│     3                prod.product_name,                               │
│     4                prod.product_price,                              │
│     5                purc.quantity,                                   │
│     6                pers.first_name,                                 │
│     7                pers.last_name                                   │
│     8        FROM    plsql101_product   prod,                         │
│     9                plsql101_person    pers,                         │
│    10                plsql101_purchase  purc                          │
│    11        WHERE   prod.product_name = purc.product_name            │
│    12                AND                                              │
│    13                pers.person_code = purc.salesperson              │
│    14        )                                                        │
│    15    ;                                                            │
│                                                                       │
│ 7 rows created.                                                       │
│                                                                       │
│ SQL>                                                                  │
│ SQL> SELECT * FROM plsql101_purchase_log;                            │
│                                                                       │
│ PURCHASE_ PRODUCT_NAME            PRODUCT_PRICE  QUANTITY SALES_FIRST_NAM S │
│ --------- ---------------------- ------------- --------- --------------- - │
│ 14-JUL-03 Small Widget                      99         1 Charlene      A │
│ 14-JUL-03 Medium Wodget                     75        75 Bobby         B │
│ 14-JUL-03 Chrome Phoobar                    50         2 Gary          A │
│ 15-JUL-03 Small Widget                      99         8 Gary          A │
│ 15-JUL-03 Medium Wodget                     75        20 Laren         B │
│ 16-JUL-03 Round Chrome Snaphoo              25         5 Charlene      A │
│ 17-JUL-03 Small Widget                      99         1 Charlene      A │
│                                                                       │
│ 7 rows selected.                                                      │
│                                                                       │
│ SQL>                                                                  │
└─────────────────────────────────────────────────────────────────────┘
```

FIGURE 7-1. *Copying records from one table to another*

Creating a New Table Based on an Existing One

The method you just learned for copying data from one table to another assumes that the destination table already exists. That's appropriate for day-to-day additions to the destination table—but there's a way to make the creation of that table easier, too. It's a variation on the CREATE TABLE command. The syntax is as follows:

```
CREATE TABLE new_table_name AS
    SELECT statement
;
```

In this case, the *SELECT statement* portion of the command will be the same SELECT statement you used to populate the first destination table a moment ago. Enter the following code to create a second destination table with this technique, and compare your results with those shown in Figure 7-2:

```
CREATE TABLE plsql101_purchase_log2 AS
      SELECT purc.purchase_date,
             prod.product_name,
             prod.product_price,
             purc.quantity,
             pers.first_name,
             pers.last_name
      FROM   plsql101_product   prod,
             plsql101_person    pers,
             plsql101_purchase  purc
      WHERE  prod.product_name = purc.product_name
             AND
             pers.person_code = purc.salesperson
  ;

SELECT * FROM plsql101_purchase_log2;
```

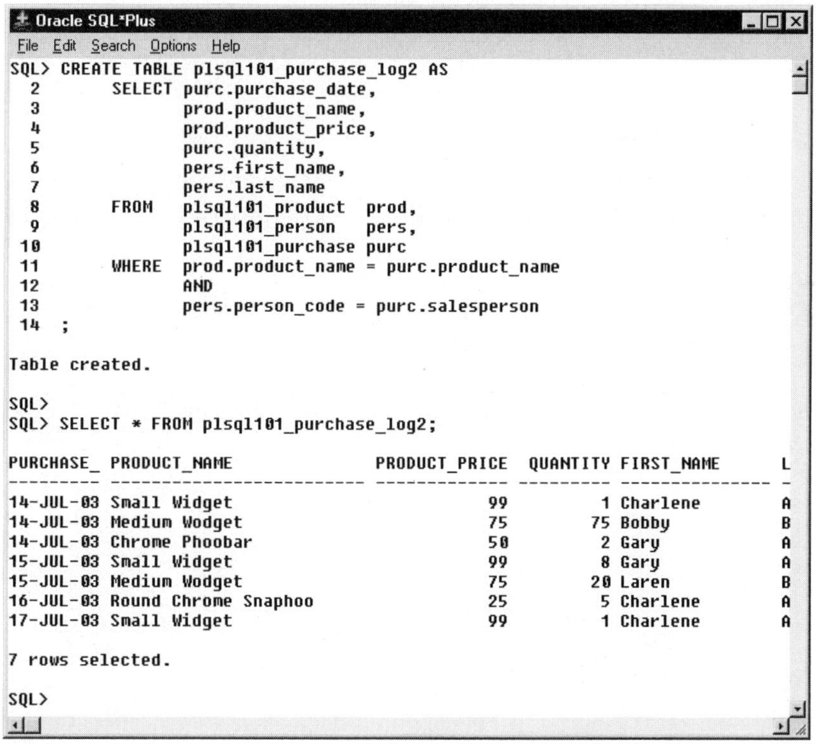

FIGURE 7-2. *Creating a new table based on one or more existing tables*

Renaming Tables

From time to time you will be called on to change the names of existing tables. It's very easy to do. The syntax is as follows:

RENAME *old_table_name* TO *new_table_name*;

Apply this to your own tables now by entering the following command:

```
RENAME plsql101_purchase_log2 TO plsql101_log;
```

Altering a Table's Structure

As a database evolves, the business needs that it must satisfy can change. This often creates reasons to change the structure of tables the database already contains. Fortunately, certain types of changes are simple to make: adding new columns, changing the datatypes of existing columns, and changing whether columns allow null values.

Adding Columns

You can add columns to a table at any time. New columns are appended to the end of the table's structure after all the existing columns. The syntax to do this is as follows:

ALTER TABLE *table_name*
ADD *new_column_name datatype* [NOT NULL]
;

Try out this new command by adding a new column to the PLSQL101_LOG table with the following code. Compare the results you get with those shown in Figure 7-3.

```
DESC plsql101_log

ALTER TABLE plsql101_log
ADD data_load_date VARCHAR2(8);

DESC plsql101_log
```

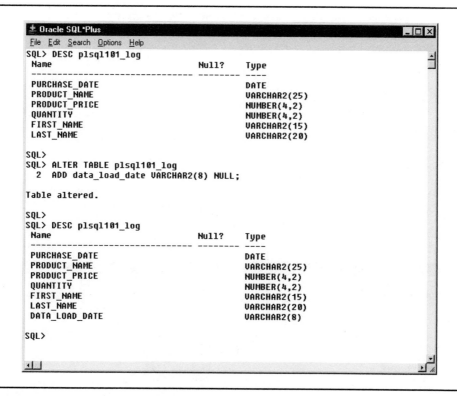

FIGURE 7-3. *Adding a column to an existing table*

Changing Column Datatypes

You may have wondered why the column you just added is a text column, when its name suggests it is supposed to contain dates. The answer: so you can change the new column's datatype to one that is more appropriate.

The syntax to change the datatype of an existing column is as follows:

ALTER TABLE *table_name*
MODIFY *column_name new_datatype*
;

To apply this to your PLSQL101_LOG table, enter the following code. Compare your results with those shown in Figure 7-4.

```
DESC plsql101_log

ALTER TABLE plsql101_log
MODIFY data_load_date DATE;

DESC plsql101_log
```

Changing Null Options

Often when a database is being designed, the users are not yet sure which columns will be required and which will not. In these instances, it's common to initially

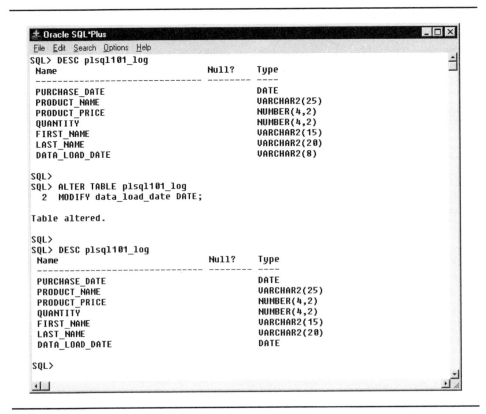

FIGURE 7-4.   *Changing the datatype of an existing column*

create the columns so they allow null values, and then later change them so they do not. (You can change NOT NULL columns to NULL too, of course.) The syntax to do this is as follows:

```
ALTER TABLE table_name
MODIFY column_name NOT NULL
;
```

Before you can modify your new column so it requires data, you must fill that column in the table's existing records. The following set of commands accomplishes this and then modifies the column so it will no longer accept null values. Enter the commands and compare their results with those shown in Figure 7-5.

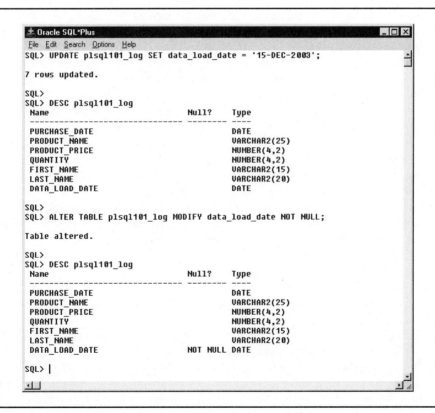

FIGURE 7-5. *Changing the null option of an existing column*

```
UPDATE plsql101_log SET data_load_date = '15-DEC-2003';

DESC plsql101_log

ALTER TABLE plsql101_log MODIFY data_load_date NOT NULL;

DESC plsql101_log
```

Views

The concept of a *view* is simple: Define a query that is going to be used frequently, store it in the Oracle database, and allow users to call it by name, as they would a table. When users select records from the view, Oracle runs the view's stored query, organizes the resulting records in whatever way is specified by the view, and presents them to the user. From the user's point of view, the view looks exactly like a table: data appears to be retrieved from it. In reality, the data is actually coming *through* the view, from one or more other sources.

Why are views useful? A variety of reasons. One very common use for a view is to join data from two or more tables and present it to users in one easy-to-read list. By simplifying the record-retrieval process so that users don't have to understand how to join tables, you make the data available to a larger number of people.

Views are also useful for enforcing security, because they allow you to limit the columns and rows returned to the user. If you don't want them to see a personnel table's salary column, just don't include that column when defining the view. As far as the user of the view is concerned, the column will not exist. The same is true for limiting rows: just include a WHERE clause when defining the view, and the records returned will be filtered in whatever way you want.

Finally, views can provide a convenience factor for you and other users. Certainly you would never design a table whose columns have hard-to-understand names or are in a bizarre order—but other people do, and sooner or later you will have to use their tables. Because a view is just a stored query, you can utilize a query's ability to change the names assigned to columns, as well as change the order in which the columns are displayed. For instance, recently I was given the task of analyzing an existing database with hundreds of columns with names like ID101, ID205, ID3322, and so on. I had a reference guide explaining what each column contained, but continually referring to that reference would have wasted a lot of time, and users who didn't have the reference would have been out of luck. For each table in the database, I created a view that presented that table's columns using clear, easy-to-understand names. As a result, nobody tries retrieving data directly from the tables; everyone is retrieving from the views instead, because when they look at the column names they understand what they're getting.

Creating a View

The method for creating a view is simplicity itself. Essentially, you specify the name of the view, and then the SELECT statement that the view will execute. The syntax is as follows:

```
CREATE OR REPLACE VIEW view_name AS
SELECT statement
;
```

Note that this command has a new component: OR REPLACE. This addition allows the command to create a new view even if a view with the same name already exists. (The existing view gets overwritten in this case, of course.)

To see a view in action, enter the following commands and compare your results with those shown in Figure 7-6:

```
SELECT * FROM plsql101_purchase;

CREATE OR REPLACE VIEW plsql101_sales_by_atlas_v AS
SELECT *
FROM    plsql101_purchase
WHERE   salesperson = 'CA'
;

SELECT * FROM plsql101_sales_by_atlas_v;
```

To see how to create a view that presents data from joined tables, enter the following commands:

```
CREATE OR REPLACE VIEW plsql101_sales_per_person_v AS
SELECT pers.first_name || ' ' || pers.last_name SALESPERSON,
       purc.product_name,
       purc.purchase_date,
       purc.quantity
FROM   plsql101_person   pers,
       plsql101_purchase purc
WHERE  pers.person_code = purc.salesperson (+)
;

SELECT * FROM plsql101_sales_per_person_v
ORDER BY salesperson, product_name, purchase_date;
```

Note that the prior example includes an ORDER BY clause in the SELECT statement that retrieves data from the view, but not in the view itself. Up until

```
± Oracle SQL*Plus                                                    _ □ ×
 File  Edit  Search  Options  Help
SQL> SELECT * FROM plsql101_purchase;

PRODUCT_NAME              SALESPERSON               PURCHASE_  QUANTITY
------------------------  ------------------------  ---------  ---------
Small Widget              CA                        14-JUL-03         1
Medium Wodget             BB                        14-JUL-03        75
Chrome Phoobar            GA                        14-JUL-03         2
Small Widget              GA                        15-JUL-03         8
Medium Wodget             LB                        15-JUL-03        20
Round Chrome Snaphoo      CA                        16-JUL-03         5
Small Widget              CA                        17-JUL-03         1

7 rows selected.

SQL>
SQL> CREATE OR REPLACE VIEW plsql101_sales_by_atlas_v AS
  2  SELECT *
  3  FROM    plsql101_purchase
  4  WHERE   salesperson = 'CA'
  5  ;

View created.

SQL>
SQL> SELECT * FROM plsql101_sales_by_atlas_v;

PRODUCT_NAME              SALESPERSON               PURCHASE_  QUANTITY
------------------------  ------------------------  ---------  ---------
Small Widget              CA                        14-JUL-03         1
Round Chrome Snaphoo      CA                        16-JUL-03         5
Small Widget              CA                        17-JUL-03         1

SQL>
```

FIGURE 7-6.   *Creating a simple filtering view*

Oracle 8*i*, views could not include an ORDER BY clause. In 8*i* and subsequent versions, you can cause the view to sort the records it shows by including the ORDER BY clause right after the WHERE clause, just like you would in a standard SELECT statement.

Dropping Views

Dropping a view is as easy as dropping a table (but less destructive—since a view doesn't contain any data, the worst that can happen if you accidentally drop a view is having to re-create it). The syntax to drop a view is as follows:

    DROP VIEW *view_name*;

Try the syntax now by using it to drop the view you just created. The command to do this is:

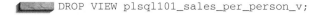

```
DROP VIEW plsql101_sales_per_person_v;
```

Altering a View's Definition

Oracle does not provide a way to alter an existing view. The only way to change a view is drop it and re-create it. For this reason, it's a good idea to store all of your view-creation commands in .sql script files. That way, if you need to change a view, it's easy to open the script file, change the command it contains, and re-run the CREATE VIEW command.

Top *N* Analysis

Once you see how to make SQL show you the top 1, 10, or 100 records matching whatever criteria and sorting you specify, the technique is so easy you may prefer to simply use the technique manually, rather than creating a view that encapsulates it. Doing it for other users can score you big points, though, and increased user satisfaction equals increased job security and higher pay. OK, maybe this technique won't get you a raise, but it might get you a free beverage of your choosing.

This technique leverages the fact that Oracle dynamically assigns row numbers to every row returned by each query it processes. This means that no matter where a row resides in its table, if it is the first (or only) row returned by a SELECT statement, it will have a row number of 1 within that query. You can refer to these row numbers in a SELECT statement's WHERE clause. If you write your SELECT statement to sort its results in a way you care about, you can get Oracle to show you the 5, 50, or 500 most important records by including a WHERE clause statement that restricts the row number to the number of records you want.

The syntax to perform this is as follows:

```
SELECT column_name_1[, column_name_2…]
FROM table_name
WHERE ROWNUM <= numbers_of_records_you_want
ORDER BY column_with_value_you_care_about
;
```

Applying this to the small number of records contained in your sample tables for this book won't produce impressive results, but it will demonstrate how the technique works. The following command shows how to create a view that shows the three products whose stock quantities are the highest:

NOTE
This view will only work in Oracle versions 8i and later, because those versions allow views to include an ORDER BY clause.

```
CREATE OR REPLACE VIEW plsql101_overstocked_items AS
SELECT product_name, quantity_on_hand
FROM    plsql101_product
WHERE   ROWNUM <= 3
ORDER BY quantity_on_hand
;

SELECT * FROM plsql101_overstocked_items;
```

Other Database Objects

The final section of this chapter covers an assortment of techniques that you could end up using every day. In the pages that follow, you will learn how to use sequences, synonyms, and the Oracle data dictionary.

Sequences

Databases are all about keeping things in order, and one way to keep records in order is to assign them sequential numbers. Oracle allows you to create counters called *sequences* that increment each time they are used. By referring to the sequence when inserting records, you can ensure that a new unique number is assigned to each record inserted.

Creating a Sequence

The syntax to create a sequence is as follows:

```
CREATE SEQUENCE sequence_name;
```

This simple command creates a sequence that starts at 1 and increments by 1 each time it is used. This is often all you will require from a sequence. However, there are many optional parameters you can use when defining a sequence. Take a look at the following syntax to see some of the more useful parameters:

```
CREATE SEQUENCE sequence_name
[INCREMENT BY increment_quantity]
```

```
[START WITH starting_value]
[MAXVALUE highest_value]
[MINVALUE lowest_value]
[CYCLE]
;
```

The INCREMENT BY parameter allows you to create sequences that jump in intervals other than 1. The values for this parameter can have up to 28 digits (although there won't be many opportunities to use an increment like that!). If you specify a negative value here, the sequence will decrement in value each time it is used.

The START WITH parameter enables you to create a sequence whose first value is something other than 1. This can be handy when you are creating a sequence for a table that already contains records: You can tell the sequence to start at the next value after the highest existing record ID.

The MAXVALUE and MINVALUE parameters allow you to define limits for the numbers the sequence generates. If you use these in conjunction with the CYCLE parameter, you can create a sequence that loops repeatedly through a set of values you define.

By far, the most common sequences increment by 1 and have no limit on their values. Execute the following command to create such a sequence, and then proceed to the next topic to put it to use:

```
CREATE SEQUENCE plsql101_test_seq;
```

Using a Sequence

To get values from a sequence, you must refer to it like a table. Sequences contain two "pseudocolumns" named CURRVAL and NEXTVAL that return the sequence's current and next value, respectively. Selecting from the NEXTVAL column causes the sequence to automatically increment to its next number.

To see this in action, enter the following commands and compare your results with those shown in Figure 7-7:

```
SELECT plsql101_test_seq.nextval FROM DUAL;
SELECT plsql101_test_seq.nextval FROM DUAL;
SELECT plsql101_test_seq.nextval FROM DUAL;
```

Now that you have seen how a sequence operates, it is time to learn the method for populating a table's column from a sequence. You can accomplish this by including a reference to the sequence as a value in the INSERT statement. To see

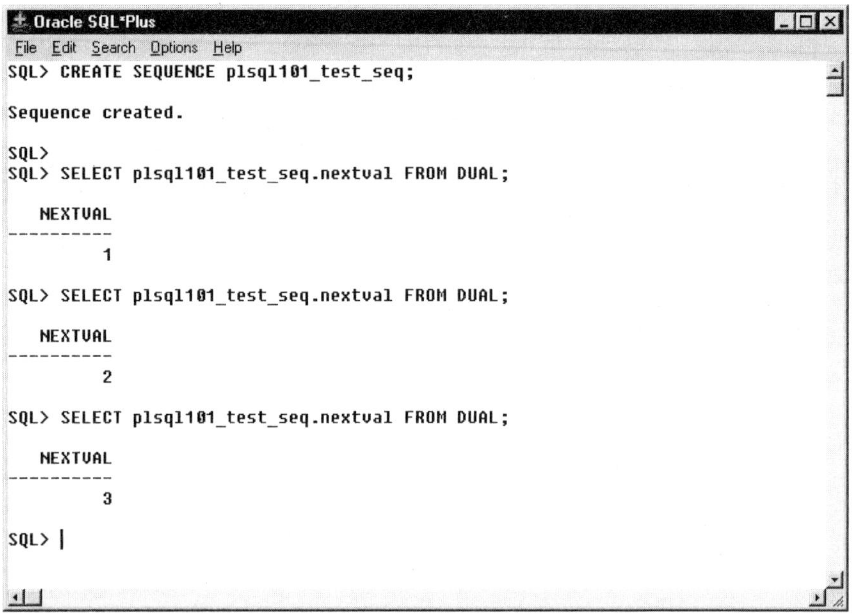

FIGURE 7-7. *Using a sequence from the command line*

how this works, enter the following commands and compare the results you see
with those in Figure 7-8:

```
CREATE TABLE plsql101_test (
      record_id    NUMBER(18,0),
      record_text VARCHAR2(10)
);

INSERT INTO plsql101_test VALUES (
     plsql101_test_seq.nextval,
     'Record A'
);

INSERT INTO plsql101_test VALUES (
     plsql101_test_seq.nextval,
     'Record B'
);

SELECT * FROM plsql101_test;
```

```
± Oracle SQL*Plus                                                    _ □ ×
File  Edit  Search  Options  Help
SQL> CREATE TABLE plsql101_test (
  2        record_id   NUMBER(18,0),
  3        record_text VARCHAR2(10)
  4  );

Table created.

SQL> INSERT INTO plsql101_test VALUES (
  2        plsql101_test_seq.nextval,
  3        'Record A'
  4  );

1 row created.

SQL> INSERT INTO plsql101_test VALUES (
  2        plsql101_test_seq.nextval,
  3        'Record B'
  4  );

1 row created.

SQL> SELECT * FROM plsql101_test;

 RECORD_ID RECORD_TEX
---------- ----------
         4 Record A
         5 Record B

SQL>
```

FIGURE 7-8.   *Using a sequence to populate a table's column*

NOTE
*While a sequence is usually designed to be used
by one table, there is no restriction in Oracle that
requires this. A sequence is an independent object.
It can be used by one table, many tables, or no
tables at all.*

The method you just employed demonstrates how to utilize a sequence in an
INSERT statement by referring to the sequence explicitly. It is also possible to have
the sequence referenced automatically, so it does not have to be referenced in the
INSERT statement. The technique for doing this is introduced in Chapter 9.

Modifying an Existing Sequence

Once a sequence has been created, you can modify it in a number of ways. You can alter the increment value, adjust or remove minimum and maximum values, or change whether it loops when it reaches its limits, among other things.

The syntax for making these changes to an existing sequence is very similar to what you used to create the sequence in the first place. The syntax is as follows:

```
ALTER SEQUENCE sequence_name
[INCREMENT BY increment_quantity]
[MAXVALUE highest_value | NOMAXVALUE]
[MINVALUE lowest_value | NOMINVALUE]
[CYCLE | NOCYCLE]
;
```

To see this in action, compare Figure 7-9 with the results you get from entering the following commands:

```
ALTER SEQUENCE plsql101_test_seq
MAXVALUE 10
;

SELECT plsql101_test_seq.nextval FROM DUAL;
SELECT plsql101_test_seq.nextval FROM DUAL;
SELECT plsql101_test_seq.nextval FROM DUAL;
SELECT plsql101_test_seq.nextval FROM DUAL;
SELECT plsql101_test_seq.nextval FROM DUAL;
SELECT plsql101_test_seq.nextval FROM DUAL;
```

Synonyms

A *synonym* allows you to refer to an Oracle object by a name other than its actual name. You can apply synonyms to a table, view, or sequence, as well as to objects you will learn about later in this book, such as functions, procedures, and packages. The rest of this discussion will talk about synonyms as they relate to tables, but the information also applies to synonyms assigned to other objects.

Why would you want to create a synonym for something? The main reason is convenience: If you frequently refer to a table that has a long name, you might appreciate being able to refer to it with a shorter name without having to rename the table and alter code referring to that table.

Synonyms can also increase convenience by making it easier for other people to access your data. Tables are organized by the Oracle user ID of the person who created them, and if another user wants to reference a table you have created, they

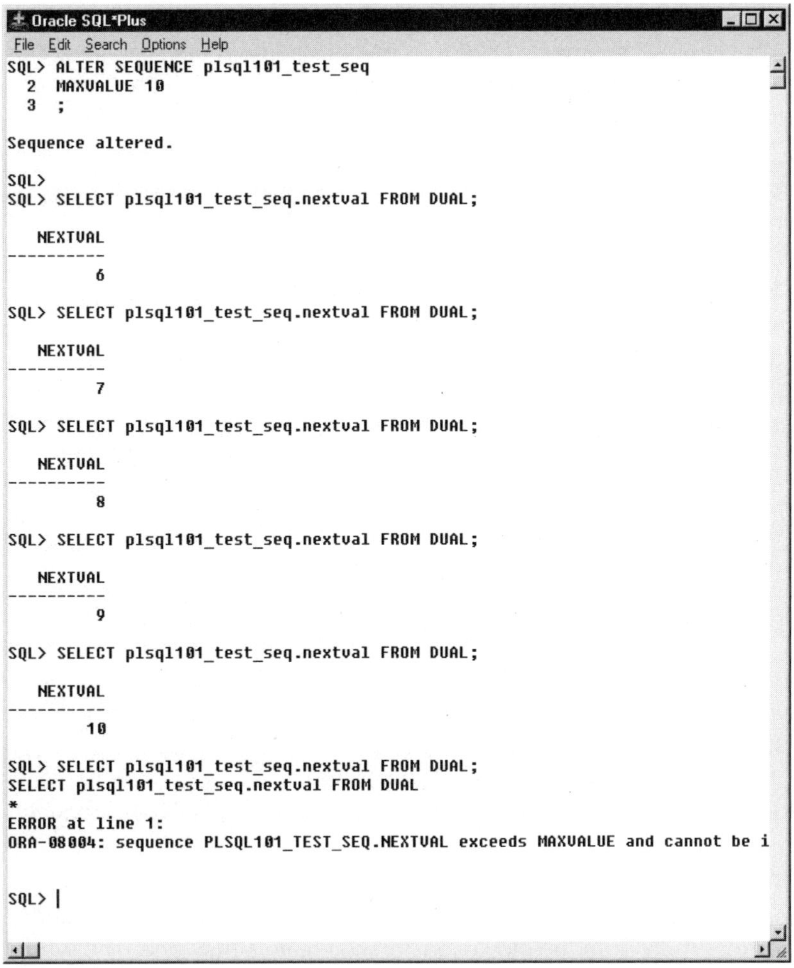

```
Oracle SQL*Plus                                                    _ □ ×
File  Edit  Search  Options  Help
SQL> ALTER SEQUENCE plsql101_test_seq
  2   MAXVALUE 10
  3   ;

Sequence altered.

SQL>
SQL> SELECT plsql101_test_seq.nextval FROM DUAL;

   NEXTVAL
----------
         6

SQL> SELECT plsql101_test_seq.nextval FROM DUAL;

   NEXTVAL
----------
         7

SQL> SELECT plsql101_test_seq.nextval FROM DUAL;

   NEXTVAL
----------
         8

SQL> SELECT plsql101_test_seq.nextval FROM DUAL;

   NEXTVAL
----------
         9

SQL> SELECT plsql101_test_seq.nextval FROM DUAL;

   NEXTVAL
----------
        10

SQL> SELECT plsql101_test_seq.nextval FROM DUAL;
SELECT plsql101_test_seq.nextval FROM DUAL
*
ERROR at line 1:
ORA-08004: sequence PLSQL101_TEST_SEQ.NEXTVAL exceeds MAXVALUE and cannot be i

SQL> |
```

FIGURE 7-9.   *Altering an existing sequence*

generally have to place your username in front of the name of the table, as
demonstrated here:

SELECT * FROM *your_user_name.your_table_name;*

This can get tedious, and if the table is moved to a different user, then any existing code referencing the table must be changed. Synonyms have an option enabling the table to be "visible" to anyone even if its owner's name is not specified. This allows you to write SQL statements that will continue to work even if the tables they refer to move to another user.

Creating a Synonym
The syntax to create a synonym is as follows:

```
CREATE [PUBLIC] SYNONYM synonym_name
FOR object_name
;
```

To see how a synonym works, issue the following commands. Figure 7-10 shows the results you should see.

```
SELECT * FROM prod;

CREATE SYNONYM prod FOR plsql101_product;

SELECT * FROM prod;
```

If you simply want to make a table available to other users, you can create a synonym that has the same name as the table. An example of this type of command follows:

```
CREATE PUBLIC SYNONYM plsql101_product FOR plsql101_product;
```

Modifying an Existing Synonym
Because a synonym is so simple, Oracle does not offer any means of altering one. Instead, you simply drop the old synonym and create a new one. The syntax is:

```
DROP [PUBLIC] SYNONYM synonym_name;
```

To drop the first synonym you created enabling the PLSQL101_PRODUCT table to be referred to as PROD, execute this command:

```
DROP SYNONYM prod;
```

To drop the public synonym you created, issue this command:

```
DROP PUBLIC SYNONYM plsql101_product;
```

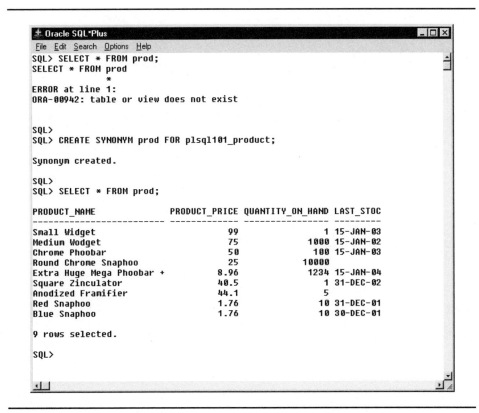

```
 Oracle SQL*Plus                                                    _ □ ×
File  Edit  Search  Options  Help
SQL> SELECT * FROM prod;
SELECT * FROM prod
              *
ERROR at line 1:
ORA-00942: table or view does not exist


SQL>
SQL> CREATE SYNONYM prod FOR plsql101_product;

Synonym created.

SQL>
SQL> SELECT * FROM prod;

PRODUCT_NAME               PRODUCT_PRICE QUANTITY_ON_HAND LAST_STOC
-------------------------- ------------- ---------------- ---------
Small Widget                          99                1 15-JAN-03
Medium Wodget                         75             1000 15-JAN-02
Chrome Phoobar                        50              100 15-JAN-03
Round Chrome Snaphoo                  25            10000
Extra Huge Mega Phoobar +           8.96             1234 15-JAN-04
Square Zinculator                   40.5                1 31-DEC-02
Anodized Framifier                  44.1                5
Red Snaphoo                         1.76               10 31-DEC-01
Blue Snaphoo                        1.76               10 30-DEC-01

9 rows selected.

SQL>
```

FIGURE 7-10. *Creating a synonym for a table*

Oracle Data Dictionary

You probably recognize by now that an Oracle database is made up of many different objects: tables, columns, views, relationships, constraints, sequences, and so on. Oracle keeps track of all of these objects by storing information about them in its *data dictionary*. The data dictionary is a collection of tables and views which are maintained by Oracle so they always have up-to-date information about every object and user in the database. The data dictionary contains every characteristic you specified when creating an object, as well as behind-the-scenes information such as the amount of space allocated to the object, the amount of that space currently in use, and the rights users have related to that object.

Querying the Data Dictionary to Acquire User and Database Information

The complete list of data dictionary objects is available by querying a view named DICT. Using the following command, you can see the list of data dictionary objects containing useful information. (The list includes information about synonyms that is not relevant to this discussion, so the following command includes a WHERE clause to omit synonyms from the list.) The list may be longer than your screen can show, so the end of the list will look like what you see in Figure 7-11.

```
SELECT table_name, SUBSTR(comments, 1, 45)
FROM   dict
WHERE  SUBSTR(comments, 1, 7) <> 'Synonym'
;
```

Using Different Data Dictionary Views

Because Oracle has so many different data dictionary views, an entire book could be written on how to use all of them (in fact, many books written for database administrators devote a substantial amount of time to some of Oracle's more intricate data dictionary views related to system parameters). Within the scope of this book, the two most useful data dictionary views are those that will show you lists of the tables and views you own. The following command will show you a list of all of your tables:

```
SELECT table_name FROM user_tables;
```

This command produces a list of all the views you have created:

```
SELECT view_name FROM user_views;
```

These commands are handy when you don't remember exactly what you named a table or view, as well as when you want to determine whether a table or view has already been created.

Chapter Summary

This chapter introduced a variety of tips and tools that make your knowledge of SQL more complete. It began by showing you how to transfer data between tables using an INSERT statement that has a SELECT statement where you would normally place the values to be inserted. You can also transfer data by executing a CREATE TABLE statement whose column definitions are replaced by a SELECT statement.

After learning how to rename tables using the simple syntax RENAME *old_table_name* TO *new_table_name*, you saw how to alter a table's structure to

```
± Oracle SQL*Plus                                                    _ □ ×
File  Edit  Search  Options  Help
USER_REPPRIORITY_GROUP           Information about user's priority groups
USER_REPPROP                     Propagation information about the current use
USER_REPRESOLUTION               Description of all conflict resolutions for u
USER_REPRESOLUTION_METHOD        All conflict resolution methods accessible to
USER_REPRESOLUTION_STATISTICS    Statistics for conflict resolutions for user'
USER_REPRESOL_STATS_CONTROL      Information about statistics collection for c
USER_REPSCHEMA                   N-way replication information about the curre
USER_REPSITES                    N-way replication information about the curre
USER_RESOURCE_LIMITS             Display resource limit of the user
USER_ROLE_PRIVS                  Roles granted to current user
USER_SEGMENTS                    Storage allocated for all database segments
USER_SEQUENCES                   Description of the user's own SEQUENCEs
USER_SNAPSHOTS                   Snapshots the user can look at
USER_SNAPSHOT_LOGS               All snapshot logs owned by the user
USER_SNAPSHOT_REFRESH_TIMES      Snapshots and their last refresh times for ea
USER_SOURCE                      Source of stored objects accessible to the us
USER_SYNONYMS                    The user's private synonyms
USER_SYS_PRIVS                   System privileges granted to current user
USER_TABLES                      Description of the user's own relational tabl
USER_TABLESPACES                 Description of accessible tablespaces
USER_TAB_COLUMNS                 Columns of user's tables, views and clusters
USER_TAB_COL_STATISTICS          Columns of user's tables, views and clusters
USER_TAB_COMMENTS                Comments on the tables and views owned by the
USER_TAB_HISTOGRAMS              Histograms on columns of user's tables
USER_TAB_PRIVS                   Grants on objects for which the user is the o
USER_TAB_PRIVS_MADE              All grants on objects owned by the user
USER_TAB_PRIVS_RECD              Grants on objects for which the user is the g
USER_TRIGGERS                    Triggers owned by the user
USER_TRIGGER_COLS                Column usage in user's triggers
USER_TS_QUOTAS                   Tablespace quotas for the user
USER_TYPES                       Description of the user's own types
USER_TYPE_ATTRS                  Description of attributes of the user's own t
USER_TYPE_METHODS                Description of methods of the user's own type
USER_UPDATABLE_COLUMNS           Description of updatable columns
USER_USERS                       Information about the current user
USER_VIEWS                       Description of the user's own views
AUDIT_ACTIONS                    Description table for audit trail action type
COLUMN_PRIVILEGES                Grants on columns for which the user is the g
DICTIONARY                       Description of data dictionary tables and vie
DICT_COLUMNS                     Description of columns in data dictionary tab
GLOBAL_NAME                      global database name
INDEX_HISTOGRAM                  statistics on keys with repeat count
INDEX_STATS                      statistics on the b-tree
NLS_DATABASE_PARAMETERS          Permanent NLS parameters of the database
NLS_INSTANCE_PARAMETERS          NLS parameters of the instance
NLS_SESSION_PARAMETERS           NLS parameters of the user session
RESOURCE_COST                    Cost for each resource
ROLE_ROLE_PRIVS                  Roles which are granted to roles
ROLE_SYS_PRIVS                   System privileges granted to roles
ROLE_TAB_PRIVS                   Table privileges granted to roles
SESSION_PRIVS                    Privileges which the user currently has set
SESSION_ROLES                    Roles which the user currently has enabled.
TABLE_PRIVILEGES                 Grants on objects for which the user is the g

286 rows selected.

SQL>
```

FIGURE 7-11.   *Seeing the objects in the Oracle data dictionary*

add new columns, change the datatypes of existing columns, and change whether columns accept null values. Next you learned about views, which are essentially stored queries. Views allow you to write the command to create a customized result from one or more tables and store that command so it can easily be used over and over. As an example, you created a view that showed products with the highest numbers of items in stock.

Next you learned about sequences, which are Oracle's mechanism for generating sequential numbers for use as record IDs and other counting operations. The CREATE SEQUENCE command allows you to specify parameters such as the starting value, lowest and highest values, increment quantity, and whether the sequence loops back to its beginning value once it reaches its limit. You can incorporate a sequence's value into an INSERT statement by including a reference to *sequence_name*.nextval in the values to be inserted.

Next you learned about synonyms, which allow you to refer to an Oracle object by a name other than its actual name. Synonyms also enable you to make a table or other object available to all users of a database without them needing to know who owns the table.

The final topic in this chapter was the Oracle data dictionary, which is Oracle's internal method for keeping track of users, database objects, and other information needed to keep the database up and running. In this topic you learned how to get a list of all data dictionary views. You also saw how to get a list of your tables and views by selecting from data dictionary views named USER_TABLES and USER_VIEWS.

The information in this chapter, and those that preceded it, forms a strong base of knowledge about how to use SQL in powerful and efficient ways. Now you are ready to learn how to write sophisticated programs using Oracle's superset of SQL, PL/SQL. In today's job market, knowing how to write PL/SQL programs is like money in the bank.

Chapter Questions

1. Which of the following commands would transfer data from a table named PRODUCT to a table named PRODUCT_ARCHIVE?

   A. INSERT INTO product (
       SELECT *
       FROM product_archive
)
     ;

   B. COPY * FROM product TO product_archive;

    C. CREATE TABLE product_archive AS
        SELECT * FROM product;

    D. INSERT INTO product_archive (SELECT * FROM product);

2. Which of the following commands will rename a table?

    A. RENAME *table_name new_table_name*;

    B. RENAME *table_name* TO *new_table_name*;

    C. RENAME TABLE *table_name new_table_name*;

    D. RENAME TABLE *table_name* TO *new_table_name*;

3. Which of the following commands will add a required text column named NEW_COLUMN to a table named TAB1?

    A. ALTER TABLE tab1
        ADD new_column VARCHAR2(10) NOT NULL;

    B. ADD new_column VARCHAR2(10) NOT NULL
        TO tab1;

    C. ALTER tab1
        ADD new_column VARCHAR2(10) NOT NULL;

    D. ADD new_column VARCHAR2(10) NOT NULL
        TO TABLE tab1;

4. Which of the following is *not* a benefit offered by views?

    A. Can rename columns to more readable names than those used in the underlying table

    B. Can join information from multiple tables

    C. Can filter data so only certain rows or columns are displayed

    D. Can speed up data access by referring directly to the columns needed

5. Which of the following commands would *not* result in the creation of a sequence?

    A. CREATE SEQUENCE new_seq1 NOMAXVALUE;

    B. CREATE SEQUENCE 2new_seq START WITH 2;

    C. CREATE SEQUENCE new3_seq MIN 1 MAX 100 CYCLE;

    D. CREATE SEQUENCE new_4seq INCREMENT BY -1;

6. Which of the following are benefits of using table synonyms?

A. Can increase data throughput speed

B. Allows column to be referred to by a different name

C. Allows table to be referred to by a different name

D. Enables other users to reference a table without knowing its owner

Answers to Chapter Questions

1. C, D. CREATE TABLE product_archive AS
           SELECT * FROM product;
           INSERT INTO product_archive (SELECT * FROM product);

Explanation   Choice A has the correct syntax, but it has the source and destination tables reversed. Choice B is not valid syntax. Choices C and D are both valid ways of copying data from PRODUCT to PRODUCT_ARCHIVE.

2. B. RENAME *table_name* TO *new_table_name*;

Explanation   This is one of the few SQL commands that does not require you to identify the type of object being acted upon. You do, however, have to include the word TO between the original table name and the new one.

3. A. ALTER TABLE tab1
          ADD new_column VARCHAR2(10) NOT NULL;

Explanation   For a refresher on the ALTER TABLE syntax, review the section titled "Adding Columns."

4. D. Can speed up data access by referring directly to the columns needed

Explanation   The explanation of choice D sounds somewhat like a benefit offered by indexes. It is not, however, relevant to views. A view does not substantially affect the amount of time it takes to access data.

5. B, C. CREATE SEQUENCE 2new_seq START WITH 2;
        CREATE SEQUENCE new3_seq MIN 1 MAX 100 CYCLE;

Explanation   Choice B will fail because the sequence name begins with a number (remember the guideline on naming objects?). Choice C will fail because the parameters to set a sequence's limits are MINVALUE and MAXVALUE, not MIN and MAX. If you thought that choice D would fail because its increment value is a negative number, remember that that's the way to create a sequence that decrements in value instead of increments.

6. C, D. Allows table to be referred to by a different name, Enables other users to reference a table without knowing its owner

Explanation   For a refresher on this subject, refer to the section titled "Synonyms."

PART
III

Creating Programs
Using PL/SQL

CHAPTER
8

Introduction to PL/SQL

toring and retrieving information is just one part of any real-life application. Even the simplest applications need to do some processing that is difficult or impossible using SQL alone. Just think of how complex the computations are when the government's share of your earnings needs to be computed every year! OK, maybe you want to think of another example instead. In any case, SQL alone isn't up to the task.

What Is PL/SQL?

You may ask why SQL doesn't have features that allow you to do more sophisticated computations on data. The reason is partly historical: SQL came into existence as a database query language (Structured Query Language) and has evolved and been optimized for doing exactly that: querying databases. Different providers of database software have agreed to certain SQL standards, but they did not agree on how to give users more sophisticated SQL-oriented programming capabilities. Thus, each database software provider has come up with proprietary or semi-proprietary products. Oracle calls its solution *PL/SQL*. You can think of this as standing for "Programming Language for SQL."

In this chapter you will be introduced to the basics of PL/SQL. You will learn the difference between SQL, SQL*Plus, and PL/SQL. You will also start writing simple PL/SQL procedures, as well as functions using basic PL/SQL constructs like variables, loops, and cursors. Then you will learn about the important art of handling errors in a way the user can easily understand.

If you just started reading in this chapter and have not done any of the exercises in the preceding chapters, you will need to create the sample tables built in prior chapters before you can do the exercises in this chapter. You can accomplish this by entering the following SQL commands:

```
DROP TABLE plsql101_purchase;
DROP TABLE plsql101_product;
DROP TABLE plsql101_person;
DROP TABLE plsql101_old_item;
DROP TABLE plsql101_purchase_archive;

CREATE TABLE plsql101_person (
     person_code VARCHAR2(3) PRIMARY KEY,
     first_name  VARCHAR2(15),
     last_name   VARCHAR2(20),
     hire_date   DATE
     )
```

```
;

CREATE INDEX plsql101_person_name_index
ON plsql101_person(last_name, first_name);

ALTER TABLE plsql101_person
ADD CONSTRAINT plsql101_person_unique UNIQUE (
      first_name,
      last_name,
      hire_date
      )
;

INSERT INTO plsql101_person VALUES
      ('CA', 'Charlene', 'Atlas', '01-FEB-02');
INSERT INTO plsql101_person VALUES
      ('GA', 'Gary', 'Anderson', '15-FEB-02');
INSERT INTO plsql101_person VALUES
      ('BB', 'Bobby', 'Barkenhagen', '28-FEB-02');
INSERT INTO plsql101_person VALUES
      ('LB', 'Laren', 'Baxter', '01-MAR-02');
INSERT INTO plsql101_person VALUES (
      'LN', 'Linda', 'Norton', '01-JUN-03');

CREATE TABLE plsql101_product (
      product_name    VARCHAR2(25) PRIMARY KEY,
      product_price   NUMBER(4,2),
      quantity_on_hand NUMBER(5,0),
      last_stock_date  DATE
      )
;

ALTER TABLE plsql101_product ADD CONSTRAINT positive_quantity CHECK(
      quantity_on_hand IS NOT NULL
      AND
      quantity_on_hand >=0
      )
;

INSERT INTO plsql101_product VALUES
      ('Small Widget', 99, 1, '15-JAN-03');
INSERT INTO plsql101_product VALUES
      ('Medium Wodget', 75, 1000, '15-JAN-02');
INSERT INTO plsql101_product VALUES
      ('Chrome Phoobar', 50, 100, '15-JAN-03');
INSERT INTO plsql101_product VALUES
      ('Round Chrome Snaphoo', 25, 10000, null);
INSERT INTO plsql101_product VALUES
```

```
                ('Extra Huge Mega Phoobar +',9.95,1234,'15-JAN-04');
INSERT INTO plsql101_product VALUES ('Square Zinculator',
     45, 1, TO_DATE('December 31, 2002, 11:30 P.M.',
                    'Month dd, YYYY, HH:MI P.M.')
     )
;
INSERT INTO plsql101_product VALUES (
     'Anodized Framifier', 49, 5, NULL);
INSERT INTO plsql101_product VALUES (
     'Red Snaphoo', 1.95, 10, '31-DEC-01');
INSERT INTO plsql101_product VALUES (
     'Blue Snaphoo', 1.95, 10, '30-DEC-01')
;


CREATE TABLE plsql101_purchase (
     product_name  VARCHAR2(25),
     salesperson   VARCHAR2(3),
     purchase_date DATE,
     quantity      NUMBER(4,2)
     )
;

ALTER TABLE plsql101_purchase
ADD PRIMARY KEY (product_name,
                 salesperson,
                 purchase_date
                 )
;

ALTER TABLE plsql101_purchase ADD CONSTRAINT reasonable_date CHECK(
     purchase_date IS NOT NULL
     AND
     TO_CHAR(purchase_date, 'YYYY-MM-DD') >= '2000-06-30'
     )
;

ALTER TABLE plsql101_purchase
     ADD CONSTRAINT plsql101_purchase_fk_product FOREIGN KEY
     (product_name) REFERENCES plsql101_product;

ALTER TABLE plsql101_purchase
     ADD CONSTRAINT plsql101_purchase_fk_person FOREIGN KEY
     (salesperson) REFERENCES plsql101_person;

CREATE INDEX plsql101_purchase_product
ON plsql101_purchase(product_name);
```

```
CREATE INDEX plsql101_purchase_salesperson
ON plsql101_purchase(salesperson);

INSERT INTO plsql101_purchase VALUES
     ('Small Widget', 'CA', '14-JUL-03', 1);
INSERT INTO plsql101_purchase VALUES
     ('Medium Wodget', 'BB', '14-JUL-03', 75);
INSERT INTO plsql101_purchase VALUES
     ('Chrome Phoobar', 'GA', '14-JUL-03', 2);
INSERT INTO plsql101_purchase VALUES
     ('Small Widget', 'GA', '15-JUL-03', 8);
INSERT INTO plsql101_purchase VALUES
     ('Medium Wodget', 'LB', '15-JUL-03', 20);
INSERT INTO plsql101_purchase VALUES
     ('Round Chrome Snaphoo', 'CA', '16-JUL-03', 5);
INSERT INTO plsql101_purchase VALUES (
     'Small Widget', 'CA', '17-JUL-03', 1)
;

UPDATE plsql101_product
SET    product_price = product_price * .9
WHERE  product_name NOT IN (
       SELECT DISTINCT product_name
       FROM   plsql101_purchase
       )
;

CREATE TABLE plsql101_old_item (
     item_id   CHAR(20),
     item_desc CHAR(25)
     )
;

INSERT INTO plsql101_old_item VALUES
     ('LA-101', 'Can, Small');
INSERT INTO plsql101_old_item VALUES
     ('LA-102', 'Can, Large');
INSERT INTO plsql101_old_item VALUES
     ('LA-103', 'Bottle, Small');
INSERT INTO plsql101_old_item VALUES
     ('LA-104', 'Bottle, Large');
INSERT INTO plsql101_old_item VALUES
     ('NY-101', 'Box, Small');
INSERT INTO plsql101_old_item VALUES
     ('NY-102', 'Box, Large');
INSERT INTO plsql101_old_item VALUES
     ('NY-103', 'Shipping Carton, Small');
INSERT INTO plsql101_old_item VALUES
```

```
          ('NY-104', 'Shipping Carton, Large');


CREATE TABLE plsql101_purchase_archive (
     product_name  VARCHAR2(25),
     salesperson   VARCHAR2(3),
     purchase_date DATE,
     quantity      NUMBER(4,2)
     )
;

INSERT INTO plsql101_purchase_archive VALUES
     ('Round Snaphoo', 'BB', '21-JUN-01', 10);
INSERT INTO plsql101_purchase_archive VALUES
     ('Large Harflinger', 'GA', '22-JUN-01', 50);
INSERT INTO plsql101_purchase_archive VALUES
     ('Medium Wodget', 'LB', '23-JUN-01', 20);
INSERT INTO plsql101_purchase_archive VALUES
     ('Small Widget', 'ZZ', '24-JUN-02', 80);
INSERT INTO plsql101_purchase_archive VALUES
     ('Chrome Phoobar', 'CA', '25-JUN-02', 2);
INSERT INTO plsql101_purchase_archive VALUES
     ('Small Widget', 'JT', '26-JUN-02', 50);
```

Describing PL/SQL

PL/SQL provides the features that allow you to do sophisticated processing of information. Every night you want to transfer the day's business summary into a day's summary table—*PL/SQL packages* can help you do this. You want to know whether you need to arrange for extra supplies for purchase orders that are really large—PL/SQL provides *triggers* that will notify you as soon as any order placed is found to be larger than certain limits decided by you. You can use *PL/SQL stored procedures* to compute the your employees' performance to help you decide about bonuses. A nice *PL/SQL function* can calculate the tax withholdings for an employee.

PL/SQL lets you use all the SQL data manipulation, cursor control, and transaction control commands, as well as all the SQL functions and operators. So, you can manipulate Oracle data flexibly and safely. Also, PL/SQL fully supports SQL datatypes. That reduces the need to convert data passed between your applications and the database. PL/SQL also supports dynamic SQL, an advanced programming technique that makes your applications more flexible and versatile. Your programs can build and process SQL data definition, data control, and session control statements "on the fly" at run time.

Before we proceed to learn more about some of these power tools, I will give you some idea about how PL/SQL, SQL, and SQL*Plus relate to each other.

Who's Who in SQL, PL/SQL, and SQL*Plus

Think of a restaurant. You go in and hopefully a well-trained waiter or waitress waits on you. You look through the menu and place an order. The waiter writes down your order and takes it into the kitchen. The kitchen is huge—there are many chefs and assistants. You can see a lot of food—cooked, partially cooked, and uncooked—stored in the kitchen. You can also see people with various jobs: they take the food in and out of storage, prepare a particular type of food (just soups or just salads, for instance), and so forth. Depending on what menu items you ordered, the waiter takes the order to different chefs. Some simple orders are completed by one chef, while more complex orders may require help from assistants, or even multiple chefs. In addition, some orders are standard items—a waiter can just tell a chef "mushroom pizza"—while other orders are custom creations requiring a detailed list of exactly what ingredients you want.

Now alter this scenario a little. Think of an Oracle database as the restaurant's kitchen, with SQL*Plus serving as the waiter taking our orders—scripts, commands, or programs—to the kitchen, or database. Inside the kitchen are two main chefs: SQL and PL/SQL. Like a waiter, SQL*Plus knows what orders it can process on its own, as well as what orders to take to specific chefs. In the same way that a waiter can bring you a glass of water without having to get it from a chef, SQL*Plus can adjust the width of the lines shown on its screen without needing to go to the database.

The commands or programs you enter and execute at the SQL*Plus prompt are somewhat like your special-order pizza. For custom orders the chefs have to do some thinking each time. Just like the chef has the recipe for cheese pizza stored in his or her brain, you can have PL/SQL store "recipes" for your favorite orders. These stored PL/SQL elements are called triggers, stored functions, stored procedures, and packages. You will learn more about them soon.

As I mentioned earlier, some orders require more than one chef to prepare them. Most of the interesting and useful database applications you create will have SQL and PL/SQL working together, passing information back and forth between them to process a script or program. In a restaurant, after an order is prepared it goes to a waiter to be taken to your table. Similarly, when SQL and PL/SQL process commands, the results go to SQL*Plus (or a custom front-end form) to be displayed to the user.

Stored Procedures, Functions, and Triggers

PL/SQL procedures, functions, and triggers all help you build complex business logic easily and in a *modular* fashion (meaning piece by piece, with the pieces being reusable by other pieces). Storing these in the Oracle server provides two immediate benefits: they can be used over and over with predictable results, and they execute very rapidly because server operations involve little or no network traffic.

Stored Procedures

A *stored procedure* is a defined set of actions written using the PL/SQL language. When a procedure is called, it performs the actions it contains. The procedure is stored in the database, which is the reason it is called a stored procedure.

A stored procedure can execute SQL statements and manipulate data in tables. It can be called to do its job from within another PL/SQL stored procedure, stored function, or trigger. A stored procedure can also be called directly from a SQL*Plus prompt. As you read through the pages that follow, you will learn how to employ each of these methods for calling a stored procedure.

A procedure consists of two main parts: the specification and the body. The *procedure specification* contains the procedure's name and a description of its inputs and outputs. The inputs and outputs we are talking about are called the procedure's *formal parameters* or *formal arguments*. If a call to a procedure includes command-line parameters or other inputs, those values are called *actual parameters* or *actual arguments*.

Now let's take a look at some samples of procedure specifications. (Remember, the specification doesn't contain any code; it just names the procedure and defines any inputs and outputs the procedure can use.)

```
run_ytd_reports
```

This simple specification contains only the procedure's name. It has no parameters.

```
increase_prices (percent_increase NUMBER)
```

A value can be passed to this procedure when it is called. Within the procedure, the value will be addressed as PERCENT_INCREASE. Note that the value's datatype has been specified: NUMBER.

```
increase_salary_find_tax (increase_percent IN      NUMBER := 7,
                          sal              IN OUT NUMBER,
                          tax                     OUT NUMBER
                          )
```

Here we have a procedure with three formal parameters. The word IN after a parameter's name indicates that the procedure can read an incoming value from that parameter when the procedure is called. The word OUT after a parameter's name indicates that the procedure can use that parameter to send a value back to whatever called it. Having IN OUT after a parameter's name says that the parameter can bring a value into the procedure and also be used to send a value back out.

The INCREASE_PERCENT parameter in this example gets assigned a *default value* of 7 by including := 7 after the datatype. Because of this, if the procedure is called without specifying any increase percentage, it will increase the salary given by 7 percent and calculate the tax based on the new salary.

NOTE
Datatypes in a procedure cannot have size specifications. For instance, you can specify that a parameter is a NUMBER datatype, but not a NUMBER(10,2) datatype.

The *procedure body* is a block of PL/SQL code, which you will learn about in the next section of this chapter.

Stored Functions

A PL/SQL function is similar to a PL/SQL procedure: It has function specification and a function body. The main difference between a procedure and a function is that a function is designed to return a value that can be used within a larger SQL statement.

For instance, think for a moment about a function designed to calculate the percentage difference between two numbers. Ignoring the code that would perform this calculation, the function specification would look like this:

```
calc_percent(value_1 NUMBER,
             value_2 NUMBER) return NUMBER
```

This function accepts two numbers as input, referring to them internally as VALUE_1 and VALUE_2. Once the body of this function was written, it could be referred to in a SQL statement in the following way:

```
INSERT INTO employee VALUES (3000, CALC_PERCENT(300, 3000));
```

Triggers

A *trigger* is a PL/SQL procedure that gets executed automatically whenever some event defined by the trigger—the *triggering event*—happens. You can write triggers that fire when an INSERT, UPDATE, or DELETE statement is performed on a table; when DDL statements are issued; when a user logs on or off; or when the database starts, encounters an error, or shuts down.

Triggers differ from PL/SQL procedures in three ways:

■   You cannot call a trigger from within your code. Triggers are called automatically by Oracle in response to a predefined event.

- Triggers do not have a parameter list.

- The specification for a trigger contains different information than a specification for a procedure.

You will learn more about triggers and their uses in the next chapter.

Stored Procedures and SQL Scripts

While SQL scripts reside on your computer's hard disk, stored procedures reside within your Oracle database. A SQL script contains a series of SQL commands that are executed, one by one, when you invoke the script. In contrast, a stored procedure can contain flow-control commands allowing it to iterate through a particular section of code over and over; branch to another code section when particular situations occur; and respond to error conditions in a way you specify.

Structure of a PL/SQL Block

In this section you will learn about the PL/SQL *basic block*. Everything in PL/SQL that actually does work is made up of basic blocks. After learning about the basic blocks, you will see examples of complete procedures, functions, and triggers in the next section.

A PL/SQL basic block is made up of four sections: the *header section*, an optional *declaration section*, the *execution section*, and the optional *exception section*.

An *anonymous block* is a PL/SQL block with no header or name section, hence the term anonymous block. Anonymous blocks can be run from SQL*Plus and they can be used within PL/SQL functions, procedures, and triggers. Recall that PL/SQL procedures, functions, and triggers are all made up of basic blocks themselves. What this means is that you can have a basic block within a basic block. You will learn more about this later in this section.

Perhaps the best way to begin to understand a basic block is to examine a sample. First type the following command so that information printed by programs can be made visible in SQL*Plus.

```
set serveroutput on
```

Now try the following sample code to create an anonymous block. Compare your results with Figure 8-1.

```
DECLARE
        Num_a NUMBER := 6;
        Num_b NUMBER;
```

```
BEGIN
        Num_b := 0;
        Num_a := Num_a / Num_b;
        Num_b := 7;
        dbms_output.put_line(' Value of Num_b ' || Num_b);
EXCEPTION
        WHEN ZERO_DIVIDE
THEN
                dbms_output.put_line('Trying to divide by zero');
                dbms_output.put_line(' Value of Num_a ' || Num_a);
                dbms_output.put_line(' Value of Num_b ' || Num_b);
END;
/
```

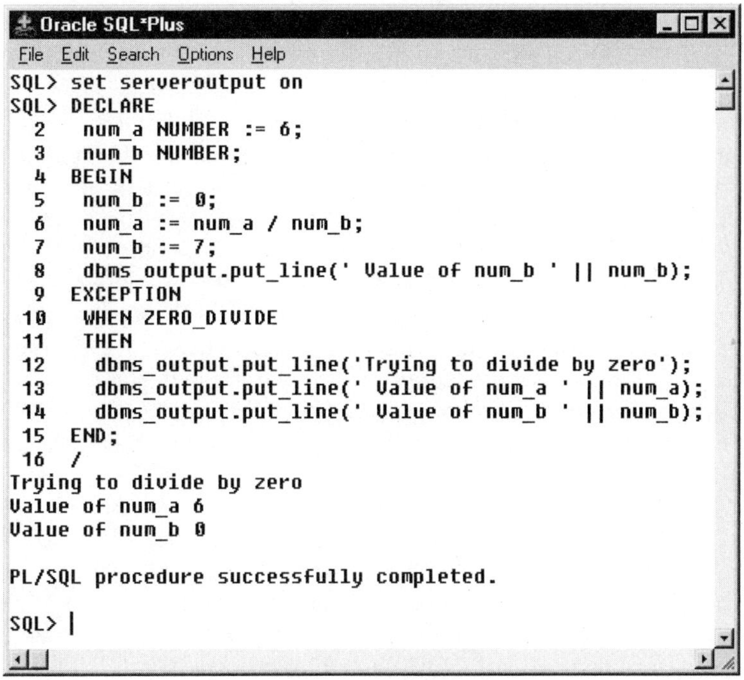

```
Oracle SQL*Plus                                          _ □ ×
File  Edit  Search  Options  Help
SQL> set serveroutput on
SQL> DECLARE
  2    num_a NUMBER := 6;
  3    num_b NUMBER;
  4  BEGIN
  5    num_b := 0;
  6    num_a := num_a / num_b;
  7    num_b := 7;
  8    dbms_output.put_line(' Value of num_b ' || num_b);
  9  EXCEPTION
 10    WHEN ZERO_DIVIDE
 11    THEN
 12    dbms_output.put_line('Trying to divide by zero');
 13    dbms_output.put_line(' Value of num_a ' || num_a);
 14    dbms_output.put_line(' Value of num_b ' || num_b);
 15  END;
 16  /
Trying to divide by zero
Value of num_a 6
Value of num_b 0

PL/SQL procedure successfully completed.

SQL> |
```

FIGURE 8-1. *Example of an anonymous PL/SQL block*

Header Section

The header section for a block varies based on what the block is part of. Recall that procedures, functions, triggers and anonymous blocks are made up of basic blocks. In fact, each has one basic block that makes up its body. This body block may contain more basic blocks inside it. The header for this top-level basic block of a function, procedure, or trigger is the specification for that function, procedure, or trigger. For anonymous blocks the header contains only the keyword DECLARE. For labeled blocks the header contains the name of the label enclosed between << and >>, followed by the keyword DECLARE, as shown here:

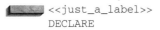
```
<<just_a_label>>
DECLARE
```

Block labels help make it easier to read code. In a procedure using nested blocks (blocks inside other blocks), you can refer to an item in a specific block by preceding the item's name with the name of the block (for example, *block_label.item_label*).

Declaration Section

The declaration section is optional. When used, it begins after the header section and ends at the keyword BEGIN. The declaration section contains the declarations for PL/SQL variables, constants, cursors, exceptions, functions, and procedures that will be used by the execution and exception sections of the block. All variable and constant declarations must come before any function or procedure declarations within the declaration section. You will learn more about PL/SQL variables and constants in the following sections. A declaration tells PL/SQL to create a variable, constant, cursor, function, or procedure as specified in the declaration.

The declaration section in the example shown in Figure 8-1 tells PL/SQL to create two number type variables called Num_a and Num_b. It also assigns a value of 6 by default to Num_a.

When a basic block has finished its run, everything declared within the declaration section stops existing. Things declared within the declaration section of a basic block can be used only within the same block. Thus, after running the example block in SQL*Plus there is no way to pass Num_a to another PL/SQL procedure. Num_a and Num_b just go out of existence as soon as the block finishes its run. However, if you call a PL/SQL function or procedure within the execution or exception section of the block, you can pass Num_a and Num_b to them as actual parameters.

The long and short of the story is, whatever is in the declaration section is the private property of the block—to be used by and visible only to itself. Thus what is in the declaration section of the block only lives as long as the block. In technical terms, Num_a and Num_b are said to have the *scope* of the block in which they are declared. The scope of the block starts at the beginning of the block's declaration section and ends at the end of its exception section.

Execution Section

The execution section starts with the keyword BEGIN and ends in one of two ways. If there is an exception section, the execution section ends with the keyword EXCEPTION. If no exception section is present, the execution section ends with the keyword END, followed optionally by the name of the function or procedure, and a semicolon. The execution section contains one or more PL/SQL statements that are executed when the block is run. The structure for the executable section is shown below.

```
BEGIN
    one or more PL/SQL statements
[exception section]
END [name of function or procedure];
```

The executable section in the example block contains three PL/SQL assignment statements. The assignment statement is the most commonly seen statement in PL/SQL code. The first statement assigns the value of zero to Num_b. The colon followed by an equal sign (:=) is the assignment operator. The assignment operator tells PL/SQL to compute whatever is on its right-hand side and place the result in whatever is on its left-hand side.

The second statement assigns Num_a the value of Num_a divided by Num_b. Note that after this statement is executed successfully the value of Num_a will be changed.

The third statement assigns the value of 7 to Num_b.

Exception Section

It is possible that during the execution of PL/SQL statements in the execution section, an error will be encountered that makes it impossible to proceed with the execution. These error conditions are called *exceptions*. The procedure's user should be informed when an exception occurs and told why it has occurred. You may want to issue a useful error to the user or you may want to take some corrective action and retry whatever the procedure was attempting before the error happened. You may want to roll back changes done to the database before the error occurred.

For all these situations PL/SQL helps you by providing *exception handling* capabilities. Exceptions are so important for good applications that I have a special section at the end of this chapter where you will learn more about them. As an introduction, here is the structure for the exception section.

```
EXCEPTION
    WHEN exception_name
    THEN
        actions to take when this exception occurs
    WHEN exception_name
    THEN
        actions to take when this exception occurs
```

The exception section begins at the keyword EXCEPTION and ends at the end of the block. For each exception there is a WHEN *exception_name* statement that specifies what should be done when a specific exception occurs. Our example has three funny-looking statements that have the effect of making text display on your SQL*Plus screen. A little more information is needed to understand what they are doing but we will leave the details for Chapter 9. The DBMS_OUTPUT package and PUT_LINE procedure are part of the Oracle database; together they cause text to display on your SQL*PLUS screen one line at a time.

All the statements between the statement that causes the exception and the exception section will be ignored. So, in the case of the example block, the assigning of 7 to Num_b is not executed. You can verify this by looking at the value for Num_b that the example code prints out.

When an exception is dealt with by a statement in the exception section, we refer to the action as *exception handling*.

Detecting that the error occurred and which exception best describes it and then taking appropriate steps to inform PL/SQL about it so as to make it possible for PL/SQL to find the exception section for that exception is called *raising exception*. In the example code the exception is raised by PL/SQL on its own by detecting that there is an attempt at division by zero. PL/SQL has a predefined name for this exception—ZERO_DIVIDE. In many situations the error must be detected by your code, not by PL/SQL.

Creating a Simple PL/SQL Procedure

We have all the ingredients to try out writing a complete PL/SQL procedure. You know about the basic block and you have learned about procedure specifications. Try out the following code.

```
CREATE PROCEDURE my_first_proc IS
        greetings VARCHAR2(20);
BEGIN
```

```
        greetings := 'Hello World';
        dbms_output.put_line(greetings);
END my_first_proc;
/
```

The syntax for creating a stored procedure is

CREATE PROCEDURE *procedure_specification* IS *procedure_body*

In our sample, the procedure specification is just the name of the procedure and the body is everything after it up to the last semicolon. For functions you will use the keyword FUNCTION instead of PROCEDURE.

CREATE FUNCTION *function_specification* IS *function_body*

The forward slash (/) tells SQL*Plus to go ahead and process the commands in the program. You can re-create the same procedure or function by changing the command CREATE to CREATE OR REPLACE. This will destroy the old definition of the procedure or function and replace it with the new one. If there is no old definition it will simply create a new one.

CREATE OR REPLACE PROCEDURE *procedure_specification*
IS *procedure_body*

Now let us see how this procedure can be called from SQL*Plus:

```
set serveroutput on
EXECUTE my_first_proc;
```

SERVEROUTPUT ON allows you to see the printed output. The command EXECUTE actually executes the procedure. You can call the procedure from within an anonymous block as follows. Compare your results with those shown in Figure 8-2.

```
BEGIN
        my_first_proc;
END;
/
```

Calling Procedures and Functions

A procedure or function may or may not have formal parameters with default values. In fact, it may not have any formal parameters at all. For each case the way

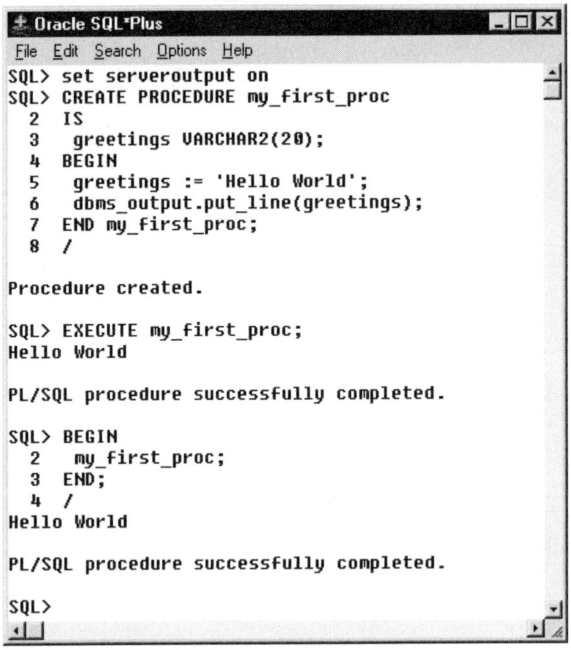

```
Oracle SQL*Plus                                    _ □ X
File  Edit  Search  Options  Help
SQL> set serveroutput on
SQL> CREATE PROCEDURE my_first_proc
  2  IS
  3    greetings VARCHAR2(20);
  4  BEGIN
  5    greetings := 'Hello World';
  6    dbms_output.put_line(greetings);
  7  END my_first_proc;
  8  /

Procedure created.

SQL> EXECUTE my_first_proc;
Hello World

PL/SQL procedure successfully completed.

SQL> BEGIN
  2    my_first_proc;
  3  END;
  4  /
Hello World

PL/SQL procedure successfully completed.

SQL>
```

FIGURE 8-2. *Simple "Hello World" PL/SQL procedure*

the procedure or function is called is different. However, the following applies regardless of the parameters.

■ The datatypes for the actual parameters must match or should be convertible by PL/SQL to the datatypes of corresponding formal parameters.

■ Actual parameters must be provided for all formal parameters that do not have default values.

When calling a function without any parameters, you can just use the name with or without parentheses, like this:

procedure_name();

    or

procedure_name;

The same syntax is used when dealing with a function, except a semicolon will not be used when the function is called as part of an expression.

When a procedure has formal parameters with default values and when they are all at the end of the list of formal parameters in the procedure specification, the procedure may be called without specifying values for the last few formal parameters for which default values exist. However, all the formal parameters for which actual parameters are being supplied at call time must be listed before all of the formal parameters for which no actual parameters are being supplied. The call will then look like this:

```
procedure_name(actual_param1,
               actual_param2,
               ...
               actual_paramN);
```

N may be less than or equal to the number of formal parameters for the procedure and *N* must be greater than or equal to the number of formal parameters for which default values do not exist.

When the default-valued formal parameters are not the last parameters in the specification, or when you wish to avoid having PL/SQL figure out which actual parameter corresponds to which formal parameter using its order in the list, you can specifically tell PL/SQL which actual parameter is for which formal parameter using the following syntax:

```
procedure_name(formal_param1 => actual_param1,
               formal_param2 => actual_param2,
               ...
               )
;
```

This is called *named notation* for calling functions and procedures. The earlier notation is called *positional notation* as the parameters are matched by their position in the list.

The same calling methods apply to functions. Functions, however, can appear within other expressions and may not have any semicolon at the end. You will see an example for named notation in the next section. It is possible to mix two notations but the positional list must precede the notational list in the call.

PL/SQL Variables and Constants

You have seen some examples of PL/SQL variables in previous sections. Now we will discuss them in greater detail. Variables are essentially containers with name tags. They can contain or hold information or data of different kinds. Based on the kind of data they can hold, they have different datatypes and to distinguish them from one another they have names. Just as oil comes in a bottle and flour in a paper bag, PL/SQL will store numbers in variables of the NUMBER datatype and text in CHAR or VARCHAR2 datatype variables. Taking it a step further, imagine the refrigerator in your company's break room. It's filled with brown paper bags that contain your lunch and the lunches of your co-workers. How will you find your noontime feast amongst all the other bags? Right! You'd put your name on the bag. Variables are given names, too, in order to avoid confusion. Further, if your lunch consisted of only bananas you may eat them and put the peels back into the brown paper bag. Now the contents of the bag have changed. Similarly, the contents of variables can be changed during the execution of PL/SQL statements.

Declaring PL/SQL Variables

The syntax for declaring a variable in PL/SQL is either of the following:

variable_name data_type [[NOT NULL] := *default_value_expression*];

variable_name data_type [[NOT NULL] DEFAULT *default_value_expression*];

variable_name is any valid *PL/SQL identifier*. A valid PL/SQL identifier is:

■ Up to 30 characters long and has no white space of any form in it (as space or tabs).

■ Made up of letters, digits 0 to 9, underscore (_), dollar ($) and pound (#) signs.

■ Starts with a letter.

■ Is not the same as a *PL/SQL* or *SQL reserved word,* which has special meaning for PL/SQL or SQL. For example, a variable name cannot be BEGIN. BEGIN has a special meaning telling PL/SQL that here starts the beginning of a basic block execution section.

data_type is any valid SQL or PL/SQL datatype. More information on datatypes can be found in the next section.

The use of NOT NULL requires that the variable have a value and, if specified, the variable must be given a default value.

When a variable is created it can be made to have a value specified by the default value expression. It is just a shorthand way to assign values to variables.

You already know about SQL datatypes—NUMBER, VARCHAR2, and DATE. PL/SQL shares them with SQL. PL/SQL has additional datatypes that are not in SQL. For a complete list, please refer to Oracle PL/SQL references.

Declaring PL/SQL Constants

The syntax for declaring a constant is:

variable_name data_type CONSTANT := *constant_value_expression*;

Unlike variables, constants must be given a value and that value cannot change during the life or scope of the constant. Constants are very useful for enforcing safe and disciplined code development in large and complex applications. For example, if you want to ensure that the data passed to a PL/SQL procedure is not modified by the procedure, you can make that data a constant. If the procedure tries to modify it PL/SQL will return with an exception.

Assigning Values to Variables

There are three ways a variable can get its value changed. Assignment of a valid expression to it using the PL/SQL assignment operator is one. You have seen a number of examples of this kind. The syntax is:

variable_name := *expression* ;

Second, a variable can be passed as the actual parameter corresponding to some IN OUT or OUT formal parameter when calling a PL/SQL procedure. After the procedure is finished the value of the variable may change. The following example shows the named notation for calling procedures. Refer to Figure 8-3 for the expected output.

```
CREATE   PROCEDURE hike_prices (old_price NUMBER,
                                percent_hike NUMBER := 5,
                                new_price OUT NUMBER)
IS
BEGIN
        new_price := old_price + old_price * percent_hike / 100;
END hike_prices;
/
```

The following procedure shows the variables changing their values:

```
DECLARE
        price_to_hike NUMBER(6,2)  := 20;
        hiked_price NUMBER(6,2)  := 0;
BEGIN
        dbms_output.put_line('Price before hike ' || price_to_hike);
        dbms_output.put_line('hiked_price before hike ' || hiked_price);
        hike_prices (old_price => price_to_hike,
                new_price => hiked_price);
        dbms_output.put_line('price_to_hike after hike ' || price_to_hike);
        dbms_output.put_line('hiked_price after hike ' || hiked_price);
END;
/
```

```
± Oracle SQL*Plus                                                    _□×
File  Edit  Search  Options  Help
SQL> set serveroutput on
SQL> CREATE  PROCEDURE hike_prices (old_price NUMBER,
  2                                 percent_hike NUMBER := 5,
  3                                 new_price OUT NUMBER)
  4  IS
  5  BEGIN
  6         new_price := old_price + old_price * percent_hike / 100;
  7  END hike_prices;
  8  /

Procedure created.

SQL> DECLARE
  2          price_to_hike NUMBER(6,2) := 20;
  3          hiked_price NUMBER(6,2) := 0;
  4  BEGIN
  5          dbms_output.put_line('Price before hike ' || price_to_hike);
  6          dbms_output.put_line('hiked_price before hike ' || hiked_price);
  7          hike_prices (old_price => price_to_hike,
  8                       new_price => hiked_price);
  9          dbms_output.put_line('price_to_hike after hike ' || price_to_hike);
 10          dbms_output.put_line('hiked_price after hike ' || hiked_price);
 11  END;
 12  /
Price before hike 20
hiked_price before hike 0
price_to_hike after hike 20
hiked_price after hike 21

PL/SQL procedure successfully completed.

SQL>
```

FIGURE 8-3.   *Assigning values to PL/SQL variables by using them as actual parameters*

The third way of changing or assigning values to variables will be discussed in detail in the next chapter. Here is a quick example and Figure 8-4 shows the results.

```
DECLARE
product_quant          NUMBER;
BEGIN
      SELECT   quantity_on_hand
      INTO     product_quant
      FROM     plsql101_product
      WHERE    product_name = 'Small Widget';
dbms_output.put_line ('Small Widget ' || product_quant);
END;
/
```

product_quant is assigned the value equal to the quantity of small widgets.

```
+ Oracle SQL*Plus                                          _ □ X
File  Edit  Search  Options  Help
SQL> set serveroutput on
SQL> DECLARE
  2    product_quant NUMBER;
  3  BEGIN
  4    SELECT  quantity_on_hand
  5    INTO    product_quant
  6    FROM    plsql101_product
  7    WHERE   product_name = 'Small Widget';
  8
  9    dbms_output.put_line ('Small Widget    ' || product_quant);
 10  END;
 11  /
Small Widget   1

PL/SQL procedure successfully completed.

SQL>
```

FIGURE 8-4. *Assigning values to PL/SQL variables using SQL*

Using Variables

Variables are the very basic units of PL/SQL programs. They are used to hold results of computations, to return values from function calls, as actual parameters for calling functions and procedures, and so on. Variables should be used to make your application clean and easier to read, thereby creating a lower maintenance, more efficient program.

Suppose you want to perform a number of calculations using the current quantity of small widgets—compare it with the quantity from three months ago, or to the quantity of medium widgets. By using the variable to hold the value, you avoid the delay that would come from getting the quantity from the table again and again.

By naming variables in a way that makes sense to you, you can make your code easy to read and understand. The same principle applies when you use variables to hold the results of some very complex expressions instead of repeating the expressions in the code in multiple places.

Control Structures in PL/SQL

Many times you want to do one thing if something is true and something else if it is not true. For example, if a purchase order exceeds a certain dollar amount you would like to take 5 percent off the order, and maybe 10 percent off if the order exceeds some other amount. This kind of logic may be required inside your application that prints out the final invoice for your customers. This is *conditional processing* of data. Based on the condition, different parts of the code need to be executed.

Recall the case where you need to compute income tax for each employee. You need to complete a function for each employee such as finding the earnings and filing status and then applying the correct formula to find the tax. The correct formula differs for each employee based on filing status and all of the other factors. This is an example of an *iterative operation*.

PL/SQL provides you with the ability to do conditional and iterative processing. The constructs it provides are said to cause change of *program flow* and so control *the flow of the execution*.

IF Statement

The syntax for an IF statement is as follows:

```
IF condition_1 THEN
    actions_1;
[ELSIF condition_2 THEN
    actions_2;]
...
[ELSE
    actions_last;]
END IF;
```

actions_1 to *actions_last* represent one or more PL/SQL statements. Each set of statements gets executed only if its corresponding condition is true. When one of the IF conditions is determined to be true, the rest of the conditions are not checked.

Enter the following example and see that your results match those of Figure 8-5.

```
-- Compute discounts on orders.
-- Input order amount. Returns discount amount (zero for wrong inputs).
CREATE FUNCTION compute_discounts (order_amt NUMBER)
RETURN NUMBER IS
        small_order_amt NUMBER := 400;
        large_order_amt NUMBER := 1000;
        small_disct NUMBER := 1;
        large_disct NUMBER := 5;
BEGIN
        IF (order_amt < large_order_amt
           AND
           order_amt >= small_order_amt)
        THEN
            RETURN (order_amt * small_disct / 100);
        ELSIF (order_amt >= large_order_amt)
        THEN
```

```
                RETURN (order_amt * large_disct / 100);
        ELSE
                RETURN(0);
        END IF;
END compute_discounts;
/
```

```
 Oracle SQL*Plus                                                        _ □ X
File  Edit  Search  Options  Help
SQL> CREATE FUNCTION compute_discounts (order_amt NUMBER)
  2   RETURN NUMBER
  3   IS
  4           small_order_amt NUMBER := 400;
  5           large_order_amt NUMBER := 1000;
  6           small_disct NUMBER := 1;
  7           large_disct NUMBER := 5;
  8   BEGIN
  9           IF (order_amt < large_order_amt
 10               AND
 11               order_amt >= small_order_amt)
 12           THEN
 13                   RETURN (order_amt * small_disct / 100);
 14           ELSIF (order_amt >= large_order_amt)
 15           THEN
 16                   RETURN (order_amt * large_disct / 100);
 17           ELSE
 18                   RETURN(0);
 19           END IF;
 20   END compute_discounts;
 21   /

Function created.

SQL> DECLARE
  2           tiny NUMBER := 20;
  3           med NUMBER := 600;
  4           big NUMBER := 4550;
  5           wrong NUMBER := -35;
  6   BEGIN
  7           dbms_output.put_line (' Order      AND      Discount ');
  8           dbms_output.put_line (tiny || '  ' || compute_discounts(tiny));
  9           dbms_output.put_line (med || '  ' || compute_discounts (med));
 10           dbms_output.put_line (big || '  ' || compute_discounts (big));
 11           dbms_output.put_line (wrong || '  ' || compute_discounts (wrong));
 12   END;
 13   /
Order      AND      Discount
20  0
600  6
4550  227.5
-35  0

PL/SQL procedure successfully completed.

SQL>
```

FIGURE 8-5.   *Example of an IF statement*

This function will give a 1 percent discount for orders between 400 and 1000 and a 5 percent discount on orders above 1000. It will return zero for all other amounts including wrong values. For example, someone may try to use a negative value for *order_amt*, which is meaningless.

Observe at the start how the function is clearly documented. You should always consider all possibilities when writing your code and either clearly state in your documentation what you are going to do about error conditions or, if the conditions are severe enough, give appropriate error messages. Suppose in our case—however unimaginable it is—that this function may be called with a negative value for the *order_amt*, we have documented what the function will do in such a case.

You can test the function by calling it in an anonymous block. Be sure you have serveroutput on. Refer once again to Figure 8-5 for this example.

```
DECLARE
        tiny NUMBER := 20;
        med NUMBER := 600;
        big NUMBER := 4550;
        wrong NUMBER := -35;
BEGIN
        dbms_output.put_line (' Order      AND      Discount ');
        dbms_output.put_line (tiny || ' ' || compute_discounts(tiny));
        dbms_output.put_line (med || ' ' || compute_discounts (med));
        dbms_output.put_line (big || ' ' || compute_discounts (big));
        dbms_output.put_line (wrong || ' ' || compute_discounts (wrong));
END;
/
```

Loops

PL/SQL provides three different iteration constructs. Each allows you to repeatedly execute a set of PL/SQL statements. You stop the repeated executions based on some condition.

LOOP

The syntax for the LOOP construct is:

```
<<loop_name>>
LOOP
    statements;
    EXIT loop_name [WHEN exit_condition_expression];
    statements;
END LOOP ;
```

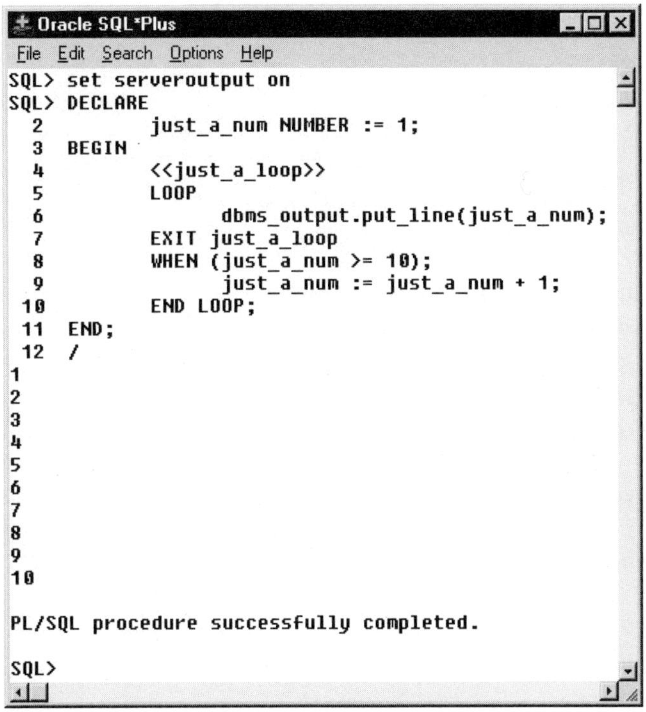

```
Oracle SQL*Plus                                          _□X
File  Edit  Search  Options  Help
SQL> set serveroutput on
SQL> DECLARE
  2             just_a_num NUMBER := 1;
  3   BEGIN
  4             <<just_a_loop>>
  5             LOOP
  6                     dbms_output.put_line(just_a_num);
  7             EXIT just_a_loop
  8             WHEN (just_a_num >= 10);
  9                     just_a_num := just_a_num + 1;
 10             END LOOP;
 11   END;
 12   /
1
2
3
4
5
6
7
8
9
10

PL/SQL procedure successfully completed.

SQL>
```

FIGURE 8-6. *Example of a simple LOOP*

All the statements within the loop are executed repeatedly and during each
repetition or *iteration* of the loop the exit condition expression is checked for positive
value if the WHEN condition is present. If the expression is true the execution skips all
statements following the EXIT and jumps to the first statement after END LOOP within
the code. No more iterations are done. If the WHEN condition is not present the effect
is to execute statements between LOOP and EXIT only once. You will obviously be
doing something illogical if you are not using the WHEN condition. After all, the idea
of a loop is to potentially loop through the code.

Try out the loop example below and compare the results with Figure 8-6. It
simply prints out the first ten numbers.

As usual, do not forget to set serveroutput on to see the output.

```
DECLARE
        just_a_num NUMBER := 1;
```

```
BEGIN
        <<just_a_loop>>
        LOOP
                dbms_output.put_line(just_a_num);
        EXIT just_a_loop
        WHEN (just_a_num >= 10);
                just_a_num := just_a_num + 1;
        END LOOP;
END;
/
```

Each iteration increments the variable *just_a_num* by 1. When 10 is reached, the exit condition is satisfied and the loop is exited.

WHILE Loop

Another type of loop is the WHILE loop. A WHILE loop is well suited for situations when the number of loop iterations is not known in advance, but rather is determined by some external factor. The syntax for a WHILE loop is as follows:

WHILE *while_condition_expression*
LOOP
    statements;
END LOOP;

Practice creating a WHILE loop by entering the following code. Your results should match those of Figure 8-7.

```
DECLARE
        just_a_num NUMBER := 1;
BEGIN
        WHILE (just_a_num <= 10) LOOP
            dbms_output.put_line(just_a_num);
            just_a_num := just_a_num + 1;
        END LOOP;
END;
/
```

Every time before entering the loop the condition for the WHILE must be true.

FOR Loop

The FOR loop uses a counter variable, also called a *loop index*, to count the number of iterations. The counter is incremented starting from the lower limit specified or

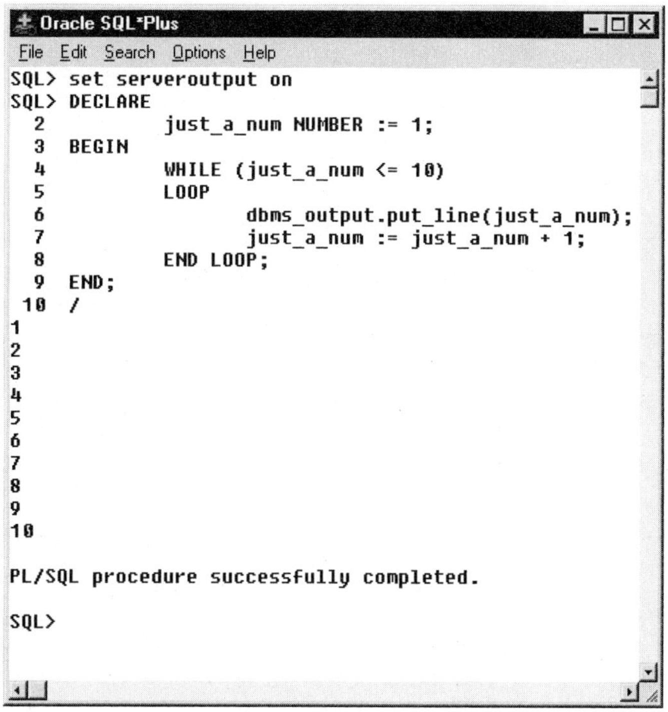

```
± Oracle SQL*Plus                                    _ □ ×
 File  Edit  Search  Options  Help
SQL> set serveroutput on
SQL> DECLARE
  2             just_a_num NUMBER := 1;
  3    BEGIN
  4             WHILE (just_a_num <= 10)
  5             LOOP
  6                      dbms_output.put_line(just_a_num);
  7                      just_a_num := just_a_num + 1;
  8             END LOOP;
  9    END;
 10    /
1
2
3
4
5
6
7
8
9
10

PL/SQL procedure successfully completed.

SQL>
```

FIGURE 8-7.   *Example of a WHILE loop*

decremented starting from the upper limit specified at the end of each iteration or loop. If it is out of the range the looping stops. The syntax for the FOR loop is as follows:

FOR *counter* IN [REVERSE] *lower_bound .. upper_bound*
LOOP
    statements;
END LOOP;

Now create your first FOR loop using the following code. See Figure 8-8.

```
BEGIN
        FOR just_a_num IN 1..10
        LOOP
```

```
                dbms_output.put_line(just_a_num);
        END LOOP;
END;
/
```

Now for fun and experience, try using the command REVERSE in your FOR loop. Your results should show the numbers in reverse order from 10 to 1.

Cursors

The cursor is an extremely important PL/SQL construct. It is the heart of PL/SQL and SQL cooperation and stands for "current set of records." A cursor is a special PL/SQL element that has an associated SQL SELECT statement. Using a cursor, each row of the SQL statement associated with the cursor can be processed one at a time. A cursor is declared in the declaration section of a basic block. A cursor is opened using the command OPEN and rows can be fetched using the command FETCH.

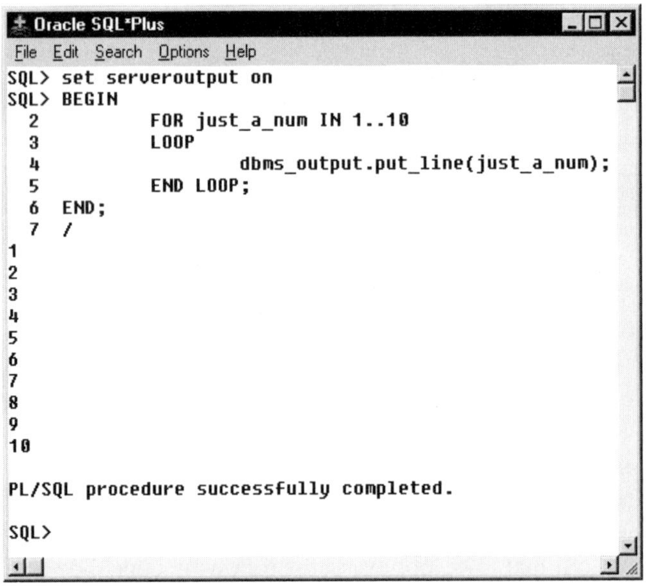

FIGURE 8-8. *Example of a FOR loop*

After all processing is done, the cursor is closed using the command CLOSE. Closing the cursor releases all of the system resources that were used while the cursor was open. You can lock the rows selected by a cursor to prevent other people from modifying them while you are using them. Closing the cursor or executing an explicit COMMIT or ROLLBACK will unlock the rows.

PL/SQL uses hidden or *implicit cursors* for SQL statements within PL/SQL code. We discuss them more in the next chapter. In this section we will focus on *explicit cursors*, which simply means cursors that have been assigned a name.

We will write a simple procedure that uses a cursor to compute the commissions for all salespersons. Before we do that, however, take a look at the syntax for an explicit cursor.

Cursor Declaration and Cursor Attributes

A cursor is declared within a PL/SQL procedure in the following manner:

```
CURSOR cursor_name [( [parameter1 [, parameter2 ...])]
[RETURN return_specification]
IS
    select_statement
        [FOR UPDATE
            [OF table_or_col1
                [, table_or_col2 ...]
            ]
        ]
    ;
```

The parameters are similar to procedure parameters but they are all IN parameters. They cannot be OUT or IN OUT because the cursor cannot modify them. The parameters are used in the WHERE clause of the cursor SELECT statement. The return specification tells what type of records will be selected by the SELECT statement. You will learn more about PL/SQL records in the next chapter. The *table_or_col* is a column name you intend to update or a table name from which you intend to delete or update rows and it must be taken from the names of tables and columns used within the cursor SELECT statement. It is used to clearly document what may potentially be modified by the code that uses this cursor. The commands FOR UPDATE lock the rows selected by the SELECT statement when the cursor is opened and they remain locked until you close the cursor in the ways already discussed.

A cursor has some indicators to show its state and they are called *attributes of the cursor*. The attributes are shown in Table 8-1.

Attribute	Description
cursor_name%ISOPEN	Checks if the cursor is open. It returns TRUE if the cursor *cursor_name* is already open.
cursor_name%ROWCOUNT	The number of table rows returned by the cursor SELECT statement.
cursor_name%FOUND	Checks whether the last attempt to get a record from the cursor succeeded. It returns TRUE if a record was fetched.
cursor_name%NOTFOUND	Opposite of the FOUND attribute. It returns TRUE when no more records are found.

TABLE 8-1. *Cursor Attributes*

PL/SQL Records

Although PL/SQL records will be discussed in greater detail in the next chapter, you'll need to know a little something about them before we proceed. So let's start with a brief introduction in this chapter.

A PL/SQL record is a collection of data of basic types and can be accessed as a single unit. You access the individual fields of the record using the *record_name.field_name* notation you are already familiar with for use with table columns. Records are of three types and you can declare variables of record types. The three types of records are:

- **Table-Based**   The record has fields that match the names and types of the table columns. So if a cursor selects the entire row—by using SELECT* from *some_table,* for example—the records it returns can be directly copied into the variable of the table-based record type for *some_table.*

- **Cursor-Based**   The record fields match in name, datatype, and order to the final list of columns in the cursor's SELECT statement.

- **Programmer-Defined**   These are records in which you define a record type.

Using OPEN, FETCH, and CLOSE Cursor

Here is the syntax for opening, fetching from, and closing a cursor:

OPEN *cursor_name*;

FETCH *cursor_name* INTO *record_var_or_list_of_var*;

CLOSE *cursor_name*;

When opened, a cursor contains a set of records if the cursor's SELECT statement was successful and resulted in fetching selected rows from the database. Each FETCH then removes a record from the open cursor and moves the record's contents into either a PL/SQL variable—of a record type that matches the record type of the cursor record—or into a different set of PL/SQL variables such that each variable in the list matches in type with the corresponding field in the cursor record.

You will check if there are any more records left in the cursor before trying to fetch one from the cursor using the FOUND and NOTFOUND attributes of the cursor. Fetching from an empty cursor will fetch the last fetched record over and over again and will not give you any error. So make sure you use FOUND or NOTFOUND if you are using FETCH.

The actual processing of records from a cursor usually occurs within a loop. When writing the loop, it's a good idea to start by checking whether a record has been found in the cursor. If so, the code proceeds to perform whatever processing you need; if not, the code exits from the loop. There is a more compact way to do the same where PL/SQL takes care of opening, fetching, and closing without your needing to do it—the cursor FOR loop.

Cursor FOR Loop
The syntax for the cursor FOR loop is:

```
FOR cursor_record IN cursor_name LOOP
    statements;
END LOOP;
```

This cursor FOR loop continues fetching records from the cursor into the *cursor_record* record type variable. You can use *cursor_record* fields to access the data within your PL/SQL statements in the loop. When all the records are done, the loop ends. The cursor is automatically opened and closed for your convenience by PL/SQL.

You will receive an *invalid cursor* message if you try to fetch from a cursor that is not open. If you do not close cursors you may end up eventually running into the maximum number of open cursors that the system allows. Note that the implicit cursors—which will be discussed later—also count toward this limit.

WHERE CURRENT OF
When the cursor is opened in order to update or delete the rows it selects, you can use

WHERE CURRENT OF *cursor_name*

to access the table and row corresponding to the most recently fetched record in the WHERE clause of the UPDATE or DELETE statement. For example, to reduce the prices in the PLSQL101_PRODUCT table by 3 percent, type the following code and check your results against those in Figure 8-9.

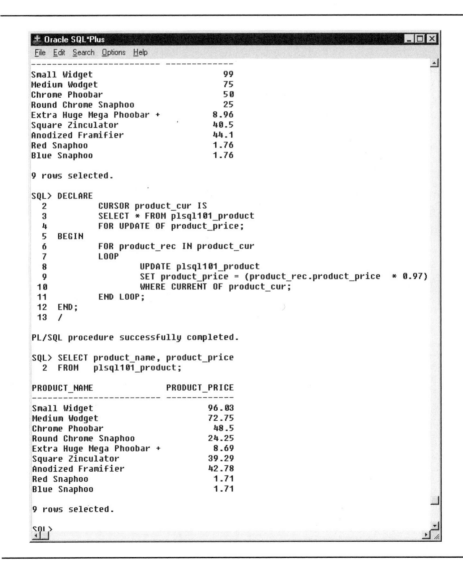

```
Oracle SQL*Plus

File  Edit  Search  Options  Help
─────────────────────────  ─────────────
Small Widget                          99
Medium Wodget                         75
Chrome Phoobar                        50
Round Chrome Snaphoo                  25
Extra Huge Mega Phoobar +           8.96
Square Zinculator                   40.5
Anodized Framifier                  44.1
Red Snaphoo                         1.76
Blue Snaphoo                        1.76

9 rows selected.

SQL> DECLARE
  2         CURSOR product_cur IS
  3         SELECT * FROM plsql101_product
  4         FOR UPDATE OF product_price;
  5  BEGIN
  6         FOR product_rec IN product_cur
  7         LOOP
  8                UPDATE plsql101_product
  9                SET product_price = (product_rec.product_price  * 0.97)
 10                WHERE CURRENT OF product_cur;
 11         END LOOP;
 12  END;
 13  /

PL/SQL procedure successfully completed.

SQL> SELECT product_name, product_price
  2  FROM   plsql101_product;

PRODUCT_NAME             PRODUCT_PRICE
───────────────────────  ─────────────
Small Widget                     96.03
Medium Wodget                    72.75
Chrome Phoobar                    48.5
Round Chrome Snaphoo             24.25
Extra Huge Mega Phoobar +         8.69
Square Zinculator                39.29
Anodized Framifier               42.78
Red Snaphoo                       1.71
Blue Snaphoo                      1.71

9 rows selected.

SQL>
```

FIGURE 8-9. *Examples of a cursor FOR loop and WHERE CURRENT OF clause*

```
SELECT product_name, product_price
FROM   plsql101_product;

DECLARE
     CURSOR product_cur IS
     SELECT * FROM plsql101_product
     FOR UPDATE OF product_price;
BEGIN
     FOR product_rec IN product_cur
     LOOP
          UPDATE plsql101_product
          SET    product_price = (product_rec.product_price * 0.97)
          WHERE  CURRENT OF product_cur;
     END LOOP;
END;
/

SELECT product_name, product_price
FROM   plsql101_product;
```

Nested Loops and Cursor Example

The following code demonstrates complete use of cursors and loops within loops or *nested loops*. Enter the following code:

```
-- This procedure computes the commissions for salespersons.
-- It prints outthe salesperson's code, his or her total sales,
-- and corresponding commission.
-- No inputs. No errors are reported and no exceptions are raised.
/* Logic: A cursor to create a join between PLSQL101_PRODUCT and
PLSQL101_PURCHASE on PRODUCT_NAME column is done.
The result is ordered by salesperson.
Outer loop starts with a new salesperson and inner loop
processes all rows for one salesperson.
*/
CREATE OR REPLACE PROCEDURE do_commissions IS
     commission_rate NUMBER   := 2   ;
     total_sale      NUMBER   := 0   ;
     current_person  CHAR(3) := ' ' ;
     next_person     CHAR(3)         ;
     quantity_sold   NUMBER   := 0   ;
     item_price      NUMBER   := 0   ;
     CURSOR sales_cur IS
          SELECT tab1.salesperson,
                 tab1.quantity,
                 tab2.product_price
          FROM   plsql101_purchase tab1,
```

```
                    plsql101_product  tab2
            WHERE  tab1.product_name = tab2.product_name
            ORDER BY salesperson;
BEGIN
     OPEN sales_cur;
     LOOP
          FETCH sales_cur INTO
               next_person, quantity_sold, item_price;
          WHILE (next_person = current_person
                AND
                sales_cur%FOUND)
          LOOP
              total_sale :=
                   total_sale + (quantity_sold * item_price);
                 FETCH sales_cur INTO
                    next_person, quantity_sold, item_price;
          END LOOP;
          IF (sales_cur%FOUND)
          THEN
               IF (current_person != next_person)
               THEN
                    IF (current_person != ' ' )
                    THEN
                         dbms_output.put_line
                            (current_person ||
                             ' ' ||
                             total_sale ||
                             ' ' ||
                             total_sale * commission_rate / 100);
                    END IF;
                    total_sale := quantity_sold * item_price;
                    current_person := next_person;
               END IF;
          ELSE IF (current_person != ' ')
          THEN
                dbms_output.put_line(current_person ||
                             ' ' ||
                             total_sale ||
                             ' ' ||
                             total_sale * commission_rate / 100);
               END IF;
          END IF;
          EXIT WHEN sales_cur%NOTFOUND;
          END LOOP;
          CLOSE sales_cur;
     END do_commissions;
/
```

First look at the cursor's SELECT statement. It lists, from the PLSQL101_PURCHASE table, the quantities of items sold. It also shows their corresponding prices from the PLSQL101_PRODUCT table. This is achieved by creating a join. The result is ordered by salesperson so that we have all of the records for a particular salesperson together.

Once the cursor is opened and the first row is fetched, the condition for WHILE is checked. The first FETCH command for the current person has a value that cannot match any salesperson code; recall that its default value is a single space ( ). Therefore, the loop is skipped and we jump to the first IF statement. The IF statement checks to see if the last FETCH command returned any records. If records were returned, a check is made to see whether the *current_person* and *next_person* values match. If they don't match, we know that the last FETCH is the start of a new salesperson and it is time to print out the commissions for the current salesperson. Note that the first record for *current_person* is not valid; therefore, the IF check will fail and nothing will print.

The next statement sets the value for *total_sale* to be equal to the cost for the very first product. The statement after that stores the *next_person* value into the *current_person* variable. Now we will be back to the first FETCH in the loop as the loop's EXIT condition is not yet true. This FETCH may result in the same value for *next_person* as the *current_person*, in which case we have more than one entry for the current person in our list of sales. When that is the case, the WHILE loop is entered and the cost for items is added to the total sale amount. This loop will keep adding costs by fetching new records from the cursor until a new salesperson is identified. This process repeats over and over until there are no records left in the cursor. At that point, the validity of the *current_person* is checked. If the *current_person* is valid, then the very last IF statement prints out sales and commissions for that person; the commissions are calculated using the value in the *commission_rate* constant.

To test the procedure, enter the following commands and compare your results with those in Figure 8-10. The first command shows the raw records in the PLSQL101_PURCHASE table, while the second command causes the DO_COMMISSIONS procedure to subtotal the sales in those records and calculate appropriate commissions for each salesperson.

```
SELECT  tab1.salesperson,
        tab1.quantity,
        tab2.product_price
FROM    plsql101_purchase tab1,
        plsql101_product   tab2
WHERE   tab1.product_name - tab2.product_name
ORDER BY salesperson;

EXECUTE do_commissions;
```

```
± Oracle SQL*Plus                                    _ □ ×
File  Edit  Search  Options  Help
 61                          END IF;                        ▲
 62                  END IF;
 63
 64                  EXIT WHEN sales_cur%NOTFOUND;
 65          END LOOP;
 66          CLOSE sales_cur;
 67  END do_commissions;
 68  /

Procedure created.

SQL>        SELECT
  2                  tab1.salesperson,
  3                  tab1.quantity,
  4                  tab2.product_price
  5          FROM    plsql101_purchase tab1,
  6                  plsql101_product tab2
  7          WHERE   tab1.product_name = tab2.product_name
  8          ORDER BY salesperson;

SAL   QUANTITY PRODUCT_PRICE
---  ---------- -------------
BB          75        72.75
CA           1        96.03
CA           5        24.25
CA           1        96.03
GA           8        96.03
GA           2         48.5
LB          20        72.75

7 rows selected.

SQL> EXECUTE do_commissions;
BB  5456.25 109.125
CA  313.31 6.2662
GA  865.24 17.3048
LB  1455 29.1

PL/SQL procedure successfully completed.

SQL>                                                        ▼
◄                                                          ► //
```

FIGURE 8-10. *Example of nested loops*

Error Handling

It is important to issue user-friendly error messages when error conditions occur. Earlier in this chapter the section on basic PL/SQL blocks included a mention of exceptions; now it is time to get into more detail.

Exceptions

An exception is an error state that is activated—or *raised*—when a specific problem occurs. There are many different exceptions, each relating to a different type of problem. When an exception is raised, the code execution stops at the statement that raised the exception, and control is passed to the exception-handling portion of the block. If the block does not contain an executable section, PL/SQL tries to find an executable section in the *enclosing basic block*, which is an outer block of code surrounding the block in which the exception was raised. If the immediate enclosing block does not have an exception handler to accommodate the raised exception, then the search continues to the next enclosing block and so on until a proper exception handler is found or, if not found, execution is halted with an unhandled exception error.

The exception-handling portion of a block is the perfect opportunity to issue meaningful error messages and clean up anything that could cause confusion or trouble later. A typical cleanup could involve issuing the ROLLBACK statement if an exception is raised during a procedure that has inserted rows into a table.

Once control is passed to the exception handler, control is not returned to the statement that caused the exception. Instead, control is passed to the enclosing basic block at the point just after the enclosed block or procedure/function was called.

System-Defined Exceptions

You are familiar with the ZERO_DIVIDE exception predefined by PL/SQL. There are quite a few other system-defined exceptions that are detected and raised by PL/SQL or Oracle. Table 8-2 provides a more complete list of system-defined exceptions.

PL/SQL has two ways of showing a user information about an error. One option is the use of the command SQLCODE, which returns the error code. An error code is a negative value that usually equals the value of the corresponding ORA error that would be issued if the exception remains unhandled when an application terminates. The other option returns a text message regarding the error. Not surprisingly, this command is SQLERRM. You can use both SQLCODE and SQLERM in the exception handler. Note: not all system-defined exceptions are named.

System-Defined Exception	Description
CURSOR_ALREADY_OPEN	Tried to open an already open cursor.
DUP_VAL_ON_INDEX	Attempted to insert duplicate value in column restricted by unique index to be unique.
INVALID_CURSOR	Tried to FETCH from cursor that was not open or tried to close a cursor that was not open.
NO_DATA_FOUND	Tried to SELECT INTO when the SELECT returns no rows (as well as other conditions that are outside the scope of this book).
PROGRAM_ERROR	Internal error. Usually means you need to contact Oracle support.
STORAGE_ERROR	Program ran out of system memory.
TIME_OUT_ON_RESOURCE	Program waited for some resource to be available for too long.
TOO_MANY_ROWS	SELECT INTO in PL/SQL returns more than one row.
VALUE_ERROR	PL/SQL encountered invalid data conversions, truncations, or constraints on data.
ZERO_DIVIDE	Attempt at division by zero.
OTHERS	All other exceptions or internal errors not covered by the exceptions defined in the basic block. Used when you are not sure which named exception you are handling but you do want to handle whichever exception was raised.

TABLE 8-2. *System-Defined Exceptions*

Now try the previous example again, but this time use SQLCODE and SQLERRM. Enter the following code and compare your results with those shown in Figure 8-11.

```
DECLARE
    Num_a NUMBER := 6;
    Num_b NUMBER;
BEGIN
    Num_b := 0;
```

```
    Num_a := Num_a / Num_b;
    Num_b := 7;
    dbms_output.put_line(' Value of Num_b ' || Num_b);
EXCEPTION
    WHEN ZERO_DIVIDE THEN
        DECLARE
            err_num NUMBER         := SQLCODE;
            err_msg VARCHAR2(512) := SQLERRM;
        BEGIN
            dbms_output.put_line('ORA Error Number '  || err_num );
            dbms_output.put_line('ORA Error message ' || err_msg);
            dbms_output.put_line(' Value of Num_a '   || Num_a);
            dbms_output.put_line(' Value of Num_b '   || Num_b);
        END;
END;
/
```

```
Oracle SQL*Plus                                                    _ □ ×
File  Edit  Search  Options  Help
SQL> set serveroutput on
SQL> DECLARE
  2    num_a NUMBER := 6;
  3    num_b NUMBER;
  4  BEGIN
  5        num_b := 0;
  6        num_a := num_a / num_b;
  7        num_b := 7;
  8        dbms_output.put_line(' Value of num_b ' || num_b);
  9  EXCEPTION
 10        WHEN ZERO_DIVIDE
 11        THEN
 12            DECLARE
 13                    err_num NUMBER := SQLCODE;
 14                    err_msg VARCHAR2(512) := SQLERRM;
 15            BEGIN
 16                    dbms_output.put_line('ORA Error Number ' || err_num );
 17                    dbms_output.put_line('ORA Error message ' || err_msg);
 18                    dbms_output.put_line(' Value of num_a ' || num_a);
 19                    dbms_output.put_line(' Value of num_b ' || num_b);
 20            END;
 21  END;
 22  /
ORA Error Number -1476
ORA Error message ORA-01476: divisor is equal to zero
Value of num_a 6
Value of num_b 0

PL/SQL procedure successfully completed.

SQL>
```

FIGURE 8-11. *Using SQLCODE and SQLERRM for system-defined exceptions*

Programmer-Defined Exceptions

One handy feature of PL/SQL is that it allows you to create your own exception conditions and names. When raising and handling your own exceptions, they must be named and declared just like any other PL/SQL entity.

Here is a complete example of how to name and define your own exception. Enter the following code and compare your results with those shown in Figure 8-12.

```
set serveroutput on
DECLARE
        quantity1 NUMBER := -2;
        quantity2 NUMBER := 3;
        total NUMBER := 0;
        quantity_must_positive EXCEPTION;
        FUNCTION find_cost (quant NUMBER) RETURN NUMBER IS
        BEGIN
            IF (quant > 0)
            THEN
                RETURN(quant * 20);
            ELSE
                RAISE quantity_must_positive;
            END IF;
        END find_cost;
BEGIN
        total := find_cost (quantity2);
        total := total + find_cost(quantity1);
EXCEPTION
        WHEN quantity_must_positive
        THEN
            dbms_output.put_line('Total until now: ' || total);
            dbms_output.put_line('Tried to use negative quantity ');
END;
/
```

The exception is declared in the declaration section. Just like any other PL/SQL variable declared there, the life of the exception is valid only for this block. Since *find_cost* is also in this block or is enclosed by this block, it can use the exception name. If the same function was defined as, say, a stored function you could not use the same exception name.

You can use your own exceptions for application-specific exception conditions that otherwise cannot be detected by the system or have no meaning for the system. For example, the system does not know that quantities ordered must be positive integer values. Your application should know this, however, and you can enforce it by catching values that are not positive integers as an exception while doing computations based on quantities. This is a very simple example, but you can imagine and will certainly come across more complex cases in real-life applications.

```
Oracle SQL*Plus                                                      _ □ ×
File  Edit  Search  Options  Help
SQL> set serveroutput on
SQL> DECLARE
  2          quantity1 NUMBER := -2;
  3          quantity2 NUMBER := 3;
  4          total NUMBER := 0;
  5          quantity_must_positive EXCEPTION;
  6          FUNCTION find_cost (quant NUMBER) RETURN NUMBER IS
  7          BEGIN
  8                  IF (quant > 0)
  9                  THEN
 10                          RETURN(quant * 20);
 11                  ELSE
 12                          RAISE quantity_must_positive;
 13                  END IF;
 14          END find_cost;
 15  BEGIN
 16          total := find_cost (quantity2);
 17          total := total + find_cost(quantity1);
 18  EXCEPTION
 19          WHEN quantity_must_positive
 20          THEN
 21                  dbms_output.put_line('Total until now: ' || total);
 22                  dbms_output.put_line('Tried to use negative quantity ');
 23  END;
 24  /
Total until now: 60
Tried to use negative quantity

PL/SQL procedure successfully completed.

SQL>
```

FIGURE 8-12.   *Programmer-defined exception*

Summary

This chapter served as an introduction to the wonderful world of PL/SQL—a powerful programming language that works hand in hand with SQL. We explored PL/SQL variables. PL/SQL variables are used to hold the results of computations and to carry those results from one computation task to another.

We discussed the aspects of the PL/SQL basic block. All PL/SQL program units are made up of one or more basic blocks. A basic block is made up of header, declaration, execution, and exception sections. The header section contains identifying information for the block. For anonymous blocks, the header section is empty. The declaration section contains declarations for variables, constants, exceptions, cursors, functions, and procedures to be used within the block's execution and exception sections; if none of these are used, the declaration section will be empty. The execution section contains PL/SQL executable statements. The execution section is not optional and must be present to form a block. The exception section is used to handle error, or exception, conditions occurring within the execution section. This includes exceptions that may not be handled within any enclosed or nested blocks and within functions or procedures called.

We discussed how to create and call functions and procedures. You learned the meaning and use of formal and actual parameters.

Recall that PL/SQL program flow control constructs allow you to conditionally execute a piece of code once or repeatedly. The IF statement allows conditional execution once. The LOOP, WHILE loop, and FOR loop allow for repeated execution of the same set of statements. Cursors are the means for PL/SQL to communicate with SQL and hence the database. The cursor FOR loop allows you to process rows of tables one at a time.

Finally, you learned how to define your own exceptions and to raise or handle them by issuing friendly error messages. Another option is to remove what's causing the error and try again to create a successful program.

We have covered a lot of ground in this chapter and it has been the foundation for Chapter 9. You are probably eager to play with PL/SQL's powerful features. Have some fun, and then jump right into the next chapter.

Chapter Questions

1. Which of the following are true about PL/SQL procedures and functions?

    A. There is no difference between the two.

    B. A function has a return type in its specification and must return a value specified in that type. A procedure does not have a return type in its specification and should not return any value, but it can have a return statement that simply stops its execution and returns to the caller.

    C. Both may have formal parameters of OUT or IN OUT modes but a function should not have OUT or IN OUT mode parameters.

    D. Both can be used in a WHERE clause of SQL SELECT statement.

2. Which is the correct output for a run of the following code sample?

```
<<outer_block>>
DECLARE
    scope_num NUMBER := 3;
BEGIN
    DECLARE
        scope_num NUMBER := 6;
        Num_a     NUMBER := outer_block.scope_num;
    BEGIN
```

```
        dbms_output.put_line(scope_num);
        dbms_output.put_line(Num_a);
    END;
    dbms_output.put_line(scope_num);
END;
```

A. 6 3 3

B. Gives error saying duplicate declaration and aborts execution

C. 3 3 3

D. 6 3 6

3. Which of the following is true about IF statements?

A. At most one set of executable statements gets executed corresponding to the condition that is TRUE. All other statements are not executed.

B. It depends. Sometimes more than one set of statements gets executed as multiple conditions may be TRUE and then statements for each of them should get executed.

4. Which of the following LOOPs will be entered at least once?

A. Simple LOOP

B. WHILE loop

C. FOR loop

D. Cursor FOR loop

5. Which one of the following is not true about exceptions?

A. Exceptions raised within the declaration section are to be handled in the enclosing block, if you want to handle them.

B. Statements in the execution section just after the statement responsible for raising exceptions are executed once the exception handler has finished execution.

C. When system raises exceptions and they are not handled by the programmer, all the committed changes made to database objects like tables by the execution section within which the exception occurred are not automatically rolled back by the system.

D. Exceptions raised within a called procedure not handled by the procedure will roll back the changes done to IN OUT or OUT parameters by the procedure before the exception occurred.

Answers to Chapter Questions

1. B, C.

Explanation   A is certainly not true. D is false because procedures do not return values whereas functions do by utilizing the WHERE clause. Functions compute and return a single value, but do not modify its inputs so C is true. B is true as a matter of PL/SQL legal syntax.

2. A. 6 3 3

Explanation   This is an example of scope. The outer block *scope_num* is overridden inside the inner block by its own *scope_num.* Thus the value for *scope_num* inside the inner block is 6. This inner *scope_num* is not visible to the outer block so once the inner block has run, the *scope_num* used is the outer *scope_num* resulting in the last value of 3. To get at the outer *scope_num,* we use the label name inside the inner block while assigning value to Num_a.

3. A. At most one set of statements is executed.

Explanation   The IF, ELSE, and ELSIF constrain the execution so that the conditions are mutually exclusive. Only one statement can be true. When no statements are true, no statements are executed.

4. A. Simple LOOP

Explanation   The simple LOOP checks the condition for exiting the loop inside the loop body so it must get inside at least once. All other loops check the condition before entering the loop.

5. B.

Explanation   If not handled, exceptions will abort the execution of the execution section and return control to the enclosing block. Therefore, the statements in the culprit execution section after the statement that raises exception will not be executed. All other choices are true.

CHAPTER
9

More PL/SQL Tools

he previous chapter covered many of the PL/SQL basics. You can now write complete PL/SQL procedures and functions. You can also use cursors to interact with the database. This chapter focuses on implicit cursors and triggers and further explores functions and procedures. This chapter introduces PL/SQL packages as well as demonstrates how to interact with Oracle using non-Oracle products. Specifically, you will see how to transfer data between an Oracle database and Microsoft's Access and Excel products. You will also learn how to measure program execution speed and determine the amount of time a process takes to complete. Then it will be time to get down and dirty—time to write interesting, useful projects. We'll begin the chapter by discussing what it takes to turn ordinary code into truly stellar programming by covering code-writing conventions.

Take a minute or two now for a self-check. You need to be well versed in Chapter 8's content before continuing with Chapter 9. Are you ready? If you feel you need to review, by all means, take the time now to re-read Chapter 8 before delving into this fun- and fact-filled chapter. Also, if you haven't created the tables and other database objects that were in Chapter 8, you'll need to do that now. You can use the following SQL script to create those objects.

```
-- Script to be executed before completing exercises in Chapter 9.
-- ======================= PERSON ===================================
DROP TABLE plsql101_person;
CREATE TABLE plsql101_person (
     person_code VARCHAR2(3) PRIMARY KEY,
     first_name  VARCHAR2(15),
     last_name   VARCHAR2(20),
     hire_date   DATE
     )
;

CREATE INDEX plsql101_person_name_index
ON plsql101_person(last_name, first_name);

ALTER TABLE plsql101_person
ADD CONSTRAINT plsql101_person_unique UNIQUE (
     first_name,
     last_name,
     hire_date
     )
;

INSERT INTO plsql101_person VALUES
     ('CA', 'Charlene', 'Atlas', '01-FEB-02');
```

```
INSERT INTO plsql101_person VALUES
     ('GA', 'Gary', 'Anderson', '15-FEB-02');
INSERT INTO plsql101_person VALUES
     ('BB', 'Bobby', 'Barkenhagen', '28-FEB-02');
INSERT INTO plsql101_person VALUES
     ('LB', 'Laren', 'Baxter', '01-MAR-02');
INSERT INTO plsql101_person VALUES (
     'LN', 'Linda', 'Norton', '01-JUN-03');

-- ================= PRODUCT ======================
DROP TABLE plsql101_product;
CREATE TABLE plsql101_product (
     product_name     VARCHAR2(25) PRIMARY KEY,
     product_price    NUMBER(4,2),
     quantity_on_hand NUMBER(5,0),
     last_stock_date  DATE
     )
;

ALTER TABLE plsql101_product ADD (
     CONSTRAINT positive_quantity CHECK(
         quantity_on_hand IS NOT NULL
         AND
         quantity_on_hand >=0
         )
     )
;

INSERT INTO plsql101_product VALUES
     ('Small Widget', 99, 1, '15-JAN-03');
INSERT INTO plsql101_product VALUES
     ('Medium Wodget', 75, 1000, '15-JAN-02');
INSERT INTO plsql101_product VALUES
     ('Chrome Phoobar', 50, 100, '15-JAN-03');
INSERT INTO plsql101_product VALUES
     ('Round Chrome Snaphoo', 25, 10000, null);
INSERT INTO plsql101_product VALUES
     ('Extra Huge Mega Phoobar +',9.95,1234,'15-JAN-04');
INSERT INTO plsql101_product VALUES ('Square Zinculator',
     45, 1, TO_DATE('December 31, 2002, 11:30 P.M.',
                    'Month dd, YYYY, HH:MI P.M.')
     )
;
INSERT INTO plsql101_product VALUES (
     'Anodized Framifier', 49, 5, NULL);
INSERT INTO plsql101_product VALUES (
     'Red Snaphoo', 1.95, 10, '31-DEC-01');
```

```
INSERT INTO plsql101_product VALUES (
     'Blue Snaphoo', 1.95, 10, '30-DEC-01')
;


-- =================== PURCHASE ========================
DROP TABLE plsql101_purchase;
CREATE TABLE plsql101_purchase (
     product_name  VARCHAR2(25),
     salesperson   VARCHAR2(3),
     purchase_date DATE,
     quantity      NUMBER(4,2)
     )
;


ALTER TABLE plsql101_purchase
ADD PRIMARY KEY (product_name,
                 salesperson,
                 purchase_date
                 )
;


ALTER TABLE plsql101_purchase ADD (
     CONSTRAINT reasonable_date CHECK(
         purchase_date IS NOT NULL
         AND
         TO_CHAR(purchase_date, 'YYYY-MM-DD') >= '2000-06-30'
         )
     )
;


ALTER TABLE plsql101_purchase
     ADD CONSTRAINT plsql101_purchase_fk_product FOREIGN KEY
     (product_name) REFERENCES plsql101_product;

ALTER TABLE plsql101_purchase
     ADD CONSTRAINT plsql101_purchase_fk_person FOREIGN KEY
     (salesperson) REFERENCES plsql101_person;

CREATE INDEX plslq101_purchase_product
ON plsql101_purchase(product_name);

CREATE INDEX plsql101_purchase_salesperson
on plsql101_purchase(salesperson);
```

```
INSERT INTO plsql101_purchase VALUES
     ('Small Widget', 'CA', '14-JUL-03', 1);
INSERT INTO plsql101_purchase VALUES
     ('Medium Wodget', 'BB', '14-JUL-03', 75);
INSERT INTO plsql101_purchase VALUES
     ('Chrome Phoobar', 'GA', '14-JUL-03', 2);
INSERT INTO plsql101_purchase VALUES
     ('Small Widget', 'GA', '15-JUL-03', 8);
INSERT INTO plsql101_purchase VALUES
     ('Medium Wodget', 'LB', '15-JUL-03', 20);
INSERT INTO plsql101_purchase VALUES
     ('Round Chrome Snaphoo', 'CA', '16-JUL-03', 5);
INSERT INTO plsql101_purchase VALUES (
     'Small Widget', 'CA', '17-JUL-03', 1)
;

UPDATE plsql101_product
SET    product_price = product_price * .9
WHERE  product_name NOT IN (
       SELECT DISTINCT product_name
       FROM   plsql101_purchase
       )
;

-- ========================== OLD_ITEM ===============================
DROP TABLE plsql101_old_item;
CREATE TABLE plsql101_old_item (
     item_id   CHAR(20),
     item_desc CHAR(25)
     )
;

INSERT INTO plsql101_old_item VALUES
     ('LA-101', 'Can, Small');
INSERT INTO plsql101_old_item VALUES
     ('LA-102', 'Can, Large');
INSERT INTO plsql101_old_item VALUES
     ('LA-103', 'Bottle, Small');
INSERT INTO plsql101_old_item VALUES
     ('LA-104', 'Bottle, Large');
INSERT INTO plsql101_old_item VALUES
     ('NY-101', 'Box, Small');
INSERT INTO plsql101_old_item VALUES
     ('NY-102', 'Box, Large');
INSERT INTO plsql101_old_item VALUES
     ('NY-103', 'Shipping Carton, Small');
```

```
INSERT INTO plsql101_old_item VALUES
     ('NY-104', 'Shipping Carton, Large');

-- ========================= PURCHASE_ARCHIVE =========================
DROP TABLE plsql101_purchase_archive;
CREATE TABLE plsql101_purchase_archive (
     product_name  VARCHAR2(25),
     salesperson   VARCHAR2(3),
     purchase_date DATE,
     quantity      NUMBER(4,2)
     )
;

INSERT INTO plsql101_purchase_archive VALUES
     ('Round Snaphoo', 'BB', '21-JUN-01', 10);
INSERT INTO plsql101_purchase_archive VALUES
     ('Large Harflinger', 'GA', '22-JUN-01', 50);
INSERT INTO plsql101_purchase_archive VALUES
     ('Medium Wodget', 'LB', '23-JUN-01', 20);
INSERT INTO plsql101_purchase_archive VALUES
     ('Small Widget', 'ZZ', '24-JUN-02', 80);
INSERT INTO plsql101_purchase_archive VALUES
     ('Chrome Phoobar', 'CA', '25-JUN-02', 2);
INSERT INTO plsql101_purchase_archive VALUES
     ('Small Widget', 'JT', '26-JUN-02', 50);

-- ================== Reduce Prices (for update cursor) ============
DECLARE
        CURSOR product_cur IS
        SELECT * FROM plsql101_product
        FOR UPDATE OF product_price;
BEGIN
        FOR product_rec IN product_cur
        LOOP
                UPDATE plsql101_product
                SET product_price = (product_rec.product_price * 0.97)
                WHERE CURRENT OF product_cur;
        END LOOP;
END;
/
```

Coding Conventions

Throughout this book, you have seen a systematic choice of fonts, distance between the lines and words, the way pages are numbered, and the way figures are shown.

A specific font size has been used for all the chapter headings. Font sizes have not changed arbitrarily from chapter to chapter. These formatting choices were made, of course, to create an organized, easy-to-read body of text. When writing code, a good programmer will use standard formatting practices—or *conventions*—in order for his or her program to be easily understood. Table, index, function, and procedure names were chosen carefully throughout this book. Attempts were made to be as descriptive as possible when choosing names so that those names would reflect the purpose of the entity. For example, the purpose of the function named COMPUTE_DISCOUNTS in Chapter 8 was to—you got it—compute discounts.

Most real-life applications are made up of hundreds and thousands of program pieces or modules and can easily run into a few hundred thousand lines of code and many times even millions of lines of code. Usually, several developers work on a piece of code together. The code keeps changing as time goes by. Developers come and go and new developers need to be able to understand and modify old code without disabling an existing application. Such a disruption could cause a critical activity, such as the day-to-day activities of a major financial institution, to come to a screeching halt. If each developer wrote code in a style of his or her whims, that type of shutdown is exactly the sort of thing that could happen because the varying styles of code would become difficult—if not impossible—to read. Utilizing coding conventions helps standardize the code. In fact, conventions are so vitally important for successful long-term development that many organizations have special departments and committees devoted only to developing and enforcing a set of conventions.

Even if you're the only person who reads your code, you'll regret not using standard conventions once you've been away from the program long enough to forget its finer (and sometimes not-so-fine) points.

Some of the conventions you've seen in this book so far are:

- All SQL and PL/SQL commands are in uppercase.

- All names are in lowercase.

- For SQL, each logical piece of the statement starts on a separate line. For example, the list of columns in a SELECT statement starts with the command SELECT on a line of its own, each column name is on a line of its own, and so on.

- Similar rules are followed in PL/SQL. Function and procedure specifications stand out from the body. The indentation for nested blocks clearly indicates block boundaries.

- A space is always placed after comma.

When writing code, keep in mind the conventions outlined in this chapter as well as other factors, such as clear, self-explanatory object names, the 30-character limit on object names, and the maximum screen width (if your code lines are longer than the screen width they will either get chopped off or wrap around in an ugly, hard-to-read fashion on the screen). Take a few minutes to look at the previous chapters, and you will notice how coding conventions such as these were used.

More on PL/SQL and Oracle Server Interaction

You've already learned to use explicit cursors to fetch and modify data in the database. In this section we'll further explore PL/SQL records and how they are used with cursors. Then you'll read about using implicit cursors within PL/SQL. Finally, we will consider which type of cursor—implicit or explicit—is better to use in a given situation.

Allow me to return to the restaurant analogy for a moment. Imagine a kitchen with two chefs. One chef is tasked with getting raw food items out of the refrigerator and placing them on a tray in an arrangement that makes sense for the dish being prepared. The second chef takes the items from the tray, submits those items to cooking steps such as peeling, chopping, boiling, and spicing, and then places the prepared items back on the tray. At this point the first chef takes the prepared items from the tray and gives them to a food server.

This analogy actually matches what goes on inside a PL/SQL procedure. (I realize this may seem like a stretch, but stay with me.) The first chef's actions—taking raw items out of storage, making them available for processing, and moving the processed items to the person who will serve them—match those taken by SQL in a procedure when it retrieves data from a table, filters and sorts it, and makes it available to PL/SQL. The second chef's actions—processing the raw food into desired results—match what PL/SQL does. The tray that the two chefs use to move food back and forth between each other is analogous to cursors.

Whenever PL/SQL and SQL interact, they do so via a cursor. When we give the cursor a name by declaring it, it is an *explicit cursor*. When PL/SQL creates a cursor on its own to handle an operation, it is called an *implicit cursor*. (You'll read more about implicit cursors soon.)

Declaring Variable Types Dynamically and PL/SQL Records

In Chapter 8 you fetched data from a cursor into PL/SQL variables. In this chapter, PL/SQL records will be put to work to do some cool stuff. As you have seen, PL/SQL records allow you to gather different pieces of data into a single unit, hiding the complexity of the data. It's also less convenient to pass several PL/SQL variables than it is to use one record whose fields can contain the information from all of your variables.

The concept is similar to that of the large crates that revolutionized the shipping industry. Each crate can hold a myriad of goods that can be transported all at once. When you want to add or remove something from the inventory, all you do is open the crate and put the object in or take the object out. The crane that moves the crate from one place to another doesn't need to do anything differently. Similarly, a PL/SQL program unit specification doesn't necessarily need to change if the structure of a record it uses changes. If the changes to the record do not affect the data being used by your program, then the program does not need to change. For example, if a function takes a record but only uses the first two fields of it, the function does not need to change if you add a third field to the record. The function does need to change, however, if you remove the record's first field. This is very convenient and important in real applications.

PL/SQL has another very powerful feature: the dynamic type—or *anchored variable type*—declaration for PL/SQL variables that automates finding out which stored PL/SQL program units need to change if the database objects they depend on have changed. PL/SQL will try to compile all those program units automatically and the ones that fail to compile will be put in an unusable or invalid state. If you try to use an invalid program unit you will get an error. You can then modify that unit to make it conform to the changes to the database objects. For example, if a stored function used a record based on a table and you removed a column from the table that the function was using, you will need to rewrite the function body.

Imagine you want to create a record that has the same fields as the columns in a single row of a table, or you want to create a variable that has the same type as a column in a table, or you want a record that has the same fields as the columns selected by a cursor. Well, lucky for you, PL/SQL has ways of allowing you to do all of those things:

- Syntax to declare a PL/SQL variable of a column type:

  variable_name table_name.column_name%TYPE ;

- Syntax to declare a record with fields that are the same as a row in a table:

  record_name table_name%ROWTYPE ;

- Syntax to declare a record with fields that are the same as columns in a cursor:

  record_name cursor_name%ROWTYPE ;

In a cursor FOR loop we use a cursor-based record that is automatically created by PL/SQL for us. All we do is give it a name. The example record given in Chapter 8 that reduces prices uses the name product_rec. It has fields that match the order, name, and type of the columns selected by the cursor.

To create your own record you need to first tell PL/SQL what the name of the record is going to be, followed by what the structure will be for the record. You do this by using the following syntax in the declaration section:

TYPE *record_type_name* IS
(*field_1_name field_1_type,*
 field_2_name field_2_type,
 …
);

The actual declaration of the record follows:

record_variable record_type_name;

The following example puts all the pieces together. Create the following SQL script and run it in SQL*Plus. See Figure 9-1.

```
/* Performance is current average per order amount as a percentage of the
historical average per order sale amount for a salesperson. Status returns the
status of errors if any.
*/
SET SERVEROUTPUT ON
DECLARE
    TYPE performance_type IS RECORD
        (person_code     plsql101_person.person_code%TYPE,
         person_name     plsql101_person.last_name%TYPE,
         current_sales   NUMBER(8,2),
         perform_percent NUMBER(8,1),
         status          varchar2(30)
        );

    one_perform performance_type;

    CURSOR person_cur IS
        SELECT *
        FROM   plsql101_person;

    /* This procedure computes the performance and current total sales by
       one salesperson. The information for the salesperson is passed in
       as a record named a_person. If there are no sales for the day by the
```

```
    person then current_sales is set to zero. If the person has no
    history, for example, the person just joined today, then the
    perform_percent is set to zero.
 */
PROCEDURE current_performance
    (a_person plsql101_person%ROWTYPE,
     a_perform OUT performance_type)
IS
    CURSOR history_cur (person varchar2) IS
        SELECT   AVG(tab2.product_price * tab1.quantity) avg_order
        FROM     plsql101_purchase_archive tab1,
                 plsql101_product tab2
        WHERE    tab1.product_name = tab2.product_name
        GROUP BY tab1.salesperson
        HAVING   tab1.salesperson = person;

    hist_rec history_cur%ROWTYPE;
    current_avg_sales NUMBER(8,2) := 0;

BEGIN
    a_perform.person_code := a_person.person_code;
    a_perform.person_name := a_person.last_name;
    a_perform.status := NULL;

    BEGIN
        SELECT   SUM(tbl2.product_price * tbl1.quantity),
                 AVG(tbl2.product_price * tbl1.quantity)
        INTO     a_perform.current_sales,
                 current_avg_sales
        FROM     plsql101_purchase tbl1,
                 plsql101_product tbl2
        WHERE    tbl1.product_name = tbl2.product_name
        GROUP BY tbl1.salesperson
        HAVING   tbl1.salesperson = a_person.person_code;
    EXCEPTION
        WHEN NO_DATA_FOUND
        THEN
            a_perform.status := 'Current purchases exception';
            a_perform.current_sales := 0;
    END;

    OPEN history_cur (a_person.person_code);
    FETCH history_cur INTO hist_rec;
    IF (history_cur%NOTFOUND)
    THEN
        a_perform.perform_percent := 0;
        IF (a_perform.status IS NULL)
        THEN
            a_perform.status := 'Erroneous or no history';
```

```
                END IF;
        ELSE
            a_perform.perform_percent :=
                 100 * (current_avg_sales-hist_rec.avg_order)/
                                           hist_rec.avg_order;
            a_perform.status := 'All fine';
        END IF;
        CLOSE history_cur;
    EXCEPTION
        WHEN NO_DATA_FOUND
        THEN
            a_perform.status := 'Exceptions found';
    END current_performance;

BEGIN
    FOR person_rec IN person_cur
    LOOP
        current_performance(person_rec, one_perform);

        dbms_output.put_line(one_perform.person_code ||
                        ' ' ||
                        one_perform.person_name ||
                        ' ' ||
                        one_perform.current_sales ||
                        ' ' ||
                        one_perform.perform_percent ||
                        ' ' ||
                        one_perform.status);
    END LOOP;
END;
/
SELECT * FROM plsql101_person;
SELECT * FROM plsql101_purchase;
SELECT * FROM plsql101_purchase_archive;
SELECT * FROM plsql101_product;
```

Let's review what you just did here. First you declared a record type called
PERFORMANCE_TYPE. Because the declaration employs %TYPE on the fields being
drawn from the PLSQL101_PERSON table, you guaranteed that the datatypes in
the table and procedure will always match, even if those in the table are changed in
the future! Next, you declared a record variable called ONE_PERFORM, followed
by a simple cursor that selects all rows from the PLSQL101_PERSON table.

The procedure CURRENT_PERFORMANCE takes two parameters. One
parameter is the person record, which has exactly the same type as a row of the
PLSQL101_PERSON table and which is also the same as the type of the records
fetched by the PERSON_CUR cursor declared earlier. So it is safe to pass
records from PERSON_CUR cursor to this procedure.

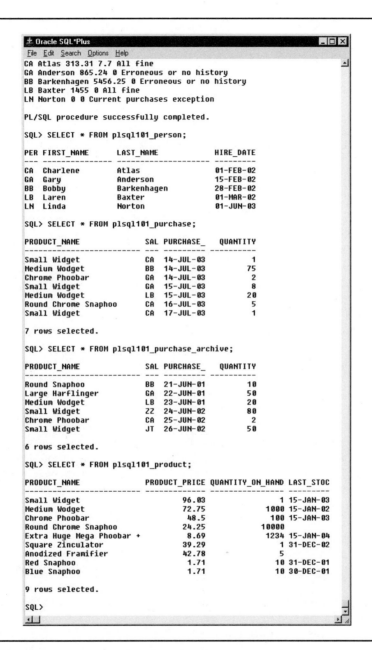

```
Oracle SQL*Plus                                          _ □ ×
File  Edit  Search  Options  Help
CA Atlas 313.31 7.7 All fine
GA Anderson 865.24 0 Erroneous or no history
BB Barkenhagen 5456.25 0 Erroneous or no history
LB Baxter 1455 0 All fine
LN Norton 0 0 Current purchases exception

PL/SQL procedure successfully completed.

SQL> SELECT * FROM plsql101_person;

PER FIRST_NAME        LAST_NAME            HIRE_DATE
--- ---------------   -------------------- ---------
CA  Charlene          Atlas                01-FEB-02
GA  Gary              Anderson             15-FEB-02
BB  Bobby             Barkenhagen          28-FEB-02
LB  Laren             Baxter               01-MAR-02
LN  Linda             Norton               01-JUN-03

SQL> SELECT * FROM plsql101_purchase;

PRODUCT_NAME             SAL PURCHASE_   QUANTITY
------------------------ --- ---------   ----------
Small Widget             CA  14-JUL-03          1
Medium Wodget            BB  14-JUL-03         75
Chrome Phoobar           GA  14-JUL-03          2
Small Widget             GA  15-JUL-03          8
Medium Wodget            LB  15-JUL-03         20
Round Chrome Snaphoo     CA  16-JUL-03          5
Small Widget             CA  17-JUL-03          1

7 rows selected.

SQL> SELECT * FROM plsql101_purchase_archive;

PRODUCT_NAME             SAL PURCHASE_   QUANTITY
------------------------ --- ---------   ----------
Round Snaphoo            BB  21-JUN-01         10
Large Harflinger         GA  22-JUN-01         50
Medium Wodget            LB  23-JUN-01         20
Small Widget             ZZ  24-JUN-02         80
Chrome Phoobar           CA  25-JUN-02          2
Small Widget             JT  26-JUN-02         50

6 rows selected.

SQL> SELECT * FROM plsql101_product;

PRODUCT_NAME             PRODUCT_PRICE QUANTITY_ON_HAND LAST_STOC
------------------------ ------------- ---------------- ---------
Small Widget                     96.03                1 15-JAN-03
Medium Wodget                    72.75             1000 15-JAN-02
Chrome Phoobar                    48.5              100 15-JAN-03
Round Chrome Snaphoo             24.25            10000
Extra Huge Mega Phoobar +         8.69             1234 15-JAN-04
Square Zinculator                39.29                1 31-DEC-02
Anodized Framifier               42.78                5
Red Snaphoo                       1.71               10 31-DEC-01
Blue Snaphoo                      1.71               10 30-DEC-01

9 rows selected.

SQL>
```

FIGURE 9-1. *An example of anchored or dynamic types*

The second parameter is OUT, which means the parameter will be written into by the procedure. The procedure will fill up the a_perform parameter. The procedure has HISTORY_CUR as an explicit cursor. This cursor joins the PLSQL101_PRODUCT and PLSQL_101_PURCHASE_ARCHIVE tables to find the average amount per order for a given salesperson. This is the archived or historical data, hence the name HISTORY_CUR. This value will be used to find out how well the salesperson has done with his current sales. hist_rec is a record variable based on the HISTORY_CUR cursor. CURRENT_AVG_SALES is the average of all current orders for a salesperson.

In the execution section of the procedure you wrote code that copied the salesperson's last name and code into the OUT parameter A_PERFORM. You also set the initial status to NULL.

Next, you created the implicit cursor, which we will discuss at greater length in the next section. In this case, the implicit cursor computed the total current sales and the current average sales per order for the salesperson that we obtained from the A_PERSON IN parameter. We have enclosed this portion of the code in its own basic block so that we can catch exceptions raised only by this portion. As you can see, there is indeed an exception for Linda Norton. She has no current sales, so no data is found for her.

Next, you opened the HISTORY_CUR cursor and fetched from it. Note that a single fetch was done, as there can be no more than one summary for a single salesperson. Also note the use of the column alias AVG_ORDER. The cursor here takes the salesperson's name as a parameter. So the cursor code can be reused for different salespeople. It is possible that there may be no data for a salesperson in archives because he or she is a new hire. It is also possible that there are other errors that cause the cursor to return no records. In this case the two items Large Harflinger and Round Snaphoo have no data in the PLSQL101_PRODUCT table. That is why we set the status to "erroneous or no history," not just "no history." If we do find valid historical data, we compute the percentage the current average amount per order is of its historical value and put this into the a_perform.perform_percent field.

Finally, you closed the HISTORY_CUR cursor. The exception section is for capturing unforeseen NO_DATA_FOUND exceptions not captured before.

The execution section of the main anonymous block simply looped through the PERSON_CUR and called the procedure for each person record and printed the results.

You executed the final SELECT statements in order to verify that the program did what it was supposed to and to see what error conditions occurred.

This is a complete example that covers a lot of new stuff. The same example with modifications will be used later to demonstrate some other topics covered in this chapter. If you're not completely comfortable with what was done here, go back now and review so that you'll be ready for the rest of the chapter.

DML in PL/SQL or Implicit Cursors

In this section we will study the implicit cursors we used and talked about. Take a look at the last example. The SELECT statement that finds the current average amount per order is a simple SELECT statement with the added keyword INTO. The INTO part of the statement is required in order to put the values returned by the SELECT statement into the corresponding PL/SQL variables. In our example the PL/SQL variables are CURRENT_AVG_SALES and the A_PERFORM.CURRENT_SALES. We can use this SELECT only if it returns a maximum of one record. If it returns more than one record, the TOO_MANY_ROWS exception will be raised. PL/SQL uses an implicit cursor that it calls "SQL" for this SELECT statement. This cursor has attributes that you can refer to learn information about the most recently performed SQL action. For instance, if you execute SQL%FOUND it will tell you whether or not the latest SELECT statement fetched any records at all. When there are two consecutive SELECT statements, SQL%FOUND only gives the status for the second one.

Let's correct the exceptions that were raised in the previous example by inserting some purchase data for Linda using an INSERT from within PL/SQL. Compare your results with Figure 9-2.

```
DECLARE
    quant NUMBER := 20;
BEGIN
    INSERT INTO plsql101_purchase
    VALUES ('Medium Wodget',
            'LN',
            '18-AUG-02',
            quant);
    IF (SQL%NOTFOUND)
    THEN
        dbms_output.put_line('Insert error?!');
    END IF;
END;
/
SELECT * FROM plsql101_purchase;
```

You can use a PL/SQL variable to insert a value. However, the column destined to hold the value must be of the same type as the PL/SQL variable or must be convertible from the PL/SQL variable to the column type. Remember, in SQL and PL/SQL data items can interact only if their types match.

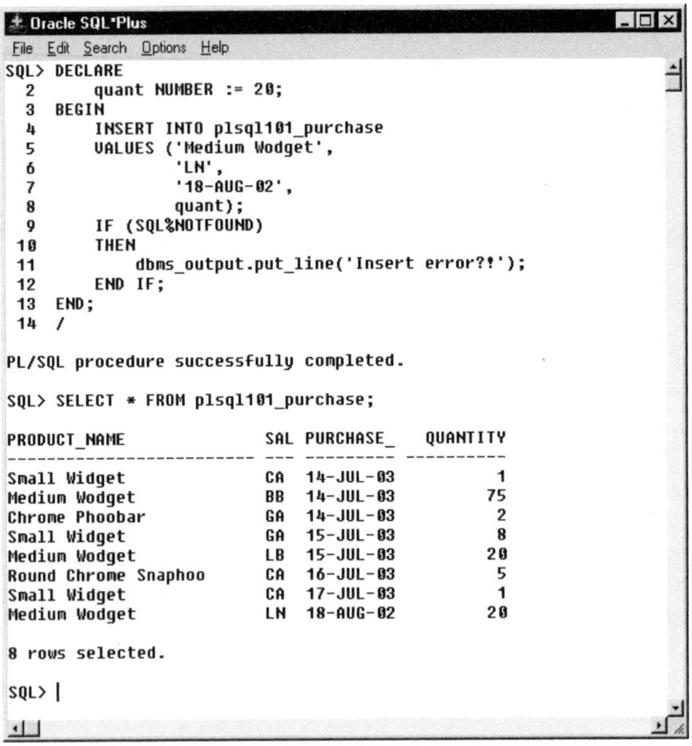

```
Oracle SQL*Plus                                        _ □ ✕
File  Edit  Search  Options  Help
SQL> DECLARE
  2       quant NUMBER := 20;
  3  BEGIN
  4       INSERT INTO plsql101_purchase
  5       VALUES ('Medium Wodget',
  6              'LN',
  7              '18-AUG-02',
  8              quant);
  9       IF (SQL%NOTFOUND)
 10       THEN
 11           dbms_output.put_line('Insert error?!');
 12       END IF;
 13  END;
 14  /

PL/SQL procedure successfully completed.

SQL> SELECT * FROM plsql101_purchase;

PRODUCT_NAME             SAL PURCHASE_   QUANTITY
------------------------ --- ---------- ----------
Small Widget             CA  14-JUL-03          1
Medium Wodget            BB  14-JUL-03         75
Chrome Phoobar           GA  14-JUL-03          2
Small Widget             GA  15-JUL-03          8
Medium Wodget            LB  15-JUL-03         20
Round Chrome Snaphoo     CA  16-JUL-03          5
Small Widget             CA  17-JUL-03          1
Medium Wodget            LN  18-AUG-02         20

8 rows selected.

SQL> |
```

FIGURE 9-2.   *Inserting a record using PL/SQL*

Now, using a SQL statement, insert two rows into the PLSQL101_PRODUCT
table. See Figure 9-3 for results.

```
INSERT INTO plsql101_product
VALUES ('Large Harflinger',
        21,
        100,
        '29-AUG-01');

INSERT INTO plsql101_product
VALUES ('Round Snaphoo',
        12,
        144,
        '21-JUL-01');
SELECT * FROM plsql101_product;
```

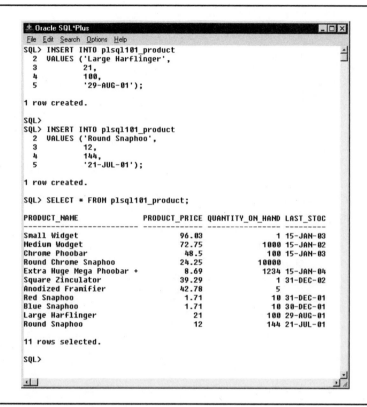

FIGURE 9-3.   *New rows in the PLSQL101_PRODUCT table*

Now update from within PL/SQL. See Figure 9-4.

```
CREATE OR REPLACE PROCEDURE update_prod (
     prod_rec plsql101_product%ROWTYPE
     ) IS
BEGIN
     UPDATE plsql101_product
     SET    last_stock_date = prod_rec.last_stock_date,
            quantity_on_hand = quantity_on_hand
                               +
                               prod_rec.quantity_on_hand
     WHERE product_name = prod_rec.product_name;
END update_prod;
/
DECLARE
```

```
        a plsql101_product%ROWTYPE;
BEGIN
    a.product_name := 'Small Widget';
    a.product_price := 87;
    a.quantity_on_hand := 31;
    a.last_stock_date := TO_DATE('23-NOV-01');
    update_prod(a);
END;
/
SELECT * FROM plsql101_product;
```

That was simple enough! You will always need to be aware of all possible exceptions when using SQL DML within PL/SQL. This is especially true for implicit cursors, as you do not have as much control as you get with explicit cursors.

The delete works similarly. Let us try to delete something that violates a constraint and see the results using SQL attributes. Refer to Figure 9-5.

```
set serveroutput on

BEGIN
  DELETE FROM plsql101_product
  WHERE        product_name = 'junk';
  IF (SQL%NOTFOUND)
  THEN
      dbms_output.put_line('No such product');
  END IF;
END;
/
```

Implicit Versus Explicit Cursors

Because an implicit cursor can only deal with a single row of data, you should use an explicit cursor whenever the statement filling the cursor can generate more than one row of results. In addition, explicit cursors remain in the database's memory for a while after you have executed them, and if you (or another user) issue the same cursor SELECT statement while the prior one is still in the database's memory, you will get your results much more quickly.

Note that the HISTORY_CUR cursor in our earlier example can be easily replaced by an implicit cursor, because grouping the records by salesperson guarantees that only one row of results will be produced. Later in this chapter when I show you how to put functions and procedures into packages, I will also demonstrate how to change the cursor to one that is implicit.

```
± Oracle SQL*Plus                                                _ □ ×
 File  Edit  Search  Options  Help
SQL> CREATE OR REPLACE PROCEDURE update_prod (
  2          prod_rec plsql101_product%ROWTYPE
  3          ) IS
  4   BEGIN
  5          UPDATE plsql101_product
  6          SET    last_stock_date = prod_rec.last_stock_date,
  7                 quantity_on_hand = quantity_on_hand
  8                                  +
  9                                  prod_rec.quantity_on_hand
 10          WHERE product_name = prod_rec.product_name;
 11   END update_prod;
 12   /

Procedure created.

SQL> DECLARE
  2          a plsql101_product%ROWTYPE;
  3   BEGIN
  4          a.product_name := 'Small Widget';
  5          a.product_price := 87;
  6          a.quantity_on_hand := 31;
  7          a.last_stock_date := TO_DATE('23-NOV-01');
  8          update_prod(a);
  9   END;
 10   /

PL/SQL procedure successfully completed.

SQL> SELECT * FROM plsql101_product;

PRODUCT_NAME               PRODUCT_PRICE QUANTITY_ON_HAND LAST_STOC
-------------------------- ------------- ---------------- ---------
Small Widget                       96.03               32 23-NOV-01
Medium Wodget                      72.75             1000 15-JAN-02
Chrome Phoobar                      48.5              100 15-JAN-03
Round Chrome Snaphoo               24.25            10000
Extra Huge Mega Phoobar +           8.69             1234 15-JAN-04
Square Zinculator                  39.29                1 31-DEC-02
Anodized Framifier                 42.78                5
Red Snaphoo                         1.71               10 31-DEC-01
Blue Snaphoo                        1.71               10 30-DEC-01
Large Harflinger                      21              100 29-AUG-01
Round Snaphoo                         12              144 21-JUL-01

11 rows selected.

SQL>
```

FIGURE 9-4. *Update from PL/SQL procedure using an implicit cursor*

```
Oracle SQL*Plus                                              _□×
File  Edit  Search  Options  Help
SQL> set serveroutput on
SQL>
SQL> BEGIN
  2    DELETE FROM plsql101_product
  3    WHERE       product_name = 'junk';
  4    IF (SQL%NOTFOUND)
  5    THEN
  6       dbms_output.put_line('No such product');
  7    END IF;
  8  END;
  9  /
No such product

PL/SQL procedure successfully completed.

SQL> |
```

FIGURE 9-5.   *Procedure to delete from a table using PL/SQL*

Timing Operations

This section describes how to calculate the amount of time it takes a process to execute. This is useful for finding out how good your code is. After all, speed is key when running database applications. A responsible programmer will utilize the information in this section on a regular basis.

Using a Program to Measure Time

One way of measuring how long a procedure takes to run is to have the procedure keep track of time itself. The following code demonstrates this. It employs SYSDATE to find the start time and end time for a loop that inserts 5000 records into a table. It then calculates how long one record insertion takes by dividing the total elapsed time by 5000. Here is the SQL script to do this. See Figure 9-6.

NOTE
You will see different results based on various factors, like load on the database server, actual speed of the database computer, and so on. Usually, you will run the same code again and again and then take the average to estimate the performance. Also, remember that the date shown in Figure 9-6 will be different from the date shown in your work because the code is using SYSDATE.

```
DROP TABLE plsql101_timetab CASCADE CONSTRAINTS;
CREATE TABLE plsql101_timetab (
     c1     NUMBER NOT NULL,
     c2     VARCHAR2(30) NULL,
     c3     DATE NULL
     )
;
CREATE OR REPLACE PROCEDURE test_time IS
     maxloops NUMBER := 5000;
     loopcount NUMBER(6,0) := 0;
     starttime CHAR(5) ;
     endtime CHAR(5) ;
     /* Note that since the start and end times are defined in terms
     of the number of seconds since midnight, this routine will not
     work if the run time crosses over midnight.
     */
     runtime NUMBER;
     processrate NUMBER(20,10);
BEGIN
     starttime := TO_CHAR(SYSDATE,'SSSSS');
     LOOP
          loopcount := loopcount +1;
          INSERT INTO plsql101_timetab (C1, C2,C3)
          VALUES (loopcount, 'TEST ENTRY', SYSDATE);
          COMMIT;
          IF loopcount >= maxloops THEN
               EXIT;
          END IF;
     END LOOP;
     COMMIT;
     endtime := TO_CHAR(SYSDATE,'SSSSS');
     runtime := TO_NUMBER(endtime)-TO_NUMBER(starttime);
     dbms_output.put_line(runtime || ' seconds' );
     processrate := maxloops / runtime;
     INSERT INTO plsql101_timetab (C1, C2, C3) VALUES
          (loopcount+1,
          TO_CHAR(processrate, '9999999999')||' records per second',
          SYSDATE
          );
END test_time;
/
EXECUTE test_time;
SELECT * FROM plsql101_timetab
WHERE  c1 > 5000;
```

```
Oracle SQL*Plus                                              _ □ ×
File  Edit  Search  Options  Help
Table created.

SQL> CREATE OR REPLACE PROCEDURE test_time IS
  2         maxloops NUMBER := 5000;
  3         loopcount NUMBER(6,0) := 0;
  4         starttime CHAR(5) ;
  5         endtime CHAR(5) ;
  6         /* Note that since the start and end times are defined in terms
  7         of the number of seconds since midnight, this routine will not
  8         work if the run time crosses over midnight.
  9         */
 10         runtime NUMBER;
 11         processrate NUMBER(20,10);
 12  BEGIN
 13         starttime := TO_CHAR(SYSDATE,'SSSSS');
 14         LOOP
 15              loopcount := loopcount +1;
 16              INSERT INTO plsql101_timetab (C1, C2,C3)
 17              VALUES (loopcount, 'TEST ENTRY', SYSDATE);
 18              COMMIT;
 19              IF loopcount >= maxloops THEN
 20                   EXIT;
 21              END IF;
 22         END LOOP;
 23         COMMIT;
 24         endtime := TO_CHAR(SYSDATE,'SSSSS');
 25         runtime := TO_NUMBER(endtime)-TO_NUMBER(starttime);
 26         dbms_output.put_line(runtime || ' seconds' );
 27         processrate := maxloops / runtime;
 28         INSERT INTO plsql101_timetab (C1, C2, C3) VALUES
 29              (loopcount+1,
 30              TO_CHAR(processrate, '9999999999')||' records per second',
 31              SYSDATE
 32              );
 33  END test_time;
 34  /

Procedure created.

SQL> EXECUTE test_time;
6 seconds

PL/SQL procedure successfully completed.

SQL> SELECT * FROM plsql101_timetab
  2  WHERE  c1 > 5000;

       C1 C2                                 C3
---------- ------------------------------ ---------
     5001          833 records per second 22-OCT-00

SQL>
```

FIGURE 9-6. *Measuring performance of inserts with a PL/SQL program*

Here is a test loop that will show time measurements for ten iterations of the same code. See Figure 9-7.

```
TRUNCATE TABLE plsql101_timetab;
COMMIT;
SET SERVEROUTPUT ON
BEGIN
    FOR trial_count IN 1..10
    LOOP
        test_time;
        COMMIT;
    END LOOP;
END;
/
SELECT   *
FROM     plsql101_timetab
WHERE    c1 > 5000
ORDER BY c3;
```

Using the TIMING Command to Count Real Time

When you want to do more accurate measurements, you can do so using the TIMING command. We will modify the above example slightly to show you how. Figure 9-8 shows the results. In this example the elapsed time is represented with the value 7470. This value means that 7.47 seconds elapsed between the TIMING START command and the TIMING STOP command.

```
TIMING START;
EXECUTE test_time;
COMMIT;
TIMING STOP;
```

PL/SQL Packages

What makes using a PC so easy? One of the reasons is that it combines many useful functions into one easy-to-use package. The software displays screens and you do not need to know how a mouse click communicates with the computer in order to achieve your desired result. The complexity of the behind-the-scenes activities is hidden from you; all you need to know is that when you take a particular action, a predictable result occurs. PL/SQL offers a similar efficiency in software development by providing *packages* for bundling useful functions, procedures, record types, and cursors together.

A package has a specification just like a procedure or function. It has a body just like a procedure or function. What makes a package different is that you can create the specification and body separately. You can even replace a package body with

```
Oracle SQL*Plus                                                    _ □ ×
File  Edit  Search  Options  Help
SQL> TRUNCATE TABLE plsql101_timetab;

Table truncated.

SQL> COMMIT;

Commit complete.

SQL> SET SERVEROUTPUT ON
SQL> BEGIN
  2      FOR trial_count IN 1..10
  3      LOOP
  4          test_time;
  5          COMMIT;
  6      END LOOP;
  7  END;
  8  /
7 seconds
8 seconds
7 seconds
7 seconds
7 seconds
6 seconds
7 seconds
8 seconds
7 seconds
8 seconds

PL/SQL procedure successfully completed.

SQL> SELECT    *
  2  FROM      plsql101_timetab
  3  WHERE     c1 > 5000
  4  ORDER BY c3;

     C1 C2                              C3
---------- ------------------------------- ---------
     5001            714 records per second 22-OCT-00
     5001            625 records per second 22-OCT-00
     5001            714 records per second 22-OCT-00
     5001            714 records per second 22-OCT-00
     5001            714 records per second 22-OCT-00
     5001            833 records per second 22-OCT-00
     5001            714 records per second 22-OCT-00
     5001            625 records per second 22-OCT-00
     5001            714 records per second 22-OCT-00
     5001            625 records per second 22-OCT-00

10 rows selected.

SQL>
```

FIGURE 9-7.   *Results of a ten-iteration speed test*

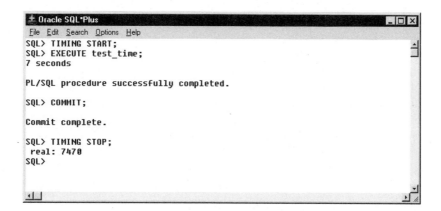

FIGURE 9-8.   *Measuring INSERT performance with the TIMING command*

a different body that conforms to the existing specifications, and the package will continue to work.

Now, why would you want to keep the body separate from the specification? The answer is really quite simple. Package users don't need to be exposed to all of the details of package implementation, so those details are hidden inside the body. The body is stored, compiled, and processed from within the database and is invisible to users of the package. Users of the package should simply use the specification for their programming purposes and be done with it. This is very important when you want your proprietary code to be secure and not accessible to hackers or competitors.

The syntax for a package specification is as follows:

CREATE PACKAGE *package_name* IS
   [*variable_and_type declarations*]
   [*cursor specifications*]
   [*function_and_procedure specifications*]
END [*package_name*] ;

To create a package body, you would use this syntax:

CREATE OR REPLACE PACKAGE BODY *package_name* IS
   [*local declarations*]
   [*full_cursors in package specification*]
   [*full_function_and_procedures in package specification*]
BEGIN
   [*executable statements*]

[EXCEPTION]
   [*exception handlers*]
END [*package_name*] ;

All variables and types declared in the package specification are accessible by users of the package. The package specification contains only enough information to identify what a package contains, as well as what variables those contents expect as input and output. The package specification's declaration section contains declarations for functions, procedures, exceptions, cursors, variables, and constants that are available for use within the package's body. The executable section of the package body contains the full definitions—without the CREATE OR REPLACE command—for all the cursors, functions, and procedures declared in its specification.

The variables that are present in the package specification are called *package variables*. They are initialized only once: when the package is first accessed. When a call is made to any of the package's contents, Oracle loads the package into memory, where it stays for as long as the user is connected to the database. When there are multiple sessions the package variables and their values are shared; the packaged objects can also be accessed more quickly in subsequent sessions.

The use of the execution section of the package is usually for the initialization of package local variables or package variables. The execution section of a package is executed once when the package is loaded, so there is not much scope for using the execution section to do things repeatedly, since it cannot be called more than once.

Users access the package's procedures, variables, and functions using the same *container.contained* notation—in this case, that means *package_name.packaged_object*. You have already used one example of a packaged function, the dbms_output.put_line function from the dbms_output package supplied by Oracle. When referring to functions from within their own package, you do not need to place the *package_name* qualification before the function name.

Ready to create a package? You bet you are. You'll just pull some of the previous examples and turn them into a package. Run the following SQL script to see the creation and use of a package. Figure 9-9 shows the SQL*Plus outputs.

```
CREATE OR REPLACE PACKAGE plsql101_pack IS
    DATE_LOADED DATE;
    /* Performance is current average per order amount as a percentage
       of the historical average per order sale amount for a
       salesperson. Status returns the status of errors if any.
     */
    TYPE pkg_perform_type IS RECORD
        (person_code       plsql101_person.person_code%TYPE,
         person_name       char(12),
         current_sales     NUMBER(8,2),
         perform_percent   NUMBER(8,1),
         status            char(30)
        );
    CURSOR PKG_PER_CUR RETURN plsql101_person%ROWTYPE;
```

```
    /* Compute discounts on orders.
       Input order amount.
       Returns discount amount (zero for wrong inputs).
     */
    FUNCTION pkg_comp_discounts (order_amt NUMBER) RETURN NUMBER;

    /* This procedure computes the performance and current total sales
       BY a salesperson. The information for the salesperson is passed
       in as a record a_person. If there are no sales for the day BY
       the person the current_sales is set to zero. If the person has
       no history, for example, the person just joined today, then
       the perform_percent is set to zero.
     */
    PROCEDURE pkg_compute_perform
        (a_person plsql101_person%ROWTYPE,
         a_perform OUT pkg_perform_type);
END plsql101_pack;
/

CREATE OR REPLACE PACKAGE BODY plsql101_pack IS
    small_order_amt NUMBER(8,2) := 400;
    large_order_amt NUMBER(8,2) := 1000;
    small_disct NUMBER(4,2)     := 1;
    large_disct NUMBER(4,2)     := 5;

    CURSOR PKG_PER_CUR
    RETURN plsql101_person%ROWTYPE
    IS
        SELECT *
        FROM plsql101_person;

    FUNCTION pkg_comp_discounts (order_amt NUMBER)
    RETURN NUMBER IS
    BEGIN
        IF (order_amt < large_order_amt
            AND
            order_amt >= small_order_amt)
        THEN
                RETURN (order_amt * small_disct / 100);
        ELSIF (order_amt >= large_order_amt)
        THEN
                RETURN (order_amt * large_disct / 100);
        ELSE
                RETURN(0);
        END IF;
    END pkg_comp_discounts;

    PROCEDURE pkg_compute_perform
        (a_person plsql101_person%ROWTYPE,
         a_perform OUT pkg_perform_type)
    IS
```

```
        hist_ord_avg NUMBER(8,2) := 0;
        current_avg_sales NUMBER(8,2) := 0;

BEGIN
    a_perform.person_code := a_person.person_code;
    a_perform.person_name := a_person.last_name;
    a_perform.status := NULL;

    BEGIN
        SELECT    SUM(tbl2.product_price * tbl1.quantity),
                  AVG(tbl2.product_price * tbl1.quantity)
        INTO      a_perform.current_sales,
                  current_avg_sales
        FROM      plsql101_purchase tbl1,
                  plsql101_product tbl2
        WHERE     tbl1.product_name = tbl2.product_name
        GROUP BY tbl1.salesperson
        HAVING    tbl1.salesperson = a_person.person_code;
    EXCEPTION
        WHEN NO_DATA_FOUND
        THEN
            a_perform.status := 'Current purchses exception';
            a_perform.current_sales := 0;
    END;

    BEGIN
    SELECT    AVG(tab2.product_price * tab1.quantity) avg_order
    INTO      hist_ord_avg
    FROM      plsql101_purchase_archive tab1,
              plsql101_product tab2
    WHERE     tab1.product_name = tab2.product_name
    GROUP BY tab1.salesperson
    HAVING    tab1.salesperson = a_person.person_code;

        a_perform.perform_percent :=
           100 * (current_avg_sales-hist_ord_avg)/hist_ord_avg;
        a_perform.status := 'All fine';

    EXCEPTION
        WHEN NO_DATA_FOUND
        THEN
            a_perform.perform_percent := 0;
            IF (a_perform.status IS NULL)
            THEN
                a_perform.status := 'Erroneous or no history';
            END IF;
    END;
EXCEPTION
    WHEN NO_DATA_FOUND
    THEN
```

```
            a_perform.status := 'Exceptions found';
     END pkg_compute_perform;

BEGIN
     /* The date the package was first loaded */
     DATE_LOADED := SYSDATE;
END plsql101_pack;
/

DECLARE
    one_perform plsql101_pack.pkg_perform_type;
    cursale char(8);
    disct   char(8);
    perf    char(8);
BEGIN
    dbms_output.put_line('Code' ||
                         ' ' ||
                         'Last Name' ||
                         ' ' ||
                         'Total Sales' ||
                         ' ' ||
                         'Discounts' ||
                         ' ' ||
                         'Performance%' ||
                         ' ' ||
                         'Errors?');
    FOR person_rec IN plsql101_pack.PKG_PER_CUR
    LOOP
        plsql101_pack.pkg_compute_perform(person_rec, one_perform);
        cursale := TO_CHAR(one_perform.current_sales);
        disct   := TO_CHAR(plsql101_pack.pkg_comp_discounts
                        (one_perform.current_sales));
        perf    := TO_CHAR(one_perform.perform_percent);

        dbms_output.put_line(one_perform.person_code ||
                         ' ' ||
                         one_perform.person_name ||
                         ' ' ||
                         cursale ||
                         ' ' ||
                         disct ||
                         ' ' ||
                         perf ||
                         ' ' ||
                         one_perform.status);
    END LOOP;

    dbms_output.put_line('Pkg load date seconds ' ||
                    TO_CHAR(plsql101_pack.DATE_LOADED, 'SSSSS'));
```

```
dbms_output.put_line('System date seconds ' ||
                     TO_CHAR(SYSDATE, 'SSSSS'));

END;
/
```

```
 Oracle SQL*Plus                                                  _ □ ×
 File  Edit  Search  Options  Help
 19      FOR person_rec IN plsql101_pack.pkg_per_cur
 20      LOOP
 21          plsql101_pack.pkg_compute_perform(person_rec, one_perform);
 22
 23   cursale := TO_CHAR(one_perform.current_sales);
 24   disct   := TO_CHAR(plsql101_pack.pkg_comp_discounts
 25       (one_perform.current_sales));
 26       perf    := TO_CHAR(one_perform.perform_percent);
 27
 28       dbms_output.put_line(one_perform.person_code ||
 29                             ' ' ||
 30                             one_perform.person_name ||
 31                             ' ' ||
 32                             cursale ||
 33                             ' ' ||
 34                             disct ||
 35                             ' ' ||
 36                             perf ||
 37                             ' ' ||
 38                             one_perform.status);
 39      END LOOP;
 40
 41      dbms_output.put_line('Pkg load date seconds ' ||
 42                           TO_CHAR(plsql101_pack.date_loaded, 'SSSSS'));
 43
 44      dbms_output.put_line('System date seconds ' ||
 45                           TO_CHAR(SYSDATE, 'SSSSS'));
 46
 47   END;
 48   /
Code Last Name Total Sales Discounts Performance% Errors?
CA  Atlas      313.31      0         7.7          All fine
GA  Anderson   865.24      8.6524    -58.8        All fine
BB  Barkenhagen 5456.25    272.8125  4446.9       All fine
LB  Baxter     1455        72.75     0            All fine
LN  Norton     1455        72.75     0            Erroneous or no history
Pkg load date seconds 39571
System date seconds 39571

PL/SQL procedure successfully completed.

SQL>
```

FIGURE 9-9. *Example of a package and its usage*

Notice that the cursor PKG_PER_CUR is required to have a return type. The use of the CHAR variable is purely for cosmetic purposes: it makes the printout look better.

I have hidden the discount rates inside the package so that the users of the package cannot modify them. DATE_LOADED is a package variable. On some computers the code executes so fast there is no difference between system time and the package loaded time. You will, however, see a difference if the execution becomes slow or the database's host computer is slow.

Triggers

Triggers were briefly introduced in Chapter 8. This section offers a short review of that material and then goes into the nitty-gritty of triggers.

A trigger is best described as a procedure that is executed automatically whenever some event defined by the trigger—the *triggering event*—happens.

You can write triggers that fire whenever one of the following operations occurs:

- DML statements on a particular schema object

- DDL statements issued within a schema or database

- User logon or logoff events, server errors, database startup, or instance shutdown.

Triggers differ from PL/SQL procedures in three ways:

- Triggers are called automatically by Oracle when the event defined for that trigger happens. You cannot call a trigger from within your code.

- Triggers do not have a parameter list.

- The syntax for a trigger specification is slightly different than a specification for a procedure.

Triggers are similar to procedures in the following ways:

- The body of a trigger looks like the body of a procedure—both are PL/SQL basic blocks.

- A trigger does not return any values.

- Triggers can be used to perform a variety of tasks.

- Triggers automatically generate derived column values. For example, every time a new order is processed the commission for the sales agent may be automatically calculated and entered into the appropriate table.

- Triggers can prevent invalid transactions. For example, a trigger can stop someone from increasing the salary of an employee by more than the budget allows. Note that this cannot be done using check constraints, because a check constraint only refers to values in the current row—and therefore cannot determine an overall budget amount.

- Triggers can be used to enforce complex security authorizations. For example, only supervisors can change the salary value, and only for the people they supervise.

- Triggers can be used to enforce complex business rules. For example, a trigger can be used to verify that an item on a purchase order is available on the shipping date and if it isn't, the trigger will automatically place a restocking order such that enough quantities arrive before the shipping date.

- Triggers can provide transparent event logging. For example, a trigger can track how many times a particular salesperson accesses an inventory table.

- Triggers can provide sophisticated auditing. For example, a trigger can be used to find out how many times on average a given salesperson needs to access the database in order to process a single purchase order.

- Triggers can gather statistics on table access. For example, a trigger can tabulate how many queries occur in one day for the small widget in the product catalog table.

As you may have realized by now, triggers are powerful tools. Triggers should be used prudently, because a trigger can fire as often as every time a table is accessed, and that puts an additional strain on the database server. A good rule of thumb is to use a trigger to perform an action that cannot be performed by any other means. For example, if you can use one or more constraints to do the job of a specific trigger, then use the constraints instead of the trigger. Similarly, if your system requires totals that can be calculated during off hours, it may be better to design the system that way instead of having triggers firing during every transaction to create the calculation. For example, suppose a bank decides when more cash is needed from a central repository by calculating how many $20 bills left the bank on a given day. That calculation can be done after office hours by counting the total bills given out that day. If a trigger fired during the business day to update the $20 bill count, the bank's transaction speeds would significantly degrade during business hours.

Triggers defined on tables are called *table triggers* and will be the subject of the rest of our trigger discussion. The syntax for a trigger is as follows:

```
CREATE OR REPLACE TRIGGER trigger_name fire_time trigger_event
   ON table_name
   [WHEN trigger_restriction]
   [FOR EACH ROW]
   [DECLARE
      declarations]
   BEGIN
      statements
   [EXCEPTION
      WHEN exception_name
      THEN ...]
END trigger_name;
```

Keep reading, and you will see how to build triggers using this syntax.

Trigger Types

The *fire_time* specifies when the trigger will fire. The choices are BEFORE or AFTER the trigger event or statement is executed. When using BEFORE, the trigger is executed before any constraint checking is done on rows affected by the triggering event. No rows are locked. This type of trigger is called, sensibly, a *BEFORE trigger*.

If you chose the keyword AFTER, then the trigger will fire after the triggering statement has done its job and after all constraint checks are done. The affected rows are locked during the execution of the trigger in this case. This type of trigger is called an *AFTER trigger*.

The *trigger_event* or triggering statement can be an INSERT, UPDATE or DELETE.

The *trigger_restriction* is one or more additional conditions to be met in order for the trigger to execute.

The optional FOR EACH ROW set of keywords executes the trigger body for every row that is affected by the triggering statement. Such triggers are called *row triggers*. When the FOR EACH ROW option is absent, the trigger is executed only once for the triggering statement or event. When this is the case, the trigger is referred to as a *statement trigger*, as it executes only once for each triggering statement.

The portion of code between DECLARE and END *trigger_name* is simply a PL/SQL basic block.

You can combine different trigger events using OR. For example:

DELETE OR INSERT *rest_of_statement*

When using UPDATE, you can specify a list of columns:

UPDATE OF *column1, column2, ...*

Also when using UPDATE in PL/SQL statements, the new row is accessed with a colon before the word "new" (:new) and the old row is identified by a colon before the word "old" (:old). Thus, :old.column_name will give you the old value for that column in the row before the triggering statement changes it. However, the trigger restriction uses the names "old" and "new" without the preceding colon.

Trigger Example

You will now create a trigger to track the activities of a sales force. Here is the SQL script you'll need. Figure 9-10 shows the end result of the example.

```
-- Add a column to the purchase table. The values will be null.
ALTER TABLE plsql101_purchase
    ADD ORDER_NUMBER NUMBER(10);

-- Create the audit table.
CREATE TABLE plsql101_audit
    (ORDER_NUMBER       NUMBER(10),
     person_code        VARCHAR2(3),
     user_name          CHAR(30),
     user_machine       CHAR(20),
     change_in_quant    NUMBER(5),
     transaction_time DATE,
     FOREIGN KEY (person_code) REFERENCES plsql101_person);

-- Sequence for order numbers
CREATE SEQUENCE order_num_seq;

CREATE OR REPLACE TRIGGER audit_trigger
BEFORE INSERT OR UPDATE ON plsql101_purchase
FOR EACH ROW
DECLARE
    no_name_change EXCEPTION;
    quant_change NUMBER(5) := 0;
BEGIN
    /* Do not allow any changes to product_name for orders.
       Raise exception and reset the values back to original.
     */
    IF (UPDATING
        AND
        (:NEW.product_name <> :OLD.product_name))
    THEN
        RAISE no_name_change;
    END IF;

    /* Create an order number for old non-numbered orders as well
       as new orders that do not have any order number.
```

```
 */
IF (((UPDATING)
     AND
     (:OLD.ORDER_NUMBER IS NULL))
     OR
     ((INSERTING)
      AND
      (:NEW.ORDER_NUMBER IS NULL)))
THEN
    SELECT order_num_seq.NEXTVAL
    INTO   :NEW.ORDER_NUMBER
    FROM   dual;
END IF;

/* Finally, populate the audit table with user name, user's
   computer or terminal name, the change he or she made to
   the quantity, and the time of the change. If inserting, then
   change to quantity is same as new quantity.
 */

IF (UPDATING)
THEN
    quant_change := :NEW.quantity-:OLD.quantity;
ELSE
    quant_change := :NEW.quantity;
END IF;

INSERT INTO plsql101_audit
VALUES (:NEW.ORDER_NUMBER,
        :NEW.salesperson,
        USER,
        USERENV('TERMINAL'),
        quant_change,
        SYSDATE);

  EXCEPTION
      WHEN no_name_change
      THEN
          dbms_output.put_line('Change of product name not allowed');
          dbms_output.put_line('Aborting and resetting to old values');
          :NEW.product_name := :OLD.product_name;
          :NEW.salesperson  := :OLD.salesperson;
          :NEW.ORDER_NUMBER := :OLD.ORDER_NUMBER;
          :NEW.quantity     := :OLD.quantity;
END audit_trigger;
/

SELECT * FROM plsql101_purchase;
```

```
SELECT * FROM plsql101_audit;
INSERT INTO plsql101_purchase
    VALUES ('Round Snaphoo', 'LN', '15-NOV-02', 2, NULL);
SELECT * FROM plsql101_purchase WHERE salesperson = 'LN';
SELECT * FROM plsql101_audit;
UPDATE plsql101_purchase SET salesperson = 'LB'
    WHERE salesperson = 'CA' AND quantity = 1;
SELECT * FROM plsql101_purchase WHERE salesperson = 'CA';
SELECT * FROM plsql101_audit;
UPDATE plsql101_purchase SET quantity = 20 WHERE salesperson = 'BB';
SELECT * FROM plsql101_purchase WHERE salesperson = 'BB';
SELECT * FROM plsql101_audit;
UPDATE plsql101_purchase SET product_name = 'Round Snaphoo'
    WHERE salesperson = 'BB';
SELECT * FROM plsql101_purchase WHERE salesperson = 'BB';
SELECT * FROM plsql101_audit;
```

Let's talk about what you just did. First you added the ORDER_NUMBER column to the purchase table. Then you created a table for audit records that holds the name of the logged-in user. The user name is entered through the USER function while his or her computer or terminal name is entered using the USERENV('TERMINAL') call to USERENV function. The values for salesperson and any changes to the quantity in the order as well as the order number and the date of change are also entered. The trigger will not allow any changes to the product_name and it will automatically generate order numbers for new orders as well as old entries in the purchase table that have no order numbers. The trigger will also insert values into the audit table when the update or insert is successful. The keywords UPDATING and INSERTING tell us whether the triggering action was an update or an insert.

The trigger was tested by first inserting a row into the PLSQL101_PURCHASE table and comparing the old values to the new by selecting from the table. You then performed two simple updates and followed by a final update that attempted to change the product name for the order.

Modifying Triggers

As with views, there is no command to modify a trigger. You simply replace an old trigger with a new one by employing a CREATE OR REPLACE TRIGGER command.

You can also drop a trigger by issuing a command using the following syntax:

DROP TRIGGER *trigger_name*;

Existing triggers can be deactivated and reactivated using commands with this syntax:

ALTER TRIGGER *trigger_name* DISABLE;
ALTER TRIGGER *trigger_name* ENABLE;

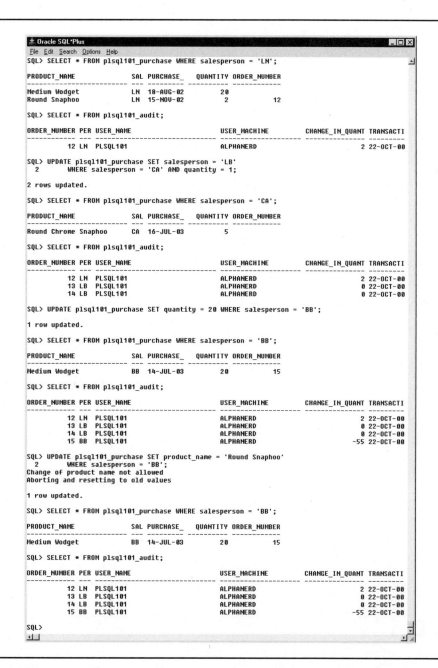

```
± Oracle SQL*Plus                                                    _ □ X
File  Edit  Search  Options  Help
SQL> SELECT * FROM plsql101_purchase WHERE salesperson = 'LN';

PRODUCT_NAME              SAL PURCHASE_   QUANTITY ORDER_NUMBER
------------------------- --- ---------  ---------- ------------
Medium Wodget             LN  18-AUG-02       20
Round Snaphoo             LN  15-NOV-02        2           12

SQL> SELECT * FROM plsql101_audit;

ORDER_NUMBER PER USER_NAME                USER_MACHINE          CHANGE_IN_QUANT TRANSACTI
------------ --- ----------------------   --------------------- --------------- ---------
          12 LN  PLSQL101                 ALPHANERD                           2 22-OCT-00

SQL> UPDATE plsql101_purchase SET salesperson = 'LB'
  2      WHERE salesperson = 'CA' AND quantity = 1;

2 rows updated.

SQL> SELECT * FROM plsql101_purchase WHERE salesperson = 'CA';

PRODUCT_NAME              SAL PURCHASE_   QUANTITY ORDER_NUMBER
------------------------- --- ---------  ---------- ------------
Round Chrome Snaphoo      CA  16-JUL-03        5

SQL> SELECT * FROM plsql101_audit;

ORDER_NUMBER PER USER_NAME                USER_MACHINE          CHANGE_IN_QUANT TRANSACTI
------------ --- ----------------------   --------------------- --------------- ---------
          12 LN  PLSQL101                 ALPHANERD                           2 22-OCT-00
          13 LB  PLSQL101                 ALPHANERD                           0 22-OCT-00
          14 LB  PLSQL101                 ALPHANERD                           0 22-OCT-00

SQL> UPDATE plsql101_purchase SET quantity = 20 WHERE salesperson = 'BB';

1 row updated.

SQL> SELECT * FROM plsql101_purchase WHERE salesperson = 'BB';

PRODUCT_NAME              SAL PURCHASE_   QUANTITY ORDER_NUMBER
------------------------- --- ---------  ---------- ------------
Medium Wodget             BB  14-JUL-03       20           15

SQL> SELECT * FROM plsql101_audit;

ORDER_NUMBER PER USER_NAME                USER_MACHINE          CHANGE_IN_QUANT TRANSACTI
------------ --- ----------------------   --------------------- --------------- ---------
          12 LN  PLSQL101                 ALPHANERD                           2 22-OCT-00
          13 LB  PLSQL101                 ALPHANERD                           0 22-OCT-00
          14 LB  PLSQL101                 ALPHANERD                           0 22-OCT-00
          15 BB  PLSQL101                 ALPHANERD                         -55 22-OCT-00

SQL> UPDATE plsql101_purchase SET product_name = 'Round Snaphoo'
  2      WHERE salesperson = 'BB';
Change of product name not allowed
Aborting and resetting to old values

1 row updated.

SQL> SELECT * FROM plsql101_purchase WHERE salesperson = 'BB';

PRODUCT_NAME              SAL PURCHASE_   QUANTITY ORDER_NUMBER
------------------------- --- ---------  ---------- ------------
Medium Wodget             BB  14-JUL-03       20           15

SQL> SELECT * FROM plsql101_audit;

ORDER_NUMBER PER USER_NAME                USER_MACHINE          CHANGE_IN_QUANT TRANSACTI
------------ --- ----------------------   --------------------- --------------- ---------
          12 LN  PLSQL101                 ALPHANERD                           2 22-OCT-00
          13 LB  PLSQL101                 ALPHANERD                           0 22-OCT-00
          14 LB  PLSQL101                 ALPHANERD                           0 22-OCT-00
          15 BB  PLSQL101                 ALPHANERD                         -55 22-OCT-00
SQL>
```

FIGURE 9-10. *Trigger that prohibits changing product name while updating orders*

Fine Points Regarding Triggers

You should keep in mind the following points when creating triggers:

- A trigger executing DML statements may result in more triggers being fired. This can potentially lead to a large number of fired triggers.

- A trigger fired by an INSERT statement has meaningful access to new column values only. Because the row is being created by the INSERT, the old values are null.

- A trigger fired by an UPDATE statement has access to both old and new column values for both BEFORE and AFTER row triggers.

- A trigger fired by a DELETE statement has meaningful access to :old column values only. Because the row no longer exists after the row is deleted, the :new values are NULL. However, you cannot modify :new values. ORA-4084 is raised if you try to modify :new values.

- ROLLBACK, COMMIT, and SAVEPOINT cannot be used inside the trigger body.

- When unhandled exceptions occur all the changes including the triggering statement are rolled back.

- If more than one trigger is defined for the same triggering event, the order of trigger firing is undefined. That is, you cannot assume in what order the triggers will fire.

- A "mutating table" error condition arises when a trigger tries to read a table and then write to it. While the intention of restricting this type of activity is reasonable, Oracle takes it further than necessary, restricting operations when a table has simply been looked at but not changed. One way around this problem is to create a second table that contains duplicates of the columns the trigger wants to read from the main table. In this scenario, the trigger gathers the values it needs from the second table, and then performs the actions it needs on the first table. When employing this approach, it is essential that all INSERT, UPDATE, and DELETE commands on the main table be mirrored by the trigger to the second table, so they stay synchronized.

ODBC

So far in this book, all of your interaction with Oracle has been through the SQL*Plus program. This is great for certain types of work, but there are likely to be other tasks that would benefit from being able to work with Oracle data in programs such as Microsoft Access or Excel. It's easy to make this happen, but it requires a type of connection that is not already present and not particularly well documented: an *ODBC* connection. This section of the book will show you how to create such a connection in Windows.

ODBC stands for Open Database Connectivity. It is an interface allowing applications such as Access and Excel to interact with many different brands of databases in a generic way. The ODBC layer allows programs to use the Oracle connectivity used by SQL*Plus. The following illustration shows how ODBC fits into the connectivity picture.

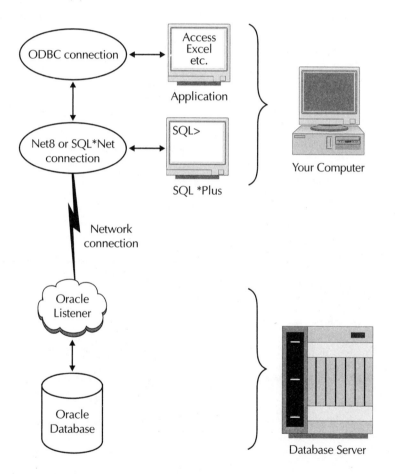

Creating an ODBC Connection

In order to create an ODBC connection, you need to know four things:

- The brand of database you are accessing

- The name of the database

- A valid user name

- A valid password

If you have done the SQL*Plus exercises in this or any other chapter in this book, then you know all four of these items. The database brand is Oracle, and the database name, user, and password are the ones you use in the SQL*Plus logon dialog box. Figure 9-11 shows the logon dialog and identifies which dialog field relates to which item.

To create an ODBC connection, take the following steps:

1. Run the Microsoft ODBC Administrator. To do this, open the Windows Start menu, navigate to Programs, and select your Oracle program group. Within it, locate and select the program named Microsoft ODBC Data Source Administrator. You should see a screen similar to the one shown in Figure 9-12.

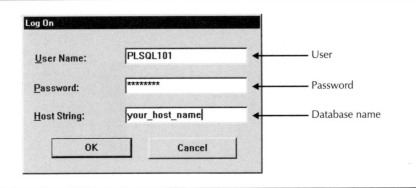

FIGURE 9-11. *SQL*Plus connection information to use when creating an ODBC connection*

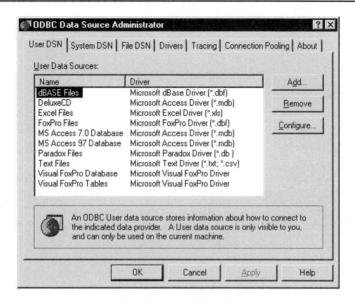

FIGURE 9-12. *Microsoft ODBC Data Source Administrator*

2. If more than one person uses your computer and you want the ODBC connection to be available to all users, click on the tab labeled System DSN at the top of the ODBC Administrator. If the ODBC connection will be used only by you, remain within the tab labeled User DSN.

3. Click the Add button. This will open a dialog named Create New Data Source, which is shown in Figure 9-13. Select the data source named Oracle ODBC Driver and click the Finish button.

4. You should now see a dialog named Oracle8 ODBC Driver Setup, as shown in Figure 9-14. The first field is labeled Data Source Name. Enter into that field the name you would like to use when referring to this particular ODBC connection. For the sake of simplicity, it's often a good idea to have the ODBC connection name be the same as the database name. With this guideline in mind, type **PLSQL101** into the Data Source Name field for the purposes of this exercise.

5. Navigate to the field named Service Name. Type into this field the Oracle database name you use when logging in with SQL*Plus. For this exercise, the value to type into this field is also **PLSQL101**.

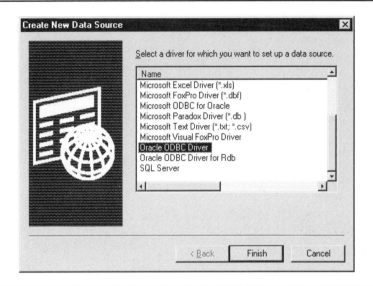

FIGURE 9-13. *Create New Data Source dialog*

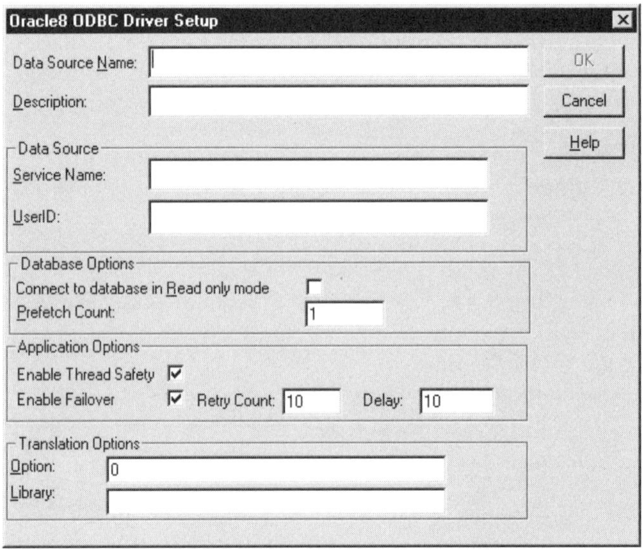

FIGURE 9-14. *Oracle ODBC driver configuration*

6. Click the OK button to complete the configuration. You will be returned to the ODBC Data Source Administrator dialog, and you should see the data source you just created in the list of sources shown.

7. Click the OK button to close the ODBC Data Source Administrator dialog.

8. To test your new ODBC connection, return to the Oracle program folder in your Windows Start menu, and select the program named Oracle ODBC Test. You will see a screen similar to the one shown in Figure 9-15.

9. Click the Connect button and you will be presented with a Select Data Source dialog, as shown in Figure 9-16.

10. Click on the tab named Machine Data Source, and locate your ODBC connection's name in the alphabetical list. Click on the connection name to select it, and then click the OK button.

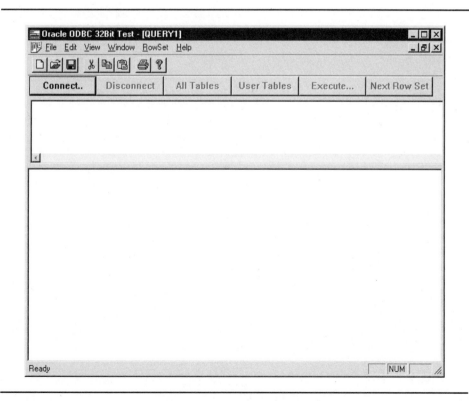

FIGURE 9-15. *Oracle ODBC Test screen*

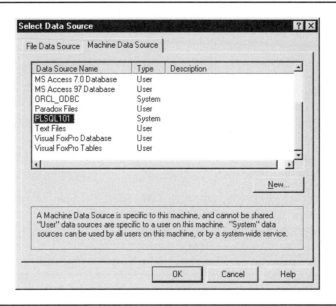

FIGURE 9-16. *Selecting an ODBC data source to test*

11. When presented with the Oracle ODBC Driver Connect dialog, enter your user name and password (notice that the database name is already entered, and is present in the first field rather than the last field as in SQL*Plus). For this exercise, type a user name of **PLSQL101** and a password of **PLSQL101**. Then click the OK button.

12. The only evidence you will see in the Oracle ODBC Test program that your connection succeeded is that the Connect button will be grayed out, while the buttons labeled Disconnect, All Tables, User Tables, and Execute will become active. Click on the button label User Tables. You should see a list of table names appear, as shown in Figure 9-17. By default, the Oracle ODBC Test program only shows five tables at a time. To make it show more, you can either click the Next Row Set button, or go to the program's menu and execute the Row Set | 100 command.

13. To exit the Oracle ODBC Test program, click the Disconnect button, and then execute the File | Exit menu command.

Congratulations! You have successfully created an ODBC connection to your Oracle database. Now let's put it to use.

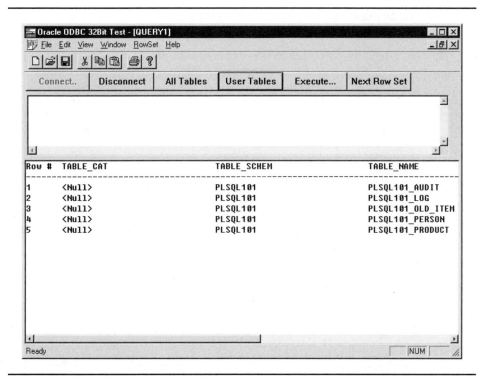

FIGURE 9-17.   *Successful ODBC connection test*

Handy Uses for an ODBC Connection

In this section you will see how to do the most common tasks requiring ODBC:
manipulating data in Access and importing data into Excel.

Viewing and Editing Data in Access

The following steps show how to create a link between your Oracle tables and
Access. As later versions of Access are released, the names of the menu items used
may vary slightly. If you encounter this, just use the overall approach outlined
below and apply it to the menu item names you see in your version. The overall
approach has been the same for the last three versions of Access and is not likely
to change in future versions.

I. Start your Access program. For the purposes of this exercise, create a new
    Access file named **PLSQL101.mdb**.

2. Execute the menu command File | Get External Data | Link. This will cause a standard file-open dialog to appear.

3. Navigate to the field named Files of Type and open its list of file types. At the bottom of the list, select the entry named ODBC Databases. You should now see the ODBC Select Data Sources dialog (as shown earlier in Figure 9-16).

4. Click on the tab labeled Machine Data Source. Locate the ODBC data source you want (PLSQL101 for this exercise), click on it, and click the OK button.

5. When presented with the logon dialog, enter your user name and password, and then click the OK button.

6. You will be presented with a list of Oracle tables and views available through that ODBC connection. The list will include objects owned by other users, and each object name will be preceded by the name of the user who owns it. Scroll down the list until you locate your user name, and then select the objects you want. For this exercise, select all of the PLSQL101 objects. Unlike most selection lists in Windows programs, the list of objects in Access does not understand CTRL-clicking or SHIFT-clicking to select multiple items. To select more than one name, you just perform a normal click on the name of each object you want.

7. To ensure that you do not have to enter a user name and password each time you use the table links you are about to create, click on the Save Password checkbox.

8. Click the OK button. Access will start reading the structure of each table and view you selected. If it encounters a table that does not have a primary key, Access will ask you to identify one or more columns in the table that uniquely identify each record in that table. For instance, the PLSQL101_AUDIT table does not have a primary key, so Access displays a dialog like the one shown in Figure 9-18. You do not have to select primary key columns for a table that doesn't already have any, but if you do not, the table will be read only through Access—you will not be able to add or change records using the Access link. In this particular case, the audit table should not get changed through Access anyway, so you can click the dialog's OK button without identifying any primary key columns.

9. You should now see a series of table entries in Access that look similar to the ones shown in Figure 9-19. Notice that the name of the owner has been appended to the name of each table. You can rename these links if you wish; the names of the underlying Oracle tables will not be affected.

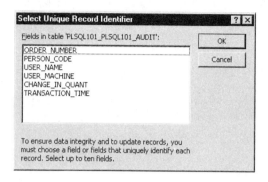

FIGURE 9-18. *Access' request to identify one or more primary key columns for a table that does not have any*

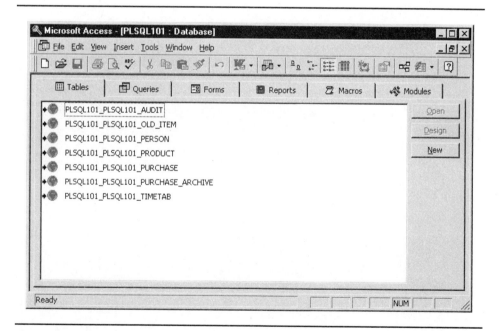

FIGURE 9-19. *Linked tables in Access*

10. Double-click on a table name to open it. For instance, double-clicking on the PLSQL101_PURCHASE table's link will create a screen similar to the one shown in Figure 9-20.

Importing Oracle Data into Excel

Unlike Access, the link between Excel and Oracle is one way only: data can be read out of Oracle into Excel, but not vice versa. This reflects Excel's common usage as an analysis tool.

To pull Oracle data into Excel, follow these steps:

1. Start your Excel program.

2. Execute the menu command Data | Get External Data | Create New Query. This will cause a dialog named Choose Data Source to appear, as shown in Figure 9-21.

3. Locate the data source you want (PLSQL101 for this exercise), click on it, and click the OK button.

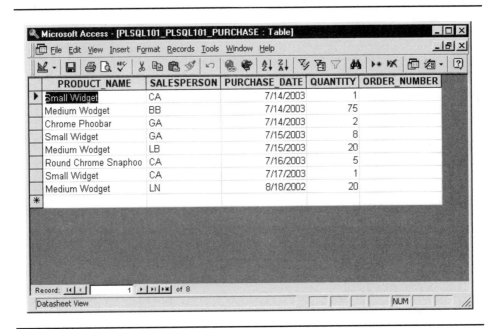

FIGURE 9-20. *Oracle data displayed through Access*

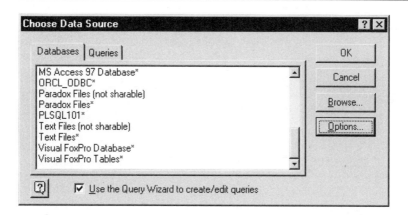

FIGURE 9-21. *Choosing a source for importing data into Excel*

4. When presented with the logon dialog, enter your user name and password, and then click the OK button.

5. You will be presented with a list of Oracle tables and views available through that ODBC connection. To the left of each table or column name is a plus sign; clicking on that plus sign will cause the list to expand so column names show. You can select all of the columns from a table or view by clicking on the table or view name and then clicking the right arrow in the center of the dialog. You can also select individual columns by expanding the list, clicking on the name of the column you want, and then clicking on the right arrow in the center of the dialog. For the purposes of this exercise, move all of the columns from the PLSQL101_PURCHASE table into the right window named Columns in Your Query. When your screen looks like the one shown in Figure 9-22, click the Next button to proceed.

6. The next dialog allows you to specify filtering criteria, similar to a WHERE clause in a SQL SELECT command. I feel confident that anyone who has made it to this point in the book will understand how to use this dialog, so for this exercise you can just click the Next button to continue.

7. The following dialog allows you to specify up to three sorting columns. Click the Next button to move forward.

8. In the last dialog of the Query Wizard, ensure that the Return Data to Microsoft Excel choice is selected, and then click the Finish button.

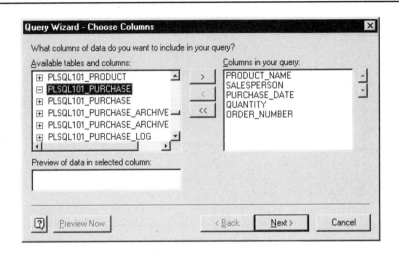

FIGURE 9-22. *Selecting Oracle columns to import into Excel*

9. Finally, you will see a dialog asking where you would like the data from Oracle to be placed. Click the OK button.

10. You should now see the Oracle data in your Excel spreadsheet, as shown in Figure 9-23.

Summary

This chapter began with a discussion of coding conventions. Coding conventions are guidelines for writing readable, maintainable, quality code. Coding conventions also facilitate successful modular development in large projects.

You furthered your studies of implicit cursors—or SQL DML within PL/SQL or SQL cursors. Implicit cursors are useful when dealing with only one row at a time. The implicit cursors are not shared across sessions. Implicit cursors allow you to select values directly into PL/SQL variables and allow the use of PL/SQL variables in the WHERE clause.

You learned more about PL/SQL records and declaring variables using anchored types. %ROWTYPE and %TYPE allow you to anchor the type of your record or variable to a specific table row type, cursor row type, or table column type.

You learned how to use TIMING commands in order to measure program execution speed and determine the amount of time a process takes to complete using the well-known SYSDATE system variable.

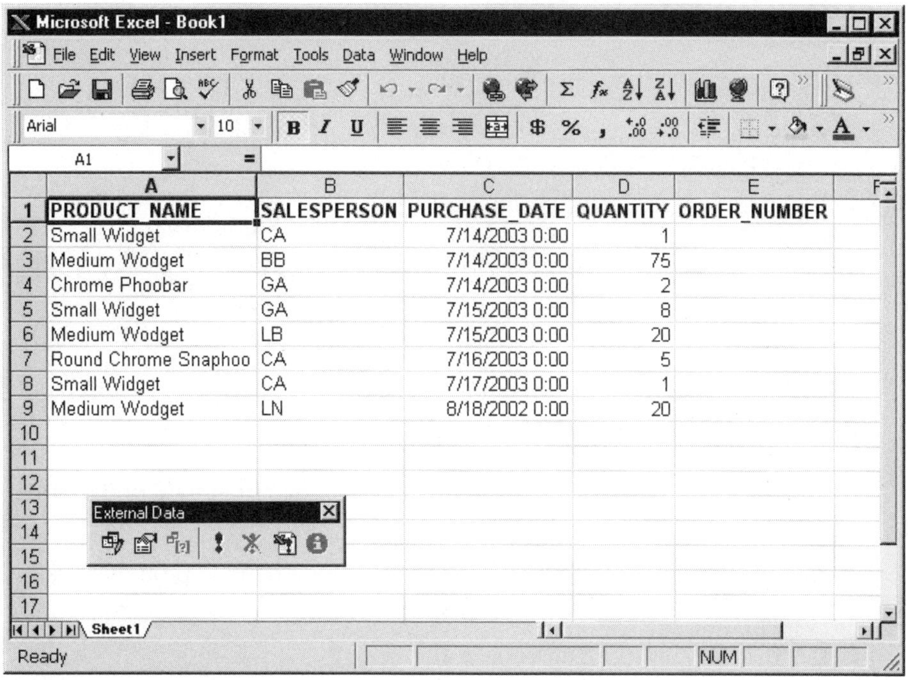

FIGURE 9-23. *Oracle data imported into Excel*

We discussed PL/SQL packages, which enable you to hide implementation details for PL/SQL modules, thus allowing for cleaner programming interfaces. Package code can be shared across multiple sessions. Packages have visible package specifications that expose all the usable parts of a package like functions and procedures.

Triggers are used to enforce complex business constraints, rules, and security measures not enforceable using other means. Triggers are fired automatically when the event that triggers them, usually a DML statement, happens. Triggers can be configured to execute before or after the triggering event is executed. Finally, triggers can be used to automate many tasks like auditing user activity or accounting.

To finish up the chapter, you created an ODBC connection to your Oracle tables. Setting up an ODBC connection is not complicated; it just requires that you know what information the ODBC configuration wants. Once established, an ODBC connection can easily be leveraged by Windows products like Access and Excel.

Congratulations! Now you know more about PL/SQL than most people you will meet. I wish you all the best in your pursuits.

Chapter Questions

1. Which of the following are true about SQL DML within PL/SQL?

    A. There are two ways to implement SQL DML: explicit cursors and implicit cursors.

    B. SQL DML cannot be implemented from within PL/SQL code.

    C. It is not possible to use explicit cursors to execute SQL DML that affects at most a single row.

    D. You can use PL/SQL variables within SQL DML inside PL/SQL code.

2. Coding conventions are important because:

    A. Following them eases the maintenance of software.

    B. They allow for better understanding between a multitude of developers of large projects.

    C. They eliminate wasteful efforts involved dealing with problems that may arise due to hard-to-read coding styles.

    D. They always make all code portable.

3. Which of the following is not true about packages?

    A. Packages can contain triggers.

    B. Package variables are variables declared in the package specification and are initialized once when the package is loaded into memory.

    C. The package execution section is mainly used for assigning values to package variables and doing some one-time work for that package.

    D. Functions and procedures declared and defined within a package body but not declared in its specification are not accessible to users of the package.

4. Which of the following are true about triggers?

    A. Triggers are automatically called by the system.

    B. Triggers can call other stored PL/SQL procedures or functions.

    C. If an exception is raised during the execution of a trigger, all the changes including the ones made by the triggering statement are rolled back if the exception is not handled.

    D. You can write triggers on packages, because they are also stored in the database.

Answers to Chapter Questions

1. A, D.

Explanation B is certainly not true; the last two chapters have contained numerous examples showing the use of DML commands within PL/SQL code. C is false because an explicit cursor may return a single row or now rows at all.

2. A, B, and C.

Explanation A, B, and C are all valid reasons to use coding conventions. D is not true. While you can write coding and naming conventions to make code portable to many platforms, you cannot guarantee the code based only on coding conventions. This is because there are vast differences between hardware and software platforms.

3. A. Packages can contain triggers.

Explanation By definition, triggers can only be fired in response to an action taken on a table. They cannot be called as part of a package.

4. A, B, and C.

Explanation D is false. Oracle does not allow you to write triggers that fire in response to package events, for the same reason that triggers cannot be placed inside packages.

PART
IV

Appendix

APPENDIX
A

Glossary

resented here is a set of brief definitions of the major terms you will encounter in this book. Every attempt has been made to ensure that all of the important terms have been included.

actual parameters   Actual variables or constants that are usually copied to the formal parameters of a function or procedure when a call is made. There are ways for not copying them not covered in this book.

after trigger   A trigger that is fired after the triggering statement has done its changes and after all the constraint checks are done. This trigger locks the rows that its triggering statement affects.

anchored type or dynamic type   The result of declaring a type of PL/SQL variable to be the same as the type of record in a cursor or as that of a row of a table using the table or cursor name followed by %ROWTYPE and the same as the type of a column in a table by column_name%TYPE.

anonymous block   A PL/SQL basic block without any name or specification. The header section is empty.

application   A collection of scripts and programs working together to perform a well-defined set of database tasks.

back end   See the meaning of **front end**. The rest of the application or program referred to there is usually called the "back end." In most cases this will be the database.

before trigger   A trigger that is fired before the triggering statement executes and before any constraint checks are done.

branch blocks   In a B*-Tree index, the non-leaf blocks that do not contain any actual records but only values for indexed fields in records to help reach the leaf blocks in as few steps as possible.

Cartesian product   A join without a WHERE clause that results in combining each record from one table with every record in the other.

character functions   ORACLE functions for manipulating text strings.

check constraint   Constraint that allows you to specify a set of conditions on incoming data for it to be accepted for insertion into the database table.

child table   The table in a parent-child relationship that references rows in the parent table.

column   A collection of one type of information stored in a table (for instance, all of the phone numbers or all of the last names).

column alias   A surrogate name assigned to a column in SQL commands. For example, in the following code "Sold By" is the column alias for column salesperson.

```
SELECT product_name || ' was sold by ' || salesperson "Sold By"
FROM   plsql101_purchase;
```

composite index   An index based on more than one column in a table.

concatenated index   See **composite index**.

concatenation   Operation of joining two pieces of text to make a single piece of text.

conditional processing   Execution of different sets of statements or pieces of code depending on a condition being satisfied or not.

constant   An expression with a fixed value, such as 6/3.

constraints   Characteristics that must be true about the data in order for it to be accepted by the database.

control flow *or* execution flow   The sequence of execution of one statement after another in a program. The sequence may be altered based on conditions. The constructs that allow this are called *flow control statements* or *constructs*. IF or LOOP statements in PL/SQL are examples of flow control statements.

cursor attributes   Properties of a cursor that tell whether it contains any rows, the count of rows it fetched, whether it is open or not, and whether it obtained any row on the last fetch.

data conversion   The operation of converting information from one datatype to another—usually between text and dates, times, or numbers.

data dictionary   A collection of tables and views maintained by a database system (ORACLE) to keep up-to-date information about all the database objects in the database.

data models   See **Entity Relationship Diagram (ERD)**.

database   A collection of related tables.

datatype   Type of data—for example, NUMBER, CHAR, and so on.

date math   Arithmetic operations with dates—for example, finding days between two dates.

default value   Value given or assigned automatically when the variable or database entity is created if no explicit assignment exists in the code or until such explicit assignment happens and overwrites the default value.

directory   A folder on the hard disk where program or script files are stored.

Entity Relationship Diagram (ERD)   A diagram depicting the design of a relational database where the tables are represented by certain standard symbols called "entities." The entities are connected using standard symbols and lines called "relationships" and they convey the nature of the relationship between the two entities (tables) that they connect.

exception   An error condition at runtime that prevents the application or program from executing any further in its normal flow of execution. If not handled, the application exits.

exception handler   Executable statements in the exception section of a PL/SQL program unit that do something when the exception occurs. They may print out an error message or try to rectify the exception.

explicit cursor or *cursor*   Cursors declared by a programmer explicitly using CURSOR ... IS syntax. Cursor is the go-between structure used by PL/SQL and SQL to interact with each other. Explicit cursors hold the set of rows selected by their SELECT statement that can be fetched from the cursor one at a time for processing by PL/SQL code.

expression   A piece of command or program construct that, when executed, results in one or more values. For example, 3 + 4 is an expression as is sales_tax / product.

field   The junction of a row and a column in a table containing a single piece of information about something.

flat file   A single large table that stores information without using relationships, repeating the information as many times as needed. For example, a sales_order flat file table will repeat all the fields for a particular product for every row for that product.

foreign key   The child table column(s) that contains the primary-key values from the parent table.

formal parameters   The list of names and datatypes for variables a function or procedure accepts from the caller that act like variables local to the function or procedure.

front end   The parts of an application or program that read in the input data and then transport it to appropriate parts of the rest of the application or program.

function   A piece of program code, either built-in or user-written, that accepts a set of data values and returns another set of data values computed based on an accepted or input set of data values.

function specification   The specification for a PL/SQL function made up of the name of the function and the list of its formal parameters and return type.

group   A collection of records, usually the result of a SQL query.

group functions   ORACLE functions that work on groups of records—for example, SUM, AVG, MIN, MAX, and so on.

group separator   A character that separates hundreds, thousands, and so on, within a number.

group values   A value or set of values common to all records in a group. Used in the HAVING clause to filter entire groups.

hard-coded   Information or values explicitly written into script or programs.

implicit cursor   A hidden cursor used by PL/SQL for DML statements within PL/SQL.

INSTEAD OF trigger   A trigger that is applied to tables underlying the view on which the trigger is defined, provided the view meets certain criteria.

iterative processing   Processing one row or record at a time. Repeated processing on different data for each repetition.

join operators   Operators for combining results from two SQL queries (SELECT statements) in various ways—for example, UNION, MINUS, INTERSECT, and so on.

Julian dates   A calendar system that counts the number of days starting from a specific day. For example, ORACLE uses January 1, 4712 BC as the starting day. Time of day is treated as a fractional part of the date. 54321.5 means noon of the 54,322nd day starting from January 1, 4712 BC.

leaf blocks   When building a B*-Tree index ORACLE analyzes the columns of the table and then splits the tables into storage units called "blocks" with each block containing the same number of records. These blocks are called "leaf blocks" in the index.

literal   Fixed text in a command or program that does not change and is interpreted literally, instead of as a name for a variable.

loop index   The variable used in a FOR loop as the loop counter. It occurs between the FOR and IN parts of the FOR statement.

modes of parameters   A means of telling whether an actual parameter may be only read or only written to or both read and written by the called function or procedure. This is specified as part of the formal parameter description using IN for read only, OUT for write only, and IN OUT for read and write both.

modular   Made up of parts or modules, each of which has a well-defined behavior and interface for interaction with other parts.

multirow subquery   A subquery that may return more than one row or record.

named notation   A way of calling a procedure or function such that each actual parameter is matched to its formal parameter by using *formal_name* => *actual_name* notation. This allows for default-valued formal parameters to be anywhere in the list, not just at the end of the list of formal parameters.

nested blocks or loops   Loops or PL/SQL blocks placed one inside another.

null   An indicator that data does not exist. Not be confused with zero or blank space, which are valid data values. Null means the value is not known at all.

object privileges   Privileges for a specific database object like a table, sequence, and so on.

ODBC   Open Database Connectivity. An industry-standard protocol for connecting and transferring data to and from database and client software.

one-to-many relationship   A relationship between tables wherein a single record in one table can be referred to by many records in another table.

operator precedence   The order in which different operations are performed in an expression with more than one operator. For example, 3 – 4 / 2 will first perform 4 / 2, which is 2, and then 3 – 2, giving the final value of 1.

operators   The technical name for mathematical operation symbols, such as the plus sign and minus sign.

PL/SQL   Procedural options to SQL. A programming language provided by ORACLE.

PL/SQL basic block   A basic PL/SQL building block made up of header, declaration, execution, and exception sections that may be compiled as a unit on its own by PL/SQL.

PL/SQL function   A PL/SQL piece of code made up of one or more PL/SQL basic blocks that computes a single value and returns it when called, and which may accept a set of inputs called "formal parameters."

PL/SQL package   A PL/SQL program unit that can contain procedures, functions, and other PL/SQL program units. A package exposes only the interfaces or specifications to its contents for use by other program units.

PL/SQL procedure   A PL/SQL piece of code made up of one or more PL/SQL basic blocks that performs a set of well-defined actions when called and that may accept a set of inputs and outputs called "formal parameters." Does not return any value.

PL/SQL record   A PL/SQL data structure made up of individual fields of basic PL/SQL types.

package body   The actual body of code containing the full definitions of objects defined in package specification and executable code to initialize package variables.

package specification   The specification for a PL/SQL package made up of the package name and package variables, functions, procedures, types, and cursors.

package variables   A variable declared within the package specification. These get initialized only once per loading of the package in memory and are shared across multiple sessions by the same user. The execution section of the package may be used to initialize these variables. They are accessible to users of packages as they are part of the package specification.

parent table   A table in a parent-child relationship where a single row or record in the table can be referenced by multiple rows (records) in the child table.

parent-child relationship   A relationship between two tables wherein a single record in one table—the parent table—can be referenced by multiple records in another table—the child table.

parsing   The process of breaking up strings into substrings.

path   The name of the disk drive and directory in which a file is to be stored.

populated   When a valid data value is stored in an attribute or a field, that attribute is said to be populated.

positional notation   A way of calling a procedure or function where the actual parameters are matched to formal parameters by their respective positions in the list of formal parameters. Formal parameters with default values must be the last ones in the list for this to work.

privileges   The ability for some users to be able to do some activity or changes to the database tables that some other users cannot. For example, some users cannot create new tables in the database while some can.

procedure specification   The specification for a PL/SQL procedure made up of the name of the procedure and the list of its formal parameters.

raising exception   Notification to PL/SQL or the system of occurrence of exception condition. This is explicitly done using RAISE by programmer code or implicitly by the system.

record   Data contained in a table row.

relational database   A database that organizes data in the form of tables and relationships amongst those tables.

relationship   An association between two or more tables made up of the columns of the table. For example, the items in the product_id column of a sales_order table must come from the values in the product_id column of the product_catalog table. This relationship between the two tables is established by making the product_id column in the sales_order table a foreign key referring to the product_id column in the product_catalog table.

result set *or* active set   A set of rows selected by a SQL DML (SELECT, INSERT, DELETE, or UPDATE) statement.

role   A set of privileges. Roles are a shorthand way of granting the same set of privileges to multiple users.

row   One line in a table.

row trigger   A trigger that executes per modified row, modified by the triggering event.

sequence   A database counter that automatically increments or decrements when you select a value from it and can be configured to start and stop at limiting values chosen. You can also configure it to recycle values when it reaches its limits.

single-row subquery   A subquery that returns at most a single row or record.

specification   A piece of information that uniquely identifies a PL/SQL program unit.

spooling   The process of writing information out to a file on a disk.

statement trigger   A trigger that gets fired once for the triggering event or statement.

string   Text.

substitution variable   A variable in SQL script used as a placeholder for user-typed input.

substring   A part of a string.

synonym   A database synonym is another name given to an existing database object.

syntax   The valid way of writing a command or language construct. Only those commands and language constructs that are correct and complete in syntax can be successful.

system privilege   Privileges for actions anywhere in the database—for example, inserting into any table.

table   A collection of rows and columns that store all information about one type of thing (for instance, people or products).

table alias   A shorthand name that may be assigned to a table name within SQL statements and that then can be used to refer to the table throughout the rest of the statement.

table trigger   A trigger defined on tables.

trigger   A PL/SQL block that gets automatically executed when the triggering event happens.

trigger action   The executable part of a trigger. The actual action that happens when the trigger is fired and it passes its restriction.

trigger event *or* triggering statement   An event such as a DML statement that may be used to trigger execution of a trigger.

trigger restriction   The condition that must be met by new and old data for the trigger to execute. For example, the new value must be greater than the old value.

trimming   The process of removing extra space from the beginning or end of a string.

unique index   An index created by ORACLE for enforcing a unique constraint.

variable   A placeholder for a portion of a command in scripts. In programs, a placeholder for an actual value or data.

view   A query stored in the database and given a name.

wildcards   A portion of text that can vary, represented by % in SQL commands. In the following example, the % wildcard character matches any text following the word "Chrome," so rows for all products with a name starting with "Chrome" are selected.

```
SELECT * FROM plsql101_product
WHERE  product_name LIKE 'Chrome%';
```

Index

NOTE: Page numbers in *italics* refer to illustrations or charts.

SYMBOLS

' (apostrophes), inserting data containing, 50–52
|| (vertical bars), connecting text columns via SELECT statements, 58

A

ACCEPT command, substitution variables and scripts, 125–126

Knowledge is power. To which we say,

crank up the power.

Are you ready for a power surge?

Accelerate your career—become an **Oracle Certified Professional (OCP)**. With Oracle's cutting-edge *Instructor-Led Training*, *Technology-Based Training*, and this *guide*, you can prepare for certification faster than ever. Set your own trajectory by logging your personal training plan with us. Go to **http://education.oracle.com/tpb**, where we'll help you pick a training path, select your courses, and track your progress. We'll even send you an email when your courses are offered in your area. If you don't have access to the Web, call us at 1-800-441-3541 (Outside the U.S. call +1-310-335-2403). **Power learning has never been easier.**

University

Get Your FREE Subscription to *Oracle Magazine*

Oracle Magazine is essential gear for today's information technology professionals. Stay informed and increase your productivity with every issue of *Oracle Magazine*. Inside each **FREE,** bimonthly issue you'll get:

- Up-to-date information on Oracle Database Server, Oracle Applications, Internet Computing, and tools
- Third-party news and announcements
- Technical articles on Oracle products and operating environments
- Development and administration tips
- Real-world customer stories

Three easy ways to subscribe:

1. Web   **Visit our Web site at www.oracle.com/oramag/. You'll find a subscription form there, plus much more!**

2. Fax   Complete the questionnaire on the back of this card and fax the questionnaire side only to **+1.847.647.9735.**

3. Mail   Complete the questionnaire on the back of this card and mail it to P.O. Box 1263, Skokie, IL 60076-8263.

If there are other Oracle users at your location who would like to receive their own subscription to *Oracle Magazine*, please photocopy this form and pass it along.

☐ **YES! Please send me a FREE subscription to *Oracle Magazine.*** ☐ **NO**

To receive a free bimonthly subscription to *Oracle Magazine*, you must fill out the entire card, sign it, and date it (incomplete cards cannot be processed or acknowledged). You can also fax your application to +1.847.647.9735. Or subscribe at our Web site at www.oracle.com/oramag/

SIGNATURE (REQUIRED)	X		DATE	

NAME _____ TITLE _____

COMPANY _____ TELEPHONE _____

ADDRESS _____ FAX NUMBER _____

CITY _____ STATE _____ POSTAL CODE/ZIP CODE _____

COUNTRY _____ E-MAIL ADDRESS _____

☐ From time to time, Oracle Publishing allows our partners exclusive access to our e-mail addresses for special promotions and announcements. To be included in this program, please check this box.

You must answer all eight questions below.

1 What is the primary business activity of your firm at this location? *(check only one)*
- ☐ 03 Communications
- ☐ 04 Consulting, Training
- ☐ 06 Data Processing
- ☐ 07 Education
- ☐ 08 Engineering
- ☐ 09 Financial Services
- ☐ 10 Government—Federal, Local, State, Other
- ☐ 11 Government—Military
- ☐ 12 Health Care
- ☐ 13 Manufacturing—Aerospace, Defense
- ☐ 14 Manufacturing—Computer Hardware
- ☐ 15 Manufacturing—Noncomputer Products
- ☐ 17 Research & Development
- ☐ 19 Retailing, Wholesaling, Distribution
- ☐ 20 Software Development
- ☐ 21 Systems Integration, VAR, VAD, OEM
- ☐ 22 Transportation
- ☐ 23 Utilities (Electric, Gas, Sanitation)
- ☐ 98 Other Business and Services _____

2 Which of the following best describes your job function? *(check only one)*

CORPORATE MANAGEMENT/STAFF
- ☐ 01 Executive Management (President, Chair, CEO, CFO, Owner, Partner, Principal)
- ☐ 02 Finance/Administrative Management (VP/Director/ Manager/Controller, Purchasing, Administration)
- ☐ 03 Sales/Marketing Management (VP/Director/Manager)
- ☐ 04 Computer Systems/Operations Management (CIO/VP/Director/ Manager MIS, Operations)

IS/IT STAFF
- ☐ 07 Systems Development/ Programming Management
- ☐ 08 Systems Development/ Programming Staff
- ☐ 09 Consulting
- ☐ 10 DBA/Systems Administrator
- ☐ 11 Education/Training
- ☐ 14 Technical Support Director/ Manager
- ☐ 16 Other Technical Management/Staff
- ☐ 98 Other _____

3 What is your current primary operating platform? *(check all that apply)*
- ☐ 01 DEC UNIX
- ☐ 02 DEC VAX VMS
- ☐ 03 Java
- ☐ 04 HP UNIX
- ☐ 05 IBM AIX
- ☐ 06 IBM UNIX
- ☐ 07 Macintosh
- ☐ 09 MS-DOS
- ☐ 10 MVS
- ☐ 11 NetWare
- ☐ 12 Network Computing
- ☐ 13 OpenVMS
- ☐ 14 SCO UNIX
- ☐ 24 Sequent DYNIX/ptx
- ☐ 15 Sun Solaris/SunOS
- ☐ 16 SVR4
- ☐ 18 UnixWare
- ☐ 20 Windows
- ☐ 21 Windows NT
- ☐ 23 Other UNIX _____
- ☐ 98 Other _____
- 99 ☐ **None of the above**

4 Do you evaluate, specify, recommend, or authorize the purchase of any of the following? *(check all that apply)*
- ☐ 01 Hardware
- ☐ 02 Software
- ☐ 03 Application Development Tools
- ☐ 04 Database Products
- ☐ 05 Internet or Intranet Products
- 99 ☐ **None of the above**

5 In your job, do you use or plan to purchase any of the following products or services? *(check all that apply)*

SOFTWARE
- ☐ 01 Business Graphics
- ☐ 02 CAD/CAE/CAM
- ☐ 03 CASE
- ☐ 05 Communications
- ☐ 06 Database Management
- ☐ 07 File Management
- ☐ 08 Finance
- ☐ 09 Java
- ☐ 10 Materials Resource Planning
- ☐ 11 Multimedia Authoring
- ☐ 12 Networking
- ☐ 13 Office Automation
- ☐ 14 Order Entry/Inventory Control
- ☐ 15 Programming
- ☐ 16 Project Management
- ☐ 17 Scientific and Engineering
- ☐ 18 Spreadsheets
- ☐ 19 Systems Management
- ☐ 20 Workflow

HARDWARE
- ☐ 21 Macintosh
- ☐ 22 Mainframe
- ☐ 23 Massively Parallel Processing
- ☐ 24 Minicomputer
- ☐ 25 PC
- ☐ 26 Network Computer
- ☐ 28 Symmetric Multiprocessing
- ☐ 29 Workstation

PERIPHERALS
- ☐ 30 Bridges/Routers/Hubs/Gateways
- ☐ 31 CD-ROM Drives
- ☐ 32 Disk Drives/Subsystems
- ☐ 33 Modems
- ☐ 34 Tape Drives/Subsystems
- ☐ 35 Video Boards/Multimedia

SERVICES
- ☐ 37 Consulting
- ☐ 38 Education/Training
- ☐ 39 Maintenance
- ☐ 40 Online Database Services
- ☐ 41 Support
- ☐ 36 Technology-Based Training
- ☐ 98 Other _____
- 99 ☐ **None of the above**

6 What Oracle products are in use at your site? *(check all that apply)*

SERVER/SOFTWARE
- ☐ 01 Oracle8
- ☐ 30 Oracle8*i*
- ☐ 31 Oracle8*i* Lite
- ☐ 02 Oracle7
- ☐ 03 Oracle Application Server
- ☐ 04 Oracle Data Mart Suites
- ☐ 05 Oracle Internet Commerce Server
- ☐ 32 Oracle *inter*Media
- ☐ 33 Oracle JServer
- ☐ 07 Oracle Lite
- ☐ 08 Oracle Payment Server
- ☐ 11 Oracle Video Server

TOOLS
- ☐ 13 Oracle Designer
- ☐ 14 Oracle Developer
- ☐ 54 Oracle Discoverer
- ☐ 53 Oracle Express
- ☐ 51 Oracle JDeveloper
- ☐ 52 Oracle Reports
- ☐ 50 Oracle WebDB
- ☐ 55 Oracle Workflow

ORACLE APPLICATIONS
- ☐ 17 Oracle Automotive
- ☐ 35 Oracle Business Intelligence System
- ☐ 19 Oracle Consumer Packaged Goods
- ☐ 39 Oracle E-Commerce
- ☐ 18 Oracle Energy
- ☐ 20 Oracle Financials
- ☐ 28 Oracle Front Office
- ☐ 21 Oracle Human Resources
- ☐ 37 Oracle Internet Procurement
- ☐ 22 Oracle Manufacturing
- ☐ 40 Oracle Process Manufacturing
- ☐ 23 Oracle Projects
- ☐ 34 Oracle Retail
- ☐ 29 Oracle Self-Service Web Applications
- ☐ 38 Oracle Strategic Enterprise Management
- ☐ 25 Oracle Supply Chain Management
- ☐ 36 Oracle Tutor
- ☐ 41 Oracle Travel Management

ORACLE SERVICES
- ☐ 61 Oracle Consulting
- ☐ 62 Oracle Education
- ☐ 60 Oracle Support
- ☐ 98 Other _____
- 99 ☐ **None of the above**

7 What other database products are in use at your site? *(check all that apply)*
- ☐ 01 Access
- ☐ 02 Baan
- ☐ 03 dbase
- ☐ 04 Gupta
- ☐ 05 IBM DB2
- ☐ 06 Informix
- ☐ 07 Ingres
- ☐ 08 Microsoft Access
- ☐ 09 Microsoft SQL Server
- ☐ 10 PeopleSoft
- ☐ 11 Progress
- ☐ 12 SAP
- ☐ 13 Sybase
- ☐ 14 VSAM
- ☐ 98 Other _____
- 99 ☐ **None of the above**

8 During the next 12 months, how much do you anticipate your organization will spend on computer hardware, software, peripherals, and services for your location? *(check only one)*
- ☐ 01 Less than $10,000
- ☐ 02 $10,000 to $49,999
- ☐ 03 $50,000 to $99,999
- ☐ 04 $100,000 to $499,999
- ☐ 05 $500,000 to $999,999
- ☐ 06 $1,000,000 and over

If there are other Oracle users at your location who would like to receive a free subscription to *Oracle Magazine*, please photocopy this form and pass it along, or contact Customer Service at +1.847.647.9630

Form 5

OPRESS